Barry Edward O'Meara

Napoleon at St. Helena

Barry Edward O'Meara

Napoleon at St. Helena

ISBN/EAN: 9783743340664

Manufactured in Europe, USA, Canada, Australia, Japa

Cover: Foto ©ninafisch / pixelio.de

Manufactured and distributed by brebook publishing software (www.brebook.com)

Barry Edward O´Meara

Napoleon at St. Helena

NAPOLEON.
DRAWN AT Sⸯ HELENA, TWO MONTHS ONLY BEFORE HIS DEATH.
LONDON. RICHARD BENTLEY & SON. 1887

NAPOLEON AT ST. HELENA

BY

BARRY EDWARD O'MEARA
HIS LATE SURGEON

NAPOLEON'S TOMB

IN TWO VOLUMES
VOL. II.

LONDON
RICHARD BENTLEY & SON, NEW BURLINGTON STREET
Publishers in Ordinary to Her Majesty the Queen
1888

A Voice from St. Helena

LIST OF ILLUSTRATIONS

PAGE

PORTRAIT OF NAPOLEON *in colour*. From a Sketch made three months before his death . . . *Frontispiece*

TOMB OF NAPOLEON AT ST. HELENA (Woodcut) *Title Page*

NAPOLEON AT ST. HELENA (Woodcut) . . . 1

VIEW OF LONGWOOD, from the road to Deadwood, *in colour*
to face page 126

VIEW OF LONGWOOD, from the Flower Garden, *in colour*
to face page 224

PORTRAIT OF NAPOLEON IN HIS GARDEN. From a Sketch (Woodcut) . . . 360

DR. O'MEARA'S DIARY

NAPOLEON AT ST. HELENA.

CHAPTER III
(CONTINUED)

1817

March 16.—Saw the Emperor in the drawing-room. He was in extremely good spirits, laughed repeatedly, joked with me on a supposed attachment to a fair damsel, and endeavoured to speak some English. Said that he had seen Lady Bingham the day before, that she could not speak French, but that she 'looked good-tempered.'

'Bertrand,' said Napoleon, 'has told me that the Governor has at last sent up his answers. I have not read them myself, but from what Bertrand tells me, they are a very poor production, and would make one pity the writer who covers over so many pages without arriving at any conclusion.'

Napoleon spoke again about Talleyrand. 'The triumph of Talleyrand,' said he, 'is the triumph of immorality. A priest united to another man's wife, and who has paid her husband a large sum of money to leave her with him! A man who has sold everything, betrayed everybody and every side! I forbade Madame Talleyrand the Court, first, because she was a disreputable character, and because I found out that some Genoese merchants had paid her four hundred thousand francs, in hopes of gaining some commercial favours through her husband. She was a very fine woman, English or East Indian, but *sotte* and grossly ignorant.

'I sometimes asked Denon, whose works I suppose you have read, to breakfast with me, as I took pleasure in his conversation, and conversed very freely with him. Many intriguers and speculators paid their court to Denon, with the view of inducing him to mention their projects or themselves in the course of his conversations with me, thinking that even being mentioned by such a man as Denon, for whom I had a great esteem, might materially serve them. Talleyrand, who was a great speculator, invited Denon to dinner. When he went home to his wife he said, " My dear, I have invited Denon to dine. He is a great traveller, and you must say something handsome to him about his travels, as he may be useful to us with the Emperor." His wife being extremely ignorant, and probably never having read any other book of travels than that of *Robinson Crusoe*, concluded that Denon could be nobody else than Robinson. Wishing to be very civil to him, she, before a large company, asked him divers questions about his man Friday! Denon, astonished, did not know what to think at first, but at length discovered by her questions that she really imagined him to be Robinson Crusoe. His astonishment and that of the company cannot be described, nor the peals of laughter which it excited in Paris as the story flew like wildfire through the city, and even Talleyrand himself was ashamed of it.[1]

'Dr. Warden has said,' continued he, 'that I turned Mahometan in Egypt. Now it is not the case. I never followed any of the tenets of that religion. I never prayed in the Mosques. I never abstained from wine, or was circumcised, neither did I ever profess it. I said merely that we were the friends of the Mussulmen, and that I respected Mahomet their prophet, which was true; I respect him now.[2] I wanted to make the Imans cause

[1] The strange career and remarkable beauty of Talleyrand's wife, and her notorious connection, when Madame Grandt, with Sir Philip Francis, are noticed at some length in a note to Bourrienne's *Memoirs of Napoleon Bonaparte*, vol. i. p. 453, 1885 edition; where also, though it is admitted that her intellect was not brilliant, she is vindicated from the charge of having inquired for Sir George Robinson's 'Man Friday.' The real perpetrator of this question is said to have been a French abbé.

[2] 'I had heard that the Emperor professed Mahometanism when in Egypt, and I had been prompted by some one to catechise him on the subject. I at once came out with the question in my Anglo-French: "Pourquoi avez-vous tourné Turque?" He did not at first understand me, and I was obliged to explain that "tourné Turque" meant changing his religion. He laughed, and said, "What is that to you? Fighting is a soldier's religion. I never changed that. The other is the affair of women and priests; *quant à moi*, I always adopt the religion of the country I am in." At a later period some Italian ecclesiastics arrived at St. Helena and were attached to Napoleon's suite.'—*Recollections of the Emperor Napoleon*, by Mrs. Abell, third edition, pp. 83, 84.

prayers to be offered up in the Mosques for me, in order to make the people respect me still more than they actually did, and obey me more readily. The Imans replied that there was a great obstacle, because their prophet in the Koran had inculcated to them that they were not to obey, respect, or hold faith with infidels, and that I came under that denomination. I then desired them to hold a consultation, and see what was necessary to be done in order to become a Mussulman, as some of their tenets could not be practised by us. Well, after deliberating and battling together for I believe three months, they finally decided that a man might become a Mussulman, and neither circumcise, nor abstain from wine; but that in proportion to the wine drunk, some good works must be done. I then told them that we were all Mussulmen and friends of the Prophet, which they readily believed, as the French soldiers never went to church, and had no priests with them. For during the Revolution there was no religion whatever in the French army. Menou,' continued Napoleon, 'really turned Mahometan, which was the reason that I left him behind.'[1]

---

[1] Napoleon, filled with ideas of subduing the world, started in 1798 to conquer as a preliminary the eastern portion of it. All through his life he betrayed an Oriental belief in fate and destiny, attributing his success more to the fidelity of fortune than to the skilfulness of his own arrangements. Shortly after his arrival in Egypt, the approach of Nelson's fleet being announced to him, he exclaimed, 'Fortune, wilt thou abandon me? What! I ask but five days.' And he is reported to have subsequently said, 'In five days

He then spoke about some of the plans that he had had in contemplation for making canals of communication in Egypt. 'I intended,' said he, 'to have made two : one from the Red Sea to the Nile at Cairo, and the other to the Mediterranean. I had the Red Sea surveyed, and found that its waters were thirty feet higher than the Mediterranean when they were highest, but only twenty-four at the lowest.[1] My plan was to have prevented any water from flowing into the canal unless at low water, and ·this in the course of a distance of thirty leagues in its passage to the Mediterranean would have been of little consequence. Besides, I would have had some sluices made. The Nile was seven feet lower than the Red Sea, when at its lowest, but fourteen feet higher (I think he said) during the inundation. The expense was calculated at eighteen millions of francs, and two years' labour.

I was master of Egypt. It was only when fortune perceived that all her favours were useless that she abandoned our fleet to its destiny.' Napoleon having landed at Alexandria, marched through the desert and encamped among the beautiful gardens of Gizeh. Here, in the presence of the Sphinx, the battle of the Pyramids took place.

His secretary relates that while in Egypt he was fond of solitude, and was given to reverie and meditation ; that when the weather was not too warm he rode about upon his horse alone. 'I used to read to him every night; when I read poetry he would fall asleep; but when he asked for the *Life of Cromwell*, I counted on sitting up pretty late.'

[1] This has been subsequently found to be incorrect. Until quite recent times also a difference of level between the Indian Ocean and Bay of Bengal was demonstrated by surveys, but was ultimately found to be due to the constant multiplication of a most minute error of visibility common to all instruments, in plotting a survey line from Bombay to Madras.

'It is only,' continued he, 'the ignorance and barbarity of the Turks which prevents your India trade from being ruined. If any European nation had possession of Egypt it would speedily be effected, and one day or another Egypt will destroy the East India Company. If Kléber had lived you would never have conquered it. He would have had the army down from Cairo in nine days, and would have overwhelmed you. If I had been there myself, I would have brought the troops down in seven days, and have been on the coast before you had disembarked. I had done so before, when the Turks landed with Sidney Smith.'

I asked if he had not saved Menou's life after the 13th of Vendémiaire? He replied, ' I certainly was the means of saving his life. The Convention ordered him to be tried, and he would have been guillotined; I was then Commander-in-Chief of Paris. Thinking it very unjust that Menou only should suffer, while three *Commissaires* of the Convention, under whose orders he acted, were left untried and unpunished, but not venturing to say openly that he ought to be acquitted (for in those terrible times a man who told the truth lost his head), I had recourse to a stratagem. I invited the Members who were trying him to breakfast, and turned the conversation upon Menou. I said that he had acted very wrongly, and deserved to be condemned to death; but that first the Commissioners of the Convention must be tried and condemned, as he had acted by their orders, and all must suffer. This had the desired effect. The Members of the Court said, "We will not allow those civilians to bathe themselves in our blood, while they allow their own Commissioners, who are more culpable, to escape with impunity." Menou was immediately declared innocent.'

I then asked how many men he supposed had lost their lives on the 13th Vendémiaire? He replied, 'Very few, considering the circumstances. Of the people there were about seventy or eighty killed, and between three and four hundred wounded; of the Conventionalists about thirty killed, and two hundred and fifty wounded. The reason so few were killed was, that after the first two discharges, I made the troops load with powder only, which had the effect of frightening the Parisians, and answered as well as killing them would have done. I made the troops at first fire ball, because to a rabble who are ignorant of the effect of firearms, it is the worst possible policy to fire powder only in the beginning. For the populace after the first discharge, hearing a great noise, are a little frightened, but looking around them and seeing nobody killed or wounded pluck up their spirits, begin immediately to despise you, become doubly outrageous, and rush on without fear, and it is necessary to kill ten times the number that it would have been had ball been used at first. With a rabble everything depends upon the first impressions made upon them. If they receive a discharge of firearms, and perceive the killed and wounded falling amongst them, a panic seizes them, and they take to their heels instantly. Therefore, when it is necesssary to fire at all, it ought to be done with ball at first. ' It is mistaken humanity to use powder only at that moment, and instead of saving the lives of men, ultimately causes an unnecessary waste of human blood.'

March 17.—Napoleon walked round the house for a short time.

A letter written by Captain Poppleton to Sir Hudson Lowe, informing His Excellency that the horses of the establishment had been three days without receiving any hay, and that for a length of time they had had no litter. Also, that the stuff sent as hay was grass recently cut, with occasionally a large portion of cow-grass[1] mixed with it. That upon allowing fifty pounds of the said miscalled hay to dry for two days, it only weighed, with the rope which bound it, twenty pounds, according to a very accurate trial made by himself. That in consequence, he had directed the grooms to go and cut some grass if they could find any, as the horses were starving.

March 18.—Napoleon joked with me for some time about St. Patrick, and endeavoured to speak some English, in which he succeeded better than I had ever observed before. I said, that I had remarked divers of his expressions in some of the French bulletins. That from having had the honour of being accustomed to speak to him, I had recognised some of them, and took the liberty of

[1] A species of inferior coarse grass, which horses will not eat.

asking him if he had not occasionally written them? He replied, 'Where have you seen them?' I answered, at the Governor's, and that I had particularly remarked his forcible expressions in the bulletin announcing the burning of Moscow. He laughed, gave me a gentle pull by the ear, and said, 'You are right. Some of them are mine.

'I am told,' said Napoleon, 'that there is £20,000 worth of iron railings sent out. It is money thrown into the sea. Before this railing can be fixed up here, I shall be underground, for I am sure that I shall not exist more than two years under the treatment that I now experience.'

Sir Hudson Lowe very busy inspecting the ditches and other works he had ordered to be thrown up about Longwood House and the stables.

March 19.—Saw Napoleon in his bath. He was reading a little book, which I perceived to be a French New Testament. I could not help observing to him that many people would not believe that he would read such a book, as it had been asserted and credited by some that he was an unbeliever. Napoleon laughed and replied, 'It is not true. I am far from an Atheist.'[1] In spite of all the iniquities

[1] 'When we were visiting Madame Bertrand we always passed our Sundays as if at home, reading the lessons for the day, and observing the prayers, etc. On Sunday morning Napoleon came bustling in, and seeing me reading aloud to my sister, asked what I was so intently engaged upon, and why I looked so much graver than usual. I told him I was learning the collect for the day, and that if I failed in saying it, my father would be very angry. I remarked: "I suppose *you* never learnt a collect or anything religious, for I am told you disbelieve the existence of a God." He seemed displeased

and frauds of the teachers of religion, who are eternally preaching that their kingdom is not of this world, and yet seize everything which they can lay their hands upon, from the time that I became Head of the Government I did everything in my power to re-establish religion. But I wished to render it the foundation and prop of morality and good principles, and not *à prendre l'essor* of the human laws. Man has need of something wonderful. It is better for him to seek it in religion than in Mlle le Normand.[1] Moreover, religion is a great consolation and resource to those who possess it, and no man can say what he will do in his last moments.'

Napoleon then made some remarks upon the conduct of the Governor, whom he declared to be a man totally unfit for his situation. ' If he were,' said he, ' he might make it pleasant and interesting. He might spend much of his time with me, and get great information with respect to past occurrences, with which no other person could be so well acquainted or so satisfactorily account for. You see what I am, *dottore*. Even unknown to myself, he would imperceptibly have opportunities of getting information from me, which would be very desirable to his Ministers, and which I am certain they have ordered him to obtain, and that he burns to know. If I had really any intention of effecting my escape

at my observation, and answered : "You have been told an untruth. When you are wiser you will understand that no one could doubt the existence of a God."'—Mrs. Abell's *Recollections*, 1873 edition, p. 174.

[1] A celebrated fortune-teller at Paris, consulted even by several crowned heads, etc.

from this place, instead of disagreeing with him I would caress and flatter him, endeavour to be on the best terms, go to Plantation House, call on his wife, and try to make him believe that I was contented, and thereby lull his suspicions asleep.'

March 20.—Saw Napoleon in his bedroom in his dressing-gown. He spoke at length about some statements in Warden's book. 'At one time I had appointed Talleyrand,' said he, 'to proceed on a mission to Warsaw, in order to arrange and organise the best method of accomplishing the separation of Poland from Russia. He had several conferences with me respecting this mission, which was a great surprise to the Ministers, as Talleyrand had no official character at the time. Having married one of his relations to the Duchess of Courland, Talleyrand was very anxious to receive the appointment, that he might revive the claims of the Duchess's family. However, some money transactions of his were discovered at Vienna, which determined me not to employ him on the intended mission. I had intended at one time to have made him a cardinal, with which he refused to comply. Madame Grandt threw herself twice upon her knees before me, in order to obtain permission to marry him, which I refused; but through the entreaties of Josephine, she succeeded on the second application.

'Ney,' said he, 'never made use of tall language at Fontainebleau in my presence; on the contrary, he was always submissive before me, although in my absence he sometimes broke out into violence, as he was a man without education. If he had made use of unbecoming language towards me at Fontainebleau, the troops would have torn him to pieces.[1]

'Lavalette,' added Napoleon, 'knew nothing of my intended return from Elba, or of what was preparing there. Madame Lavalette was of the family of Beauharnais. She was a very fine woman. My brother Louis fell in love with and wanted to marry her; to prevent which I caused her to espouse Lavalette, to whom she was attached.

'When Lavalette was Director of Posts,' continued Napoleon, 'I desired to be made acquainted with the sentiments of the nation relative to my administration. I appointed twelve persons, all of different ways of thinking, some Jacobins, some Royalists, some Republicans, others Imperialists, etc., with a salary of a thousand francs a month, whose business it was to make monthly reports to Lavalette of their own opinions and those which they had heard expressed relative to the public acts. These reports were brought to me unopened by Lavalette. After reading and making extracts when necessary, I burned them. This was conducted so secretly that even the Ministers did not know of it.

[1] Napoleon added that he had never told Ney that he had entered France with the support of England; that on the contrary he had always disclaimed the idea of returning by the aid of foreign bayonets, and had come purposely to overturn a dynasty upheld by them. That all he looked for was the support of the French nation, to which all his proclamations would bear witness.—B. E. O'M.

'Warden has given a very imperfect account of the part taken by Captain Wright in the conspiracy against me. In different nights of August, September, and December 1803, and January 1804, Wright landed Georges, Pichegru, Rivière, Coster, St. Victor, La Haye, St. Hilaire, and others, at Beville. The four last-named had been accomplices in the former attempt to assassinate me by means of the infernal machine, and most of the rest were well known to be chiefs of the Chouans. They remained during the day in a little farmhouse near to where they had landed, the proprietor of which had been bribed to assist them. They travelled only by night, pretending to be smugglers, concealing themselves in the daytime in lodgings which had been previously procured for them. They had plenty of money, and remained at Paris for some time without being discovered, although the police had some intimation that a plot was going on, through Mehée de la Touche, who, although paid as a spy by your Ministers,[1] disclosed everything to the French police. He had several conferences with Drake, your *Chargé d'affaires* at Munich, from whom he received large sums of money. Some of the brigands who had been landed were arrested and interrogated. By their answers it appeared that a man named Mussey, who lived at Offembourg,

---

[1] Napoleon informed me that Mehée had received from Mr. Drake and other official persons nearly two hundred thousand francs. —B. E. O'M.

with the Duc d'Enghien, was very active in corresponding with and sending money to those who had been secretly landed on the coasts, and most of whom could give no good reason why they had ventured to return to Paris at the imminent hazard of their lives, as they had not been included in the amnesty.

'The list of the prisoners and their answers on examination were submitted to me. I was very anxious, and on looking over it one night, I remarked that one of the number, named Querel, was stated to be a surgeon. It struck me that this man was not actuated by enthusiasm, or by a spirit of party, but by the hope of gain.[1] He would therefore be more likely to confess than any of the others; and the fear of death would probably induce him to betray his accomplices. I ordered him to be tried as a Chouan; and according to the laws he was condemned to death. It was not a mock trial, as Warden thought: on the contrary, while going to execution, he promised to make important disclosures. Querel was conducted back to prison, where he was interrogated by the *grand juge* Réal. He confessed that he had come from England, and had been landed in August 1803 from Wright's ship, along with Georges and several others. That Georges was then in Paris, planning the assassination of the First Consul. He also pointed out the houses where the other conspirators and himself had stopped on their way to Paris. Police

---

[1] Was Napoleon amusing himself with O'Meara?

officers were sent to the place he had designated; and from the result of their inquiries it appeared that he had told the truth, and that since the time he had described, two other landings of similar gentry had been effected by Wright, with the last of whom there had been some person of consequence whose name they could not discover, and that they soon expected another cargo. The Duke of Rovigo, as I told you once before, was immediately sent to Beville with a party of the police, in the hope of being able to seize them. An Emigrant, named Bouvet de Lozier, who has since been employed at the Isle of France, was also arrested. After he had been confined for some weeks he became desperate and hung himself in the prison one morning. The jailer, who heard an unusual noise in his room, went in and cut him down before life had departed. While he was recovering his senses he burst out into incoherent exclamations, that Moreau had brought Pichegru from London; that he was a traitor, and had persuaded them that all the army were for him, and that he would prove the cause of their destruction. Those expressions excited alarm. The police knew that a brother of Pichegru's, who had once been a monk, lived in Paris. He was arrested and examined. He avowed that he had seen his brother a day or two before, and asked if it were a crime? Moreau was immediately arrested, and large rewards were offered by the police for the apprehension of Georges and Pichegru.

'Pichegru was betrayed by one of his old friends, who came to the police and offered to deliver him into their hands for a hundred thousand francs paid on the spot. Georges still continued to elude the vigilance of the police. I proclaimed the city of Paris to be in a state of siege, and no person was allowed to quit it unless by day, and through certain barriers, where were stationed people to whom the persons of the conspirators were familiar. About three weeks afterwards Georges was betrayed and taken, after having shot one of the men who tried to arrest him. All his accomplices were subsequently taken. Pichegru did not deny having been employed by the Bourbons, and behaved with great audacity. Afterwards, finding his case desperate, he strangled himself in the prison. The rest of the conspirators were publicly tried in the month of May before the Tribunal of the Department of the Seine, and in the presence of all the foreign Ambassadors in Paris. Georges, Polignac, Rivière, Coster, and sixteen or seventeen others were found guilty of having conspired against the life of the Chief Magistrate of the French nation, and condemned to death. Georges, Coster, and seven or eight more were executed. Rivière was pardoned, partly through the intercession of Murat. I also pardoned some of the others. Moreau was condemned to two years' imprisonment, which was commuted into banishment to America. Jules de Polignac, confidant of the Comte d'Artois, and many others, were also condemned to imprisonment. According to the confession of some of the conspirators, the Duc d'Enghien was an accomplice, and was waiting on the frontiers of France for the news of my assassination, upon receiving which he was to have entered France as the King's lieutenant. As the police,' added Napoleon, 'did not like to trust to the evidence of Mehée de la Touche alone, they sent Captain Rose (in whose integrity they had every confidence) to Drake at Munich, with a letter from Mehée, which procured him an interview, the result of which confirmed Mehée's statement, that he was concerned in a plot to *terrasser le premier consul*, no matter by what means.'[1]

March 23.—Napoleon dressed and in the billiard-room. In very good humour. Gave him some libels upon himself. They were all in French, and amongst others were *Mémoires Secrets*, and *Bonaparte peint par lui-même*, which excited his laughter.

Napoleon then asked several questions about the Governor. I said that Sir Hudson had desired me to say, a few days ago, that he had every wish to accommodate matters, and that he thought that Las

---

[1] While the Duc d'Enghien was on his trial, Madame la Maréchale Bessières said to Colonel Ordener, who had arrested him, 'Are there no possible means to save that *malheureux*? Has his guilt been established beyond a doubt?'—'Madame,' replied Colonel Ordener, 'I found in his house sacks of papers sufficient to compromise half of France.' The Duke was executed in the morning, and not by torchlight as has been represented.

Cases, Warden, and Mrs. Skelton,[1] and some others, had been the means of producing much ill-blood, and a great deal of misunderstanding. Napoleon replied, 'He deceives himself. In the first place, it was the badness of his physiognomy; next his wanting to force me to receive the visit of an officer twice in the twenty-four hours; then the letter to Bertrand; his wishing that I should send you away, and to give me a surgeon of his own choice; the manner in which he spoke to me about the wooden house; his letters full of softness, accompanying the train of vexations which followed; and his always leaving something doubtful which he could afterwards interpret as best suited his views. In fact, he wanted, by showing that he could render things disagreeable, to compel us to yield, submissively demand pardon of him, go to Plantation House, and be his very humble servants.

'It appears that Warden has been informed,' added Napoleon, 'that I applied some lines of Shakespeare to Madame Montholon. You well know that I could not then, nor can I now, quote English verse, nor have I ever intended to convey

[1] Mrs. Skelton was accused by the Governor of having told Napoleon one day at dinner, that from experience she knew he would not always find Longwood pleasant. That at certain times of the year it was a damp, disagreeable, bleak, and unhealthy residence; as a proof of which she mentioned that she never could succeed in rearing poultry there; while down in the Company's garden, situated in a sheltered valley, about four hundred yards distant, she had no difficulty in bringing them up. Mrs. Skelton and family had resided at Longwood a few months in each year for four or five years before Napoleon arrived.

a reflection on Madame Montholon. On the contrary, I think that she possesses more firmness and *caractère* than most of her sex.'

March 24.—Napoleon complained of swellings in his legs, for which I recommended some simple remedies, which he put in practice.

He afterwards observed that he had been reading all yesterday the *Secret Memoirs* of himself, Pichon's work, etc. 'These libels,' said he, 'have done me more good than harm in France, because they irritated the nation both against the writers, and the Bourbons who paid them, by representing me as a monster, and by the improbable and scandalous falsehoods they contained against me, and the government under me, which were degrading to them as a nation. Even Châteaubriand has done me good by his work. Pichon, the author of the *State of France under Bonaparte*, had been Consul in America, and was disgraced by me for having embezzled three millions of francs, part of which he was obliged to refund, as I was very particular with consuls and other agents, and always examined their accounts myself. This Pichon, after he had published his libel, was sent by me to London as a spy after my return from Elba; at least, he was so far sent by me that I suffered it, because, although he was *un coquin*, he had some *esprit*, and on account of the nature of his writings would not be suspected. You see what dependence is to be placed upon writers of libels. This man, who in 1814 had written such a libel against me, went in

1815 as a spy for the police of the very person whom he had so grossly libelled.'

March 25.—Napoleon in his bath. His legs much better. In very good spirits. 'It appears, Mr. Doctor,' said he, 'from the books you lent me, that at a very early age I poisoned a girl; that I poisoned others for the mere pleasure of poisoning; that I assassinated Desaix, Kléber, the Duc d'Abrantès, and I know not how many others; that I went to the army of Italy, consisting of some thousand galley-slaves, who were extremely happy to see me, as being one of their fraternity. It is surprising what things are believed on both sides, in consequence of not having had communication with each other. In France, if a house was burnt down, the vulgar attributed it to the English. "Pitt! Pitt!" was the cry directly. Nothing could persuade the French *canaille* that the conflagration at Lyons had not been effected by the English. In like manner, you English believed everything bad of me, which belief was always encouraged by your Ministers.

'When I was at Elba,' added Napoleon, 'I was visited by an English nobleman, a Catholic, about thirty years old, and from Northumberland, I believe. He had dined a few weeks before with the Duc de Fleury, with whom he had a conversation relative to the sum of money to be allowed me annually by France, according to the agreement that had been signed by the Ministers of the Allied Powers. The Duke laughed at him for supposing for a moment that it would be complied with, and said, that they were not such fools. This was one of the reasons which induced me to quit Elba. I do not believe that Castlereagh thought I would have ventured to leave it, as otherwise some frigates would have been stationed about the island. If they had kept a frigate in the harbour, and another outside, it would have been impossible for me to have gone to France, except alone, which I would not have attempted. If even the King of France had ordered a frigate with a picked crew to cruise off the island, it would have prevented me.' I asked if he thought that it had been the intention of the Allies to have sent him to St. Helena?[1] 'Why,' replied the Emperor, 'it was much spoken of. However, Colonel Campbell denied it. They must have sent an army to take me; I could have held out for some months. But there were many violations of the treaty of Fontainebleau by the Allies, which authorised and obliged me to take the step I did. Besides what I have told you, it was stipulated and agreed to that all the members of my family should be allowed to follow me to Elba; but in violation of that, my wife and child were seized, detained, and never permitted to join a husband and a father. They were also to have had the duchies of Parma, Placentia, and Guastalla, which they were deprived of. By the treaty Prince Eugène was to

[1] 'A very decided intention of removing Bonaparte from the island of Elba is manifesting itself. I have proposed one of the Açores; it is five hundred leagues from any coast.'—Talleyrand, *Correspondence*, vol. i. p. 48.

have had a principality in Italy, which was never given. My mother and brothers were to receive pensions, which were also refused .to them. My own private property, and the savings which I had made on the civil list, were to have been preserved for me. Instead of that, they were seized in the hands of Labouillerie, the treasurer, contrary to the treaty, and all claims made by me rejected. The private property of my family was to be held sacred; it was confiscated. The dotations assigned to the army on the Mont Napoléon were to be preserved—they were suppressed; nor were the hundred thousand francs, which were to be given as pensions to persons pointed out by me, ever paid. Moreover, assassins were sent to Elba to murder me. Never,' continued Napoleon, 'have the terms of a treaty been more evidently violated, and, indeed, openly scoffed at, than those were by the Allies, and yet your Ministers had the impudence to tell the nation that I was the first violator of the treaty of Fontainebleau.'[1]

I observed that the Allies had given as a reason for their conduct towards him, that he had aimed at universal dominion. 'No,' replied the Emperor, 'I certainly wished to render France the most power-

---

[1] On this subject of the violation of solemn treaty engagements by the Bourbons see an interesting note by Colonel Phipps in the 1885 edition of Bourrienne's *Memoirs of Napoleon*, vol. iii. pp. 238, 239. Even the Czar of Russia, Emperor of Austria, and Lord Castlereagh remonstrated with Louis XVIII. on the point. M. Plon, in his Life of the great sculptor Thorvaldsen, gives another instance of the bad faith of the Bourbons in not taking over his contract work.

ful nation in the world, but no further. I did not aim at universal dominion. It was my intention to have made Italy an independent kingdom. There are natural limits for France, which I did not intend to overstep. It was my object to prevent England from being able to go to war with France, without assistance from some of the great Continental Powers, without which, indeed, she ought never to venture.'

Had some conversation about Ferdinand of Spain. 'When Ferdinand was at Valençay,' said Napoleon, 'he always expressed a great dislike of the English, and declared that the first thing he would do, on his return to Spain, would be to re-establish the Inquisition. You English will find one day that by restoring him you have done yourselves a great national injury. While at Valençay he said that he would prefer remaining in France to returning to Spain, and wrote several times to me, begging of me to adopt and give him a Frenchwoman in marriage.

'As your Ministers and the Bourbonists cannot any longer deny that I have done some good to France, they endeavour to get over it by saying that whatever good I effected was done through the persuasions of Josephine. For example, they say that it was Josephine who induced me to recall the Emigrants. Now Josephine was the most amiable and the best of women, but she never interfered with politics. Their object is to persuade the world that I am incapable of a good action.'

Sir Pulteney and Lady Malcolm, Captains Stanfell and Festing, of the Navy, came up and had an interview with Napoleon. When they came out, Captain —— expressed his astonishment at finding Napoleon so different a person from what he was reported. 'Instead of being a rough, impatient, and imperious character,' said he, 'I found him to be gentle in his manner, and one of the pleasantest men I ever saw. I shall *never* forget him, nor how different he is from the idea I had been led to form of him!'

Sir Pulteney Malcolm expressed to me his ardent wish that matters might be accommodated between Napoleon and the Governor, adding, that two opportunities of effecting it would soon present themselves, viz. the arrival of Lord Amherst, and of Admiral Plampin; that he much wished that *both* should be introduced by Sir Hudson Lowe, and, indeed, thought that Lord Amherst could not be introduced by any other person.

Napoleon, accompanied by Countesses Bertrand and Montholon, and their husbands, walked down into the wood. On their return, chairs were brought out and placed in front of the billiard-room, where the company remained for some time after sunset.

March 26.—Napoleon conversed a good deal about the battle of Waterloo. 'Lord Wellington,' he said, 'allowed himself to be surprised. On the 15th I was at Charleroi, and had beaten the Prussians without his knowing anything about it.[1] I had gained forty-eight hours of manœuvres upon him, which was a great object; and if some of my generals had shown that vigour and genius which they had displayed in other times, I should have taken his army in cantonments without ever fighting a battle. But they were discouraged, and fancied that they saw an army of a hundred thousand men everywhere opposed to them. I had not time enough myself,' he said, 'to attend to the *minutiæ* of the army. I reckoned upon surprising and cutting them up in detail. I knew of Bulow's arrival at eleven o'clock; but I did not regard it. I had still eighty chances out of a hundred in my favour. Notwithstanding the great superiority of force against me, I was convinced that I should obtain the victory. I had about seventy thousand men, of whom fifteen thousand were cavalry. I had also two hundred and fifty pieces of cannon; but my troops were so good that I esteemed them sufficient to beat a hundred and twenty thousand. Lord Wellington had under his command about ninety thousand, and two hundred and fifty pieces of cannon; and Bulow had thirty thousand, making a hundred and twenty thousand.[2] Of all those

[1] 'Were you not surprised, Duke, in 1815?' said, on one occasion, a lady naively at a dinner party to the victor of Waterloo. 'No, madam, but I am *now!*' was the reply.

[2] Dorsey Gardner gives the French force as nearly seventy-two thousand men, and two hundred and forty-six guns; the English force as nearly sixty-eight thousand men (including auxiliaries), and one hundred and fifty-six guns; and the Prussian force as (at 4.30 P.M., six thousand men), at 7 P.M. fifty-two thousand men, and one hundred and four guns.

troops, however, I only reckoned the English as being able to cope with my own, the others I thought little of. I believe that of English there were from thirty-five to forty thousand. These I esteemed to be as brave and as good as my own troops; the English army was well known latterly on the Continent; and besides, your nation possesses courage and energy. As to the Prussians, Belgians, and others, half the number of my troops were sufficient to beat them. I only left thirty-four thousand men to take care of the Prussians. The chief causes of the loss of that battle were, first of all, Grouchy's great tardiness and neglect in executing his orders;[1] next, the *grenadiers à cheval* and the cavalry under General Guyot, which I had in reserve, and which were never to leave me, engaged without orders and without my knowledge; so that after the last charge, when the troops were beaten, and the English cavalry advanced, I had not a single corps of cavalry in reserve to resist them; instead of one which I esteemed to be equal to double their own number. In consequence of this, the English attack succeeded, and all was lost. There was no means of rallying. The youngest general would not have committed the fault of leaving an army entirely without reserve, which however occurred here, whether in consequence of treason, or not, I cannot say. These were the two principal causes of the loss of the battle of Waterloo.'

Napoleon then spoke about the libels upon him-

[1] See footnote in vol. i. p. 334.

self which I had collected for him. 'As yet,' said he, 'you have not procured me one that is worthy of an answer. Would you have me sit down and reply to Goldsmith, Pichon, or the *Quarterly Review*? They are so contemptible and so absurdly false, that they do not merit any other notice than to write *faux, faux,* on every page. The only truth I have seen in them is, that one day I met an officer, Rapp, I believe, in the field of battle, with his face covered with blood, and that I cried, *Oh, comme il est beau!* This is true enough; and of it they have made a crime. My admiration of the gallantry of a brave soldier is construed into a crime, and a proof of my delighting in blood. But if I were such a tyrant, such a monster, would the people and the army have flown to join me with the enthusiasm they showed when I landed from Elba with a handful of men? Could I have marched to Paris and have seated myself upon the throne without a musket having been fired?

'I have,' continued he, 'been twice married. Political motives induced me to divorce my first wife, whom I tenderly loved. She, poor woman, fortunately for herself, died in time to prevent her witnessing the last of my misfortunes. Let Marie Louise be asked with what tenderness and affection I always treated her. After her forcible separation from me, she avowed in the most feeling terms to —— her ardent desire to join me, extolled with many tears both myself and my conduct to her, and bitterly lamented her cruel separation, avowing her ardent desire to join me in my exile.[1] Is this the result of the conduct of a merciless, unfeeling tyrant? A man is known by his conduct to his wife, to his family, and to those under him.'

I then told the Emperor that Lord Amherst, the late British Ambassador to China, was expected here in a few days. He said he thought the English Ministers had acted wrongly in not having ordered him to comply with the customs of the place he was sent to. I observed that the English would consider it debasing to the nation, if Lord Amherst had consented to prostrate himself in the manner required. That if such a point were conceded, the Chinese would probably not be contented, and would require ceremonies to be performed similar to those insisted upon by the Japanese, and complied with so disgracefully by the Dutch. That, besides, Lord Amherst was willing to pay the same obeisance to the Chinese Emperor as he would do to his own King. Napoleon replied, 'It is quite a different thing. One is a mere ceremony, performed by all the great men of the nation to their chief, and the other is a national degradation required of strangers, and of strangers only. In my opinion, whatever is the custom of a nation, and is practised by the first personages of that nation towards their chief, cannot degrade strangers who perform the same. Different nations have different customs. In England, at Court, you kiss the King's

---

[1] Marie Louise readily consoled herself during Napoleon's absence by 'marriages at frequent intervals.'

hand. Such a thing in France would be considered ridiculous, and the person who did it would be held up to public scorn; but still the French Ambassador who performed it in England would not be considered to have degraded himself. In England, some hundred years back, the King was served kneeling; the same ceremony now takes place in Spain. In Italy, you kiss the Pope's toe, yet it is not considered as a degradation. A man who goes into a country must comply with the ceremonies in use there, and it would have been no degradation whatever for Lord Amherst to have submitted to such ceremonies before the Emperor of China as are performed by the first Mandarins of that Empire.

'If I,' continued he, 'had sent an Ambassador to China, I would have ordered him to make himself acquainted with the ceremonies performed before the Emperor by the first Mandarins; and, if required, to do the same himself, and no more. Now, perhaps, you will lose the friendship of the nation, and great commercial advantages, through this piece of nonsense.' I said that we could easily compel the Chinese to grant good terms by means of a few ships of war; that, for example, we could deprive them altogether of salt, by a few cruisers properly stationed. Napoleon replied, 'It would be the worst thing you have done for a number of years, to go to war with an immense empire like China, and possessing so many resources. You would doubtless, at first, succeed, take what vessels they have, and destroy their trade; but you would teach them their own strength. They would be compelled to adopt measures to defend themselves against you; they would consider, and say, "We must try to make ourselves equal to this nation. Why should we suffer a people, so far away, to do as they please to us? We must build ships, we must put guns into them, we must render ourselves equal to them." They would,'continued the Emperor, 'get artificers and shipbuilders from France and America, and even from London; they would build a fleet, and, in the course of time, defeat you.'[1]

I observed that it was likely Lord Amherst would wait upon him. Napoleon replied, 'If he is to be presented by the Governor, or if the latter sends one of his staff with him, I will not receive him; if he comes with the Admiral, I shall. Neither will I receive the new Admiral if he is to be introduced by the Governor. In his last letter there is an insult to us. He says that we may go round by Miss Mason's, but that we must not go off the main road. Where is this main road? I never could find any.[2] If I stepped aside a few yards I should be exposed to be shot at by a sentinel. The Admiral, when he was here last, spoke like Sir Hudson's advocate, and wanted me to receive him with Lord Amherst. I would not receive my own son if he were to be presented by him!'

[1] This prediction of Napoleon's has since been borne out to the letter during the aggressions of the (third) French Republic upon the Chinese Empire.

[2] The *main road* is a path impassable by wheel-carriages.

March 27.—Napoleon gave me some explanations touching what had been said of his having kept secret from his soldiers in Egypt for a long time that the plague had got into the army. ' I,' said he, *once* touched a soldier in the hospital who was infected, with a view to convince the troops that the disease was not the plague; and I believe that I succeeded for fifteen days in persuading them that it was only a kind of fever. I rarely practised visiting the hospital,' continued he, 'as the extreme sensibility of my nose was such, that the smell always made me ill, on which account I was advised by Corvisart and my other physicians not to attempt it. Even during my campaigns in Europe I seldom visited them.'

March 29.—The Emperor in his bath. Conversed about the English manufacturers. ' I, myself, during my reign, gave up near five hundred convents, without any payment, to individuals, on the sole condition of their engaging to establish a manufactory in each. Moreover, I lent them out of my own pocket upwards of fifty millions of francs to enable them to go on, which they were to retain for nine years, without paying any interest, after which term the principal was to be returned. In England, your machines are so numerous, that in a short time you would have had no occasion for hands.' I observed that the prevalence of machinery was one cause of the great distress in England. ' But,' replied Napoleon, 'you were obliged to have recourse to the aid of machinery, because the necessaries of life are twice as dear in England as on the Continent, and your taxes six times greater, and also because other nations have them. Otherwise, you could not have sold your manufactures as cheap as they could, and consequently would not find purchasers. In Germany and Switzerland, for example, there were a great number of machines.'

March 31.—Dined at Plantation House in company with Count Balmaine, Baron and Baroness Sturmer, Captain Gorrequer, etc. The Commissioners very anxious to know something about Napoleon.

April 2.—Saw Napoleon, who was in tolerable spirits. I asked if it were true that he had been induced to quit Egypt by his having received private information that the Directory purposed to get him assassinated there? 'No,' replied the Emperor, 'I never heard, or thought so; neither had the Directory any intention of causing it to be done. They were jealous of me certainly, but they had no idea of the kind; and in the actual situation of France, I do not think that they wished it. I returned from Egypt because my presence was necessary to the Republic, and because the first object of the expedition had been gained by the conquest of Egypt.' I asked if the project had originated with him, or with the Directory. 'We both thought of it at the same time,' replied Napoleon.

'After the defeat of the Turks at Aboukir,' added he, 'Sidney Smith sent his secretary with a flag of truce to Alexandria as the bearer of some letters addressed to me, which one of his cruisers had taken on board of a ship, to which Sidney Smith added some English newspapers, the contents of which decided me to return to France.'

Mr. and the Misses Churchill from India came up yesterday to see Madame Bertrand, for the purpose of having an interview with Napoleon. His Excellency, however, took an effectual mode of preventing it, by sending up Sir Thomas Reade to accompany them. It is probable that Napoleon, who is very partial to female society, and was informed that the young ladies were highly accomplished, and spoke French fluently, would have managed to meet them *accidentally*, had not Sir Thomas been an attentive listener close to their side during the whole time.

Captain Cook, of the *Tortoise*, and Mr. Mackenzie, midshipman of the same ship, came up to Longwood. Mr. Mackenzie had been midshipman on board the *Undaunted*, Captain Ussher, when the Emperor took a passage in that ship to Elba. Captain Cook told me that after waiting some time on the look-out, they saw Napoleon walking in the garden, who sent for them and asked many questions. He recollected Mr. Mackenzie, observed that he had grown much since he had seen him before, and made some inquiries about Captain Ussher. He asked Captain Cook how long he had been in the service? to which he replied, 'Thirty years.' He seemed surprised at this, and asked what actions? Cook mentioned, amongst others, Trafalgar. Napoleon asked the name of the ship he belonged to, and divers questions about the battle, where he came from, and concluded by asking him where he was going to dine? 'At camp,' was the reply. 'At camp? Then take care,' said Napoleon, 'that you do not get drunk.'

April 3.—Napoleon observed that he had seen yesterday an old seaman, which he expressed in English. 'He looks,' said he, 'like a seaman *è pare un brav'uomo*. There was with him a midshipman who was on board the frigate with Ussher, when I took a passage in her to Elba. He is much grown,' continued he, 'but I recollected him.' I told him that the midshipman had said the ship's company of the *Undaunted* had liked him (Napoleon) very much. 'Yes,' replied Napoleon, 'I believe they did; I used to go amongst them, speak to them kindly, and ask different questions. My freedom in this respect quite astonished them, as it was so different from that which they had been accustomed to receive from their own officers. You English are *aristocrats*. You keep a great distance between yourselves and the people.'[1] I observed that on board a man-of-war it was necessary to keep the seamen at a great distance in order to maintain a proper respect for the officers. 'I do not think,' replied the Emperor, 'that it is necessary to keep up so much as you practise. When the officers do not

---

[1] For some interesting remarks on this subject see Count Vitzthum's *Memoirs*, vol. i. p. 126.

eat or drink, or take too many freedoms with them, I see no necessity for any greater distinctions. It was always my custom to go amongst the soldiers and the common people, to converse with them and take an interest in their plans. This I found to be of great benefit to me. On the contrary, the generals and officers kept them at a distance.

'I asked,' continued he, 'the *old seaman* where he was to dine, and cautioned him not to get drunk. He told me he was married, and had no children. I asked him what he intended to do with his money. He said that he would leave it to an hospital. I then asked him if he had any nephews or nieces, and recommended him to leave his riches to *them* instead.

'You brought a book,' said he, 'about the battle of Waterloo, to Gourgaud. The author says that I am an *imbécile*, that my army was a set of robbers, and that I committed one of the greatest blunders of which a military man could be guilty, by engaging Lord Wellington with a forest in his rear. Now the great fault in Lord Wellington was having engaged me in a position with a forest in his rear, with only one road leading to it; for in case of a defeat he could not have retreated. Another libeller says that I conquered Italy with a few thousand *galley-slaves*. Now the fact is, that probably so fine an army never had existed before. More than one-half of them were men of education, the sons of merchants, of lawyers, of physicians, or of the better order of farmers and *bourgeoisie*. Two-thirds of them knew how to write, and were capable of being made officers. Indeed, in a regiment it would have puzzled me to decide who were the most deserving subjects, or who best merited promotion, as they were all so good. Oh,' continued he with emotion, 'that all my armies had been the same! When on a march, I frequently called to the soldiers for some one to come forward and write from my dictation. I was surrounded directly by dozens eager to undertake it, as there were few who did not write like clerks.

'If,' continued he, 'the French army had even been a set of brigands, which was not the case, it ill becomes a Frenchman to say so. But for your purposes, you have found worse Frenchmen than Louis has yet found Englishmen. Perhaps there is more nationality, more public spirit than in France. You are islanders. *C'è lo spirito isolare.* And, besides, you have not had a revolution so lately as in France. To form a correct judgment of the two nations, it would be necessary to see both immediately after a revolution.'

Napoleon then asked if we kept Good Friday sacred, if we fasted, and what was our mode of doing so? I replied that we did observe it; that *Protestants* seldom fasted; but that when we practised it, we abstained altogether from food. That we did not consider avoiding animal food, and gorging with turbot, or with any other delicate fish, as fasting. 'You are right,' said the Emperor; 'if one abstains at all it ought to be from everything, or else it does not deserve the name. *O come gli uomini son bestie,* to believe that abstaining from flesh, and eating fish, which is so much more delicate and delicious, constitutes fasting. *Povero uomo!*

'Before my reign,' said he, 'the oath taken by the French Kings was *to exterminate all heretics!* At my coronation, *I* swore to *protect religion in every form!* Louis has not yet sworn, because he has not been crowned, and in all probability, through fear of you and of the Prussians, will not take the oath of extermination; not that he has not the will—on the contrary, he would with pleasure both swear and *cause it to be effected;* for the family of the Bourbons are the most intolerant upon earth.'

Napoleon afterwards spoke about Hoche. 'Hoche,' said he, 'was one of the first generals that France ever produced. He was brave, intelligent, abounding in talent, decisive, and penetrating; *intrigant* also. If Hoche had landed in Ireland, he would have succeeded. He possessed all the qualities necessary to ensure success. He was accustomed to civil war, and knew how to conduct himself under such circumstances. He had pacified La Vendée, and was well adapted for Ireland. He had a fine handsome figure, a good address; he was prepossessing and artful, but by some stupidity he was placed on board a frigate which never reached the Irish coast, while the rest of the expedition of about eighteen thousand men got into Bantry Bay, where they remained for some days masters of the means of disembarkation. But Grouchy, who, I believe, was second in com mand, did not know what to do; so that after having had it in their power to land and send the ships away, as they ought to have done, they remained a short time, did nothing, and then departed like *imbéciles*. If Hoche had arrived, Ireland was lost to you.

'If the Irish,' added he, 'had sent over honest men to me, I would have certainly made an attempt upon Ireland. But I had no confidence in either the integrity or the talents of the Irish leaders that were in France. They could offer no plan, were divided in opinion, and continually quarrelling with one another. I had but a poor opinion of the integrity of that O'Connor who was so much spoken of amongst you.'

April 4.—Napoleon dressed and in the billiard-room. In very good spirits. Spoke about the Admiralty; asked who signed the commissions of naval officers? Was surprised when I informed him that none were signed by the King. 'What, was not Nelson's commission signed by King George?' I replied in the negative, and said that none but officers of the army and marines had commissions signed by the King; that His Majesty had nothing to do with naval promotions.[1] 'Who appoints the Admiralty?' said Napoleon. I replied, 'The Sovereign.'—'Then,' said he, 'it is a humbug; for if the King wishes to give a com-

[1] Until recently many hours out of every week were taken up by the monarch in the clerical and monotonous work of signing commissions, a consumption of time detrimental to more important matters. Lately this function has been delegated to a Secretary of State.

mand to an Admiral, or to promote an officer, he has nothing more to do than to signify his desire to the Admiralty, who would not dare to refuse him, through fear of losing their own places.' I observed in reply, that it had been said that the Sovereign had at times caused the appointment of an Admiral and Commander-in-Chief not exactly agreeable to the wishes of the Admiralty; but that, in such cases, it was at the option of the Lords of the Admiralty to confirm or not the promotions made by him, excepting certain vacancies which by right or by custom were in his gift. 'Bah!' said Napoleon, 'if they did not confirm the promotions, would not the King dismiss them from their places? The King can promote whom he likes. He has great power, because he appoints the Ministers, and commands those who have the direction of everything. Ministers, unless in rare instances, love their places too well to run the risk of losing them by refusing to comply with the wishes of the Sovereign. It has happened to myself that a Minister has said, "Sire, I cannot agree to this. It is contrary to my opinion, and I will sooner resign than comply."'

I remarked that instances were not wanting in England of Ministers having given up their places rather than act against their principles in compliance with the wishes of the Crown. That the King of England had considerable power over the army and the navy; but that over independent persons not military, naval, placemen, or place-hunters, he had only the influence which arose from their being conscious of the rectitude of his measures. 'And what more had I in France?' said Napoleon. 'What could I effect unless with those classes that you have excepted?' I ventured to observe that in France there was neither liberty of speech nor of the press, and that a man might be thrown into prison for opposing the measures of Government, and detained there for an indefinite period. Napoleon replied, 'There certainly was not in France that freedom of discussion which prevails in England; although sometimes there was a very strong opposition in the Senate; nor was there so much freedom of speech or liberty of the press; but what could I have done to a banker, or to other independent persons who opposed my measures? Put them in prison, vex and annoy them by arrests? They could appeal to the Senate and to the laws. Besides, it would have been an unworthy mode of acting.

'I do not deny that the old constitution of France was a very bad one, and required to be newly modelled; but the Constitution which I gave them when I returned from Elba was excellent; indeed its only fault was that it left too little power in my hands, and perhaps too much in those of the Senate. I could not imprison a man without a decree, order a fine, impose taxes, or levy them by conscription; and there was a law for the liberty of the press.' I said that his enemies had asserted that the Constitution he had given was only for the moment; and that when firmly seated on the throne he would have brought back things to the old system. 'No, no,' replied the Emperor, 'I would have maintained the last Constitution; I was well convinced that the old one required a great change. Blacas,' said Napoleon, 'is a wicked man, and a blockhead withal. He was base enough to leave behind him at Paris letters signed by the writers themselves, containing the offers of all those in France who had betrayed me before, by which, if I had pleased, I could have executed numbers of people. I did not, however, make any use of them further than remembering their names. Now a greater proof of imbecility and of treachery could not have been given than this conduct of Blacas; those letters ought to have been the very first things put into a state of security, or destroyed. But M. Blacas was only intent upon saving his *quattrini*, and gave himself but little concern about the lives of those who had been the means of bringing himself and his master back. He was then Minister of the King's Household. Everything was trusted to him by Louis, who is himself incapable, and whose chief qualities are dissimulation and hypocrisy.' Napoleon then made some severe remarks on the King's infirm and unhealthy condition, and on the state of the palace after being occupied by him.

'These Bourbons are the most timorous race imaginable,' continued Napoleon; 'frighten them, and you may obtain anything. While I was at

Elba, an actress named Mademoiselle Raucourt died. She was greatly beloved by the public, and an immense concourse of people went to her funeral. When they arrived at the Church of St. Roche to have the funeral service performed over the corpse, they found the doors shut, and admittance was refused to it. Nor would they allow it to be buried in consecrated ground, for by the old regulations of the priests people of her profession were excluded from Christian burial. The populace broke open the doors with sledges, and perceiving that there was no priest to perform the funeral service, they became clamorous, their rage knew no bounds. They cried, "*Au château, au château des Tuileries.* What right have these priests to refuse interment to a Christian corpse?" Their fury was heightened still more by learning that the very *coquin*, the curé of St. Roche, who had refused Christian burial to the corpse of Mademoiselle Raucourt, had been in the constant habit of receiving presents from her, both for himself and for the poor, and had dined and supped with her repeatedly. Moreover, that he had actually administered the sacrament to her a few days before her demise. The populace cried out, Here is a *canaille* of a priest, who administers the sacrament to a woman, and afterwards denies her body Christian burial. If she was worthy of the sacrament, she surely is worthy of burial. He receives her benefactions, eats her dinners, and refuses her body interment.

'About fifty thousand of them went to the

Tuileries to seek redress from the King. An architect, who was in the inner apartments at the time, told me that he was present when Louis was first informed of it. Not being then aware that the mob was so numerous, Louis said, " The curé is right. Those players are ungodly, they are excommunicated, and have no right to Christian burial." A few minutes afterwards Blacas entered in great fright, and said that there were above seventy thousand furious people about the palace, and that he was afraid they would pull it down. Louis, almost out of his senses with fear, gave immediate orders to have the body buried according to the rites of the Church, and actually hurried some persons away to see them instantly carried into execution. Those priests tried an experiment of a similar nature with me respecting the body of a beautiful dancer, but *per Dio !*' (said he with emotion) 'they had not Louis to deal with. I soon settled the affair.'[1]

After this, I observed to the Emperor that it had been asserted by Sir Hudson Lowe that after having at first refused to agree to the peace proposed by the Allies at Chatillon, he had sent a messenger to inform Lord Castlereagh that he had changed his mind, and was willing to agree to the terms which had been offered; but Lord Castlereagh had replied, 'That it was too late, and that they had determined upon their measures.' Napoleon

---

[1] See vol. i. p. 169 for the similar instance of intolerance at St. Roche, in the case of Mademoiselle Chameroi.

answered, 'It is false. I never would consent to the peace at Chatillon, because I had sworn to preserve the integrity of the Empire, rather than deviate from which I wrote to Caulaincourt that I would abdicate. I would have agreed to the terms proposed at Frankfort, where the Rhine was to form the boundaries of France, as being the natural ones.'

I took the liberty to observe that it might naturally be supposed that he would not have adhered to the treaty of Paris, the terms of which were worse. 'Yes,' replied Napoleon, 'I would have strictly complied with that treaty. I would not have made it myself; but finding it made, I would have adhered to it and remained at peace.'

A part of the conversation which followed led me to make some remarks not favourable to Maréchal Davoût, and also to ask Napoleon whether he was not considered one of the best of his generals. 'No,' replied the Emperor; 'I do not think him a bad character. He never plundered for himself. He certainly levied contributions, but they were for the army. It is necessary for an army, especially when besieged, to provide for itself.[1] As to being one of the first of the French generals, he is by no means so, although a good officer.' I then asked who in his opinion was now the first? 'It is difficult to say,' replied Napoleon. 'I think, however, that Suchet is probably the first. Masséna

---

[1] In consequence of his excellent dispositions Davoût was able to retain Hamburg until after the signature of peace.

was; but you may now say that he is dead. He has a complaint in his breast which has rendered him quite another kind of man. Suchet, Clausel, and Gérard,[1] are in my opinion the first of the French generals. It is difficult to pronounce which is superior,[2] as they have not had many opportunities of commanding in chief, which is the only mode by which you can ascertain the extent of a man's talents.' He also mentioned Soult in terms of commendation.[3]

Went with Captains Poppleton, Fuller, Impett, and other officers of the 53d to a *rat hunt* in the camp. Some soldiers furnished with spades began to dig close by a ditch and a wall, infested with rats. Two dogs were in waiting, and we were provided with sticks. As soon as the rats found their premises moving about them, they sallied out and endeavoured to make their escape. They were then attacked by the dogs and men, and a most

---

[1] 'At one of his levees, after giving some orders to General Gérard, whose reputation was then beginning to attract attention, the Emperor concluded with some words evidently kindly meant, though somewhat obscure. After advancing a few paces to continue his circuit, he turned back to General Gérard, apparently having read in his countenance that he had not precisely understood him, and he said very distinctly, "I observed, that if I had many men like you, I should consider all my losses repaired, and should think myself master of my fortune."'—*Las Cases*, vol. iv., part vii., p. 253, English edition.

[2] As the Emperor was rolling the balls of the billiard-table about at this moment, I am not positive whether it was only the two last that he mentioned as not having often commanded in chief.— B. E. O'M.

[3] See also vol. i. p. 224.

animated scene of confusion took place; the rats trying to get into other holes, and the others pursuing and striking at them in every direction, and hitting each other's legs, in their eagerness to reach their prey. Some of the rats turned upon the assailants and made a desperate resistance. Fourteen of them were killed in less than half an hour.

The rats are in numbers almost incredible at Longwood. I have frequently seen them assemble like broods of chickens round the offal thrown out of the kitchen. The floors and wooden partitions that separated the rooms were perforated with holes in every direction. The partitions being for the most part double, and of one inch deal, afforded a space between them sufficiently large to allow a rat to move with facility. It is difficult for any person who has not actually heard it to form an idea of the noise caused by those animals running up and down between the partitions, and galloping in flocks in the garrets. At night, when disturbed by their entrance into my chamber, and by their running over me in bed, I have frequently thrown my boots, the bootjack, and everything I could readily reach, at them, without intimidating them in the slightest degree, and have been at last obliged to get out of bed to drive them away. We amused ourselves sometimes in the evening by removing the pieces of tin which were nailed over their holes, and allowing them sufficient time to enter, when the servants, armed with sticks, and followed by dogs, rushed in, covered the holes, and attacked the rats, who frequently made a desperate resistance, and bit the assailants severely.

However good the dogs may have been at first, they generally became indifferent, or unwilling to attack those noxious animals; and the same may be said of the cats. Poisoning them was impracticable, as the smell of their putrid carcases would render the rooms uninhabitable. Indeed, in more instances than one, it has been necessary to open a partition, for the purpose of extracting the body of a rat that had died there, and had caused an insupportable odour.[1]

The wretched and ruinous state of the building, the roofs[2] and ceilings of which were chiefly formed of wood, and covered with brown paper smeared with a composition of pitch and tar, together with the partition being chiefly of wood, greatly favoured the introduction of those reptiles,

[1] The houses are overrun with rats and mice, which abound in numbers scarcely credible to those who have not been at St. Helena; and the ravages they commit are incalculable. There are also swarms of mosquitoes of two-kinds, one called the day, and the other the night mosquito, whose bites are tormenting; numbers of cockroaches, some scorpions and centipedes, and a sort of fly, extremely annoying to the cattle and horses. Caterpillars and grubs are astonishingly numerous, and the ravages they commit upon the young green plants are almost incredible; whole plantations of vegetables are said to have been sometimes destroyed by the former in a night.

[2] All the additions made to the old building were roofed in this manner. As this book may fall into the hands of some readers who may not credit the above description of Longwood House, I beg to call the attention of respectable persons who may touch at St. Helena, to the state of the house in which the exiled Sovereign of France breathed his last after six years of captivity.—B. E. O'M.

and was productive of another great inconvenience, as the composition, when heated by the rays of the sun, melted and ran off, leaving a number of chinks open, through which the heavy tropical rains found a free entry. Countess Montholon was repeatedly obliged to rise in the night, to shift her own and her children's beds to different parts of the rooms, in order to escape being soaked. The construction of the roofs rendered this irremediable, as a few hours of sunshine produced fresh cracks.

April 6. — Napoleon in very good spirits. Mentioned the Marquis Cornwallis in terms of great praise. As 'a man of probity, a generous and sincere character.—*Un très brave homme.* He was the first man who gave me a good opinion of the English; his integrity, fidelity, frankness, and the nobleness of his sentiments, impressed me with a very favourable opinion of you. I recollect Cornwallis saying one day, "There are certain qualities which may be bought, but a good character, sincerity, a proper pride, and calmness in the hour of danger, are not to be purchased." These words made an impression upon me. I gave him a regiment of cavalry to amuse himself with at Amiens, which used to manœuvre before him. The officers of it liked him much. I do not believe that he was a man of firstrate abilities, but he had talent, great probity, and sincerity. He never broke his word. At Amiens the treaty was ready, and was to be signed by him at the

Hôtel de Ville at nine o'clock. Something happened which prevented him from going; but he sent word to the French Ministers, that they might consider the treaty as having been signed, and that he would sign it the following day. A courier from England arrived at night, with directions to him to refuse his consent to certain articles, and not to sign the treaty. Although Cornwallis had not signed it, and might have easily availed himself of this order, he was a man of such strict honour, that he said he considered his promise to be equivalent to his signature, and wrote to his Government that he had promised, and that having once pledged his word, he would keep it. That if they were not satisfied, they might refuse to ratify the treaty. *There* was a man of honour—a true Englishman. Such a man as Cornwallis ought to have been sent here, instead of a compound of falsehood, suspicion, and meanness. I was much grieved when I heard of his death. Some of his family occasionally wrote to me, to request favours for some prisoners, which I always complied with.'

He then spoke about his having given himself up to the English, and observed, 'My having given myself up to you is not so simple a matter as you imagine. Before I went to Elba, Lord Castlereagh offered me an asylum in England, and said that I should be very well treated there, and much better off than at Elba.' I said that Lord Castlereagh was reported to have asserted that he (Napoleon) had applied for an asylum in England, but that it was not thought proper to grant it. 'The real fact,' said Napoleon, 'is, that he first proposed it. Before I went to Elba, Lord Castlereagh said to Caulaincourt, "Why does Napoleon think of going to Elba? Let him come to England. He will be received in London with the greatest pleasure, and will experience the best possible treatment. He must not, however, ask permission to come, because that would take up too much time; but let him give himself up to us, without making any conditions, and he will be received with the greatest joy, and be much better than at Elba." This,' added he, 'had much influence with me afterwards.'

On asking Napoleon his opinion of Baron Stein, he replied, 'A patriot, a man of talent, and a busy, stirring character.' I observed that I had heard it asserted that Stein had done him more mischief than Metternich, or indeed any other person, and had been mainly instrumental to his fall. 'Not at all,' replied Napoleon; 'he was certainly a man of talent, but had his advice been followed, the King of Prussia would have been ruined past all redemption; Stein was always hatching intrigues, and wanted Prussia to declare prematurely against me, which would have caused her destruction. The King, however, was better advised, and did not declare himself until the proper time had arrived—that is to say, until that accident of Russia, of which he took immediate advantage.'

A pause now took place; Napoleon walked a few paces, stopped, looked at me, and said in an expressive manner, 'No one but myself ever did me any harm; I was, I may say, the only enemy to myself: my own projects, the expedition to Moscow, and the accidents which happened there, were the causes of my fall. I may, however, say, that those who made no opposition to me, who readily agreed with me, entered into all my views, and submitted with facility, were my greatest enemies; because, by the facility of conquest they afforded, they encouraged me to go too far. They were more my enemies than those who formed intrigues against me, because the latter put me upon my guard, and rendered me more careful.

'I caused Stein to be sent away from the Court of Prussia. It would, however, have been very fortunate for me if his projects had been fulfilled, as Prussia would have broken out prematurely, and I should have extinguished her like that' (raising one of his feet and stamping, as if he were putting out the snuff of a candle). 'I could,' continued he, 'have dethroned the King of Prussia, or the Emperor of Austria, upon the slightest pretext, as easily as I do this,' stretching out one of his legs. 'I was then too powerful for any man, except myself, to injure me.'

I asked him if he had ever said anything of the following tenor relative to Metternich: 'One or two lies are sometimes necessary, but Metternich is all lies. Nothing but lies, lies, lies from him!' Napoleon laughed and said, '*C'est vrai.* He is composed of nothing but lies and intrigues.' I asked if he were not a man of great talent? 'Not at all,' replied he, '*è bugiardo ed intrigante—intrigante e bugiardo.* That is the sum total of his character.¹

'Lord Whitworth,' continued Napoleon, 'in that famous interview which he had with me, during which I was by no means violent, said on leaving the room, that he was well satisfied with me, and contented with the manner in which I had treated him, and hoped that all would go on well. This he said to some of the Ambassadors of the other Powers. A few days afterwards when the English newspapers arrived with his account of the interview, stating that I had been in such a rage, it excited the astonishment of everybody; especially of those Ambassadors who remonstrated with him and said, "My Lord, how can this account be correct.² You know that you allowed to us that you were well contented and satisfied with your reception, and stated your opinion that all would

---

¹ 'Napoleon did not value sincerity, and he did not hesitate to say that he recognised the superiority of a man by the greater or less dexterity with which he practised the art of lying. On the occasion of his saying this he added, with great complacency, that when he was a child, one of his uncles had predicted of him that he should govern the world, because he was an habitual liar. "M. de Metternich," he added, "approaches to being a statesman—he lies very well!"'—*Memoirs of Madame de Rémusat,* vol. i. p. 6.

² Much exaggerated at the time.—*Vide Despatches of Lord Whitworth,* recently published.

go on well." He did not know what to answer, and said, " But this account is also true."[1]

I mentioned to Napoleon that it had been stated in one of the papers that he had once sent a shipwright to Algiers or Tunis, in order to teach the

[1] An eyewitness gives a different version of the scene :—
'A little while before our last rupture with England a rumour arose that war was about to recommence, and that the Ambassador, Lord Whitworth, was preparing to leave Paris. Once a month the First Consul was in the habit of receiving the Ambassadors and their wives in Madame Bonaparte's apartments. This reception was held with great pomp. The foreigners were ushered into a drawing-room, and when they were all there, the First Consul would appear, accompanied by his wife and attended by a prefect of the palace and a lady-in-waiting. . . . A few days before the breach of the peace the *Corps Diplomatique* met as usual at the Tuileries. Whilst they were waiting, I went to Madame Bonaparte's apartment. . . . The First Consul was sitting on the floor playing with little Napoleon, the eldest son of his brother Louis. . . . He seemed to be in the best possible humour. I remarked this, and said to him that, judging by appearances, the letters the Ambassadors would have to write, after the approaching audience, would breathe nothing but peace and concord. Bonaparte laughed, and went on playing with his little nephew. By and by he was told that the company had arrived. Then he rose quickly, the good-humour vanished from his face, and I was struck by the severe expression that suddenly replaced it; he seemed to grow pale at will, his features contracted ; and all this in less time than it takes me to describe it. " Let us go, mesdames," said he abruptly, and he walked on quickly, entered the drawing-room, and, without bowing to any one, advanced to the English Ambassador. To him he began to complain bitterly of the proceedings of his Government. His anger seemed to increase every minute ; it soon reached a height which terrified the assembly ; the hardest words, the most violent threats, came from his quivering lips. No one dared to move. Madame Bonaparte and I looked at each other, dumb with astonishment, and every one stood aghast. The impassive Englishman himself was disconcerted, and it was with difficulty he could find words to answer.'—*Memoirs of Madame de Rémusat*, vol. i. pp. 16-18.

pirates shipbuilding. He replied, 'It is possible that they may have got a Frenchman as a shipbuilder, but not with my consent. They might have procured some person from Marseilles. At Constantinople, when the Turks were at war with France, there was a shipbuilder named Le Musa. Instead of succouring the pirates, I proposed to England to exterminate them, or at least to oblige them to live like honest people, to which your Ministers would not consent. There was nobody who disliked or despised those pirates more than I did. It was not the policy of the English Ministers to destroy those barbarians, or else they would have done it long ago. By permitting them to exist and to plunder, you monopolised the greatest part of the trade of the Mediterranean; because the Swedes, Danes, Portuguese, and others were afraid to send their ships there.

'The reason you sent the expedition to Algiers was to ingratiate yourselves with the Italians, and to prevent their regretting me. For I gave the French flag to all the Italian States, and made the barbarians respect it, which has not been the case since the Bourbons mounted the throne. The Italians would have been discontented, and have cried that in Napoleon's reign they were at least free from the attacks and piracies of the corsairs. That expedition deserves no credit except for the great bravery and nautical skill displayed by the Admiral,[1] and by those under him. As to the

[1] Sir Edward Pellew, afterwards Lord Exmouth.

negotiations, Lord Exmouth has failed; he ought to have made the extinction of piracy, the surrender of their fleet, and an obligation to build no more ships of war (unless the Grand Signor made war upon some of the European powers) the *sine quâ non*. You say that it has been stipulated that only prisoners, and not slaves, are in future to be made. I fear much that if any difference be made amongst those barbarians between the lot of prisoner and of slave, it will be to the disadvantage of the former. For those wretches had some interest in preserving the lives of their slaves, in order to obtain their ransom; whereas with prisoners they will have no such expectation; and therefore giving way to their natural cruelty and deadly hatred of Christians, they will in all probability mutilate and put them to cruel deaths.

'I always had a high opinion of your seamen,'[1] continued Napoleon. 'When I was returning from Holland with the Empress Marie Louise, we stopped to rest at Givet. During the night a violent storm of wind and rain came on, which swelled the Meuse so much that the bridge of boats over it was carried away. I was very anxious to depart; and ordered all the boatmen in the place to be assembled, that I might be enabled to cross the river. They said that the waters were so high that it would be impossible to pass before

---

[1] I had observed, that in consequence of the checks we had sustained from the Americans, it was desirable that our navy should wind up by doing something brilliant.—B. E. O'M.

two or three days. I questioned some of them, and soon discovered that they were freshwater seamen. I then recollected that there were English prisoners in the barracks, and ordered that some of the oldest and best seamen amongst them should be brought before me to the banks of the river. The waters were very high and the current was rapid and dangerous. I asked them if they could join a number of boats so that I might pass over. They answered that it was possible but hazardous. I desired them to set about it instantly. In the course of a few hours they succeeded in effecting what the *imbéciles* had pronounced impossible; and I crossed before the evening was over. I ordered those who had worked at it to receive a sum of money each, a suit of clothes, and their liberty. Marchand was with me at the time.

'When I landed at Elba,' added he, 'with Ussher, my guard had not arrived, and Ussher gave me one composed of his marines under the command of a *sous officier*, who constantly remained at Porto Ferrajo, and formed my bodyguard for some days. I had every reason to be contented with them. When my own guard arrived, they contracted a friendship with the marines and the sailors. They were frequently seen rolling about in the streets drunk, locked arm in arm, singing and shaking hands with each other. I believe that not a man in the ship would have injured me if it had been in his power. When I left them, I ordered a Napoléon to be given to each, and I made Ussher a present of a box, with my picture set round with diamonds. If I had had such able seamen as Ussher for officers, the naval combats between the French ships and yours would have terminated very differently.'

April 8.—On the 7th the races were held at Deadwood, at which Madame Sturmer, the three Commissioners, and Captain Gor were present. General Gourgaud also went, and had long conversations with the Baron and Baroness Sturmer, Count Balmaine, and, latterly, the Marquis de Montchenu. During the greater part of the time no British officer listened to them. Sir Hudson Lowe and Sir Thomas Reade were *spectators* a considerable portion of the time. Lady Lowe was also present. Towards the end of the races the Commissioners, Madame Sturmer, and Baron Gourgaud went to Mrs. Younghusband's house in camp, where they remained together for some time, before any of the Governor's officers followed them. Mentioned to Sir Hudson Lowe the opinion which Napoleon had expressed of Marquis Cornwallis, to which His Excellency replied that 'Lord Cornwallis was too honest a man to deal with him.'

Napoleon went down to Count Bertrand's, where he had from the upper windows a good view of the races; he remained until they were finished, and appeared to be highly entertained.

Sir Thomas Reade expressed great anger towards Mrs. Younghusband for having invited the Commissioners and General Gourgaud together without having been accompanied, and said that the Governor had a right, and ought, to turn her off the island for it, adding, that the Commissioners themselves were mean wretches for having spoken to Gourgaud, when his master treated them with such contempt.

Napoleon walked out for some time with Counts Montholon and Bertrand. Saw him at mid-day. He asked many questions about the races, in which he appeared to take an interest. Observed that, from what he had heard, Montchenu must have been very badly educated, as he had made use of very improper language before Lady Lowe, on occasion of the breeze (which was very fresh) having interfered with some lady's drapery. 'In general,' said Napoleon, 'Frenchmen at his time of life are proverbially polite; but from what I have heard, this man never could have been brought up in good company, and has *l'air d'un sous-lieutenant de l'ancien regime.*'

Mr. Rainsford, the Inspector of Police, died on the 7th.[1]

April 14.—General Gourgaud, while going through the camp, went into the apartments of Major Fehrzen of the 53d Regiment, where he remained for a few minutes.[2]

April 15.—Sir Hudson Lowe sent for the orderly officer, and demanded 'what business

---
[1] See vol. i., p. 201.
[2] Major Fehrzen was very clever with his brush, and made many water-colour sketches of Napoleon when at St. Helena.

General Gourgaud had to enter Major Fehrzen's rooms?'

Saw Napoleon, who was reclining upon his sofa. Very anxious in his inquiries about the health of Madame Bertrand, Tristan de Montholon, and the little Napoleonne, both of whom were very unwell, especially Tristan, who laboured under a severe attack of dysentery of a highly inflammatory nature, and for which I had bled him. When I told Napoleon that the bleeding had afforded the child great relief, 'Ah,' said he, 'experience, experience is everything.'[1]

April 16.—Napoleon informed me that he was employed in writing observations upon the *Seven Years' War of the Great Frederic*, which would, when finished, form two or three volumes.

In the course of conversation he mentioned General Lallemand, whose character he described in very favourable terms. 'Lallemand,' said he, 'whom you saw in the *Bellerophon*, was employed by me at Acre as a negotiator with Sidney Smith, during which he displayed considerable address and ability. After my return from Elba, he, like Labédoyère, declared for me in a moment of the greatest danger, and excited a movement of primary importance amongst the troops of his division. Lallemand *a beaucoup de décision, est capable de faire des combinaisons*, and there are few men more qualified to lead a hazardous enterprise. He has

---

[1] Napoleon had frequently before condemned the practice of bleeding, which he maintained was abstracting so much of one's life.

the *feu sacré*. He commanded the *chasseurs de la garde* at Waterloo, and *enfonça* some of your battalions.'

Victor he described to be '*Une bête sans talens et sans tête.*' Soult, 'An excellent minister of war, a very good planner, but not so well able to execute as to arrange.'

April 20.—Count Balmaine and Captain Gor came up as far as Longwood, dogged by a serjeant of the 66th Regiment, dressed in plain clothes, who was in the employ of Sir Thomas Reade.

April 21.—Napoleon has been for some days in very good spirits. On Saturday, the 19th, several captains of East Indiamen came to see Count and Countess Bertrand. Captains Innes, Campbell, and Ripsley, with Mr. Webb, stationed themselves at the back of the house in such a situation as to be likely to see Napoleon on his return from Bertrand's, where he had gone about four o'clock. Napoleon beckoned to, and conversed with them for nearly an hour, during which time he asked many questions respecting India, the East India Company, Lord Moira, their own profits, etc.; and to the Commodore, who had a very youthful appearance, in a playful way he observed, that he was a child, and ought to be ashamed of commanding captains so much older than himself.

Asked the Emperor whether it was at Lodi or Arcola that he had seized the standard, and precipitated himself among the enemy's troops. He replied, 'At Arcola, not Lodi. At Arcola I was slightly wounded;[1] but at Lodi no such circumstance occurred. Why do you ask? Do you think me *lâche!*' said he, laughing. I begged to assure him of my thorough conviction of the contrary, which was too well known to be doubted; and that it was merely to solve a difference of opinion that had arisen between some of us English who had not the means of procuring at St. Helena any books to satisfy us at which of the two it happened, that I had taken the liberty to ask him. 'Those things,' said he, with a smile, 'are not worth mentioning.'[2]

Had a long conversation with him on medical subjects. He appeared to entertain an idea that in cases purely the province of the physician, the

[1] See note on this subject later on in the present volume.

[2] 'It became of the utmost importance to gain possession of Arcola, for, by debouching thence on the enemy's rear, we should have seized the bridge of Villa Nuova over the Alpon, which was his only retreat, and established ourselves there before it could be occupied against us. But Arcola withstood several attacks. Napoleon determined to try a last effort in person; he seized a flag, rushed on the bridge and there planted it; the column he commanded had reached the middle of the bridge when the flanking fire and the arrival of a division of the enemy frustrated the attack. The grenadiers at the head of the column, finding themselves abandoned by the rear, hesitated, but being hurried away in the flight, persisted in keeping possession of their General. They seized him by his arms and by his clothes and dragged him along with them amidst the dead, the dying, and the smoke. He was precipitated into a morass, in which he sunk up to the middle, surrounded by the enemy. The grenadiers perceived that their General was in danger; a cry was heard of "Forward, soldiers, to save the General!" These brave men immediately turned back, ran upon the enemy, drove them beyond the bridge, and Napoleon was saved.'—*History of France during the Reign of Napoleon;* dictated by the Emperor to the Comte de Montholon, 1813 edition, vol. iii. pp. 361, 362.

patient has an equal chance of being despatched to the other world, either by the doctor mistaking the complaint, or by the remedies administered operating in a different manner from what was intended, and was for trusting entirely to Nature. With respect to surgery, he professed a far different opinion, and acknowledged the great utility of that science. I endeavoured to convince him that in some complaints Nature was a bad physician, and mentioned in proof of my argument the examples that had taken place under his own eyes of the cases of Countess Montholon, General Gourgaud, Tristan, and others, who, if they had been left to Nature, would have gone to the other world. I observed that in practice we always had a *certain object* in view, and never prescribed remedies without first having considered well what we had to expect from their operation. Napoleon, however, was sceptical, and inclined to think that if they had taken no medicine, maintained strict abstinence from everything except plenty of diluents, they would have done equally well.

However, after having heard all my arguments, he said, 'Well, perhaps if ever I have a serious malady, I may change my opinion, take all your medicines, and do what you please. I should like to know what sort of a patient I should make, and whether I should be tractable, or otherwise; I am inclined to think the former.' I reasoned with him afterwards about inflammation of the lungs, and asked him if he thought that Nature, if left to herself, would effect a cure in that complaint. He appeared a little staggered at this at first ; but after asking me what were the remedies, to which I replied that venesection was the sheet-anchor, he said, ' That complaint belongs to the surgeon, because he cures it with his lancet, and not to the physician.' I then mentioned dysentery and intermittent fevers. ' The remedies given in intermittent fevers,' said he, ' frequently produce worse complaints than the disease that they remove. Suppose now that the best informed physician visits forty patients a day ; amongst them he will kill one or two a month by mistaking the disease, and in the country towns, the charlatans will kill about half of those who die under their hands. The country towns in England, as well as in France, abound with *Molière's* doctors.

' Are you a fatalist ?' I replied, ' In action I am.' —' Why not everywhere else ?' said the Emperor. I said that I believed a man's dissolution, in certain cases, to be inevitable if he did not endeavour, by the means placed in his power, to prevent his fate. For example, I said that if a man in battle saw a cannon-shot coming towards him, as sometimes happened, he would naturally step to one side, and thereby avoid an otherwise inevitable death ; which comparison I thought would hold good with certain complaints, by considering the ball to be the disease, and stepping aside the remedy.

Napoleon replied, ' Perhaps by stepping to one side, you may throw yourself in the way of another ball, which otherwise would have missed you. I remember,' added he, 'an example of what I tell you having occurred at Toulon when I commanded the artillery. There were some Marseillais artillerymen present at the siege. Now of all people in France, the Marseillais are the least brave, and, generally speaking, have but little energy. I observed an officer, like the rest, to be very careful of himself, instead of setting a good example. I therefore called out and said, "*Monsieur l'officier*, come out and observe the effect of your shot. You do not know whether your guns are well pointed or not." At this time we were firing upon the English ships. I desired him to see if our shot struck them in the hull. He was very unwilling to quit his station; but at last he came over to where I was, a little outside of the parapet, where he began to look out. Wishing, however, to make himself as small and secure as possible, he stooped down and sheltered one side of his body behind the parapet, while he looked under my arm. He had not been long in that position before a shot came close to me, and low down, which knocked him to pieces. Now, if this man had stood upright, and more exposed to danger, he would have been safe, as the ball would have passed between us, without hurting either.'

I recounted to the Emperor, after this, a circumstance which had happened in the *Victorious*, seventy-four, Captain Talbot, when I was on board her. During the action with the French line-of-battle ship *Rivoli*, a man who had been slightly wounded had crept into the heart of the cable tier in the orlop deck, and placed himself among the cables in such a manner that it appeared to be a matter of impossibility that a shot could reach him. Notwithstanding the apparent security of the place, towards the end of the action a shot struck the ship very low down, penetrated the wings, went through two or three coils of the cable, then rose upwards, struck one of the beams which supported the lower deck, and being spent, rebounded and fell upon this man's breast (who was lying on his back) and killed him. He was found afterwards with the shot (a thirty-six pounder) lying upon his chest.

'This,' said he, 'confirms what I say to you, that a man cannot avoid his destiny.' Napoleon appeared interested in this anecdote, and asked whether the man was a sailor or a soldier? I replied, a sailor.

The Emperor during the course of conversation spoke about eunuchs; the making of whom he observed was a most disgraceful and horrid practice. 'I suppressed it,' said he, 'in all the countries under my dominion; even in Rome itself I prohibited it under pain of death. It was entirely put a stop to, and I believe that although the Pope and the Cardinals are now in power, it will not be again revived. I recollect,' added he, 'an incident with respect to one of those gentry which made me laugh. There was one Crescentini, an excellent singer, who often sang before me and delighted me much. As I wished to encourage merit in every science, and as his condition was his misfortune and not his fault, I conferred upon him the Knighthood of the Iron Crown. This, however, displeased a great many, and there were many discussions about it, in which Madame Grassini,[1] whom I suppose you have heard of, took a part. Whilst others were blaming me, the Grassini said, "I really think the Emperor has done right in giving it to him." Being asked why, she replied, "I think he merits it, if it were only on account of his wounds." This sally produced the greatest laughter, and disposed of all objectors completely.'

April 23.—Yesterday Napoleon remained all day in his bedroom and ate nothing. Told me that he had risen at three in the morning and wrote or dictated all day.

I gave him two or three newspapers. He repeated his disbelief of the rumour of war being likely to take place between Russia and America, as it was contrary to the interests of both.

General Gourgaud the day before yesterday rode out towards the alarm-house, and on his way met the Russian Commissioner and Captain Gor, with whom he conversed for a considerable time. They were seen by Captain Poppleton, who was on his way to dine at Plantation House. When His Excellency was informed of this, he said at first that Captain Poppleton ought to have remained with

[1] Napoleon, when First Consul, saw Madame Grassini at a concert at Milan, and was struck with her beauty and her exquisite voice. He was introduced to her, and shortly afterwards directed Bourrienne to pay her expenses to Paris, where she became one of the singers at the Court concerts. See the 1885 edition of Bourrienne's *Memoirs of Napoleon*, vol. i. p. 408; vol. ii. p. 238.

them to listen; but when it was explained to him that he could not have done so without affronting them, as General Gourgaud knew that he was to dine at Plantation House, he acknowledged that it could not have been done.

This day, however, a note came from Major Gorrequer, stating that the Governor wanted to see Captain Poppleton directly, and that he was required to write an official statement of what he had witnessed yesterday between the Commissioner and Gourgaud. That the Governor regretted he had not followed and kept company with them, in pursuance of the conversation he had had with him (Captain Poppleton) in town on a certain day. In this conversation the Governor said he expected that he would, whenever he saw them speaking together, drop in as it were by accident, and make one of their party.

These precautions appeared curious, as the parties had a long interview together at the last races before the Governor himself and his Staff without molestation.

Saw Napoleon in the evening again, who declared himself quite well. He spoke of the time he was in the habit of devoting to business when in Paris. That occasionally he used to dictate to four different secretaries at a time, all upon different subjects, and sometimes even to five, each writing as fast as he could.[1] Made some

---

[1] Particulars of the Emperor's habits will be found in the 1885 edition of Bourrienne's *Memoirs of Napoleon*, vol. i. p. 278.

comments upon the Emperor of Austria. Observed that if he were in his power, no treatment could be too good or limits too extensive. The Emperor he pronounced to be a good and religious man, but an old blockhead.¹ A man who, though he did not want common sense, never did anything of himself, but was always led by the nose by Metternich or some one else. As long as he had a bad Minister, his Government would be bad, as he entirely trusted to him, and only paid attention to botany and gardening.

April 24.—Napoleon in very good spirits. Very curious in his inquiries about Murat's expedition against Sicily. Asked me to describe minutely the strength of the English force which had then occupied Sicily, and appeared surprised when I said that it had amounted to about twenty thousand English, Hanoverians, etc. He asked if I thought that Murat would have succeeded in

¹ 'It was reported, Sire, that one day Your Majesty, being much dissatisfied at the perusal of a despatch from Vienna, said to the Empress in a moment of ill-humour, *Your father is a blockhead* (*votre père est un ganache*). Maria Louisa, who was unacquainted with many French phrases, turned to the person nearest her, and observing that the Emperor had called her father a *ganache*, asked what the term meant. The courtier, embarrassed at this unexpected interrogatory, stammered out that the word signified a wise man, a man of judgment, and a good counsellor. Some time after the Empress, with her newly-learnt term fresh in her memory, was present at the Council of State, and the discussion becoming somewhat warm, in order to put a stop to it, she called on M. Cambacérès, who was at her side. . . . "You must set us right on this important point," said she; "you shall be our oracle; for I consider you as the greatest *ganache* in the Empire." At these words the Emperor held his sides with laughter. "What a pity," said he, "that this

taking the island, if he had landed?[1] I replied that I believed not, as, independently of the formidable English force against him, in general the Sicilians themselves hated the French, and declared that they would have caused another 'Sicilian Vespers' if they came. He asked 'how many troops Ferdinand had?' I replied, perhaps fifteen thousand men, of whom, however, we were very doubtful, and consequently kept near Palermo, with the exception of a regiment of cavalry.

He wished to know 'if our ships could have kept the channel on the night that Murat had caused a landing to be made by a small body, and whether they could have remained at anchor along the Sicilian side of the Faro?' I replied that I had no doubt the ships might have kept the channel on that night; that they might also have remained at anchor along the Faro, but at a risk during the *Scirocco* winds, as the bottom was a bad holding ground, and if the anchors went, the ships must go on shore.

'That foolish fellow Murat,' added he, 'lost me about twelve or thirteen hundred men by the rash disembarkation he made in Sicily. I know not

anecdote is not true! Only imagine the scene. The offended dignity of Cambacérès, the merriment of the whole council, and the embarrassment of poor Maria Louisa, alarmed at the success of her unconscious joke.'—*Las Cases*, vol. ii., part iii., p. 113, English edition.

[1] It may be necessary to explain to the reader that I was in a mortar-boat attached to the flotilla against Murat, under the command of Captain Coffin, R.N., during the whole of the period alluded to.—B. E. O'M.

what object he could have had in view by thus landing a few men.' I replied that Murat had said he meant to have landed with his whole army near the Faro, while this small body was intended to act as a diversion. 'Do you think that he could have landed on that night?' said Napoleon. I replied, I thought he could, as all our ships were withdrawn from their stations and locked up in the harbour of Messina.

Napoleon said, 'If I had really intended Murat to take Sicily, I would have pushed out the Toulon fleet with thirty thousand men to effect a landing near Palermo, from whence the fleet should have proceeded directly to the Faro, to cover Murat's landing. But it was only intended to keep your English army doing nothing in Sicily by means of the raw troops under Murat,[1] and not to take Sicily, as there were few French troops with him, and I was apprehensive that your army might have been employed elsewhere against me.' I asked if there had been any secret treaty between Murat and the English Admiral and General to allow Murat to withdraw with his boats and troops without molestation. 'No,' said the Emperor, 'none that I know of. Why do you ask such a question?'

---

[1] Murat was not aware of this. He was sincere in his intention of landing in Sicily; but on the night in which he wanted to embark all his army for that purpose, General Grenier, who commanded the French troops with him, showed him an order prohibiting their making the attempt. Of this I have been since informed by a person who was Minister to the unfortunate King Joachim at the time.—B. E. O'M.

I replied, ' Because so little had been done to annoy them in their retreat, that I often thought some agreement must have been made to let Murat withdraw quietly with his troops, provided he abandoned his enterprise.' He laughed and said, ' There was none,—at least to my knowledge.'

I then mentioned to him the plot to massacre the English officers and drive the English out of Sicily, said to have been discovered in 1810 (I think) by ——— ' Caroline,' said he, ' was very capable of forming such a plot. I believe, however, that ——— invented a great part of it, and also betrayed you at the time that he pretended to make such important discoveries. Murat got information from some officer in the English service.' I said that ——— had frequently gone over to Calabria disguised as a peasant. ' Very probably he betrayed you every time he went,' replied Napoleon.

He spoke about the Corsicans: observed that they were brave and revengeful by nature, the best friends and the most inexorable enemies in the world. 'Their prominent national characteristic,' added he, 'is never to forget a benefit or an injury. For the slightest insult in Corsica, *una archibugiata*. Murders are consequently very common. At the same time no people are more grateful for benefits, and they will not scruple to sacrifice their lives for the person who bestowed them.'

April 25.—Had some conversation with Napoleon relative to Count Bertrand having been stopped by the sentinel a few days back, when going down towards Mr. Wilton's cottage. Napoleon said that he supposed the sentinel had orders to stop all *suspicious* persons, similar to those given to the one at Hut's Gate, and observed in a laughing manner that the French were the only *suspicious* people in the island. Told him that a report had arrived in the island of war having been declared between Spain and America, and Russia and America. 'Russia and America?' said he; 'impossible. If it takes place, I shall never be astonished again at any circumstance that happens. The Spaniards will be well drubbed.' I said that one of the American large frigates could take a Spanish seventy-four. This he would not believe. I then said that during the war with Spain, one of our frigates, which were smaller than the American's, would not have been afraid to attack a Spanish seventy-four.[1] Napoleon looked at me in rather an incredulous manner, shook his head, laughed, and said, '*Sempre per la marina, Dottore* —she certainly would have been taken.' I replied that if the weather was bad, I did not think so. He said that there never had been an instance on record of a frigate's having taken a seventy-four.[2]

April 29.—Dined with Sir Pulteney Malcolm

---

[1] O'Meara has probably in his mind the celebrated action of the *Speedy* and the *Gamo*, in which Lord Cochrane captured a Spanish vessel of more than double his force, and in which the English surgeon on board the *Speedy* took a conspicuous part.

[2] A reference to the naval abstracts published at the end of James's *Naval History* does not show any instance of a line-of-battle ship being captured by a frigate during the Napoleonic wars.

in town. Count Balmaine[1] came to pass the evening, during the course of which he had a long conversation with me. He said that he had that day met General Gourgaud near the alarm-house, and that finding himself in a very awkward situation, he told the General that his position was very embarrassing, as it appeared that he (Balmaine) was an object of suspicion to the Governor; that he must consequently beg to decline any further communication with him beyond the customary greetings, however unpleasant it was to do so in a place where there was so little French society, until after the arrival of the *Conqueror*, by which vessel he expected instructions which would clearly point out to him the line of conduct which he was in future to pursue. That in doing this, he had rather gone beyond his present instructions, which were not to *éviter ces messieurs là*, but to treat them precisely as he did the inhabitants and other residents on the island; that he could not account for the suspicion manifested by the Governor, as it could not be supposed that *he* was sent out to intrigue.

Cipriani in town. On his return he related the obligations he was under to Sir Thomas Reade, who was busily employed in assisting him to procure some hams and other articles of provisions out of the Company's stores.

April 30.—Napoleon has been occupied for some days in dictating and writing observations

[1] Russian Commissioner.

upon the works of the Great Frederick. Told me that when finished they might probably comprise five or six octavo volumes, and would consist of military observations and reflections only, with as much detail as would be necessary for the explanation of the operations commented upon. For several mornings he has been up at 3 A.M. writing. Saw several pages of his handwriting,[1] which was much more legible than any I had before seen. He observed that formerly he had sometimes been in the habit of writing only half or threequarters of each word and running them into each other, which was not attended with much inconvenience, as the secretaries had become so well accustomed to it, that they could read it with nearly as much facility as if it were written plainly; that, however, no person, except one well acquainted with his manner of writing, could read it. Latterly, he said, he had begun to write a little more legibly, in consequence of not being so much hurried as on former occasions.

Napoleon then observed that I had made a considerable progress in French since he had first seen me, 'Though you have,' said he, 'a very bad accent. It has been said by some of the English that I understand Italian better than French which is not true. Although I speak the Italian very fluently, it is not pure. *Non parlo Toscano*, nor am I capable of writing a book in Italian,

---

[1] See note upon the Emperor's handwriting (also a facsimile) in Bourrienne's *Memoirs*, English edition of 1885, vol. i. p. 368.

nor do I ever speak it in preference to the French.'[1]

Speaking about Chateaubriand's attacks upon him, he observed, 'C'est un de ces lâches qui crachent sur un cadavre. Like Pichon and others, he is one of those insects that prey upon a corpse, which, while living, they dared not approach.'

After some other conversation I asked him if there had been a sufficiency of provisions for his army on the retreat from Moscow, whether it might not have been accomplished with a loss much smaller than that which they had sustained? Napoleon answered, 'No; the cold would have destroyed them, even if they had had a sufficiency of provisions. Those who had food died by hundreds. Even the Russians themselves died like flies.'

May 2.—General Montholon very ill. Napoleon expressed much anxiety about him.

May 4.—Baron Sturmer came to Longwood and had some conversation with the orderly officer relative to Napoleon.

[1] 'Bonaparte was deficient in education and in manners; it seemed as if he must have been destined either to live in a tent where all men are equal, or upon a throne where everything is permitted. He did not know how either to enter or to leave a room. He did not know how to make a bow, how to rise, or how to sit down. His questions were abrupt, and so also was his manner of speech. Spoken by him, Italian loses all its grace and sweetness. Whatever language he speaks, it always sounds like a foreign tongue; he appears to force it to express his thoughts. And as any rigid rule becomes an insupportable annoyance to him, and every liberty which he takes pleases him as though it were a victory, he would never yield to grammar.'—*Memoirs of Madame de Rémusat* vol. i. p. 5.

May 6.—Saw Napoleon, to whom I gave a book, entitled, *Mœurs et Coutumes des Corses*, which he ran his eye over, frequently laughing very heartily at several of the anecdotes. The author, he said, was wholly unacquainted with many circumstances relative to the history, manufactures, etc. of Corsica; in fact, that he was either a place-hunter, or a man who had been well beaten by the Corsicans. That many of the anecdotes he related respecting assassinations which had been committed were true, but that the Corsicans were not in the habit of assassinating strangers; that those who espoused a party remained unchangeable. 'Even I,' continued he, 'in the height of my power, could never induce the English party to change their opinions, although I offered to receive them all into my service.

'The Admiral,' said he, 'held a long conversation with me a day or two ago. He praised the Governor; said that I was mistaken in him; that he was an extremely well-informed man, and had at bottom a good heart. He was very anxious that I should meet him, on an opportunity that soon would be afforded by the arrival of the Ambassador, when he suggested that we might meet as if nothing had previously occurred. I told him that he did not know the Governor; that until he changed his conduct, I would not see him, unless by force. As long as he treats me *à la Botany Bay*, so long will not I see him. I certainly would *understand* not to see the Commissioners, and not to enter houses which he said he suspected.

'I told the Admiral,' continued he, 'that I hoped the Prince Regent would know of the treatment which I receive here. The Admiral said that if I thought myself aggrieved, I ought to complain, either to the Regent or to the Ministers. I think it would be a degradation to me to complain to Ministers who have treated me so ill, and who act from hatred.

'I told him also,' continued Napoleon, 'that I had been well-pleased at the capture of Copenhagen, because it made bitter enemies of the Danes, without injuring me. For it was not ships that I wanted, but naval officers and seamen who were all left behind to man my vessels. I also informed him that the capture and robbery of the Spanish frigates[1] pleased me; as it caused you to be hated in Spain, where you might have been and were popular before, and besides, was unworthy of a great nation. I told him that I did

[1] The attack upon the Spanish frigates *Medea*, *Fama*, *Clara*, and *Mercedes*, October 3, 1804, in time of peace by H.M.SS. *Indefatigable*, *Lively*, *Medusa*, and *Amphion*; Spain being believed to be on the point of declaring war against Great Britain.

'Many persons, who concurred in the expediency, doubted the right of detaining these ships; and many again to whom the legality of the act appeared clear were of opinion that a more formidable force should have been sent to execute the service, in order to have justified the Spanish Admiral in surrendering without an appeal to arms.'—James's *Naval History*, vol. iii. p. 286.

When Charles IV. was bullied into joining the French against us in the great revolutionary war, Nelson's comment on the event was that the hostility of Spain would turn a poor war into a rich one.

not receive money direct from Spain. That I got bills upon Vera Cruz, which certain agents sent by circuitous routes, by Amsterdam, Hamburg, and other places, to London (as I had no direct communication). The bills were discounted by merchants in London, to whom ten per cent, and sometimes a premium, was paid as their reward. Bills were then given by them upon different bankers in Europe for the greatest part of the amount, and the remainder in gold, which last was brought over to France by the smugglers. Even for the equipping my last expedition after my return from Elba, a great part of the money was raised in London.

'I told the Admiral,' continued Napoleon, 'that you had been the first violators of the peace of Amiens; that your Ministers, who boast so much of not having acknowledged me as Emperor, were so conscious, themselves, of having been the violators of the treaty, that they offered, through Lord Whitworth, to give thirty millions of francs, and to assist, as much as lay in their power, to make me King of France, if I would consent to the English retaining Malta.' I took the liberty of asking to whom the proposal had been made? 'To *Malouet*, who was Minister to Louis a short time ago,' replied the Emperor. 'My answer to this offer was, "Tell Lord Whitworth that I will owe nothing to strangers, or to their interference. If the French nation do not, of themselves, create me King, foreign influence shall never be employed by me to obtain it." The fact is, that your Ministry always deceived the people by false and artful representations, and are of the opinion expressed by the great Lord Chatham, "That if England acted towards France with justice for twenty-four hours, she would be ruined."

'The Admiral,' continued Napoleon, 'is very well-informed about the history of the last years; is really an Englishman, and stands up for his country whenever he can; but notwithstanding, he could not contradict several of the assertions I made to him, because they were incontrovertible facts. He returned frequently to the proposed interview with the Ambassador, which he is most desirous should take place. I am convinced that no good would arise from it. I wish,' added he, 'that he should know my sentiments on these matters.'

He was very anxious in his inquiries about Captain Meynel, who was very dangerously ill. General Montholon much better.

I showed him the *Naval Chronicle*, in which there was a long article about the death of Captain Wright. 'No person,' said Napoleon, 'asserts positively that he had seen him murdered; and the principal witness who testifies to the belief in it was a man who was himself in prison. Let him be asked for what crime he was thrown into a jail. It is not a place for honest people, or for those whose testimony can be relied upon. If I had acted properly, I should have ordered Wright to be tried by a military commission as a spy, and shot within twenty-four hours, which by the laws of war I was entitled to do. What would your Ministers, or even your Parliament have done to a French captain that was discovered landing assassins in England to murder King George? If I had, in retaliation for the assassins sent to murder me, sent others to murder —— and the Bourbon princes, what would have been done to the captain of the vessel who had landed them in England, if he were taken? They would not have been so lenient as I was with Wright. They would have had him tried and executed *sur le champ*.'

May 7.—Napoleon very particular in inquiring about Captain Meynel, whose death he observed would grieve him, as he had *l'air d'un brave homme*. Had some further conversation with him relative to the prisoners made at the commencement of the war. I said that I believed he had demanded that the ships as well as the prisoners made in them should be given up, in exchange for those detained in France. He replied that he did not recollect that he had demanded the ships. 'The only reason,' added he, 'that your Government would give as a right for detaining them as prisoners was, that they *had always done so in preceding wars*, and that it would be lessening the dignity of the Government to give them up, or to consider as prisoners of war those who had been detained by me in France. To this I answered, that they had always done so, because they had to deal with *imbéciles*, and people who knew not how to act vigorously, and were afraid to retaliate. As to the exchange of prisoners, I offered to effect it in the following manner, viz. to send three thousand men, consisting of two thousand Spaniards and Portuguese, and one thousand English, to a certain place, there to be exchanged for three thousand French, and so on until all were exchanged. Your Government would not consent to this, but required that all the English should be exchanged at first; although the others were your Allies, and were taken fighting by your side. As soon as the French prisoners in England heard of this proposal, they wrote the strongest letters possible, protesting against and praying me not to consent to such terms, alleging, that as soon as your Ministers had got all the English prisoners, amounting I believe to ten thousand, they would under some pretext break off the exchange;[1] and that they (the French prisoners), who were already treated badly enough, would then be subjected to every species of brutality and ill-treatment, as the English would no longer be afraid of reprisals.' I took the liberty of observing that I hoped he did not credit what he saw in Pillet's libel. 'No, no,' replied Napoleon, 'I believe no exaggerated statement of

[1] I have some recollection (although I cannot find it in my journal) that Napoleon also told me that he had proposed to the English Minister that both powers should simultaneously land their respective prisoners in such ports in England and France as might have been previously agreed upon, which proposal was not agreed to by His Majesty's Ministers.—B. E. O'M.

the kind. I reason from the testimonies of the prisoners themselves and from the circumstances. I would not,' continued Napoleon, 'desire a better testimonial in my favour than that of the prisoners of the different nations who have been in France. Many of your English sailors did not want to be exchanged. They did not wish to be sent again on board their floating prisons. The Russians declared that they were much better than in their own country, after they discovered that their heads were not to be cut off, which they at first had been persuaded to believe; and the Austrians would not have escaped, even if allowed.

'Another shocking act of your Ministers,' said Napoleon, 'was landing several hundred wounded and disabled soldiers who had been born in countries under me, and were wounded fighting your battles against me on the coast of Holland, where they were liable by the laws of the country to be tried and shot within twenty-four hours, for having carried arms against it. When it was reported to me, and application made to try them, I said, " Let them go on. Let them land as many as they like. They will say what treatment they have received, and will prevent others of my troops from deserting and joining the English." To say nothing of the inhumanity of the practice,' said Napoleon, raising his hands with emotion, 'it was very bad policy on the part of your Ministers, as these poor injured wretches told it everywhere; and I also caused the names, countries where wounded, etc., of many of them to be published in the *Moniteur.*'

May 11.—Told Sir Hudson Lowe what Napoleon said relative to the restrictions, and the Commissioners, etc. His Excellency asked why I had not told him this before? I replied, because it had only occurred yesterday, and that having often made him communications of a similar nature before, I had not thought it important. He observed that it was of *great* importance, as having taken place since he had sent his answer to their observations upon his restrictions. He then observed that the principal cause of all the difficulties which he had to combat with the French people had arisen from Sir George Cockburn's having, upon his own authority, and beyond his instructions, taken upon himself to grant much more indulgence, and a much greater space for limits without being accompanied by a British officer, than he had any right to do; not only had he not the right, but it was contrary to his instructions, and that on his arrival he had been astonished at Sir George Cockburn's conduct.

He then spoke for some time about the letter which had been written by Madame Bertrand to the Marquis de Montchenu, which he seemed to consider a very heinous offence. I observed that Count Bertrand had said that at the time the letter was written, there had existed no prohibition against epistolary correspondence with persons domiciled in the island as the Marquis was, and that since that letter had been written by Madame

Bertrand, six sealed letters had been received by her, amongst which was one from Sir George Bingham. His Excellency did not appear to be well pleased with this observation of Count Bertrand's.

The quantity of wood and coals allowed not being nearly sufficient, Count Montholon desired me to represent to the Governor that in the Admiral's time, when there were not by any means so many fires as at present, there was more than double the quantity of fuel allowed; that for some time they had been obliged to burn the wine-cases; and to request him, if he did not think proper to increase the quantity furnished by Government, to give directions to the purveyor to supply it, on their paying for it themselves. Went to Plantation House and explained to the Governor the above communication, particularising the number of fires; he, after some discussion, replied that he would give orders for an additional supply to be furnished.

May 12.—After some conversation about the Governor, Napoleon said, 'When I was at Elba, the Princess of Wales sent to inform me of her intention to visit me. I, however, on her own account, sent back an answer begging of her to defer it a little longer, that I might see how matters would turn out; adding, that in a few months I would have the pleasure of receiving her. I knew that at the time it could not fail to injure the Princess, and therefore I put it off. It is astonishing that she desired it, for she had no reason to be attached to me, her father and brother having been killed fighting against me. She went afterwards to see Marie Louise at ——, and I believe that they are great friends.[1]

'Prince Leopold,' continued he, 'was one of the finest young men in Paris at the time he was there. At a masquerade given by the Queen of Naples, Leopold made a conspicuous and elegant figure. The Princess Charlotte must doubtless be very contented and very fond of him. He was near being one of my aides-de-camp, to obtain which post he had made interest; but by some means, fortunately for himself, he did not succeed, as probably if he had, he would not have been chosen to be a future King of England. Most of the young princes in Germany,' continued he, 'solicited to be my aides-

[1] Sir William Gell, writing from Naples in September 1817, says: 'If fate ever puts you in the way, make my royal mistress tell you how the Empress Maria Louisa invited her to Parma; how the attendants dined in the outer room; and how, in full dress feathers, and velvet chairs with heavy gold legs and backs, the two ladies sat at a very long *tête-à-tête* before dinner at a fire. "You imagine it not very entertaining; I assure you very dull. I *yarn*, and she de same. *Mein Gott*, I balance on my chaire mit my feet 'pon de fire. What you tink? I tomble all back mit de chaire, man see nothing more als my feet. I die from laugh, and what you tink she do? She stir not, she laugh not; but mit the utmost gravity she say: 'Mon Dieu, Madame, comme vous m'avez affrayé!' I go in fits of laugh, and she repeat de same word witout variation or change of feature. I not able to resist bursting out every moment at dinner, and die to get away to my gens to tell de story. We all scream mit de ridiculousness for my situation." I don't know whether I have told you this so that you can understand it, but hope your genius will help you to imagine what must have been a duet between this bottle of frisky champagne and that jug of stale small beer.'—*Journals and Correspondence of Miss Berry*, edited by Lady Theresa Lewis, vol. iii. p. 145.

de-camp, and Leopold was then about eighteen years of age.'

Some conversation now took place relative to the infernal machine and the different plots which had been formed to assassinate him. 'Many of the plots of the Bourbons,' said he, 'and the —— were betrayed to me by Frenchmen, employed and well paid by themselves, and in their confidence, but who in reality were agents of the French police. By means of them I became acquainted with their plans and the names of the contrivers of the plot, one of whom was the Comte d'—— Louis, the present king, always refused to give his consent. These agents had conferences with the Bourbon princes, and with some of your Ministers, especially with Mr. H——, Under-Secretary of State, and rendered an account of everything to the police. If I had acted rightly, I should have followed the example of Cromwell, who, on the discovery of the first attempt made to assassinate him, the plot of which had been hatched in France, caused it to be signified to the French King, that if the like occurred again, he, by way of reprisal, would order assassins to be hired to murder him and a Stuart.[1] Now I ought to have publicly signified that on the next attempt at assassination, I would cause the same to be made upon King —— and the Bourbon princes, to accomplish which last, indeed,

[1] The Lord Protector, however, was very magnanimous to those plotting against him, and frequently gave intimation that their plans were discovered in advance of the official instructions issued for arrest. *Vide* Guizot's *Cromwell*, pp. 311, 429.

I had only to say that I would not punish the projectors.'

May 13.—Application made by me to Major Gorrequer (on the part of the *maître d'hôtel*) to request that the Governor would give directions to Mr. Breame (the Company's farmer) to let the establishment have two calves monthly, as Napoleon liked veal, and Mr. Breame had refused to supply them without leave from the Governor.

Permission was accordingly granted by Sir Hudson Lowe to let the French have two calves monthly, for which the farmer was to be paid by the French themselves.

May 14.—Napoleon in very good spirits. Asked me 'why I had dined in camp yesterday?' I replied, 'Because there was nothing to eat at Longwood.' He laughed heartily at this, and observed, '*That* certainly was the best reason in the world.'

Afterwards he conversed for some time about Moreau, and said that he was by no means a man of that superior talent which the English supposed; that he was a good general-of-division, but not adapted for the command of a great army. 'Moreau was brave,' said he, 'indolent, and a *bon vivant*. He did nothing at his *quartier général* but loll on a sofa, or walk about with a pipe in his mouth. He scarcely ever read a book. His disposition was naturally good, but he was influenced by his wife and mother-in-law, who were both intriguers. I recommended Moreau to marry her, at the desire of Josephine, who loved her because she was a Creole. Moreau had fallen greatly in public estimation on account of his conduct towards Pichegru.[1] After Leoben, the

[1] While Napoleon was at Moscow, Count Daru received a letter from Madame Moreau praying him to ask the Emperor to permit her to return to France for a few months on private and indispensable business. Daru, knowing that the best mode of obtaining anything from Napoleon was by being candid and open, showed him the letter. '*Oui*,' replied the Emperor, '*elle doit être venue, et elle doit déjà être repartie.*' Daru said that a woman could not be dangerous. '*Elle vient intriguer*,' answered Napoleon; 'perhaps you are one of those who think that Moreau is a good citizen?'—'*Sire*,' replied Daru, '*je crois que sous le rapport du civisme et du patriotisme, le caractère de Moreau est inattaquable.*'—'*Eh bien, vous vous trompez*,' said Napoleon, and the subject was dropped.

At Dresden, in 1813, while Napoleon was at breakfast with Maréchal Victor and Daru, a Russian flag of truce was announced. After the person who bore it had stated his mission, Napoleon asked him some questions relative to the disorder which he had observed in the advanced posts of the enemy's army on the preceding day, and if the Russians had not lost some officer of distinction. The officer replied, 'No.'—'*Cependant*,' said Napoleon, '*il y a eu du desordre; à tel poste on a emporté quelqu'un blessé ou tué.*'—'*Je ne sache pas*,' replied the officer, '*que nous ayons perdu personne, à moins que votre majesté ne veuille parler du Général Moreau, qui a été blessé à mort aux avant postes.*'—'*Le Général Moreau?*' repeated Napoleon, and afterwards making a sign with his head to Daru, '*eh bien!*' . . . Daru instantly recollected the conversation at Moscow, when Napoleon had made use of the same words, at which time he supposed that the Emperor's opinion had been influenced by personal motives, and was obliged to acknowledge that he had judged rightly.

'Business seemed to be M. Daru's element; he was incessantly occupied. Soon after he was appointed Secretary of State, one of his friends was expressing a fear that the immense amount of business in which he would thenceforth be absorbed might prove too much for him. "On the contrary," replied Daru, "I assure you that since I have entered upon my new functions, I seem to have absolutely nothing to do." On one occasion only was his vigour ever known to relax. The Emperor called him up after midnight to write to his dictation; M. Daru was so completely overcome by fatigue that he

Senate of Venice were foolish enough to stir up a rebellion against the French armies, without being either sufficiently strong themselves, or having adequate assistance from other powers to promise the slightest hope of success. In consequence of this, I caused Venice to be occupied by the French troops.

'An agent of the Bourbons, the Comte d'Entraigues, of whom I suppose you have heard in England, was there at the time. Fearing the consequences, he escaped from Venice, but on his way to Vienna (I think he said) he was arrested on the Brenta by Bernadotte, with all his papers. As soon as it was known who he was, he was sent to me, being considered a man of some importance. Amongst his papers we found his plans, and the correspondence of Pichegru with the Bourbons. I had them immediately attested by Berthier and two others, sealed and sent to the Directory, as they were of the

scarcely knew what he was writing; at length he could hold out no longer, and he fell asleep over his paper. After enjoying a sound nap he awoke, and, to his astonishment, perceived the Emperor by his side quietly engaged in writing. The shortness of the candles informed him that his slumber had been of tolerable duration. While he sat for a few moments overwhelmed with confusion, his eyes met those of the Emperor, who said to him, "Well, sir, you see I have been doing your work, since you would not do it yourself. I suppose you have eaten a hearty supper, and passed a pleasant evening; but business must not be neglected."—" I pass a pleasant evening, Sire!" said M. Daru; "I have been for several nights without sleep, and closely engaged. Of this Your Majesty now sees the consequence; and I am exceedingly sorry for it."—" Why did you not inform me of this?" said the Emperor; "I do not want to kill you; go to bed. Good-night, M. Daru."'—*Las Cases*, vol. iii., part vi., p. 22, English edition. (*A previous allusion has been made to this anecdote.*)

greatest consequence. I then examined d'Entraigues myself, who, when he saw that the contents of his papers were known, thought there was no use in attempting concealment any longer, and confessed everything. He even told me more than I expected; let me into the secret plans of the Bourbons, with the names of their English partizans, and, in fact, the information I obtained from him was so full and so important, that it instantly determined me how to act, and was the chief cause of the measures I then pursued, and of the proclamation which I issued to the army warning them that, if necessary, they would be called upon to cross the mountains and re-enter their native country, to crush the traitors who were plotting against the existence of the Republic.

'At this time Pichegru was Chief of the Legislative Body. The Comte d'Entraigues was so communicative that, instead of putting him in confinement, I allowed him to go where he pleased in Milan, gave him every indulgence, and did not even put him under *surveillance*. He was a man of talent and acuteness, intelligent and pleasant to converse with, though he proved afterwards to be a *mauvais sujet*. A few days afterwards I received orders from the Directory to cause him to be shot (or what in those times was equivalent to it, to try him by a military commission, and sentence to be immediately executed). I wrote to the Directory that he had given very useful information, and did not deserve such a return; and finally, that I could not execute it; that if they still insisted upon shooting him they must do it themselves.

'Shortly after this d'Entraigues escaped into Switzerland, from whence the *coquin* had the impudence to write a libel, accusing me of having treated him in the most barbarous manner, and even put him in irons; when the fact was that I had allowed him so much liberty that it was not until after he had escaped for several days that his flight was discovered, and then only by his arrival having been notified in the Swiss paper. The conduct of d'Entraigues greatly displeased all who had been witnesses of the indulgent manner in which I treated him at Milan. Amongst others, some ambassadors and diplomatic persons were so much offended that they drew up and signed a declaration contradicting these accusations. In consequence of the information gained from d'Entraigues, Pichegru was banished to Cayenne.

'Immediately after the seizure of d'Entraigues, Desaix came to see me. Conversing with him about Pichegru, I remarked that we had been greatly deceived, and expressed my surprise that his treason had not been discovered sooner. "Why," said Desaix, "we knew of it three months ago!"—"How can that be possible?" I replied. Desaix then recounted to me the manner in which Moreau, with whom he had been at that time, had found in the baggage of the Austrian General Klingspor[1] some correspondence of Pichegru's, in

[1] General Klinglin.

which his plans in favour of the Bourbons were detailed, and the false manœuvres which he intended to put in practice. I asked Desaix if this had been communicated to the Directory? He replied, "No," that Moreau did not wish to ruin Pichegru; and had desired him to say nothing about it. I told Desaix that he had done very wrongly; that he ought immediately to have sent all the papers to the Directory, as I had done; that, in fact, it was tacitly conniving at the destruction of his native country.

'As soon as Moreau was informed that Pichegru was found out, he denounced him to the army as a traitor, and sent to the Directory the papers containing the proofs of it, which he had kept concealed in his possession for some months, allowing Pichegru to be chosen Chief of the Legislative Body, although he knew that he was plotting the destruction of the Republic. Moreau was accused this time, and with justice, of double treachery. "Thou hast first," it was said, "betrayed thy country, by concealing the treason of Pichegru, and afterwards thou hast uselessly betrayed thy friend, by disclosing what thou oughtest to have made known before; but which, when concealed by thee until it was discovered by other means, ought to have ever remained a secret in thy breast." Moreau never recovered the esteem of the public.'

I mentioned the retreat of Moreau,[1] and asked

[1] In 1796.

if he had not displayed great military talents in it? 'That retreat,' replied the Emperor, 'instead of being what you say, was the greatest blunder that Moreau ever committed. If he had, instead of retreating, made a *détour*, and marched in the rear of Prince Charles (I think he said), he would have destroyed or taken the Austrian army. The Directory were jealous of me, and wanted to divide, if possible, the military reputation; and as they could not give credit to Moreau for a victory, they did for a retreat, which they caused to be extolled in the highest terms; although even the Austrian generals condemned Moreau for having made it. You may probably hereafter,' continued Napoleon, 'have an opportunity of hearing the opinion of French generals on the subject, who were present, and you will find it in agreement with mine. Instead of credit, Moreau merited the greatest censure and disgrace for it. As a general, Pichegru had much more talent than Moreau.[1]

'Moreau ridiculed the idea of the formation of the Legion of Honour. When he heard from some one that it was also intended to be given to those who had distinguished themselves in science, and not to be confined to feats of arms alone, he

---

[1] In January 1803 Lord Hartington wrote to Miss Berry: 'My Aunt Besborough is to set out from Paris the 6th of next month. Moreau has been to see her. He makes no scruples of disapproving of the present Government. My aunt asked him if he was not afraid of Bonaparte killing him, upon which he said: "*Bonaparte est un tyran, mais pas un assassin.*"'—Miss Berry's *Journal*, vol. ii. p. 235.

replied, "Well, then, I shall apply for my *chef* to be made a commander of the Order, as his talents are most superior in the science of cookery."'

In reply to some arguments which I offered to convince him that —— and the English —— were ignorant of that part of Pichegru's plot which embraced assassination, Napoleon replied, 'I do not suppose that —— or any other of the English —— actually said to Georges or Pichegru, "You must kill the First Consul;" but they well knew that such formed the chief and, indeed, the only hope of success; and yet they, knowing this, furnished them with money, and provided ships to land them in France, which, to all intents and purposes, rendered them accomplices; and if —— had been tried by an English jury, he would have been condemned as such. Lord —— took great pains to persuade the Foreign Courts that they were ignorant of the project of assassination, and wrote several letters, in which he acknowledged that the English had landed men for the purpose of overturning the French Government, but denied the other. However, he made a very lame business of it, and none of the Continental Governments gave any credit to his assertions. It was naturally condemned as, on the plea of retaliation, none of the sovereigns or rulers were safe. It was at the time that I had it in contemplation to effect a descent upon England. Your —— did not want to get rid of "Napoleon Bonaparte," but of "the First Consul."

'Fox had some conversations with me on the

subject of the 3d Nivose.¹ He too, like you, denied that the —— were privy to the scheme of assassination, but faintly, after hearing what I had to say, condemned the whole transaction. Indeed, his own measures were quite opposed to it. The conduct of the Emperor of Germany also formed a striking contrast. When I had possession of his capital, he, through religious motives, positively and with sincerity prohibited attempts of the kind, which might have been executed any day, as I often walked about without precaution.'

During this interview, I mentioned that Bernadotte had been strongly suspected of being lukewarm in the cause of the Allies, if not of playing a double part; that he was called Charles Jean Charlatan, and supposed to be likely to join him if any reverse happened to the Allies. Napoleon replied, 'Probably they called him Charlatan, because he is a Gascon, a little inclined to boasting. As to joining me if I had been successful, he would have done no more than all the rest. The Saxons, Würtembergers, Bavarians, and all those who abandoned me when I was unfortunate, would have joined me again if I had been successful. After Dresden, the Emperor of Austria went upon his knees to me,² called me *his dear son*, and begged

¹ The plot of the infernal machine, December 24, 1800.

² This is not intended to be understood, as must be evident, literally, but merely as a forcible manner of making me comprehend the earnestness with which the Emperor of Austria made the application. Napoleon frequently used the same expression in similar instances.—B. E. O'M.

for the sake of his *very dear daughter*, to whom I was married, not to ruin him altogether, but to be reconciled to him.[1] Had it not been for the desertion of the Saxons with their artillery, I should have gained a victory at Leipsic, and the Allies would have been far differently situated.'

May 16.—Napoleon in his bedroom, complained of headache, and had his feet immersed in hot water. At first he was rather melancholy, but subsequently became lively and communicative. He spoke about Egypt, and asked many questions; amongst others, whether a three-decker could enter the harbour of Alexandria without having been lightened? I replied that I thought it might, or if not, that it might be very easily lightened.[2] Napoleon observed that he had sent an officer named Julien from Cairo, with peremptory orders to Brueys to enter the harbour of Alexandria, but that unfortunately he was killed by the Arabs

---

[1] Napoleon was fond of referring to the relationships conferred on him by his Austrian alliance, and his allusions to them occasionally startled his hearers.

The Emperor Francis told the Marquis de Castellentini that some time after the marriage of Napoleon and Maria Louisa the two Emperors were talking of the Revolution of 1793: 'It came from far,' said Napoleon; 'yet it would have been easy to prevent its great catastrophe if my uncle's character had not been so essentially weak.'—' I was quite stunned,' added the Emperor of Austria, 'and much more abashed when, after a moment of reflection, I saw that he was alluding to Louis XVI.'—See *The Black Cabinet*, by Comte d'Hérisson, p. 230. Note by Baron Mounier.

[2] When at Alexandria, I saw the *Tigre* and *Canopus* enter the harbour. They were 80-gun ships of the largest class, and drew as much water as a three-decker.—B. E. O'M.

on the way. 'I called,' continued he, 'a fort which I built at Rosetta after him.'

He asked me if I knew that fort, to which I replied in the affirmative. 'It was surprising,' continued he, 'how Brueys could have thought of engaging at anchor without having first fortified the island with twenty or thirty pieces of cannon, and having brought out a Venetian sixty-four, and some frigates which he had in the fort of Alexandria. In a conversation which I had with Brueys some weeks before, on board the *Orient*, he himself demonstrated to me that a fleet ought never to engage at anchor—at least that a fleet which did so must always be beaten on account of the facility which the attacking ships would have of taking up their position; and that an order (whether from Brueys, or not, I did not understand) actually existed prohibiting it. Notwithstanding which, Brueys himself attempted it afterwards. Brueys,' continued he, 'always believed that if Nelson attacked him it would be on his right, thinking his left impregnable on account of the island, and had prepared matters accordingly. I endeavoured to convince him that a ship or two of his left might be taken by a superior force, and an opening afforded thereby for the enemy's fleet to enter.'

Napoleon added that, prior to the departure of Julien, orders had been sent to Brueys that he should not quit the coast of Egypt until after he had ascertained the physical impossibility of the fleet's being able to enter the harbour of Alexandria. If possible, he was ordered to carry it into execution; if not, to proceed to Corfu with his fleet. 'Now, Brueys,' continued he, 'not having ascertained the fact, as on the contrary, Barré asserted that it was practicable, of which I was also myself convinced, did not think himself authorised to go away, and at the same time was afraid to enter the harbour even if possible, thinking it hazardous without having been first assured that we were in full possession of the country. He was ignorant of my success at Cairo until twenty-our hours before he was attacked by Nelson. In this manner he remained in hesitation, and neglected to secure himself. Moreover, he never expected that Nelson would have attacked him with an inferior force. If he had brought out his frigates, and well fortified the island, Nelson would either never have attacked him, or would have been beaten if he had.

'It was with great difficulty that I made Brueys depart from Toulon. After sailing, he wanted to send four ships to attack Nelson, who was lying with three dismasted vessels at —— ;[1] but I would not allow it, as the success of the enterprise was of too much importance to allow the capture of two or three ships to be put into competition with it. He afterwards wished to divide the fleet, which I would not permit. Brueys was a man of unquestionable talent; but he wanted that decisive resolution that enables a man to seize an oppor-

[1] Probably at St. Pietro, a harbour in Sardinia.

tunity on the instant, which I conceive to be the most essential quality in a general or admiral. Probably from want of experience he had not that confidence in his own ability and the correctness of his plans which hardly anything else can impart. Unless Nature forms a man of so peculiar a stamp as to be enabled to decide instantaneously, nothing but experience can give it. I, myself, commanded an army at twenty-two years of age, but Nature made me different from most others. If Nelson had met Brueys' fleet in going to Egypt, I know not what might have happened, as I had placed three hundred and fifty or four hundred veterans in each line-of-battle ship, who were trained to the guns twice a day, and had given orders that each ship should engage one of yours. Your vessels were small, and I believe not well-manned, and I gave this order to prevent your obtaining any advantages by your superior skill in manœuvring.'

Here some discussion took place upon the comparative merit of the English and French seamen. I urged that English sailors fought with more confidence; that if any accidents happened to the ships in action, they would remedy them much sooner, and would fight longer than the French seamen. Napoleon said he agreed in everything but the last. '*Signor Dottore*,' said he, '*il marinaro Francese è bravo quanto l'Inglese.* The French soldiers had a great contempt for the English troops at the beginning of the war, caused, perhaps, by the failure of the expeditions under the Duke of York, the great want of alertness, etc., in the English advanced posts, and the misfortunes which befell your armies. In this they were fools, as the English were well known to be a brave nation. It was probably by a similar error that Reynier was beaten by General Stuart at Maida, as the French imagined that you would run away and be driven into the sea. Reynier was a man of talent, but more fit to give counsel to an army of twenty or thirty thousand men than to command one of five or six. Your troops, on that day, were nearly all English, and Reynier's were chiefly Poles. It is difficult to conceive how little the French soldiers thought of yours until they were taught the contrary. Of your seamen, they always spoke in terms of respect, although they would only allow that they were more expert and quick, and not more brave than their own.

'When I went to see the King of Prussia, after Tilsit, instead of a library, I found he had a large room, like an arsenal, furnished with shelves and pegs, in which were placed fifty or sixty jackets of various modes. Every day he changed his costume and put on a different one. He was a tall, dry-looking fellow, and would give a good idea of Don Quixote. He attached more importance to the cut of a dragoon or a hussar uniform than was necessary for the salvation of a kingdom. At Jena his army performed the finest and most showy manœuvres possible, but

I soon put a stop to their *coglionerie*, and taught them that to fight and to execute dazzling manœuvres and wear splendid uniforms were very different affairs. If,' added he, 'the French army had been commanded by a tailor, the King of Prussia would certainly have gained the day, from his superior knowledge in the art; but as victories depend more upon the skill of the general commanding the troops than upon that of the tailor who makes their jackets, he failed.'

The Emperor then observed that we allowed too much baggage and too many women to accompany our armies. 'Women, when they are bad,' said he, 'are worse than men, and more ready to commit crimes. The soft sex, when degraded, falls lower than the other. Women are always much better or much worse than men. Witness the *tricoteuses de Paris* during the Revolution.

'When I commanded at the Col de Tende, a most mountainous and difficult country, to enter which the army was obliged to pass over a narrow bridge, I gave directions that no women should be allowed to accompany it, as the service was a most difficult one, and required the troops to be continually on the alert. To enforce this order I placed two captains on the bridge, with instructions, on pain of death, not to permit a woman to pass. I went to the bridge myself to see that my orders were complied with, where I found a crowd of women assembled. As soon as they perceived me, they began to revile me, bawling out, "Oh, then, *petit caporal*, it is you who have given orders not to let us pass." I was then called *petit caporal* by the army. Some miles farther on I was astonished to see a considerable number of women with the troops. I immediately ordered the two captains to be put in arrest, and brought before me, intending to have them tried immediately. They protested their innocence, and asserted that no woman had crossed the bridge. I caused some of those dames to be brought, when, to my astonishment, by their own confession, I found that they had thrown the provisions that had been provided for the support of the army out of some of the casks, concealed themselves in them, and passed over unperceived.'

Napoleon observed that he did not consider the English cavalry by any means equal to the infantry. The men, by some fault, were not able to stop the horses, and were liable to be cut to pieces, if, in the act of charging, it became necessary to halt and retreat. The horses too were accustomed to be fed too luxuriously,[1] kept too warm, and from what he had learned, greatly neglected by the riders.

I offered some explanations about the quantity of baggage allowed by Wellington, which I said did not exceed a small portmanteau for each officer; that only five women to a hundred men were

[1] Napoleon studied stable economy for a time. Once, when driving into Paris from Ruelle, he complained of the length of the journey, and asked Lauriston what was necessary to abridge it in future? 'More oats' was the significant reply.

allowed to embark for foreign service; and that new regulations had been adopted to prevent the horses of the cavalry from being kept too warm or too highly pampered. Napoleon replied that he had been informed by French officers that the baggage of one English officer in France, or in Belgium, was greater than that of ten French.

May 18.—Major Fehrzen came to Longwood. Being asked why he did not call upon the Bertrands occasionally, he replied that the Governor had signified his desire that no communication, beyond that of an ordinary salutation, should take place between the officers of the 53d Regiment and the persons detained in St. Helena. He admitted that the dark and mysterious conduct pursued towards the French was of a nature likely to excite suspicion, but assured them that in the 53d Regiment there were no assassins to be found.

May 22.—Had some conversation with Napoleon about Montchenu, who, he said, would perfectly justify the idea which the English formerly held of the French, viz. that they were a nation of dancing-masters; in which opinion they must have been strengthened during the Revolution, by seeing a set of vain triflers arrive amongst them who had been expelled from their own country for their arrogance and tyranny. 'This idea,' added Napoleon, 'was impressed so strongly upon the minds of the English, that when I sent Duroc as Ambassador to Petersburg, Lord St. Helens, the English Envoy there, being curious to see what he was like, took an opportunity of observing him closely on his entrance into that capital; and on being afterwards asked his opinion of him, replied, "*Ma foi, au moins il n'a pas l'air danseur!*" expressing thereby that Duroc was the only Frenchman he had seen who had not the appearance of a dancing-master; which I can readily believe, as probably until that time he had seen no other Frenchmen than *imbéciles* like Montchenu, with whom England was overrun.'

Napoleon (who had just come out of his bath) spoke about Russia, and said that the European nations would yet find that *he* had adopted the best possible policy at the time he had intended to re-establish the kingdom of Poland, which would be the only effectual means of stopping the increasing power of Russia. It was putting a barrier to that formidable empire, which it was likely would yet overwhelm Europe. 'I do not think,' said he, 'that I shall live to see it, but you may. You are in the flower of your age, and may expect to live thirty-five years longer. I think that you will see that the Russians will either invade and take India, or enter Europe with four hundred thousand Cossacks and other inhabitants of the deserts, and two hundred thousand real Russians.

'When Paul was so violent against you, he sent to me for a plan to invade India. I sent him one, with instructions in detail.' (Here Napoleon showed me on a map the routes and the different points from whence the army was to have proceeded.) 'From a port in the Caspian Sea he was to have marched on to India. Russia,' continued he, 'must either fall or aggrandise herself, and it is natural to suppose that she will choose the latter. By invading other countries, Russia has two points to gain,—an increase of civilisation and polish, by coming into contact with other powers, the acquisition of money, and the rendering friendly to herself the inhabitants of the deserts, with whom some years back she was at war. The Cossacks, Calmucks, and other barbarians, who have accompanied the Russians into France, and other parts of Europe, having once acquired a taste for the luxuries of the South, will carry back to their deserts the remembrance of places where they met with such fine women and fine living, and not only will not themselves be able to endure their own barbarous and sterile regions, but will communicate to their neighbours a desire to conquer these delicious countries.

'In all human probability Alexander will be obliged either to take India from you, in order to gain riches and provide employment for them, and thereby prevent a revolution in Russia; or he will make an irruption into Europe, at the head of some hundred thousand of those barbarians on horseback, and two hundred thousand infantry, and carry everything before him. What I say to you is confirmed by the history of ages, during which it has been invariably observed that whenever the barbarians had once got a taste of the

South of Europe, they always returned to attempt new conquests and ravages, and finally succeeded in making themselves masters of the country. They are brave, active, patient of fatigue and bad living, poor, and desirous of enriching themselves. If Alexander succeeds in incorporating Poland with Russia (that is to say, in perfectly reconciling the Poles to the Russian Government, and not merely subduing the country), he has gained the greatest step towards the conquest of India. My opinion is that he will attempt either the one or the other of the projects I have mentioned, and I think the last the most probable.'

I observed that the distance was great, and that the Russians had not the money necessary for so great an undertaking. 'The distance is nothing,' replied the Emperor; 'supplies can be easily carried upon camels, and the Cossacks will always ensure a sufficiency of them. Money they will find when they arrive there. The hope of conquest would immediately unite armies of Cossacks and Calmucks without expense. Hold out to them the plunder of some rich cities, and thousands would flock to their banners. Europe,' continued he, 'and England in particular, ought to have prevented the union of Poland with Russia.

'A great object for England,' added Napoleon, 'ought to be to keep Belgium always separate from France; as France, having Belgium, might be said, in case of a war with England, to have possession of Hamburg, etc. It would, however, have been better for England that Austria had it than that it should be possessed by Holland, because Austria is stronger; and when France arises from her present state of nothingness, Holland, being too weak to stand alone, will always be at her feet.[1]

'If I had succeeded in my expedition to Russia,' added he, 'I would have obliged Alexander to accede to the continental system against England, and thereby have compelled the latter to make peace. I would also have formed Poland into a separate and independent kingdom.' I asked what kind of a peace he would have given to us. 'A very good one,' replied Napoleon; 'I would only have insisted upon your discontinuing your vexations at sea.' I asked if he would have left us Malta; to which he replied in the affirmative, adding, that he was tired of war, and would have employed himself in improving and adorning France, in the education of his son, and in writing his history. 'At least,' said he, 'the Allied Powers cannot take from me hereafter the great public works which I have executed, the roads which I made over the Alps, and the seas which I have united. They cannot place their feet to improve where mine have not been before. They cannot take from me the Code of Laws which I formed, and which will go down

[1] The French were only driven out of Belgium when on the point of occupying Holland in 1831, by the vigorous conduct of Lord Palmerston.

to posterity. Thank God, of these they cannot deprive me!'¹

[1] 'You wish to know the treasures of Napoleon? They are immense, it is true, but they are all exposed to light. They are:—The noble harbours of Antwerp and Flushing, which are capable of containing the largest fleets, and of protecting them against the ice from the sea; the hydraulic works at Dunkirk, Havre, and Nice; the immense harbour of Cherbourg; the maritime works at Venice; the beautiful roads from Antwerp to Amsterdam; from Mayence to Metz; from Bordeaux to Bayonne; the passes of the Simplon, of Mount Cenis, of Mount Genèvre, of the Corniche, which open a communication through the Alps in four different directions; and which exceed in grandeur, in boldness, and in skill of execution, all the works of the Romans; in that alone you will find eight hundred millions; the roads from the Pyrenees to the Alps; from Parma to Spezia; from Savona to Piedmont; the bridges of Jena, Austerlitz, Des Arts, Sèvres, Tours, Rouanne, Lyons, Turin, of the Isère, of the Durance, of Bordeaux, Rouen, etc.; the canal which connects the Rhine with the Rhone by the Doubs, and thus unites the North Sea with the Mediterranean; the canal which joins the Scheldt with the Somme, and thus joins Paris and Amsterdam; the canal which unites the Rance to the Vilaine; the canal of Arles, that of Pavia, and the canal of the Rhine; the draining of the marshes of Burgoine, of the Cotentin, of Rochfort; the rebuilding of the greater number of the churches destroyed during the Revolution; the building of others; the institution of numerous establishments of industry for the suppression of mendicity; the gallery at the Louvre; the construction of public warehouses, of the Bank, of the canal of the Ourcq; the distribution of water in the city of Paris; the numerous drains, the quays, the embellishments and the monuments of that large capital; the works for the embellishment of Rome; the re-establishment of the manufactures of Lyons; the creation of many hundreds of manufactories of cotton, for spinning and for weaving, which employ several millions of workmen; funds accumulated to establish upwards of four hundred manufactories of sugar from beetroot, for the consumption of part of France, and which would have furnished sugar at the same price as the West Indies, if they had continued to receive encouragement for only four years longer; the substitution of wood for indigo, which would have been at last brought to a state of perfection in France, and obtained as good

I said that I had been seeking for the number of ships which had been seized by the English prior to the proclamation issued by him for the detention of the English in France, and could only discover that two *chasse-marées* had been taken in Quiberon Bay. 'Two *chasse-marées!*' exclaimed Napoleon, 'why, there was property to the amount of seventy millions, and I suppose above two hundred ships detained, before I issued the proclamation! When you blockaded France, I blockaded England; and it was not a paper blockade, as I obliged you to send your merchandise round by the Baltic, and occupy a little island (Heligoland) in the North Sea, in order to smuggle.

'If,' said he, ' Lord Castlereagh were to offer

and as cheap as the indigo from the Colonies; numerous manufactories for all kinds of objects of art, etc.; fifty millions expended in repairing and beautifying the palaces belonging to the Crown; sixty millions in furniture for the palaces belonging to the Crown in France, and in Holland, at Turin, and at Rome; sixty millions of diamonds for the Crown, all purchased with Napoleon's money; *the Regent* (the only diamond that was left belonging to the former diamonds of the Crown), withdrawn from the hands of the Jews at Berlin, in whose hands it had been left as a pledge for three millions. The Napoleon Museum, valued at upwards of four hundred millions, filled with objects legitimately acquired, either by money or treaties of peace known to the whole world, by virtue of which the *chefs d'œuvres* it contains were given in lieu of territory or of contributions. Several millions amassed to be applied to the encouragement of agriculture, which is the paramount consideration for the interest of France; the introduction in France of merino, sheep, etc.; these form a treasure of several thousand millions which will endure for ages! *these* are the monuments that will confute calumny!'—*Las Cases*, vol. iii. pp. 248-251.

to place me again upon the throne of France on the same conditions that Louis fills it, I would prefer remaining where I am. There is no man more to be pitied than Louis. He is forced upon the nation as King, and instead of being allowed to ingratiate himself with the people, the Allies oblige him to have recourse to measures which must increase their hatred. Royalty is degraded by the steps they have made him adopt. *On la rend si sale et si méprisable* that it reflects upon the throne of England itself. In place of making him respectable, *on l'a couvert d'ordure*. The French nation,' continued he, 'would never willingly consent to receive the Bourbons as Kings because the Allies wish it.'

May 23.—Sent for to attend the Governor at Plantation House. Found him in the library with Sir Thomas Reade. His Excellency said, 'That the day before yesterday some newspapers of a later date than any of his own had been received by Mr. Cole, the postmaster, some of which were lent to me in violation of the Act of Parliament, which positively prohibited communication, verbal or written, with General Bonaparte, or any of his family, or those about him, without his (the Governor's) knowledge. That he therefore wished to know from myself whether I had lent those papers, or any others to General Bonaparte?' I replied that I had lent those and many others at various times to Napoleon, as I had been constantly in the habit of lending papers to him since I had been on the island. That Sir

George Cockburn had in more instances than one given me newspapers to take to Longwood before having perused them himself. Sir Hudson Lowe replied that it was a violation of the Act of Parliament. I replied that I was not included in the Act of Parliament, as I had made an express stipulation that I should not be considered or treated as one of the French, and would immediately resign my situation if I were required to hold it upon such terms.

General Lowe 'desired' me to understand that for the future I was not to lend General Bonaparte any newspaper, or be the bearer of any information —or newspapers—to him, without having previously obtained his sanction. I observed that I felt a difficulty how to act, for if, after the arrival of a ship, Napoleon asked me if there were any news, I could not possibly pretend ignorance. His Excellency said that 'as soon as a ship arrived, both Captain Poppleton and myself ought to be shut up in Longwood until the whole of the information or news brought was made known to him, and *then* I could obtain from him whatever news was proper to be communicated to General Bonaparte.' I replied that I would not remain an hour in my situation subject to such a restriction.

His Excellency observed that 'some months ago information of the greatest importance had been communicated by me to General Bonaparte, before he (the Governor) had himself known it, viz. that of the Dissolution of the Chamber of Deputies in

France; that I had myself told him that I had informed General Bonaparte of it, and concluded by asking if I had communicated this intelligence verbally, or by means of a newspaper, and if the paper had not been lent to me by Sir Pulteney Malcolm?'

I replied that at such a distance of time I could not recollect whether the communication made by me had been verbal or by means of a newspaper; that most probably it had been both, and that I did not recollect from whom I had received the newspaper. His Excellency said that 'a person possessed as I was of a memory so extraordinarily good, could not pretend want of recollection,' and repeated the question. I answered that trifles did not remain long impressed upon my memory. The Governor observed it was singular I could not recollect that it had been lent by the Admiral, and in a sneering way asked 'if it was not a *Scotch* paper?' I answered that I never had seen a Scotch paper at Longwood, and that Sir Pulteney Malcolm often had selected two or three papers of the oldest dates for me, and sent the recent ones to him (Sir Hudson).

General Lowe then demanded 'if the papers lent by the Admiral had been for myself, or if Sir Pulteney knew that they would be submitted to General Bonaparte for perusal.' I replied, 'For myself, and I do not know whether he is aware of the use I put them to or not.' Sir Hudson said that 'it was very extraordinary I could not tell if the Admiral knew of it. That by the signature of His

Majesty's Ministers, nobody but himself had any right to communicate in any manner whatever with General Bonaparte.' I observed that Sir George Cockburn had never considered it necessary to keep back newspapers from Napoleon; that the only instructions he had given to me on the subject were that it would be better not to show him anything personally very offensive.

Saw Napoleon, who spoke of Madame de Staël— 'a woman,' said he, 'of considerable talent and great ambition; but so extremely intriguing and restless as to give rise to the observation that she would throw her friends into the sea, that at the moment of drowning she might have an opportunity of saving them. I was obliged to banish her from Court. At Geneva she became very intimate with my brother Joseph, whom she won over by her conversation and writings.

'When I returned from Elba, she sent her son to be presented to me, on purpose to ask payment of two millions, which her father Neckar had lent out of his private property to Louis XVI., and to offer her services, provided I complied with this request. As I knew what he wanted, and thought that I could not grant it without unfairness to others who were in a similar predicament, I gave directions that he should not be introduced. However, Joseph would not be denied, and brought him in in spite of this order, the attendants at the door not liking to refuse my brother, especially as he said that he would be answerable for the consequences. I received him very politely, heard his business, and replied that I was very sorry it was not in my power to comply with his request, as it was contrary to the laws, and would do an injustice to many others. Madame de Staël was not, however, contented with this. She wrote a long letter to Fouché, in which she stated her claims, and that she wanted the money to portion her daughter in marriage to the Duc de Broglie, promising that if I complied with her request I might command her and hers; that she *would be black and white for me.* Fouché communicated this, and advised me strongly to comply, urging that in so critical a time she might be of considerable service. I answered that I would make no bargains.

'Shortly after my return from the conquest of Italy,' continued he, ' I was accosted by Madame de Staël in a large company, although at that time I avoided going out much in public. She followed me everywhere, and stuck so close that I could not shake her off. At last she asked me, "Who at this moment is *la première femme du monde!*" intending to pay a compliment to me, and expecting that I would return it. I looked at her and coldly replied, " She who has borne the greatest number of children," turned round, and left her greatly confused and abashed.' He concluded by observing, ' That he could not call her a *wicked* woman, but that she was an *intrigante*, possessed of considerable talent and influence.'

Saw Sir Hudson Lowe at Plantation House, with

whom I had a conversation, chiefly upon subjects connected with the Admiral. Informed him that macaroni formed a large item in the expenditure of Longwood, as for the two pounds of that article, which they consumed daily, they were obliged to pay twenty-four shillings to Mr. Solomon. His Excellency observed that there was plenty of it in the Government store.[1]

Cipriani in town making his customary purchases.

May 26.—Napoleon indisposed with catarrh, inflammation and swelling of the right cheek and gums, with headache, caused probably by exposure yesterday to the cold wind in the garden.

May 27.—Napoleon better.

'In the course of a few years,' said he, 'Russia will have Constantinople, the greatest part of Turkey, and all Greece. Almost all the cajoling and flattering which Alexander practised towards me was to gain my consent to effect this object. I would not consent, foreseeing that the equilibrium of Europe would be destroyed. In the natural course of things, in a few years Turkey must fall to Russia. The greatest part of her population are Greeks, who, you may say, are Russians. The Powers it would injure, and who could oppose it, are England, France, Prussia, and Austria. Now as to Austria, it will be very easy for Russia to engage her assistance by giving her Servia and other provinces bordering upon the Austrian dominions, reaching nearly to

---

[1] When some was sent up a few days after, it was found to have been rendered unfit for use from long keeping.—B. E. O'M.

Constantinople. The only basis on which France and England can ever be allied with sincerity will be in order to prevent this.[1] But even this alliance would not avail. France, England, and Prussia united could not prevent it. Russia and Austria can at any time effect it. Once mistress of Constantinople, Russia gets all the commerce of the Mediterranean, becomes a great naval power, and God knows what may happen. She quarrels with you, marches off to India an army of seventy thousand good soldiers, which to Russia is nothing, and a hundred thousand *canaille*, Cossacks and others, and England loses India. Above all the other powers, Russia is the most to be feared, especially by you. Her soldiers are braver than the Austrians, and she has the means of raising as many as she pleases. In bravery the French and English soldiers are the only ones to be compared to them. The Russians are beginning already with you; I see that they have prohibited the introduction of your merchandise. England is falling. Even Prussia prohibits your goods. What a change for England! Under the great Chatham, you forbade the most powerful sovereign in Europe, the Emperor of Germany, to navigate the Scheldt, or to establish an extensive commerce at Ostend; this was unjust, but you had the power to prevent it, because it was against the interests of England. *Now* Prussia shuts her ports against you! What a falling off! In my opinion the only thing which can save

[1] As witness the Crimean War.

England will be abstaining from meddling in continental affairs, and withdrawing her army from the Continent.¹ Then you may insist upon whatever is necessary to your interests without fear of reprisals being made upon your army. You are superior in maritime force to all the world united; and while you confine yourself to that arm, you will always be dreaded. You have the great advantage of declaring war when you like, and of carrying it on at a distance from your home. By means of your fleets you can menace an attack upon the coasts of those powers who disagree with you, and interrupt their commerce without their being able materially to retaliate. By your present mode of proceeding you forfeit all those advantages. Your most powerful arm is given up, and you send an army to the Continent, where you are inferior to Bavaria in that species of force. You put me in mind of Francis the First, who had a formidable and beautiful artillery at the battle of Pavia. But he placed his cavalry before it, and thus masked the battery which, could it have fired, would have ensured him the victory. He was beaten, lost everything, and made prisoner.² So it is with you. You forsake your

¹ Hanover.
² 'The Spanish general found the French drawn up in order of battle and covered by a formidable force of artillery. . . . The vanguard of the Imperialists suffered severely as they began to traverse the level plain, while the main body . . . and the rearguard were each in turn exposed to the same galling fire. Del Guasto, who commanded the vanguard, then instructed his men to scatter themselves and make their way individually to the walls of the city . . . a manœuvre which completely misled Francis, who no sooner

ships, which may be compared to Francis's batteries, and throw forty thousand men on the Continent, which Prussia, or any other power who chooses to prohibit your manufactures, will fall upon and cut to pieces if you menace or make reprisals.

'So silly a treaty as that made by your Ministers for their own country,' continued the Emperor, 'was never known before. You give up everything, and gain nothing. All the other powers gained acquisitions of country and millions of souls, but you give up colonies. For example, you gave up the Isle of Bourbon to the French. A more impolitic act you could not have committed. You ought to endeavour to make the French forget the way to India and all Indian policy, instead of placing them halfway there. Why did you give up Java? Why Surinam, or Martinique, or the other French colonies? To avoid doing so you had nothing more to say than that you would retain them for the five years the Allied Powers were to remain in France. Why not demand Hamburg for Hanover? Then you would have an *entrepôt* for your manufactures. In treaties an ambassador ought to take advantage of everything for the benefit of his own country.'

Napoleon then said that if I were asked any questions by the Ambassador[1] about a reception at Longwood, I should say that he (Napoleon) was not

witnessed this apparent confusion than he gave an order to charge . . . and the whole body of his cavalry galloped to the front, thus suspending the operations of the artillery.'—See Miss Pardoe's *Life of Francis the First*, 1887 edition, vol. ii. pp. 159, 160.

[1] Lord Amherst.

on good terms with the Governor, and could not think of receiving him with that person. That if he were desirous of being introduced, he would receive him presented by Count Bertrand or by the Admiral. 'I have no doubt,' added he, 'that this Governor will tell him that I am very much dissatisfied with him for doing his duty, and that I am sulky. That having myself been so long used to command, I have not philosophy enough to bear restraint. That I have been treated very well, and have made a very bad return for it. If the Ambassador asks you, you may say that I have my own way of receiving persons who wish to be introduced to me. That I do not wish to affront him—far from it—but that I cannot see the Governor.'

May 28.—A servant, named William Hall, dismissed from Longwood. After leaving it he underwent a long interrogation at Plantation House by the Governor relative to what he had seen and heard during his residence at Longwood.

The *Ocean, Experiment*, and another ship arrived from England yesterday.

Saw Sir Hudson Lowe, who told me, with some embarrassment, that 'his conduct had undergone a parliamentary investigation, and that I should see in the newspapers an account of a motion relative to General Bonaparte, that had been made by Lord Holland in the House of Lords, but that *he* had not as yet received any official account of it from Lord Bathurst. That the reports of his lordship's reply, as given in the newspapers, might be incorrect or unfaithful, which I had better say, if General Bonaparte asked me any questions.'

May 30.—Napoleon sent for me to his bedroom to explain several passages in the *Times* newspaper, particularly in the speech imputed to Lord Bathurst in reply to Lord Holland's motion for the production of papers relative to him. Having read those parts which stated that every change which had taken place in the situation of the complainant had been for his own benefit; that the reason for lessening his limits had been his tampering with soldiers or inhabitants; that he had only received one letter; that the communication with officers and inhabitants was unrestricted and free; that people had gone to Longwood in disguise, etc.,—'*Je suis bien aise*,' said Napoleon, '*de voir que le ministre Anglais a justifié sa conduite atroce envers moi au parlement, à sa nation et à l'Europe avec des mensonges; triste ressource, qui ne dure pas long temps.* The reign of lies will not last for ever,' continued he. I felt greatly ashamed, and stammered out the excuse that had been suggested to me by Sir Hudson Lowe. 'It is even worse,' said he, 'in the *Morning Chronicle*. In the *Times* it appeared as if *prepared* for publication in a ministerial office; but in the *Chronicle* it looks as if coming from his own mouth. I have ordered Bertrand,' added he, 'to make a faithful translation of it, and to consult you about any phrase of the sense of which he may be doubtful.

'Lord Bathurst,' continued he, 'has shown great indelicacy in having shown or told to Montchenu in

London the contents of a letter written by Gourgaud to his mother, which the old blockhead repeated to all the world here. He asserts that I only received one letter, that from my brother Joseph, which is false. He ought to act like a confessor, to hear everything, and divulge nothing; but it is of a piece with the rest of his outrageous conduct. If the Governor questions you, tell him what I have said.'

Napoleon then observed it was strange that a Sovereign, who by the grace of God was born lord and master of so many millions, could not receive a sealed letter. 'How,' said he, 'can complaints be made to the Sovereign of a corrupt or vile minister if such be the rule? In time of war, if a minister betrays and sells his country, how can it be known to the King, if the complaint must go through the hands of the persons complained of, at whose option it will be either to varnish and colour it over as best suits his views, or suppress it altogether?'

May 31.—Gave Napoleon a translation I had made by his desire of a letter which appeared in the *Courier* newspaper. After reading it, he expressed his opinion that it had been written by the Governor himself, and that the seeming incorrectness of one part was only to mask the real author.

'You were greatly offended with me for having called you a *nation of shopkeepers*. Had I meant by this that you were a nation of cowards, you would have had reason to be displeased; but no such thing was ever intended. I meant that you were a nation of merchants, and that all your great riches, and your grand resources arose from commerce, which is true. What else constitutes the riches of England? It is not extent of territory, or a numerous population. It is not mines of gold, silver, or diamonds. Moreover, no man of sense ought to be ashamed of being called a shopkeeper. But your Prince and your Ministers appear to wish to change altogether *l'esprit* of the English, and to render you another nation; to make you ashamed of your shops and your trade, which have made you what you are, and to sigh after nobility, titles, and crosses; in fact, to assimilate you with the French. What other object can there be in all those cordons, crosses, and honours, which are so profusely showered. You are all nobility now, instead of the plain old Englishmen. You are ashamed of yourselves, and want to be a nation of nobility and *gentlemen*. Nothing is to be seen or heard of now in England, but "Sir John," and "My lady." All those things did very well with me in France, because they were conformable to the spirit of the nation; but believe me, it is contrary both to the spirit and the interest of England. Stick to your ships, your commerce, and counting-houses, and leave cordons, crosses, and cavalry uniforms to the Continent, and you will prosper. Lord Castlereagh himself was ashamed of your being called a nation of merchants, and frequently said in France that it was a mistaken idea to suppose that England depended upon commerce, or was indebted to it for her riches; and added that it was not by any means necessary to her. How I laughed when I heard of this false pride! He betrayed his country at the Peace. I do not mean to say,' continued he, laying his hand over his heart, 'that he did it from here, but he betrayed it by neglecting its interests. He was in fact the *commis* of the Allied Sovereigns. Perhaps he wanted to convince them that you were not a nation of merchants, by showing clearly that you would not make any advantageous bargain for yourselves; by magnanimously giving up everything, that nations might cry, "Oh! how nobly England has behaved!" Had he attended to the interests of his own country, had he stipulated for commercial treaties, for the independence of some maritime states and towns, for certain advantages to be secured to England, to indemnify her for the waste of blood, and the enormous sacrifices she had made, why then they might have said, "What a mercenary people, they are truly a nation of merchants; see what bargains they want to make;" and Lord Castlereagh would not have been so well received in the *drawing-rooms!*

'Talent he may have displayed in some instances,' continued the Emperor, 'and great pertinacity in accomplishing my downfall; but as to knowledge of, or attention to, the interests of his own country, he has manifested neither the one nor the other. Probably for a thousand years such another opportunity of aggrandising England will not occur. In the position of affairs nothing could have been refused to you.'

I told Napoleon that in one of the *Couriers* sent him by the Governor, I had observed a speech attributed to Sir Francis Burdett, accusing him of having established eight *bastilles* in France. Napoleon replied, 'In some respects it is true. I established a few prisons, but they were for certain persons who were under sentence of death; as I did not like to have the capital punishment executed, and could not send them to a Botany Bay, as you were masters of the sea and would have released them, I was obliged to keep them in prison.

'There were,' continued he, 'some Vendean chiefs, Chouans, and others, who had been arrested for rebellion and other crimes, to whom the choice was given, either to be tried, or to remain in prison as long as the Government might think it necessary for the safety of the State. Those gaols were inspected twice a year by a committee composed of a councillor of State and two judges, who each time offered the prisoners the choice of continuing in prison as they were, or of being brought to trial; but they always preferred the former. They were allowed three francs a day for their subsistence. No abuses,' continued he, 'were known to be committed in the prisons; and, in fact, instead of being a crime, as imputed to me in that paper, it was a mercy. But,' added he, 'where is the country without gaols; are there not some in England?'

June 2.—An orderly dragoon brought a letter, directing me to proceed immediately to Plantation House. Found His Excellency in the library, who asked what were General Bonaparte's remarks upon the discussions in Parliament. I repeated Napoleon's expressions (as I had been desired to do). When I mentioned the remarks he had made upon the assertion imputed to Lord Bathurst, that every change which had taken place had been for the benefit of the complainant, also his observations on the indelicacy of disclosing the contents of letters, Sir Hudson Lowe took up a number of the *Times* newspaper, and, with a countenance in which embarrassment was visible, observed, 'That Lord Bathurst was right in having asserted that whatever alterations had been made had been for the better, because his lordship must have alluded to the different manner in which letters were now sent to Longwood; for *instead of passing through the hands of inferior officers* as before, they were now only seen and read by himself (the Governor).'

Some conversation then took place relative to the quantity of provisions allowed to Longwood. Sir Hudson Lowe maintained that the quantities had been fixed by Count Montholon, and that he (Sir Hudson) had never heard any complaints made of a deficiency. I explained to His Excellency that Count Montholon had not fixed the quantities, and also called to his recollection that the scantiness of the allowance had been frequently reported to him by the orderly officer, by the purveyor, by myself, and also by the *maître d'hôtel*. Sir Hudson Lowe persisted that the quantities had been specified by Count Montholon, and sent for Major Gorrequer to prove the correctness of his assertion. Major Gorrequer, however, did not support His Excellency, as he declared that the quantity of the wine only had been fixed by the Count, and that of the remaining articles by a scale framed by orders of His Excellency himself.

Notwithstanding a little confusion produced by this, Sir Hudson Lowe persisted in asserting that he was ignorant of the insufficiency of the allowance of provisions; upon which I thought it necessary to enumerate the days on which representations to that effect had been made to him by myself, by Mr. Balcombe, and by the *maître d'hôtel;* and also observed that the assistance rendered by Sir Thomas Reade twice a week in procuring divers kinds of eatables for Longwood, for which payment had been frequently made in his presence by Cipriani, could not have left Sir Thomas in ignorance respecting the wants of the French. The Governor sneeringly observed, ' It appeared that I should be the best witness *those* people could call.'

June 4.—An increase of twenty-eight pounds daily in the meat furnished by Government to Longwood ordered by Sir Hudson Lowe.

Independently of the usual guard, an officer has been stationed at Hut's Gate since the arrival of the ships from England, with orders to inspect

VIEW OF LONGWOOD, FROM THE ROAD TO DEADWOOD.

minutely every one approaching Longwood, and to allow '*no suspicious persons*' to pass.

June 5.—Count and Countess Montholon went to town shopping, and to pay a visit to Admiral and Lady Malcolm. The officer who accompanied them was ordered by the Governor to 'follow them into the Admiral's, and to pay attention to their conversation.'

June 6.—Saw Napoleon, who was in very good spirits. Told me that Count Montholon had been informed yesterday that a person who had seen the Grand Llama had just arrived in the island; he therefore desired that as soon as I went to town I should endeavour to get acquainted with him, and inquire what ceremonies had been made use of; whether adoration was practised, and inform myself of every possible particular. 'I am,' said he, 'very curious to get some information about this Grand Llama. I have never read any accounts about him that I could rely upon, and sometimes have doubted of his existence.'[1]

Saw Sir Hudson Lowe in town, with whom I had some conversation relative to Napoleon's observations on Lord Bathurst's speech. His Excellency gave me a message to be delivered to him in reply. Mentioned to him that Napoleon had also remarked, when speaking of Lord Bathurst, 'Almost all ministers are liars. Talleyrand is their corporal, next come Castlereagh, Metternich, Hardenberg.'

---

[1] A portrait of the Grand Llama in costume appears in the recently published travels of the Russian artist Verestchagin.

Shortly afterwards I met Captain Balston, of the Hon. Company's Marine Service, who reminded me of our former acquaintance. By him I was informed that a gentleman had arrived from China, with a letter of introduction to me from Mr. Urmston of Macao, with whom I had been on terms of intimacy. On seeing the gentleman afterwards, I found that his name was Manning, and that he was the person of whom I was in search. He wore a long black beard, and had travelled through the kingdom of Thibet as far as the frontiers of China. I told him that the Emperor had expressed great curiosity about the Grand Llama, and that if he came up to Longwood, there was every probability that he would see him.

Mr. Manning told me that he had been a prisoner in France, and had been released by Napoleon, and furnished with a passport as soon as the Emperor had learned that he was a person travelling for information, which might ultimately benefit society; that as a mark of his gratitude for this favour, he had sent some little presents to the Governor for him, with a request that they might be forwarded, and that he would ask a pass for the purpose of endeavouring to see him.

A report current in town, that a marble bust of young Napoleon was brought out in the *Baring*, and that Sir Thomas Reade had recommended the captain of the vessel to throw it overboard and say nothing about it. This was asserted as a positive fact to Cipriani and to me by Captain ——, who said that the captain of the *Baring* had confessed that insinuations to that effect had been made to him.

June 7.—Mr. Manning, accompanied by Captain Balston, came up to Count Bertrand's. The former told me that he had been directed by the Governor, for what reason he could not divine, not to communicate to the Count that he had sent a few presents to him for Napoleon. After they had been about an hour at Count Bertrand's, Napoleon came in, accompanied by General Montholon. He accosted Captain Balston first, and observed, 'Oh, I have seen you here before!' He then asked Mr. Manning some questions. Manning said that he was one of the persons who had been detained in France in 1805; that he had written a letter to Napoleon, stating that he was travelling for the benefit of the world at large, which had procured his release.[1] 'What protection had you?' asked Napoleon. 'Had you a letter from Sir Joseph Banks[2] to me?' Manning replied that he had no protection whatever, nor letter from Sir Joseph Banks, nor had he any friends to interest themselves in his behalf; that he had merely written a letter to him stating his situation. 'Was it your letter only which obtained your liberty?' asked Napoleon. 'It was my simple letter,' replied Manning, 'that induced you to grant it to me, for which I am very

[1] Unlike the great Australian explorer Flinders, who was detained a prisoner in the isle of France for seven years during the Consulate and Empire.

[2] In addition to his English honours, Sir Joseph Banks was a Corresponding Member of the French Institute.

grateful, and beg to thank you.' Napoleon asked him where he had lived, and looked at the map of the countries in the atlas of Las Cases, asking a variety of questions about the route he had taken; whether he had seen the Grand Llama; the manners, customs, etc. of the countries he had passed through.

Manning gave a clear and concise reply to every question, said that he had seen the Llama, whom he described to be an intelligent boy of seven years old, and had performed the same ceremonies in his presence as were done by others who were admitted to it. Napoleon said, 'How did you escape being taken up as a spy?'—'I hope,' replied Manning, 'that there is nothing in my countenance which would indicate my being a spy;' at which Napoleon laughed and said, 'How came it to pass that you, being *profane* according to their ideas, could gain admission to the presence of the Llama?' Mr. Manning answered that he honoured and paid respect to all religions, and thereby gained admission. Napoleon desired to know if he had passed for an Englishman, and observed that the shape of his nose would indicate his being an European? The other replied that he had passed for a native of Calcutta, but he believed it was known that he was an Englishman; that there were some races of men there who had a similar formation of nose.

Napoleon then observed with a smile that '*Messieurs les voyageurs* frequently told *contes*, and that the existence of the Grand Llama had been denied by several.' Manning answered, '*Je ne suis pas du nombre de ces voyageurs là;* that truth was not falsehood,' at which Napoleon laughed, and asked many other questions. Manning related that the chief part of the revenues of the Grand Llama arose from presents made to him by the princes and others who believed in him; that temporally, however, he was subject to the Chinese; that he never married, neither did his priests; that the body into which, according to their belief, the spirit passed, was discovered by signs known only to the priests. Napoleon then asked several questions about the Chinese language, if the Russians had ever penetrated in that direction, and whether he intended to publish an account of his travels; after which he asked Balston some questions about his ship, wished them good morning, and departed.

Gave Napoleon a copy of Santini's pamphlet in French, which he read, observing as he went through it, according as the passages seemed to deserve it, 'true,' 'partly true,' 'false,' 'stuff,' etc.

He observed that they had spelt his name with an *u* (*Buonaparte*), and told me that when he first commanded the army of Italy, he had used the *u* in order to please the Italians; that, however, either the one or the other was equally proper; that after his return from Egypt he had dropped it; that, in fact, the heads of the family and those of highest rank had spelt their names with the *u*, adding, 'That a mighty affair had been made of so trifling a matter.'[1]

---

[1] The original proof-sheets of Sir Walter Scott's works were enlivened by a running commentary in the margin of notes and

June 8.—Mr. Cole (of the firm of Balcombe and Co., the purveyors) came up to Longwood by order of Major Gorrequer, to acquaint General Montholon that the liveries of the servants must be changed from green to blue, and the quantity of gold lace upon the coats diminished.

For some time back complaints have been made by the *maître d'hôtel* of the badness of the mutton, of the fowls, the indifferent quality and want of variety of the vegetables, etc. Mr. Cole informed me that it was not their fault, as, by order of Sir Hudson Lowe, the purveyor was obliged to take the sheep from the H.E.I. Company's stockyard. That this day permission had been received to purchase from the farmers, restricting them however to a certain price; that the vegetables furnished were received from the garden of the Governor.

June 9.—An official complaint made in writing by Captain Poppleton to Major Gorrequer of the badness of the above-mentioned articles; also that Mr. Cole said that the vegetables were furnished from Plantation House garden.

June 10.—Saw Napoleon in his bedroom. Told him that I had received a Portsmouth paper, in which were contained extracts from a work published

---

replies by author and printer. To a criticism by Ballantyne : ' Would to God you would alter this quote,' Scott replies : ' Would to God I could, I certainly should.'

In the second note to the Ode appears the word Bonaparte, against which appears the following marginal note : ! I would spell the accursed name correctly as an Italian word, and not as the miscreant himself wished to use it, as a French one.'

in London under his name. He looked over it, and observed that he had not written a line of it, though some parts resembled his manner. He added that there was a Scotchman, whose name he did not recollect, who had written several articles so much in his style, that when in France he had caused some of his works to be translated into French.

I informed him that Colonel Macirone, aide-decamp to Murat, had published some anecdotes of his late master. 'What does he say of me?' said Napoleon. I replied that I had not seen the book, but had been informed by Sir Thomas Reade that he spoke ill of him. 'Oh,' said he laughing, 'that is nothing; I am well accustomed to it. But what does he say?' I answered, it was asserted that Murat had imputed the loss of the battle of Waterloo to the cavalry not having been properly employed, and had said that if he (Murat) had commanded them, the French would have gained the victory.[1] 'It is very probable,' replied Napoleon, 'I could not be everywhere; and Murat was the best cavalry officer in the world. He would have given more impetuosity to the charge. There wanted very little, I assure you, to gain the day. *Enfoncer deux ou trois bataillons*, and in all probability Murat would have effected that. There were not, I believe, two such officers in the world as Murat for the cavalry, and Drouot for the artillery!

'Murat was a most singular character. Four and

[1] If Paris could have been trusted without Davoût, events might have been very different.

twenty years ago, when he was a captain, I made him my aide-de-camp, and subsequently raised him to be what he was. He loved, I may almost say adored, me. In my presence he was as it were struck with awe, and ready to fall at my feet. I did wrong in having separated him from me, as without me he was nothing. With me he was my right arm. Order Murat to attack and destroy four or five thousand men in such a direction, it was done in a moment; but leave him to himself, he was an *imbécile* without judgment. I cannot conceive how so brave a man could be so *lâche*. He was nowhere brave unless before the enemy. *There* he was probably the bravest man in the world. His boiling courage carried him into the midst of the enemy, *couvert de pennes jusqu'au clocher*, and glittering with gold. How he escaped is a miracle, being, as he was, always a conspicuous mark, and fired at by everybody. Even the Cossacks admired him on account of his extraordinary bravery. Every day Murat was engaged in single combat with some of them, and never returned without his sabre dripping with the blood of those whom he had slain. He was a paladin, in fact a Don Quixote in the field; but take him into the Cabinet, he was without judgment or decision.

'Murat and Ney were the bravest men I ever met with. Murat, however, was a nobler character than Ney. Murat was generous and open; Ney partook of the *canaille*. Strange to say, however,

Murat, although he loved me, did me more mischief than any other person in the world. When I left Elba, I sent a messenger to acquaint him with what I had done. He thought me already master of France, Belgium, and Holland, and that he must not adopt half-measures. Like a madman he attacked the Austrians with his rabble, and ruined me. For at that very time there was a negotiation going on between Austria and me, stipulating that the former should remain neutral, which would have been finally concluded, and I should have reigned undisturbed. But as soon as Murat attacked the Austrians, the Emperor supposed he was acting by my directions, and indeed it will be difficult to make people believe the contrary. Metternich said, "Oh, the Emperor Napoleon is the same as ever! A man of iron. The trip to Elba has not changed him. Nothing will ever alter him : all or nothing for him." Austria joined the coalition, and I was lost! Murat was unconscious that my conduct was governed by circumstances. He was like a man gazing at the shifting scenes at the opera, without ever thinking of the machinery behind, by which the whole is moved. He never thought that his secession in the first instance would have been so injurious to me, or he would not have joined the Allies. He concluded that I should be obliged to give up Italy and some other countries, but never contemplated my total ruin.'

Sir Hudson Lowe at Longwood. Went to

Count Bertrand's, where he remained for some time. In the evening Napoleon sent for me, and said that Sir Hudson Lowe had been to Bertrand, to inform him that Lady Holland had sent out some presents for Madame Bertrand's children, two books for himself, and some other articles, with a letter; that although it was contrary to the regulations, which prescribed that everything should come through the Secretary of State's Office, he would take it upon himself to send them. That Mr. Manning had also left some trifling presents for him (Napoleon), which he wished to know if he would accept. That there was also another circumstance still more embarrassing, viz. that a sculptor at Leghorn had made a bad bust of young Napoleon, which he had forwarded to St. Helena by the *Baring*, in charge of a man now very ill with a fever, with a letter, stating that the artist had been already satisfied, but that if he (Napoleon) wished to pay any more, one hundred guineas was the price, which he considered a large sum of money for a badly executed bust. That he wished to be informed if Napoleon desired to have it. 'Bertrand,' continued Napoleon, 'replied that doubtless the Emperor would wish to see the bust of his son. He regretted it had not been forwarded at an earlier period. That it would be better to send it that evening than detain it until to-morrow, and that the Emperor would be happy to receive Mr. Manning's presents. Bertrand says Lowe looked disturbed and appeared to attribute

great merit to himself for having offered to send
up those things, because they had not passed
through the hands of the Secretary of State. I
do not know what he meant by saying that a
hundred guineas was too much for the bust, or if
he intended it as an insult, or as a reflection upon
us. Surely no sum could be too much for a *father*
to pay under similar circumstances.[1] But this man
has no feeling!'

Napoleon then asked me if I knew anything
about the bust? I replied that I had heard of
it some days before. 'Why did you not tell me?'
asked the Emperor. I felt confused, and answered
that I expected the Governor would have sent it
up. Napoleon said, 'I have known of it for several
days. I intended, if it had not been given, to have
made such a complaint as would have caused every
Englishman's hair to stand on end with horror, and
the mothers of England to execrate him as a monster
in human shape. I have been informed that he
has been deliberating about it, and also that his
Prime Minister, Reade, ordered it to be broken. I
suppose that he has been consulting with that
little major, who has pointed out to him that it
would brand his name with ignominy for ever, or
that his wife has read him a lecture at night about

---

[1] 'When he had finished dressing, and was choosing between two
or three snuff-boxes which lay before him, he abruptly gave one to
his *valet de chambre* (Marchand): "Put that by," said he; "it is
always meeting my eye, and it hurts me." I know not what was on
this snuff-box; but I imagine it was a portrait of the King of Rome.'
—*Las Cases*, vol. i., part ii., p. 44, English edition.

the atrocity of such a proceeding. He has done enough however to dishonour his name by retaining the bust so long,[1] and by even allowing a doubt to exist of its being sent up.'

The Emperor afterwards spoke of his own family. 'My excellent mother,' said he, 'is a woman of courage and of great talent, more of a masculine than a feminine nature, proud, and high-minded.[2] She is capable of selling everything, even to her *chemise*, for me. I allowed her a million a year, besides a palace, and made her many presents. To the manner in which she formed me at an early age, I principally owe my subsequent elevation. My opinion is, that the future good or bad conduct of a child entirely depends upon the mother.[3] She is very rich. Most of my family considered that I might die, that

[1] The bust had been in the island for fourteen days, during several of which it was at Plantation House.

[2] Madame Mère, when I had the honour of seeing her at Rome in 1819, was still the remains of a fine woman. Her manners were dignified and commanding, and her deportment such as one would expect to find in a queen, or in the mother of Napoleon. Her thoughts were divided between her God and her son. She saw but little company, and I believe that the Duke of Hamilton and myself were the only Britons who had dined at her table. Her establishment was splendid, though private and unostentatious.—B. E. O'M.

[3] Napoleon once said to Madame Campan: 'The old systems of education were good for nothing. What do young women stand in need of, to be well brought up in France?'—'Of *mothers*,' answered Madame Campan. 'It is well said,' replied Napoleon. 'Well, madame, let the French be indebted to you for bringing up mothers for their children.'—See the Memoir of Madame Campan, prefixed to the *Private Life of Marie Antoinette*, vol. i. p. xlix., 1883 edition.

accidents might happen, and consequently took care to secure something. They have preserved a great part of their property.

'Josephine died worth about eighteen millions of francs. She was the greatest patroness of the fine arts that had been known in France for a series of years. She had frequently arguments with Denon, and even with myself, as she wanted to procure fine statues and pictures for her own gallery instead of the Museum. Now, I always acted to please the people; and whenever I obtained a fine statue, or a valuable picture, I sent it there for the benefit of the nation.

'When the Pope was in France,' added Napoleon, 'I allotted him a superb palace at Fontainebleau, and one hundred thousand crowns a month for his expenses. Fifteen carriages were kept for himself and the Cardinals, though he never went out. He was a good man, but a fanatic. He was greatly annoyed by the libels which had been published, containing assertions of my having ill-treated him, and contradicted them publicly, stating that, except politically, he had been very well treated. At one time,' continued the Emperor, 'I contemplated taking away all his temporal power, and making him my almoner, and Paris the capital of the Christian world.'

June 11.—This day a beautiful white marble bust of young Napoleon was sent up, about life-size, and very well executed, with an inscription, Napoléon François Charles Joseph, etc., and decorated with the Grand Cross of the Legion of Honour. The presents from Lady Holland and Mr. Manning accompanied it. Napoleon did not eat anything until eight o'clock in the evening.

Some time after the bust arrived Napoleon sent for me. It was placed on the mantelpiece in the drawing-room. 'Look at that,' said Napoleon, 'look at that image. That countenance would melt the heart of the most ferocious wild beast. The man who gave orders to break that image, would plunge a knife into the heart of the original, if it were in his power.' He gazed on the bust for several minutes with great satisfaction and delight; his face covered with smiles, and strongly expressive of paternal love and pride. I watched his countenance narrowly, while he was contemplating attentively the beautiful features sculptured on the marble. No person who had witnessed this scene could deny that Napoleon was animated by the tender affection of a father.

Napoleon afterwards commented on the alleged order for the destruction of the bust. When I endeavoured to reason upon the uncertainty of the fact, and that the order assuredly had not been given by the Governor, he interrupted me by saying, 'That it was in vain to attempt to deny a known fact. The bust,' continued he, 'was worth a million to me, although this Governor contemptuously said that a hundred pounds was a great price for it.'

Mr. Balcombe came up to Count Bertrand's about some money matters, and had an interview afterwards with Napoleon, who walked with Count Bertrand and him to the end of the wood.

June 12.—Saw Napoleon in his bath, in which he remained for four hours and a half. Gave him *M. Macirone's Interesting Facts respecting Joachim Murat.* With very little assistance from me he read it through, making observations occasionally. 'He will not be pitied,' said he, 'because he was a traitor. He never mentioned to me that he was determined to defend his kingdom; neither had I ever told him that my intentions were to unite the kingdoms of Italy and Naples, take them from him, and make him Constable of the Empire. I certainly made an instrument of him to effect great projects that I had in view for Italy, and intended, as I told you before, to have dispossessed Murat of the crown of Naples; but the time was not come; and besides, I would have given him a suitable indemnification. His letter to Macirone was ridiculous. What reason had he to complain of the Emperor of Austria, who had offered him an asylum, wherever he pleased, in his dominions, subject to no other restriction than that of not quitting it without permission, which was very necessary. In the actual state of things, what more, in God's name, could he desire! I, myself, never should have expected more in England. It was a generous act on the part of the Emperor of Austria, and a return of good for evil, as Murat had endeavoured to deprive him of Italy; had published proclamations exciting insurrection amongst the Italians; attacked the Emperor's troops like a blockhead without reason; and like a madman engaged without judgment in an expedition without a plan, and so badly arranged, that he never had been able to unite even his own guard. In his proclamations to the Italians, he never mentioned my name, although he knew that they adored me.

'Murat had not acted in that double manner in his correspondence with me, of which he has been accused. The papers shown to prove it were falsified. At that time Murat had no understanding with me. Lord Exmouth appears to have acted fairly and honourably, by candidly informing him that he would receive him on no other terms than as a prisoner of war. I do not believe that he offered a thousand louis for the arrest of Murat. *Belle armée*, indeed,' repeated he, using an expression of contempt, alluding to Murat's expression about the Neapolitan army; 'you know what the Neapolitans are. Murat undertook an expedition *da coglione al fondo*, to invade Naples with two hundred Corsicans at the time that it was occupied by twenty thousand Austrians.'

June 13.—Saw Napoleon in the billiard-room. He was in very good spirits. Spoke about the possibility of his having remained in France after the battle of Waterloo, in spite of the efforts of the Allied Powers. 'My own opinion was,' said he, 'that I could not have done so, without having shed the blood of hundreds. Had the Legislative Body displayed courage, I might have succeeded, but they were frightened and divided amongst each other;

La Fayette was one of the chief causes of the success of the enemies of France. To have given me a chance, I must have had recourse to the most sanguinary measures. The conduct of the Allies, in declaring that they waged war against me alone, had a great effect. Had it been possible to have rendered me inseparable from the nation, no efforts of the Allied Powers would have succeeded; but as it was, by isolating me, and declaring that if I were once removed, all obstacles to a peace would cease, people became divided in their sentiments, and I determined to abdicate, and remove, as far as I was concerned, every difficulty. Had the French nation guessed at the intentions of the Allies, or that they would have acted as they have done since, they would have rallied round me.

'Many were of opinion that I ought to have fought to the last. Others said that fortune had abandoned me—that Waterloo had closed my career of arms for ever. My own opinion is, that I ought to have died at Waterloo; perhaps a little earlier. The smiles of fortune were at an end. I experienced little but reverses afterwards; hitherto I had been unconquered. I ought to have died at Waterloo. But the misfortune is, that when a man seeks death most, he cannot find it. Men were killed around me, before, behind, everywhere, but there was no bullet for me.'

A letter written to Sir Hudson Lowe by Count Bertrand, stating that he had not yet seen the captain of the vessel who had brought the bust, and expressing a wish that he might be permitted to come to Longwood.

Napoleon walked in the evening for some time with Count Montholon.

June 18.—A reply was returned by the Governor to Count Bertrand's note, stating that the bust had not been brought out by the captain of the *Baring*. A request was however again made by the Count, that he should be permitted to visit Longwood, and on this day Captain Lamb (a half-pay lieutenant of the navy) came to see Count Bertrand. On his return I asked him to favour me with some information about the bust. He stated that it had been passed and sent on board from the custom-house, in charge of the gunner of his ship, an Italian, who formerly had been for many years in the British navy. That the day after his arrival at St. Helena, he had mentioned the circumstance at a gentleman's house, and had asked to be informed of the best mode of transmitting it to Bonaparte, when he was directed to apply to Sir Thomas Reade, who had made numerous inquiries on the subject; amongst others, whether he had mentioned the circumstance to any person in the island, to which he answered that he had spoken of it at a dinner-party. He was then asked how he could think of bringing out such an article, it being contrary to the instructions; and was finally desired by Sir Thomas Reade to say nothing about the matter, and also to request those to whom he had mentioned it to be equally silent. I observed that he must be aware of the report which was current in the island, relative to a recommendation said to have been made to him to throw it overboard, or break it into pieces,—a contradiction of which I was anxious to hear from his own mouth. Captain Lamb replied that he had heard the report, which was very general, but not true, and professed that he did not know what it could have arisen from.

On this gentleman's return to town he alighted at Sir Thomas Reade's, and after a stay of a few minutes proceeded to Plantation House on one of the Governor's horses.

June 19.—The *Podargus* brought the intelligence that the *Conqueror*, with the new Admiral (Plampin), had arrived at the Cape. Letters received for Count Bertrand, General Gourgaud, and Marchand.

The Admiral and Lady Malcolm, with Major Boys of the Marines, and Captain Jones, Royal Navy, paid a visit to Napoleon. Colonel Fagan, formerly Judge Advocate in India, had also an interview with him afterwards. The Colonel, who spoke French like a native, said that Napoleon asked him many questions in his profession which puzzled him, and that he was extremely shrewd in his remarks.

Saw Napoleon in the evening. He informed me that he had seen Sir Pulteney and Lady Malcolm, also Colonel Fagan. 'The Admiral,' said he, 'endeavoured to support the Governor, and said that I might depend upon it he had sent my observations on the restrictions to England. Indeed, he advocated his conduct so much, that I told him he was like the rest of the English, *trop égoïste;* that, not being myself an Englishman, their laws did not protect me, and I had no justice to expect from them. *È troppo Inglese.* I told him that in Lord ———'s speech there were three calumnies and ten lies, and that I intended to answer it. He tried to excuse him in the same manner the Governor did, by stating that the report of the speech in the newspapers might not be correct or faithful, and was not to be depended upon. He is mistaken, however. In France, even during the time of the revolutionary fury, the speeches were faithfully reported. I gave *Milédi* one of my fine porcelain cups, with a figure of Cleopatra's needle upon it, as a mark of the esteem which I entertain for her, and the sense I have of her attentions. She insisted upon taking it down herself. I cannot,' added he, 'conceive how the Admiral can think of attempting to excuse a man so unlike himself, and whose conduct I know he cannot in his heart approve.'

Napoleon then said that he had asked Colonel Fagan several questions about the military penal code. 'Of this subject,' added he, 'I am master, as I framed many of the laws myself. I am a Doctor of Laws, and while the Code Napoléon was forming, I had repeated disputes and discussions with the compilers, who were astonished at the knowledge which I possessed on the subject. I also originated many of the best of its laws.'[1]

---

[1] 'It is calculated that Napoleon's Government in the space of fourteen years and five months presented sixty-one thousand one

June 20.—An order received by Captain Poppleton from Sir Hudson Lowe, to reply by signal, *yes* or *no*, whether Lady Malcolm, Major Boys, and Captain Jones had been with General Bonaparte at the same time with the Admiral.

Learned that the Governor appeared to be very uneasy that some observations made by Napoleon on Lord Bathurst's speech should have been repeated by a captain in the navy at Solomon's shop; which circumstance had been reported to him by Sir Thomas Reade immediately after it occurred.

An official report again made to His Excellency by the orderly officer, of the quality of the bread supplied to Longwood, which was so bad that for a considerable time Napoleon had been obliged to make use of biscuit.

June 24.—Some uneasiness manifested at Plantation House at the declaration made by two captains in the navy of their intentions towards Sir Thomas Reade, whom they accused of some practices of espionage towards them, which had not been warranted either by their situation or conduct.

June 28.—Lord Amherst, who arrived yesterday, and suite, accompanied by the Governor, paid a visit to Count and Countess Bertrand.

Napoleon observed that the civilities of the Governor were those of a gaoler. 'When he came to Bertrand's with the Ambassador,' said he, ' he merely introduced him as Lord Amherst, and then,

hundred and thirty-nine deliberations of the Council of State on different subjects.'—Montvérant's *Histoire Critique et Raisonnée*.

without sitting down or conversing for a moment like a gentleman, turned about and took his leave, like a gaoler or a turnkey who points out his prisoners to visitors, then turns the key, and leaves them together. Having come up with Lord Amherst, he ought to have remained for a quarter of an hour and then left them.'

July 3.—Admiral Plampin, who arrived two or three days ago in the *Conqueror*, came to Longwood with Captain Davie (his flag-captain) and his secretary, Mr. Elliot. They were introduced to Napoleon by Sir Pulteney Malcolm.

Saw Napoleon afterwards, who remarked the singular difference of appearance between Sir Pulteney Malcolm and his successor. 'Few men,' said he, 'have so prepossessing an exterior and manner as Malcolm; but the other reminds me of one of those drunken little Dutch *schippers* that I have seen in Holland, sitting at a table with a pipe in his mouth, a cheese, and a bottle of Geneva before him.'

On my return from town, dined with the Emperor *tête-à-tête* in his writing-room. He was in very good humour. Spoke about Sir Pulteney and Lady Malcolm; asked if I had seen the new Admiral; made some remarks on the late attacks made on the validity of his title to the crown. 'By the doctrines put forth by your Government writers,' said he, 'upon the subject of legitimacy, every throne in Europe would be shaken from its foundation. If I was not a legitimate sovereign, William the Third was an usurper of the throne of England, as he was brought in chiefly by the aid of foreign bayonets.[1] George the First was placed on the throne by a faction, composed of a few nobles; I was called to that of France by the votes of nearly four millions of Frenchmen. In fact, calling me an usurper is an absurdity which your Ministers will in the end be obliged to abandon. If my title to the crown of France was not legitimate, what is that of George the Third?'

The dinner was served on a little round table. The Emperor sat on the sofa, and I on a chair opposite. 'I was very hungry, and did great justice to what was presented to me. Napoleon said that he should like to see me drunk, and ordered Marchand to bring a bottle of champagne, of which he took one glass himself and made me finish the rest, calling out in English several times, '*Doctor, drink, drink.*'

July 4.—Sir Pulteney and Lady Malcolm sailed for England in the *Newcastle* frigate.

[Having mislaid some sheets of my journal, I have been under the necessity of chiefly trusting to my recollection for the following details. The manner in which Captain Lamb had related the history of the bust had, instead of dissipating the suspicions at Longwood, rather convinced them that some such proposal or insinuation had been made. This was confirmed by the visit at Longwood of two

---

[1] Literally,—bayonets had just then been introduced into the army.

of the captains of the lately arrived storeships, both of whom saw Napoleon in the garden. One, whose name it is not *now* necessary to mention, assured Napoleon himself, and other residents of Longwood, that he had heard Captain Lamb say that some suggestions had been made to him that the bust should be thrown overboard, the gunner who brought it confined to his ship, and nothing more said of the matter. Previously to this, I succeeded in persuading Napoleon that the charge against Sir Thomas Reade was unfounded, and even obtained his permission to communicate his sentiments on the subject to that officer. The affair was whispered about the island, and gained considerable credit.

It was reported that the bust in question had been executed at Leghorn by orders of the Empress Marie Louise, and that she had sent it to her husband by the gunner, as a silent though convincing proof that her affections were unchanged. Napoleon, who was extremely attached to the Empress, was inclined to believe this supposition, which in itself was very probable, and made him very anxious to ascertain the truth. To accomplish this object, he directed Count Bertrand to apply for permission to be granted to the gunner to come to Longwood. After some delays and assertions that the man was ill, during which time he was examined on oath at Plantation House and minutely searched, it was signified to Bertrand that leave was granted to him to go to Longwood. A few minutes after his arrival at Count Bertrand's, and while speaking to the Countess, Captain Poppleton was sent into the room by the Governor, with orders not to allow him to speak to any of the French unless in his presence. This proceeding, combined with the disingenuous manner in which it was executed, was considered as an insult, and the gunner was immediately directed to withdraw.[1]

Two or three days after Lord Amherst's arrival I had the honour of dining in company with him at Plantation House. I conceived myself bound to inform him that if he went to Longwood with a view of seeing Napoleon, accompanied by the Governor or by any of his staff, he would certainly meet with a refusal, which, although far from the intention of Napoleon, might by others be construed into an insult. That if his lordship came up with only his own staff, I had little doubt but that he would be received, provided Napoleon should be sufficiently recovered from a swelling in his cheek, with which he was then afflicted.

At the end of June, or beginning of July, Count Bertrand waited upon Lord Amherst, and informed

[1] Mr. Forsyth, in his *Captivity of Napoleon*, vol. ii. pp. 145-153, says, on the authority of Prince Esterhazy, that the bust could not have been taken from life in Leghorn, as 'the young prince had never left Vienna since his arrival there;' that Captain Lamb did not know the bust was on board his ship until about the time of his arrival at St. Helena; that the delay in forwarding it was primarily occasioned by the illness of the gunner who had charge of it; that although Sir Hudson Lowe was at first inclined to communicate with Lord Bathurst before forwarding it, Sir Thomas Reade dissuaded him from waiting to do so, and that it was accordingly sent to Longwood or the day after that on which it was landed.

him that Napoleon had been unwell for several days, and was at that moment suffering from toothache. He added, however, that if the Emperor should be in a state to see visitors before his lordship's departure, he would receive him.

Accordingly, on the 2d or 3d his lordship proceeded to Longwood, accompanied by his suite, and by Captain Murray Maxwell, of His Majesty's late ship the *Alceste*. About half-past three the Ambassador was introduced to Napoleon, with whom he remained alone for nearly two hours. Previous to leaving him, his lordship presented the members of his suite and Captain Maxwell, to each of whom Napoleon addressed some observations. Mr. Ellis, the secretary, conversed with him about a quarter of an hour. He observed to Captain Maxwell that he had taken a frigate of his off the island of Lissa, in the Adriatic, in 1811,[1] which would amply compensate for the loss of the *Alceste*.[2] To Mr. Griffiths, the chaplain, he also addressed several questions, and smilingly recommended him to his lordship's patronage.]

July 9.—Some packages and cases containing a superb set of chessmen and table, two magnificent carved ivory work-baskets, and a set of ivory counters and box, all of Chinese manufacture, sent to Count Bertrand for Napoleon. They were accompanied by a letter, stating that they had been

---

[1] The *Pomone*, taken Nov. 29, 1811, after a hard-fought action.
[2] The *Alceste* was wrecked February 18, 1817, off the island of Pulo Leat in the China Seas. The crew were saved.

made by the especial order of the Hon. Mountstuart Elphinstone, for the purpose of being presented to the distinguished personage whose initials they bore, as a mark of the gratitude entertained by the donor for the extraordinary humanity displayed by him, which was the means of saving the life of a beloved brother.[1] A letter from Sir Hudson Lowe also came with them, stating, that when he had promised Count Bertrand a day or two before that they should be sent, he was little aware that, on opening them, he should have discovered something so objectionable, and which, according to the letter of his instructions, ought to prevent their being sent.

It appeared that on the presents was engraved the letter *N*, surmounted by a crown, which His Excellency considered highly objectionable and dangerous. Captain Heaviside, who had brought them from China, on having obtained permission to visit Longwood soon after his arrival, was ordered by the Governor to maintain a strict silence on the subject to all the French.

In the evening Napoleon looked at these articles, which he greatly admired, and signified his intention to send the work-baskets to the Empress Marie

[1] The day before the battle of Waterloo, Captain Elphinstone had been severely wounded and made prisoner. His situation attracted the personal attention of Napoleon, who immediately ordered his surgeon to dress his wounds; and perceiving that he was faint from loss of blood, sent him a silver goblet full of wine from his own canteen. On the arrival of the *Bellerophon* in England, Lord Keith sent his grateful thanks to Napoleon for having saved his nephew's life.

Louise, the box of counters to his mother, the chessmen and superb table to his son.

July 11.—Saw Napoleon in his writing-room. Had some conversation touching Ferdinand of Spain and the Baron Kolli. 'Kolli,' said he, 'was discovered by the police, by his always drinking a bottle of the best wine, which so ill corresponded with his dress and apparent poverty, that it excited a suspicion amongst some of the spies, and he was arrested, searched, and his papers taken from him. Amongst them was a letter from ——, inviting him to escape, and promising every support. A police agent was then dressed up, instructed to represent Kolli, and sent with the papers taken from him to Ferdinand, who, however, would not attempt to effect his escape, although he had no suspicion of the deceit practised upon him.

'While at Bayonne I offered him permission to return to Spain, informing him however at the same time that immediately on his arrival in his own country I should declare war against him. Ferdinand refused to return unless under my protection. No force or compulsion was employed to induce him to sign his abdication; neither was he confined at the time, but had his friends, and as many of the nobles as he thought proper, about him.

'I liked Fox,' said the Emperor a little later on, 'and was fond of conversing with him.'[1] A circumstance occurred which, although accidental, must

[1] Fox on one occasion only was in France.

have been very flattering to him. As I paid him every attention, I gave orders that he should have free admission everywhere. One day he went with his family to see St. Cloud, in which there was a private cabinet of mine, that had not been opened for some time, and was never shown to strangers. By some accident Fox and his wife opened the door and entered. There he saw the statues of a number of great men, chiefly patriots, such as Sidney, Hampden, Washington, Cicero, etc., Lord Chatham, and amongst the rest his own, which was first recognised by his wife, who said, "My dear, this is yours." This little incident, although trifling and accidental, gained him great honour, and spread directly through Paris. The fact was, that a considerable time before, I had determined upon forming a collection of statues of the greatest men, and the most distinguished for their virtues, of all nations. I did not admire them the less because they were enemies, and had actually procured busts of some of the greatest enemies of France, amongst others that of Nelson. I was afterwards diverted from this intention by occurrences which did not allow me time to attend to the collecting of statues.'

I asked him his opinion of Lord Whitworth. '*Un homme habile, un intrigant*,' said he, 'as far as I could observe him. A man of address, *un bel homme*. Your Ministers had no reason to complain of him, for he answered their purposes well. The account which was published by your Ministers of his interview with me was *plein de faussetés*. No violence of manner or impropriety of language was used by me. The ambassadors could not conceal their surprise when they read such a mass of misrepresentation, and publicly pronounced it to be false.[1] His wife, the Duchess of Dorset, was greatly disliked by the English in Paris. They said publicly that she was *sotte* with pride. There was much disagreement between her and many English ladies about presentation at Court. She refused to introduce any who had not previously been presented at St. James's. Now there were many of your countrywomen who either could not or would not be presented there, but were anxious to be presented to me, which was refused by her and her husband. This excited great ill-will towards them. Your *charge d'affaires* also, Mr. Merry, was disliked by the English for the same reason. Some of them threatened to horsewhip him publicly, and he made application to me to protect him against his own countrymen.'

Napoleon then recounted the noble manner in which Fox had made known to him the proposal that had been made to assassinate him, which generous act he did not fail to compare with the treatment he now received, and with the attempts made upon his life by wretches paid by —— in 1803, and landed in France in British men-of-war.

---

[1] The incident appears to have been much exaggerated at the time. *Vide* the recently published (1887) *Journals of Lord Whitworth*.

He also mentioned that his assassination had been recommended in the English ministerial papers of the time as a meritorious action.

He subsequently related some anecdotes of General Wurmser. 'When I commanded at the siege of Mantua,' said he, 'a short time before the surrender of that fortress, a German was taken endeavouring to effect an entrance into the town. The soldiers, suspecting him to be a spy, searched, but found nothing upon him. Then they threatened him in French, which he did not understand. At last a Frenchman, who spoke a little German, was brought, who threatened him with death in bad German, if he did not immediately tell all he knew. He accompanied his menaces with violent gestures, drew out his sword, and said that he would run him through. The poor German, frightened, and not understanding perfectly the broken jargon spoken by the French soldier, concluded, when he saw him point at his belly, that his secret was discovered, and confessed that he was the bearer of despatches to Wurmser, which he had swallowed when he perceived himself in danger of being taken. He was immediately brought to my headquarters and locked up in a room, and two officers of the staff appointed to take charge of him, one of whom constantly remained with him. In a few hours the wished-for article was found. It was rolled up in wax, and was not much bigger than a hazelnut. When unrolled, it proved to be a despatch from the Emperor Francis to Wurmser, written with his own hand, enjoining him to be of good heart, to hold out a few days longer, and that he would be relieved by a large force which was coming in such a direction under the command of Alvinzi.

'Upon this, I immediately broke up with the greatest part of my troops, marched in the route indicated, met Alvinzi at the passage of the Po, totally defeated him, and returned again to the siege.[1] Wurmser then sent out General ——— with proposals to treat for the evacuation of the fortress. He stated that though the army had provisions for four months, he was willing to surrender upon honourable terms. I signified to him that I was so well pleased with the noble manner in which Wurmser had defended the fortress, and entertained so high an opinion of him that, although I knew he had not provisions for three days more, I was willing to grant him an honourable capitulation; in fact, that I would concede to Wurmser everything he desired. He was greatly astonished at the information I possessed of the deplorable state of the troops, and still more at the good terms

[1] The General-in-Chief, when in the neighbourhood of Pizzighitone, met a great fat German captain or colonel, who had been made prisoner. Napoleon took a fancy to question him, without being known, and inquired how affairs were going on. 'Very badly,' replied the officer; 'I know not how it will end; but no one seems to understand what is doing; we have been sent to fight a young blockhead, who attacks you on the right and left, in front and in the rear, so that there is no knowing how to proceed. This mode of carrying on war is intolerable; and, for my part, I am very glad to have done with it.'—*Las Cases*, vol. i., part ii., p. 3, English edition.

I offered, acquainted as I was with his distress.
Wurmser was won by it, and ever afterwards
entertained a great esteem and regard for me.[1]
After we had agreed upon the principal conditions, I sent an officer into the town, who found
that there was only one day's provisions remaining
for the garrison. Previous to this, Wurmser used
to call me *un garçon*. He was very old, brave as
a lion, but so extremely deaf that he could not
hear the balls whistling around him. He wanted
me to enter Mantua after we had agreed upon the
capitulation; but I considered that I was better
where I was. Besides, I was obliged to march
against the Pope's troops, who had made a treaty
with me and afterwards broke it.

'Wurmser saved my life afterwards. When I
got to Rimini, a messenger overtook me with a
letter from him, containing an account of a plan
to poison me, and where it was to be put in
execution. It was to have been attempted at
Rimini, and was framed by some scoundrels of
priests. It would in all probability have succeeded
had it not been for this information. Wurmser, like
Fox, acted a noble part.'

Napoleon then informed me of the precautions
which he made his army take when before Mantua,
in order to preserve their health in that unhealthy
country, one of which was burning large fires all
night and obliging the troops to remain by them.
He spoke about the measures which he had caused

[1] Wurmser did not long survive his gallant defence of Mantua.

to be taken at Jaffa. 'After the assault,' said he, 'it was impossible to restore any kind of discipline until night. You know what kind of people the Turks are. A few of them kept up firing in the streets. The soldiers, who desired nothing more, whenever a shot was discharged, cried out that they were fired upon from certain houses, which they immediately broke open, and violated all the women they found. This, together with their having stolen pelisses and other articles of Turkish dress, many of which were infected, produced the plague amongst them. The following day I gave orders that every soldier should bring his plunder into the square, where all articles of apparel were burnt. But the disease had been already disseminated. I caused the sick to be immediately sent to the hospitals, where those infected with the plague were separated from the rest.'

July 17.—Saw Sir Hudson Lowe in town, with whom I had a long conversation, part of it not of a very agreeable nature. He said that it did not appear 'that I had made use of arguments of a nature sufficiently forcible to undeceive General Bonaparte; and that he would write to Lord Bathurst, that all the time General Bonaparte was so much in the *dark* respecting *his* character, no Englishmen excepting Admiral Malcolm and myself had access to him.'

I informed His Excellency that Sir Pulteney Malcolm had done everything in his power to conciliate and to reconcile matters, and had endeavoured by all means to justify his (Sir Hudson's) conduct; so much so indeed that Napoleon had expressed his discontent at it; as to myself, I had often exerted myself to the utmost of my ability to the same effect. I also suggested to His Excellency that if Captain Lamb were to make an affidavit of the falsehood of the charge relative to the supposed proposal to break the bust, it would effectually silence all calumniators. Sir Hudson Lowe replied, 'I judge from effects, sir. You do not appear to have testified sufficient indignation at what General Bonaparte said and did. *You ought to have told him that he was guilty of a base action!*'

His Excellency then said that Napoleon had caused Bertrand to write him the most impertinent letter which he had ever received, in reply to one written by him relative to the chess-men, and another equally so for the purpose of being given to the gunner of the *Baring*. That he was empowered to turn General Bertrand off the island for his impertinence. He then desired me to 'express to General Bonaparte that he had sent for me in order to inquire who was the author of a report so false as that the gunner who had brought out the bust had been prevented from going on shore and disposing of his goods, and had in consequence sustained losses and suffered bad treatment. Also, that he was greatly astonished at the tenour of the last letter he had received, more so indeed than at that of any that had been sent to him since he arrived on the island.'

July 18.—Saw Napoleon, to whom I communicated the message I had been ordered to deliver by Sir Hudson Lowe. He replied that the gunner had declared before Madame Bertrand that he had been prevented from going on shore for several days, and consequently had been obliged to sell his little venture to Solomon, or some other shopkeeper, for half-price, and had thereby sustained a great loss. 'I have been informed, and I believe it,' continued the Emperor, 'that this bad treatment was caused by his having brought out the bust of my son. The Governor has expressed astonishment at the tenour of the letters sent to him. I want nothing from his caprice. He says that, according to the *réglemens établis en vigueur*, he was not authorised to send up those presents. Where are those regulations? I have never seen them. If they are new restrictions, let them be made known. To a dungeon, to chains upon his legs and arms, a man may accustom himself, but not to another's caprice—it is impossible. I do not desire any favour from him. Perhaps he requires that I should write him a letter of thanks daily for the air which I breathe. *Un uomo che m'ommazza ogni giorno;* and then desires that I should thank him for it. He reminds me of a German *bourreau*, who, while flogging with all his might an unfortunate sufferer, cried after each blow, "*Pardon, Monsieur, pour la grande liberté que je prends!*"'

After this, he said that he had informed Lord Amherst of the conduct pursued towards him. 'The Ambassador,' said he, 'declared that such were not the intentions of the Bill; that the object of it was not to render worse, but to ameliorate my situation as a prisoner, and that he would not fail to make known the representations I had made to him, to the Prince Regent, to Lord Liverpool, and to Lord Bathurst. He asked permission to report what I said to the Governor; I replied, "Certainly." I told him that I had observed the Governor taking him round the new road he had made, but that I supposed he had not communicated to him that I could neither quit it nor go into any houses; and that a prohibition had formerly existed which debarred me from speaking to such persons as I might meet. At this he was greatly struck. He proposed that I should see the Governor; I replied, "Neither your prince, nor both your Houses of Parliament, can oblige me to see *mon geolier et mon bourreau. Ce n'est pas l'habit qui fait le geolier, c'est la manière et les mœurs.*" I told him that he had pushed matters to such an extremity that, in order to leave nothing in his power, I had confined myself to my room, expecting that he would surround the house with sentinels. I left nothing for him to effect, except violating my privacy, which he could not have done without walking over my corpse.[1] That I would not commit suicide, but would exult in being assassinated by an Englishman. Instead of drawing back, it would be a consolation to me in my last moments.'

---

[1] The Emperor was so firmly impressed with the idea that an attempt would be made forcibly to intrude on his privacy, that from a short time after the departure of Sir George Cockburn he always

The Emperor concluded by telling me that he had no objection that the Governor should be acquainted with every sentiment which he had expressed to me.

July 18.[1]—Went to town in pursuance of Sir Hudson Lowe's directions, to whom I repeated the message which I had been ordered to deliver. His Excellency commenced his reply by denying that he had ordered me to say, 'That he, the Governor, was surprised at the tenour of the two last notes he had received, and that he had called out to me, on leaving the room, to repeat the former only;' he then said, darting a furious look at me, 'General Bonaparte's expressions convince me, sir, more and more, that means have not been taken to justify my character to him. Tell him,' continued he, not in the most moderate tone of voice, 'that to show I am not afraid to send anything home, I shall send what he has stated to the Ministers.'

He then ordered me to communicate anything else I was charged with. When I came to that part in which Napoleon (describing what he had stated to Lord Amherst) had said, 'But I suppose he did not tell you that I was not permitted to leave

kept four or five pairs of loaded pistols and some swords in his apartments, with which he was determined to despatch the first who entered against his will.—B. E. O'M.

[1] Pages 161 and 164. The same difficulty about the dates (both being July 18) occurs in the French edition; but in that at the bottom of the page containing the second July 18, is the following note:—

'In some pages of my Diary this conversation bears the date of the 19th.'

the road,' His Excellency started up, and, with a degree of violence which considerably impeded his utterance, exclaimed, '"Tis false! 'Tis false! I did tell him.' When he had recovered a little his powers of speech, he reproached me, in a violent manner, with not having contradicted the assertion, also with having manifested little warmth in his defence. After he had expended some portion of his wrath, I observed that I had attempted his defence to the best of my ability, but that I did not think he ought to be much surprised at Napoleon's not being upon good terms with him, when he considered what material alterations had taken place in his situation since his arrival, all of which tended to render it more unpleasant. He then desired me to give my opinion respecting Lord Bathurst's speech. I pointed out that many of his lordship's positions were at variance with the truth. He concluded by telling me that 'I was not permitted for the future to hold any conversation with General Bonaparte, unless upon professional subjects, and ordering me to come to town every Monday and Thursday, in order to report to him General Bonaparte's health and his habits.'

July 21.—Had another conversation with Sir Hudson Lowe, of a nature nearly similar to that of yesterday. A long and very disagreeable discussion took place, with which I shall not fatigue the reader further than by stating that I requested him to remove me from my situation.

July 24.—Went to town, according to Sir

Hudson Lowe's orders. His Excellency made me undergo an interrogation before Sir Thomas Reade and Major Gorrequer, during which he expressed much anger because my sentiments did not accord with his own.

Finding that Sir Hudson Lowe made me in a manner responsible for all Napoleon's actions and expressions, and took every opportunity of venting upon me all the ill-humour he could not personally discharge upon his prisoner, and perceiving that all hope of accommodation between the parties had vanished when Admiral Malcolm departed, and that all my efforts to ameliorate the situation of the captive were fruitless, I determined to confine myself as much as possible to my medical duties, and to avoid all unnecessary communication with a man who could avail himself of his irresponsible situation to insult an inferior officer.

August 2.—Went to report Napoleon's health as usual.

Saw the Emperor on my return, who observed that he had seen in the papers some extracts from a work written by the Duke of Rovigo (Savary), detailing several circumstances relative to Pichegru, Wright, etc. He lamented the death of Réal,[1] and remarked that Savary and Réal were the persons, especially Réal (at that time the Duke of Rovigo was not in a situation to enable him to know

[1] Réal, a *Conseiller d'État*, and employed in the Department of the Police, was charged by the Emperor to discover the nature of the plot, and his death had been reported in the last papers that arrived at St. Helena; it was afterwards contradicted.—B. E. O'M.

personally the circumstances relative to those two), who from their employments knew the names of the gaolers, turnkeys, gendarmes, and others, and could say, 'Such a man was present, let him be examined. Perhaps he is now in the service of the King.' In the exalted situation which I occupied, I could know nothing of those minute details. 'Savary,' added he, 'relates a circumstance which is perfectly true, and appears to have preserved some order that I wrote on the occasion, as well as recollected some of my expressions. I did not like to have it publicly mentioned. I did not wish to have it known that one so nearly allied by blood to my son could be capable of proposing so atrocious an act as a second Sicilian Vespers.[1] The agent who was the bearer of the proposal was at once arrested, and must have been found amongst others in the prisons that were allotted for State criminals. It was my intention, whenever I made a peace with England, to have sent him over to your Government for examination.'

[1] See also p. 71. 'The aged Queen Caroline of Naples was living in Sicily, overwhelmed with vexation and steeped in humiliations. The English had unworthily sacrificed her to their ambitious views upon Sicily. She was thirsting for vengeance, and her imagination—degraded by all the blood which she had caused to be shed when the unskilfulness of the Directory reopened to her the gates of Naples—could not be restrained within any bounds when she thought she saw a ray of hope. The marriage of one of her daughters with the Duke of Orleans was made subservient to the policy of the moment. On the birth of the Duc de Chartres she conceived the infernal idea of offering him as a holocaust in order to buy back the crown of Naples. "This child," she wrote to the Emperor, " will one day

August 10.—Had some conversation with Napoleon about a report contained in one of the papers relating to his removal to Malta, to which he did not give any credit, observing that he should create less alarm in England than in Malta. .

'The Emperors of Austria, Russia, and the King of Prussia,' he continued, 'have all three told me that I was much mistaken in believing that they had received large subsidies from England. They alleged that they had never actually obtained more than one half of the sums which they were nominally supposed to have received, through the deductions made for freightage, poundage, and numbers of other charges, and that frequently a large portion was paid in merchandise.'

Napoleon informed me that the Governor had sent answers to the letter which had been written about the Chinese articles and to the gunner; but that he had ordered Bertrand not to bring them to him until he asked for them.

Saw his reply to Lord Bathurst's speech, commencing in the following manner: '*Le Bill du*

become a dangerous rival of your son; he will fully represent a principle of conciliation between interests which you have amalgamated in appearance, but which your death will separate anew. Restore to me the Crown of Naples, and I will at the same time serve your cause and satiate my hatred of the English by new Sicilian Vespers, which will swallow up a whole race of rivals of your dynasty." The Emperor was filled with indignation, and caused the bearer of this execrable message to be conveyed to a State prison; there he would have long remained had not the events of 1814 restored him to liberty.'—*History of the Captivity of Napoleon*, by Count Montholon, 1846 edition, vol. ii. p. 243.

parlement anglais, n'est ni une loi, ni un jugement;' and proceeding to compare it with the proscriptions of Sylla and Marius, '*Aussi juste, aussi nécessaire, mais plus barbare;*' that Sylla and Marius issued their decrees '*avec la pointe encore sanglante de leurs épées;*' but that of the English Parliament was issued in time of peace, and sanctioned by the sceptre of a great nation.

August 11.—Told Sir Hudson Lowe again (having mentioned it to him before about a fortnight ago) that Napoleon wished to have the garden freed from spurge, a weed with which it is now overrun, and desired that it should be converted into grass, or sown with oats or barley. That he wished to have something green to look at out of his window, and to see something growing about him. That if it were not done within a fortnight, the season would be over. His Excellency replied that he would go to Longwood in a day or two.

August 14.—Went yesterday to Plantation House, in consequence of an order from the Governor that I should go there on Tuesdays and Saturdays, instead of Mondays and Thursdays in town. The Governor, after having asked some questions, said that I had on a former occasion mentioned that General Bonaparte told me he had made use of observations concerning him to Lord Amherst, which he desired I would repeat. Although I foresaw the consequences, I did not think myself authorised to refuse, as I had been permitted to communicate them to him; and having previously warned him that what he insisted upon might cause an access of irritation, I repeated what Napoleon had observed, viz. 'Neither your Prince nor both your Houses of Parliament can oblige me to see *mon geôlier et mon bourreau. Ce n'est pas l'habit qui fait le geôlier, c'est la manière et les mœurs.*'

Sir Hudson Lowe walked about for a few moments, looking very angry, and asked me to give him General Bonaparte's reasons for making use of such expressions. I replied that this was out of my power. He then began, as I had foreseen, to vent upon me all the ill-humour which he entertained towards the author of the epithets; brought up the old affair of the Scotch newspaper, and concluded by saying, 'You are not authorised, sir, by me, to communicate with General Bonaparte on any other than medical subjects; and if you hold any other communications with him, it is at your own peril, unless you make them known to me, and thereby free yourself from the responsibility. Your business is not to act from your own judgment or discretion, but to ask what you may be permitted to do.'

Napoleon has been up at four o'clock for several mornings writing, without calling any of his generals to assist him. He took a walk of two hours, and appeared to be in good spirits. Saw him on his return in the billiard-room. Had some conversation about Egypt, and some of the individuals who had accompanied him there. He mentioned one

Poussielgue, who had served under him during the campaigns of Italy. 'Poussielgue,' said he, 'had been employed by me upon diplomatic and other services from Milan to Genoa, during which time he acquired my confidence. He was then sent to Malta to feel the way before I attacked it. The information he obtained was very useful. He accompanied me to Egypt, where I appointed him to an office high in the commissariat, and loaded him with favours. When I quitted Egypt, Poussielgue, who was left behind, for some unaccountable reason bore a grudge against me, and wrote letters *pleines d'horreurs* of me to the Directory. I was then appointed First Consul, which was unknown to Poussielgue, and was the person who opened his letters. Although astonished and indignant at his conduct, I took no notice of it. When I was made Emperor, Poussielgue's brother, who was a distinguished surgeon, and well known to me, came to beg employment for him, admitting that, at the same time, his brother had behaved most ungratefully to me. " Poussielgue betrayed General Bonaparte, but the Emperor knows him not." I replied, " I will grant him no favour myself, but if the Minister of Finance chooses to select him, I will sign the nomination." His brother went to the Minister, told him what I had said, a recommendation for a lucrative situation was made out, which I signed, and he enjoyed it for several years.'

He afterwards spoke about the Mamelukes, and said that in the combats between the French cavalry and them, whenever the numbers of the parties engaged exceeded a hundred men, the superiority of discipline procured victory for the French, but under that number, or individually, the Mamelukes prevailed.

August 15.—Napoleon's birthday. He was dressed in a brown coat. All the generals and ladies dined with him at two o'clock; also all the children, excepting the two infants of Counts Bertrand and Montholon, who were brought in for a short time. To each of the children he gave a present, and amused himself for some time playing with them.

August 17.—Saw Napoleon at two o'clock. He was in extremely good humour, and very pleasant, joking upon various subjects, and rallying me about a young lady in the island.

Told me that when he was at Boulogne two English sailors arrived there, who made their escape from Verdun, and had passed through the country undiscovered. 'They had remained there for some time. Having no money, they were at a loss how to effect their escape, and there was such a vigilant watch kept upon the boats that they despaired of being able to seize upon one. They made a sort of vessel of little ribs of wood, which they formed with their knives, living as well as they could upon roots and fruits. This bark of theirs they covered with calico, which they stretched over the ribs. When finished, it was not more than about three feet and a half in length, and of a proportionate breadth, and so light that one of them carried it on his shoulders. In this machine they determined to attempt their passage to England. Seeing an English frigate approach very near to the shore, they launched their bark, and attempted to join her; but before they had proceeded very far they were discovered by the *douaniers*, seized, and brought back.

'The story transpired in consequence of the astonishment excited at seeing two men venture out to sea in such a fragile conveyance. I heard of it, and ordered them with their little boat to be brought before me. I was, myself, struck with astonishment at the idea of men trusting their lives to such an article; and asked them if it was possible they could have intended to go to sea in that? They replied that, to convince me of it, they were ready that moment to attempt it again in the same vessel. Admiring the boldness of the attempt, and the bluntness of the reply, I ordered that they should be set at liberty, some Napoléons given to them, and a conveyance to the English squadron provided for them. Previously to this, they were going to be tried as spies, as several persons had seen them lurking about the camp for some days.

'When I made my triumphal entry into Berlin,' said Napoleon, 'the mother of the Prince of Orange, the sister of the King, was left behind ill in the upper apartments of the palace, very badly off, and neglected by almost everybody. A day or two after my arrival there, some of her attendants came to ask for assistance, as they had not wherewithal to procure even fuel for her use. The King, indeed, had neglected her most shamefully. The moment it was made known to me, I ordered a hundred thousand francs to be instantly sent, and went to see her myself afterwards. I caused her to be furnished with everything befitting her rank,[1] and we had frequent interviews. She was much obliged to me, and a kind of friendship commenced between us. I liked her conversation.

'When her son, the Prince of Orange, was aide-de-camp to Wellington, he went over from Spain or Portugal to London, at the time that his marriage to the Princess Charlotte was in contemplation. From London he wrote several letters to his mother, giving a description of the whole of the royal family, beginning with the Queen, and going through every branch nominately, filled with horrors and follies, especially of the ——— [Regent?], against whom he appeared to be particularly indignant. Those letters he sent by an agent to Hamburg, for the purpose of being forwarded to his mother. This agent was arrested, his papers seized, and despatched to Paris, where they were examined and laid before me. I read them in a cursory manner, and laughed very heartily at their contents.

---

[1] This was not a solitary instance of Napoleon's chivalrous spirit. ,' Napoleon had the gallant consideration the day after his return (in 1815) to renew the Guard of Honour at the Hôtel of the Dowager-Duchess of Orleans, to whom he has always accorded the respect due to royalty.'—Bourrienne's *Napoleon*, English edition of 1885, vol. iii. p. 299.

Afterwards, in order to retaliate a little for all the abuse heaped upon me, I ordered them to be sent to the *Moniteur* and published. Meanwhile, however, the agent acquainted the Prince's mother with his arrest and the seizure of his papers, with the contents of which he was partly acquainted. Before the publication was completed, I received a letter from her, conjuring me not to make them public, stating what injury it would do to her son and her family, and calling to my recollection the time I had been at Berlin. I was touched by her appeal, and countermanded the publication of the letters, which would have made a great noise in Europe, and have been extremely disagreeable to the persons described in them.'

Napoleon then spoke of the late Queen of Prussia in very high terms, said that he had an esteem for her, and that if the King had brought her at first to Tilsit, it would in all probability have procured him better terms. 'She was elegant, ingenuous, and extremely well informed,' continued Napoleon. 'She bitterly lamented the war. "Ah," said she to me, "*la mémoire du grand Frédéric nous a fait égarer. Nous nous crûmes pareils à lui, et nous ne le sommes pas.*" '[1]

[1] 'The Queen of Prussia is really a charming woman. She is fond of coquetting with me; but do not be jealous; I am like a cerecloth, along which everything of this sort slides without penetrating. It would cost me too dear to play the gallant.'—Letter to Josephine, quoted in *Las Cases*, vol. i., part ii., p. 49, English edition.

Napoleon is said to have expressed himself with less gallantry soon after the celebrated interview. 'His language to the Emperor (Alexander),' writes Sir George Jackson in July 1807, 'as I know

I observed to the Emperor that his enemies had accused him of having treated her very barbarously. 'What,' said he, 'do they say that I poisoned her too?' I replied, No; but that they asserted that he had been the means of her death in consequence of the misfortunes which he had caused to befall her country. 'Why,' replied Napoleon, 'it is very probable that grief for the fallen situation of her husband and her country, and for the losses they had sustained, and the humiliations they were reduced to, may have accelerated her death. But that was not my fault. Why did her husband declare war against me? However, instead of treating her barbarously, nobody could have paid her more attention or respect, or have esteemed her more, for which I received her thanks.' He then made some remarks upon the Princess of Salms, and was not insensible to the charms of her person; nor did he fail to pay a tribute to her wit, placing her, however, on many accounts far below her sister.

from excellent authority, was: "A few hours will suffice to settle *our* business. You wish for Moldavia and Wallachia; why then *ménager* a power that has acted treacherously towards us both? Beyond that we have no point of contest. Lay down our arms, and we are at peace." As regards Prussia he said, "C'est un vilain roi; une vilaine nation; une vilaine armée; une puissance qui a trompée tout le monde et qui ne mérite pas d'exister. Tout ce qu'elle garde elle le doit à vous. Voila ce dont, moi, j'ai besoin," and he pointed towards those countries, in a map, named in the Prussian treaty, "le reste est à vous, vous n'avez qu'eu disposer. Je ferai tout par amitié pour vous, je ne ferai rien pour les beaux yeux de la reine."'
—*Diaries and Letters of Sir George Jackson, from the Peace of Amiens to the Battle of Talavera*, edited by Lady Jackson, vol. ii. p. 172.

Napoleon then made some observations about Malta, an abode with which he declared he would be satisfied for some years, professing at the same time his disbelief of such being the intentions of Government. He added that the best thing our Government could do would be to make a treaty with him, by which he would bind himself not to quit Malta for a certain number of years without the permission of the Prince Regent, with a condition that at the expiration of the time he should be received in England. This would save the nation six or eight millions of francs yearly. 'It would,' added he, 'have been much more honourable for England (and indeed for the Allied Powers) and more humane to have caused me to be shot on board the *Bellerophon*, on the spur of the moment, than to have condemned me to be exiled to such a rock as this. They might have excused themselves by saying, " It is necessary for the tranquillity of Europe to put this man out of the way." This would have at once freed them from all alarm, and saved millions to their treasury.

'When the discussions about the sentence on Louis the Sixteenth took place, Condorcet declared that his conscience would not allow him to vote for death, but in place of that he voted that the unfortunate Louis should be condemned to the galleys for life. This proposal met with universal disapprobation, even from the most violent of the Jacobins, and great odium was thrown upon Condorcet for having voted for that which, in the opinion of all, was worse than death. Now, exile here, particularly under the man they have chosen, is infinitely worse than condemnation to the galleys. For there you have the sun of Europe, and if you have money, can enjoy a comparatively tolerable existence.

'I recollect at Toulon' (I think he said) 'a colonel who had been condemned to the galleys for life. He was certainly confined, but he never was obliged to work, and had everything allowed him, at his own expense, which could render his situation supportable. The keeper, unless he was like this Governor, would never degrade a man who had held such a situation by obliging him to labour. Besides, for money a man can always get somebody to work for him. I really think that Lord —— imagined that by a series of ill-treatment and humiliation, they would induce me to commit suicide, and for that purpose found *son homme*. The very idea of this, if I ever had any thoughts of doing so, would effectually prevent my putting it into execution.'

August 22.—Saw Napoleon at twelve o'clock. He has continued to rise at four o'clock in the morning, and to employ his time in reading and writing. Pointed out to me that he had been obliged to cause his coat to be turned, as there was no green cloth on the island except of what the French call *couleur merde d'oie*.[1]

'What do you think,' said he, 'of all things in the world would give me the greatest pleasure?' I was

[1] A tint between green and yellow.

on the point of replying removal from St. Helena, when he said, 'To be able to go about *incognito* in London and other parts of England, to the *restaurateurs*, with a friend, to dine in public at the expense of half a guinea or a guinea, and listen to the conversation of the company; to go through them all, changing almost daily, and in this manner, with my own ears, to hear the people express their sentiments, in their unguarded moments, freely and without restraint; to hear their real opinion of myself, and of the surprising occurrences of the last twenty years.' I observed that he would hear much evil and much good of himself. 'Oh, as to the evil,' replied he, 'I care not about that. I am quite used to it. Besides, I know that public opinion will be changed. The nation will be just as much disgusted at the libels published against me as they formerly were greedy in reading and believing them.

'This,' added he, 'and the education of my son, would form my greatest pleasure. It was my intention to have done this had I reached America. The happiest days of my life were from sixteen to twenty, during the *semestres*, when I used to go about, as I have told you I should wish to do, from one *restaurateur* to another, living moderately, and having a lodging, for which I paid three louis a month. I was always so much occupied that I may say I never was truly happy upon the throne. Not that I have to reproach myself with doing evil whilst seated there; on the contrary, I restored fifty thousand families to their country, and the improvements I made in France will speak for themselves. I made war certainly; of this there is no doubt; but in almost every instance I was either forced to it, or I had some great political object in view.

'Had I died at Moscow,' continued he, 'I should have left behind me a reputation as a conqueror without a parallel in history.[1] A ball ought to have put an end to me there: whereas, when a man like me dies in misfortune, his reputation is lessened. *Then* I had never received a check. No doubt afterwards at Lutzen and Bautzen, with an army of recruits and without cavalry, I re-established my reputation, and the campaign of 1814, with such an inferior force, did not lessen it.'

I observed that the generality of the world was surprised that he had not made a peace at Châtillon when circumstances were apparently desperate for him. Napoleon replied, 'I could not consent to render the Empire less than what it was when I mounted the throne; I had sworn to preserve it.

---

[1] 'If ever man bore a charmed life, surely it is Bonaparte! At Bautzen he exposed himself recklessly, and bullets and balls flew around him, but none touched him. Many companies and regiments march to meet him with a conviction amongst the men that they are led out to encounter a foe that can never be conquered or killed. To this conviction amongst the men, and even in some of their officers, the many panics that have ensued—in the Prussian ranks especially —may be said to have been chiefly due. How often has it happened that after desperate fighting and on the very eve of success an unexpected advantage gained by the French has dispelled all the valour which they had warmed up to; and like men in despair they have turned tail and fled—their officers unable, or making no attempt, to rally them.'—*Diaries and Letters of Sir George Jackson*, from 1809 to 1816, edited by Lady Jackson, vol. ii. pp. 110, 111.

Moreover, the Allied Powers each day brought forth some condition more inadmissible than on the preceding one. You may think it strange, but I assure you that I would not sign it now. Had I remained on the throne after the return from Elba, I would have kept it, because I found it made, but I would not have made it myself originally. My great fault was in not having made peace at Dresden. My error was in having made that armistice. Had I pushed on at that time, my father-in-law would not have been arrayed against me.'

Napoleon then said that notwithstanding the occupation of Paris by the Allies, he should still have succeeded had it not been for the treachery of Marmont, and have driven them out of France.[1] His plan was arranged. He was to have entered Paris in the dead of night. The whole of the lower orders of the city were at the same time to attack the Allies from the houses, who, fighting against troops acquainted with the localities, would have been cut to pieces and obliged to abandon the city with immense loss. The mob were all ready. (I think he also said that he would have cut off the Allies from their park of artillery.) Once driven from Paris, the mass of the nation would have risen against them. 'I

---

[1] General Daumesnil (who had lost a leg in the battle of Wagram) commanded the fortress of Vincennes at the time of the invasion in 1814. The capital had been for some weeks occupied by the Allies, and Daumesnil still held out. Nothing was then talked of in Paris but his obstinate defence, and his humorous reply, when summoned by the Russians to surrender: 'Give me back my leg, and I will give up my fortress.'

mentioned this plan,' added he, 'to Baron Köller, who admitted the danger of it. Marmont will be an object of horror to posterity. As long as France exists, the name of Marmont will not be mentioned without shuddering. He feels it,' added Napoleon, 'and is at this moment probably the most miserable man in existence. He cannot forgive himself, and he will terminate his life like Judas.'[1]

I took the liberty of asking what he considered to be the happiest time of his life since his elevation to the throne. 'The march from Cannes to Paris,' was his reply.

'When Castlereagh was at Châtillon with the Ambassadors of the Allied Powers, after some successes of mine, and when I had partly encircled the town, he was greatly alarmed lest I might seize and make him a prisoner; not being accredited as an Ambassador, nor invested with any diplomatic character to France, I might have treated him as an enemy. He went to Caulaincourt, to whom he mentioned that he 'laboured under considerable apprehensions that I should cause violent hands to

[1] The Hon. J. W. Ward (afterwards Lord Dudley), one of the 'three or four English' present when Louis the Eighteenth gave the 'Charter of the Constitution' to the Senate, received a very different impression. 'The King,' he says, 'was seated on Napoleon's throne—but the names of fifty-six battles won by him were effaced from the canopy on which, a fortnight ago, I saw them inscribed in letters of gold. . . . I was chiefly employed in watching the countenances of the marshals. Marmont seemed pleased with his own appearance (and to do him justice he is a very handsome, manly-looking fellow), and satisfied with the price of his treason to a master, one of whose few weaknesses it was to have shown towards him favours far more than proportioned to his merits.'—*Dudley Letters*, 1840 edition, p. 41.

be laid upon him,' as he acknowledged I had a right to do. It was impossible for him to get away without falling in with my troops. Caulaincourt replied, that so far as his own opinion went, he should say that I would not meddle with him, but that he could not answer for what I might do. Immediately after Caulaincourt wrote to me what Castlereagh had said and his own answer. I signified to him in reply, that he was to tell Lord Castlereagh to make his mind easy and stay where he was; that I would consider him as an Ambassador.

I ventured to express my surprise to Napoleon that the Empress Marie Louise had not made some exertions on his behalf. 'I believe,' replied the Emperor, 'that Marie Louise is just as much a state prisoner as I am myself, except that more attention is paid to decorum in the restraints imposed upon her. I have always had occasion to praise the conduct of my good Louise, and I believe that it is totally out of her power to assist me; moreover, she is young and timorous.[1] It was, perhaps, a misfortune to me that I had not married a sister of the

---

[1] There is abundant evidence that Marie Louise was not too 'young and timorous' to fight for her own position. In the 'Bath Archives' we find Count Otto Löwenstern writing in February 1815: 'The Arch-Duchess has silently renounced the title of Empress. All the Imperial arms and ciphers have been effaced from her carriages, etc. . . . Marie Louise will have Parma for herself. She seems to have demanded and insisted in a manner quite Napoleonic, and the above arrangement was come to only after much persuasion from her father and a very animated discussion on her behalf in Congress. The Emperor was much disposed to take her view of the business and to support her claims rather warmly, but in the end

Emperor Alexander, as proposed to me by Alexander himself at Erfurth. But there would have been inconveniences in such a union, arising from her religion. I did not like to allow a Russian priest to be the confessor of my wife, as I considered that he would have been a spy in the Tuileries for Alexander. It has been said that my union with Marie Louise was made a stipulation in the Treaty of Peace with Austria, which is not true. I should have spurned the idea. It was first proposed by the Emperor Francis himself, and by Metternich, to Narbonne.

'Of all the Ambassadors I ever employed,' added Napoleon, 'Narbonne[1] was the ablest. He had *beaucoup d'esprit*, and his moral character was unexceptionable. While he was at Vienna, France was never duped by Metternich as she had been before. He penetrated Metternich's projects in a few days. Had such a man as Narbonne been sent to Alexander in 1812, it is probable that peace would have been made. Russia demanded Dantzic, and an indemnification for the Duke of Oldenburg. Romanzoff persuaded Alexander that I would make any sacrifices to avoid war, and that the favourable moment for him to make demands had arrived. After the first success I had gained, Alexander sent

left it to the other Powers to make such arrangements for his daughter and her son as they deemed advisable.'—*Diaries and Letters of Sir George Jackson*, from 1809 to 1816, edited by Lady Jackson, vol. ii. p. 473.

[1] I was informed by Cipriani that Narbonne was the natural son of Louis the Fifteenth.—B. E. O'M.

a message to me, that if I would quit his territory and retreat to the Niemen, he would treat with me. However, I did not believe that he was sincere, and thought it a *ruse*, otherwise we might have treated in person at Wilna, and settled everything.'

August 23.—General Gourgaud informed me this day, that at the close of the battle of Waterloo, when the charge made by the French had failed, and the English charged in their turn, a part of the cavalry of the latter, with some *tirailleurs* intermingled with them, approached to within a hundred or a hundred and fifty toises[1] of the spot where the Emperor was standing, with only Soult, Drouot, Bertrand, and himself. Close to them was a small French battalion drawn up in a square. Napoleon ordered Gourgaud to fire some shots from two or three field-pieces which belonged to the battalion, to drive away the cavalry, which were approaching nearer. This was put into execution, and one of these shots carried away the Marquis of Anglesea's leg.

Napoleon then placed himself with the column and wanted to charge, exclaiming, '*Il faut mourir ici, il faut mourir sur le champ de bataille.*' At this time the English *tirailleurs* were firing at them, and they expected every moment to be charged. Labédoyère was galloping about like a madman, with his arms extended before him, seeking to be killed. Napoleon was prevented from throwing himself amongst the enemy by Soult, who laid hold of his bridle, exclaiming that he would not be killed

[1] About 200 or 300 yards.

but taken prisoner, and who with the aid of others finally succeeded in compelling him to leave the field; at the time there was only the above-mentioned small column left to oppose the Prussians who were advancing.

Napoleon was so fatigued that on the road to Jemappes and Philippeville he would have frequently fallen from his horse had he not been supported by Gourgaud and two others, who were then the only persons with him. He was silent for a long time. When on the road to Paris it was decided, at one moment, that the Emperor should, on his arrival, go instantly booted and spurred to the Senate, which would have had a great effect, but this resolution unfortunately was not acted upon.

August 25.—Napoleon in high spirits. Saw him in the drawing-room, dressed in a gray double-breasted coat. He was very facetious in his remarks about the Governors of Benguilla, the Cape de Verde Islands, etc.

Had some conversation with him relative to Spain. I asked if it were true that the Queen had said to Ferdinand in his presence, that he was *her* son, but not the son of the King, thus proclaiming her own infamy? Napoleon assured me that she had never made use of such expressions before him. That she had told him he was *not worthy of being* the son of the King. I observed that it had been asserted that he had offered to give Ferdinand one of his relations in marriage, and make him King of Naples; to marry another of his relations to Don

Carlos, and to grant him a sovereignty. Napoleon replied, 'All those assertions are false. Ferdinand himself repeatedly asked me to give him one of my relations in marriage, but I never asked him.' I said that in a publication of great circulation it was broadly asserted that he had given Ferdinand the choice between abdication and death; that in consequence of this and the threats of King Charles, against himself and his followers, he had abdicated. 'That also is false,' replied Napoleon. 'There was no threat made use of, or compulsion.'

He then spoke about the battle of Essling (or Eylau, I forget which), and observed that there was a great deal to be said of it on both sides. He had remained on the field of battle, but had retired in the night, and it might be thought that he had sustained a reverse. Lutzen[1] and Bautzen, he observed, he had most decidedly gained.

'When only seventeen,' said Napoleon, 'I composed a little history of Corsica, which I submitted to the Abbé Raynal, who praised and wished that I would publish it; adding that it would do me much credit, and render great service to the cause then in agitation. I am very glad that I did not, as it was written in the spirit of the day, at a time when the rage for republicanism existed, and contained the strongest doctrines that could be promulgated in support of it. I afterwards mislaid it. When at Lyons in 1786 I gained a gold medal

---

[1] General Gourgaud informed me that at Lutzen the Emperor had only two regiments of cavalry.—B. E. O'M.

from the college on the following theme: "What are the sentiments most advisable to be recommended, in order to render men happy." When I was seated on the throne a number of years afterwards, I mentioned this to Talleyrand, who sent off a courier to Lyons to procure the treatise, which he easily obtained, by knowing the theme, as the author's name was unknown. One day afterwards, when we were alone, Talleyrand took it out of his pocket, and thinking to please and pay his court to me, put it into my hands, and asked if I knew it. I immediately recognised the writing, and threw it into the fire, where it was consumed in spite of Talleyrand's endeavours to save it. He was greatly mortified, as he had not taken the precaution of causing a copy to be made previous to showing it to me. I was very much pleased, as the style of the work was similar to that on Corsica, abounding in Republican ideas and exalted sentiments of liberty, suggested by the warmth of a fervid imagination at a moment when youth and the rage of the times had inflamed my mind. The sentiments in it were too visionary ever to be put into practice.'

I asked his opinion about Robespierre. 'Robespierre,' replied Napoleon, 'was by no means the worst character who figured in the Revolution. He opposed the trial of the Queen. He was not an atheist; on the contrary, he had publicly maintained the existence of a Supreme Being, in opposition to many of his colleagues. Neither was he of opinion that it was necessary to exterminate all priests and nobles like many others. Marat, for example, maintained that to ensure the liberties of France it was necessary that six hundred thousand heads should fall. Robespierre wanted to proclaim the King *hors de la loi*, and not to go through the ridiculous mockery of trying him.

'Robespierre was a monster, but he was incorruptible and incapable of robbing, or of causing the deaths of others, either from personal enmity or a desire of enriching himself. He was an enthusiast, but one who really believed that he was acting rightly, and died not worth a sous. All the crimes committed by Hébert, Chaumette, Collot d'Herbois, and others, were imputed to him.

'Marat,' continued he, 'Billaud de Varennes, Fouché, Hébert, and several others, were infinitely worse than Robespierre. It was truly astonishing,' added Napoleon, 'to see those fanatics, who, bathed up to the elbows in blood, would not for the world have taken a piece of money, or a watch, belonging to the victims they were butchering. There was not an instance in which they had not brought the property of their victims to the *Comité* of Public Safety. They scrupled to commit the very slightest act of dishonesty at a time when a man's life was no more regarded by them than that of a fly. At the very time that Marat and Robespierre were committing those massacres, if Pitt had offered them two hundred millions, they would have refused it with indignation. They even tried and guillotined some of their own number (such as Fabre d'Eglantine) who were guilty of plundering.

'Not so Talleyrand, Danton, Barras, Fouché: they were *figurants*, and would have espoused any side for money. Talleyrand, *c'est le plus vil des agioteurs, homme corrompu, sans opinion, mais homme d'esprit*. A *figurant* ready to sell himself and everything to the best bidder. Barras was such another. When I commanded the army of Italy, Barras made the Venetian Ambassador pay to him something like two hundred thousand dollars for writing a letter, begging me to be favourable to the Republic of Venice, which I put into my waste basket.[1] I never paid any attention to such letters. From the outset of my career, I always commanded myself. Talleyrand, in like manner, sold everything. Fouché in a less degree; his traffic was in an inferior line.'

I asked how it had been possible that Barrère had escaped during the different ebullitions of the Revolution? 'Barrère?—*parceque c'est un homme sans caractère*. A man who changed and adapted himself to every side. He has the reputation of being a man of talent, but I did not find him so. I employed him to write, but he did not display ability. He used many flowers of rhetoric, but no solid argument. Nothing but *coglionerie* wrapped up in high-sounding language.

'Of all the sanguinary monsters,' added the Emperor, 'who reigned in the Revolution, Billaud de

---

[1] See also p. 300 of this volume.

Varennes was the worst. Carnot, *c'est le plus honnête des hommes*. He left France without a sous.

'After the events in Brumaire,' said he, 'I had a long conversation with Sieyès, during which I entered fully into the state of France and divers political matters. Sieyès went immediately after to sup with some stern Republicans, his most intimate friends. After the servants had left the room, he took off his cap, and throwing it upon the ground, "*Messieurs*," said he, "*il n'y a plus de république, elle est déjà morte*. I have conversed to-day with a man who is not only a great general, but of himself capable of everything, and who knows everything. He wants no councillors, no assistance; politics, laws, the art of governing, are as familiar to him as the manner of commanding an army. He is young and determined. The Republic is ended."—"But," cried the Republicans, "if he becomes a tyrant, *il faut le poignard de Brutus, etc.*"—"*Hélas, mes amis, alors nous tomberons dans les mains des Bourbons, ce qui est pire.*"

'Fouché,' added he, 'never was my confidant. Never did he approach me without bending to the ground. For *him* I never had esteem. As a man who had been a Terrorist and a chief of Jacobins, I employed him as an instrument to discover and get rid of the Jacobins, Septembrists, and others of his old friends. By means of him I was enabled to send into banishment to the Isle of France two hundred of his old associate Septembrists, who disturbed the tranquillity of France. He betrayed and sacrificed his old *camarades* and participators in crime. He never was in a situation to demand my confidence, or even to speak to me without being questioned, nor had he the talents requisite for it. Not so Talleyrand. Talleyrand really possessed my confidence for a long time, and was frequently acquainted with my projects a year or two before I put them into execution. Talleyrand is a man of great talent, although wicked, unprincipled, and so covetous of money as not to care by what means he obtains it. His rapacity was so great that I was obliged, after having in vain warned him several times, to dismiss him from his employments. Sieyès also possessed my confidence, and was a man of great talent, but, unlike Talleyrand, Sieyès was an upright man. He loves money, but he will not obtain it otherwise than by legitimate means; unlike the other, who will grasp at it in any form.[1]

[1] 'Talleyrand grants, very liberally, permissions to return to France, to those emigrants who can find means to pay him liberally; whilst Fouché and his police are active in searching out reasons for arresting a great number of these unfortunate persons when they arrive. The enmity that exists between these two Ministers is occasioned no less by the opposition of their personal characters than by the difference in their public views. Talleyrand is considered the head of the aristocratic party, Fouché of the Jacobinical. Talleyrand has something of severity in his manners, and from former habits is disposed to everything that partakes of refinement, even in his vices. Fouché, on the contrary, is as vulgar in deportment as coarse-minded and ferocious in disposition. He is, more or less, connected with every species of malefactor, and gratifies his thirst for power and riches by favouring one party to the prejudice of another.'—*Diaries and Letters of Sir George Jackson, from the Peace of Amiens to the Battle of Talavera*, vol. i. p. 66.

'Madame Campan,' continued Napoleon, 'had a very indifferent opinion of Marie Antoinette. She told me that a person, well known for his attachment to the Queen, came to see her at Versailles on the 5th or 6th of October, where he remained all night. The palace was stormed by the populace. Marie Antoinette fled, undressed, from her own chamber to that of the King for shelter, and the lover descended from the window. On going to seek the Queen in her bedroom, Madame Campan found that she was absent, but discovered a pair of breeches which the favourite had left behind in his haste, and which were immediately recognised.'[1]

September 1.—Yesterday the *Maria* transport arrived from the Cape with mails. A letter from young Las Cases was sent to Madame Bertrand, stating that they had at length obtained permission to quit the Cape, and were on the point of embarking on board a brig for England, but were ignorant if permission to land would be granted them; that his father was very unwell, and expressed his fears that he would fall a victim to his complaint before he arrived, as there was no medical officer in the brig. He added that no letter had been received from Longwood since his father and himself had arrived at the Cape. A letter also arrived for Count Bertrand from Messrs.

[1] Madame Campan was so consistently a Royalist—at risk even of her life—that it is difficult to credit her with the statement. Count Fehrsen is probably alluded to.

Baring, Brothers, and Co. of London, informing him that two years ago the sum of £12,000 had been deposited in their hands for his use.

Napoleon has been in good spirits for several days, and has taken rather more exercise than formerly. On the 30th he went to the sentry-box on the left of the house, where he remained for some time looking at the progress which had been made in a new road, greatly to the surprise of the sentinel, who stood gazing at him at the distance of a few yards.

In one of the Cape newspapers which I received there was an article stating that his sister Caroline had married a certain General Macdonald.[1] Upon this Napoleon remarked that after the recent assassination of her husband, he did not think it possible that his sister would marry, especially in so public a manner, unless she were mad, or had been forced to it with a pistol at her throat; 'especially,' said he, 'when I consider that my sister is a woman arrived at an age when her passions are no longer *brulantes;* that she has four children, and is possessed of a strong, masculine understanding, and talents superior to the generality of her sex. However,' continued Napoleon, 'there is no accounting for the actions of a woman.'

Some extracts from a pamphlet, said to have been published by the Duc de Rovigo (Savary) upon the death of Captain Wright, now attracted

---

[1] General François Macdonald de Klor Renal, formerly in Murat's service at Naples.

his observation. 'Sidney Smith,' said he, 'has acted in a manner unworthy of himself, and unworthy of a man of honour, in the epitaph which he wrote upon Wright. For in it he leaves room to suppose that Wright was secretly despatched, although he does not dare to say it openly. After having made every search and inquiry in his power, after having exhausted all his means in endeavouring to prove that he was murdered, after having had an opportunity of examining the gaolers and turnkeys, and finding that nothing of the kind had happened, he ought, like a man of honour, to have openly declared "that there was no proof to admit of such an accusation," instead of making insinuations, especially when his old enemy, against whom he had so often fought, was in the hands of his countrymen. Sidney Smith, above all men, knew, from having been so long in the Temple, that it was impossible to have assassinated a prisoner without the knowledge of such a number of persons as would have rendered concealment impossible, and also must have been aware that nobody could have entered the prison unless by an order from the Minister of Police.

'Have you ever heard,' said he, 'that Lord Wellington was the person who first proposed to send me to St. Helena?'[1] I replied that I had.

[1] It is said that the Duke of Wellington returned to England from India in a frigate commanded by Captain (afterwards Sir George) Cockburn, and remained at St. Helena for some days, during which time he narrowly escaped death by drowning, having been upset in a boat in one of the squalls so prevalent at that anchorage; also that

but did not give the report any credit. 'If it be true,' said he, 'it will reflect but little honour upon him.'

September 2.—Went to Plantation House according to Sir Hudson Lowe's direction. After acquainting him with Napoleon's state of health, I proceeded to ask him, by General Bertrand's desire, respecting the measures necessary to be taken towards obtaining a certificate for Countess Bertrand, and a power of attorney for the Count, and begged to know whether Mr. Brooke (the Secretary to the Council) was not the person who performed the duties of Notary Public. Sir Hudson Lowe replied roughly, 'Let Count Bertrand ask Captain Blakeney.' Soon afterwards, however, he said that he would not let me return without an answer, and desired me to say that there was no Public Notary on the island; that Mr. Brooke was not vested with powers sufficient to allow him to take such a deposition; that to legalise acts, they must be signed by him as Chief Magistrate of the island.

He then asked, 'What motives could Count Bertrand have in wishing to perform it before Mr. Brooke? Why not have asked me, as Chief Magistrate?' I replied that one of Count Bertrand's

---

when Napoleon was at Elba, His Grace suggested to the Congress that he should be removed from thence to St. Helena, urging the latter place to be the best adapted for his perpetual imprisonment, from his own local knowledge. I merely give this report as an *on dit*. The Duke certainly was reluctant to permit Napoleon to leave St. Helena.—See anecdote in the *Life of Bishop Wilberforce*, vol. iii. p. 234.

motives was to spare Madame Bertrand the inconvenience of going five miles from Longwood in the bad weather which prevailed, especially as she was in an extremely delicate state of health. That Count Bertrand, in the supposition that Mr. Brooke performed the duties of Notary Public, had desired me to inquire, and if so, to ask permission for him to come to Longwood.

'Those are not his motives, sir,' said Sir Hudson Lowe; 'he wants to get the Marquis de Montchenu to Longwood, in order to have an opportunity of conversing with him before Mr. Brooke, who does not understand French. Do you not think, sir, that that is their motive?' I replied that it had never occurred to me that such was their intention. 'Then it does you but little credit, sir. You are very sharp at finding out and observing everything to their advantage;' and added that I was an instrument in their hands. I observed to His Excellency that if asking for information from himself constituted me an instrument, I must plead guilty. That I was at a loss to conceive why they should have recourse to so much trouble to have a conversation with Marquis Montchenu in Longwood, when they had frequently met and conversed, for a long time, with all the Commissioners outside of it, as he must well know, without any British officers being present. Sir Hudson said very gruffly that the less communication I had with them (the French), unless on professional subjects, the better. After repeating his insinuations, and sarcastically expressing his surprise that I should not have discovered their real motive (which I could have told him was solely the invincible repugnance everybody at Longwood had to his presence), he asked if I had anything to communicate from General Bonaparte? I replied in the negative. He then asked how many conversations with him I had had, and for how long? I replied that I did not recollect how many, or how long— they might have lasted for an hour, perhaps longer; and took my departure.

September 3.—Found the Emperor in the drawing-room reading the Old Testament aloud. In very good spirits. Told me that he had seen Mr. Cole at Madame Montholon's a few days since, and had taken him for a Jew. 'I asked Madame Montholon,' said he, 'what Jew is that? *Vraiement il a l'air d'Isaac. Il appartient à la famille d'Abraham.*'

Napoleon then made some observations upon the formalities which the Governor obliged Bertrand to go through, in order to get the bills which Las Cases had left upon London cashed, and the examination which every little bill, account, and receipt went through. 'Even the bills and salaries of the servants,' said he, 'are minutely examined, and every trifling sum obliged to be accounted for. Useless vexations; as every man of sense must know that it would not be by means of any small sum which I might get here that I could escape; and that although I have no money here, I have it at the extremity of my fingers. But this man has the spite to meddle in everything. If he had his will, he would order me to breakfast at a certain hour, dine at another, go to bed at a time prescribed by him, and come himself to see it carried into execution. All will recoil upon himself one day. He does not know that what passes here will be recorded in history.

'Cipriani informs me,' said Napoleon, 'that the Governor took great pains to make him comprehend that the Burgundy sent here some time back came from him. I ordered him never to bring me any more of it. . I do not blush to drink the wine or eat the bread of John Bull, but I will accept nothing from hands that have become so odious to me.'

He observed that he had caught a cold by having sat for a quarter of an hour yesterday on the steps in front of the billiard-room, and had been sneezing and coughing all the evening. Made some remarks on the *tempaccio*, and told me that since breakfast yesterday he had eaten nothing until the same meal this day.

He said that Count Montholon had met Madame Sturmer, and found that she was not so handsome as Betsy (Miss E. Balcombe); that she had *la tournure d'une grisette*.

September 4.—The weather has been extremely wet for several days, and Napoleon ordered that a fire should kept in the four rooms which he is accustomed to use himself. He cannot bear the smell of coals, and there was a great deficiency of wood. Found Noverraz breaking up a bedstead and some shelves to burn. Cipriani applied to Captain Blakeney to send a letter to the purveyors requesting that they would send up three thousand-weight of wood, to be paid for by themselves, as the Governor would not allow more than three hundred-weight daily, being about a third of what was wanted, in consequence of the great humidity of Longwood.

Saw Napoleon at breakfast in his bath. Expected to have found him discontented on account of the occurrences of the morning, but he was in a very good humour. He was eating some lentils, of which he asked the English name, and if I had ever seen any before. I replied that I had seen some in Egypt, but none in England. 'That arch libeller, Pillet,' said he, laughing, 'asserts that you have none in England, and, in fact, that you have no good vegetables.' I replied that it was on a par with the rest of Pillet's falsehoods. That in no country in Europe were there better vegetables or a more plentiful supply. Napoleon laughed at the warmth with which I expressed myself, and said, 'Oh, that atrocious libeller, Pillet! You English do not like to hear anything bad of your own country, although you are so fond of abusing other nations. I fancy that if Pillet had gone to England after the publication of that book he would have had his brains beaten out by you.' I said that he would certainly have been treated with the contempt which he deserved.

Napoleon then remarked that the Northern people

required the stimulus of the bottle to develop their ideas; that the English appeared in general to prefer the bottle to the ladies, as was exemplified by our allowing them to go away from table, and remaining for hours to intoxicate ourselves. I replied that although we did sit sometimes for hours after the ladies withdrew, it was more for the sake of conversation than for wine, of which last there was not so much drunk as formerly; that, moreover, it was optional to retire immediately after the ladies or to remain. He said that were he in England, he would always leave with the ladies. 'It appears to me,' said he, 'that you do not pay regard enough to the ladies. If your object is to converse instead of to drink, why not allow them to be present? Surely conversation is never so lively or so witty as when ladies take a part in it. If I were an Englishwoman, I should feel very discontented at being turned out by the men to wait for two or three hours while they were guzzling their wine. Now in France society is nothing unless ladies are present. They are the life of conversation.'

I endeavoured to show that our conversation after dinner frequently turned upon politics and other matters, with which ladies seldom meddled; moreover, that in well-regulated society the gentlemen soon followed them. This did not, however, satisfy him. He maintained that it was a custom which could not be justified — that women were necessary to civilise and to soften the other sex.

He spoke about Maréchal Jourdan, of whose military talents he had a poor opinion.[1] I observed that I had been told by some English officers who had been present at the battle of Albuera, that if Maréchal Soult had advanced after the attack made by the lancers, he would have cut the English army to pieces. Napoleon acquiesced in this, and said that he had censured Soult for having neglected to do so. He then adverted to the English mode of besieging towns, and said that Lord Wellington, at sieges, was *le bourreau des hommes;* that the immense sacrifice of men at Ciudad Rodrigo and Badajoz [and Burgos] was by no means compensated by the capture of those places. He observed that the storming of Bergen-op-Zoom was a most daring attempt, but that it ought not, or could not have succeeded, the number of the garrison being greater than that of the assailants. I observed that the failure was in part to be attributed to one of the generals not having taken the precaution to communicate the orders which had been given to him to any one else; so that when he was mortally wounded the troops did not know how to act. Napoleon replied that even if no accident of the kind had occurred, the attempt ought not to have succeeded, unless the party attacked became, as sometimes happened, panicstruck. Graham, he

[1] Napoleon refused, when asked by his brother Joseph, to create Jourdan Duke of Fleurus (see *Du Casse*). After the misfortunes in Spain, for which he was only partially responsible, Napoleon even annulled his rank of Marshal for a time.

observed, had been commissary with the army at the time of his first career of arms at Toulon. 'A daring old man,' said he, and asked if he were not the same who had commanded in the battle of Barossa near Cadiz.

September 5.—Had some conversation in the morning with Napoleon relative to the deficiency of fuel at Longwood, and with General Montholon on the same subject.

Went to Plantation House by order of Sir Hudson Lowe, to whom I communicated the deficiency of fuel, and the observations I had been desired to make upon the subject. Had a long discussion with His Excellency, and explained that there were twenty-three fires in all at Longwood, which he thought much too numerous. He answered in his accustomed manner 'that they had no business with so many.' I explained to him that Longwood was very damp, and that the French ladies and children required constant fires. He said that 'Lady Lowe had no fire in *her* room.' I observed that the French were natives of a more southern climate than ours, and consequently more susceptible to cold, and that there could be no comparison made between the comfort of such a building as Plantation House and Longwood. His Excellency said that 'he did not see any necessity for so many fires, and that he had seen a fire burning in the Countess Bertrand's room in the middle of summer.' I told him I had no observation to make upon that circumstance. I explained to him that I had done everything in my power to explain to the French that he thought the allowance which he had ordered for Longwood was sufficient, as he had made it nearly double what was consumed at Plantation House. I also told His Excellency that Napoleon could not bear the smell of coals; and suggested that instead of sending wood to the soldiers in camp, coals might be furnished, and the wood sent to Longwood; to which he replied that 'he did not like to humour any person's whims.'

Saw Napoleon in his bath. After some conversation respecting the deficiency of fuel, he said that he had seen Admiral Plampin, who had brought him a book that the Admiral said had been sent out by Lord Bathurst, 'which,' added Napoleon, 'I suppose his lordship has sent in order to discover the author, as in the letter which the Admiral said he saw it was attributed to Benjamin Constant, or Madame de Staël.'

Napoleon then observed that he had spoken to the Admiral about ships of war and their interior economy. 'The Admiral says that a seventy-four gunship will take about eighty tons more water by means of tanks used in lieu of casks. Had I known this in 1806 or 1808, I would have sent an army of thirty thousand men to invade India. I had made several calculations about the possibility of sending so large a body of men to India, but always found that they would have been short of water for a month.'

I asked what his plan was? 'In Brest,' said the

Emperor, 'I had at one time as many as fifty-six sail of the line, and often forty-six. In forty of these line-of-battle ships I intended to have dispersed thirty thousand soldiers, eight hundred in each, and only four hundred sailors. There were to have been a proportionate number of frigates and other smaller vessels. Ten of the line-of-battle ships would have been old and of little value. They were also to take on board six or eight hundred dismounted cavalry and a portion of artillery, with everything necessary for an army to take the field, and be provisioned for four months. They were to make the best of their way to the Isle of France, where they would have watered and provisioned afresh, landed their sick, and taken on board some other troops to replace them, with three thousand blacks to form colonial regiments. From thence they were to have proceeded to India, and to have disembarked in the nearest possible place, so as to have allowed the Mahrattas, with whom I had an understanding, to join them. They were to form the cavalry of the army. A few of the French were also to be mounted, and all the horses they could procure purchased. After landing, they were to have burnt the ten old ships, and divided their crews amongst the rest, who would have been thus fully manned. They would then proceed in different directions, and do you all possible mischief in your settlements. I had,' continued he, 'an understanding with the Mahrattas and others in India, by the way of Bassorah, Bagdad, Mocha, Surat; their communications were made to the Consuls at Aleppo, through the Ambassador in Persia, etc. I had frequently earlier intelligence from India than you had in England. The Shah of Persia was favourably disposed towards us. All this plan, however, was frustrated by the calculations I had made, which showed me that the ships must fall short of water by a month. Had I known of those tanks, I certainly would have made the attempt.'

Napoleon then calculated the number of tons which would have been gained by the tanks, and found that the ships would have had more than sufficient water. 'For a power which is inferior by sea,' said he, 'it is an invention of great importance, as it will prevent the necessity of their going into harbour to water.'

I mentioned Toussaint Louverture, and observed that, amongst other calumnies, some of his enemies had asserted that he had caused him to be put to death privately in prison.[1] 'It does not deserve an answer,' replied Napoleon. 'What possible interest could I have in putting a negro to death after he had arrived in France? Had he died in St. Domingo, then indeed something might have been suspected, but after he had safely arrived in France, what object could have been in view?'

[1] 'As for the hero of the black race we know now that, drawn into an ambush by General Leclerc, who acted with a heavy heart in accordance with the reiterated injunctions of Bonaparte, he was sent to France and shut up in the freezing dungeons of the Fort of Joux, where he perished at the end of a few months. . . . *A natural death*, assert our historians, referring to the reports to which this premature

'One of the greatest errors I ever was guilty of,' continued the Emperor, 'was sending that army out to St. Domingo. I committed a great oversight in not having declared St. Domingo free, acknowledged the black Government, and before the peace of Amiens sent some French officers to assist them. Had I done this, it would have been more consonant with the principles under which I was acting. It would have done you incalculable mischief. You would have lost Jamaica, and your other colonies would have followed. Having once acknowledged them, I could not have sent an army out there during the peace. But after the peace, I was continually beset with applications from proprietors of estates in the colony, merchants, and others. Indeed, the nation was crazy to regain St. Domingo, and I was obliged to comply with it; but had I, previous to the peace, acknowledged the blacks, I could under that plea have refused to make any attempts to retake it, in doing which I acted contrary to my own judgment.'

September 6.—Informed Count Montholon, by direction of Sir Hudson Lowe, that the latter had regulated the quantity of fuel necessary for Longwood by a comparison with that consumed at Plantation House, and thought that, by giving twice as much coal as was used there, and three

death gave rise—as if the prolonged sufferings, to which this son of the tropics was subjected, were not a thousand times more cruel than a legal execution !'—Lanfrey's *History of Napoleon*, English edition, 1872, vol. ii. p. 151.

hundredweight of wood daily, he had allowed sufficient. That, however, if any application had been made, he would have increased the quantity. I also showed him a letter from Major Gorrequer, stating the quantity used at Plantation House. Count Montholon replied that they were not bound to regulate the quantity of fuel they thought it necessary to burn at Longwood by that consumed by Sir Hudson Lowe at Plantation House, where there were only four or five fireplaces, while there were twenty-three at Longwood. That, moreover, they were natives of a warmer and a drier climate than the English, and stood in need of more heat; that the dampness of Longwood rendered fires absolutely necessary for the preservation of their health. That both his own and the Countess's clothes were spoiled by the damp, in spite of the fires which were used. As to asking for more, he did not like to subject himself to slights or refusals.

Napoleon for some days has eaten no dinner. Told me that he intended to accustom himself to only one meal a day. Mentioned in the course of conversation that he once had it in contemplation to have sent five thousand men to invade Surinam, and asked me (as I had been there) if I thought it would have succeeded? I replied that I thought not. First, on account of the difficulty of approaching the coast, as large ships could not come nearer than seventeen or eighteen miles, and the channel for vessels (not drawing more than eighteen feet water) was only practicable at high water, was very difficult, intricate, and required the aid of a skilful pilot. Besides, that the country itself was full of marshes and very inaccessible. That there was a garrison of three regiments besides the colonial militia. Fort Amsterdam was strong, and could for some time sustain a regular siege.

The weather has not been so bad this day as for some time past. Napoleon went out as far as Count Bertrand's. '*Veramente*,' said he yesterday when speaking of the weather, '*non è paese Cristiano.*'

September 7.—Napoleon complained of rheumatic pains and slight headache, which he attributed, and with reason, to the dampness of the climate and the house. 'Every evening,' said he, 'when I leave my little sitting-room, where there is a fire, and enter my sleeping-room,[1] where there is none, I experience a sensation as if I were going into a damp cellar. If it were not for the room that Cockburn built, which is light, airy, and built of dry wood, where I walk about and exercise, I should have been under ground before now.'

He then made some remarks upon the *Manuscrit venu de Ste Hélène*,[2] and observed that there was such ignorance of chronology displayed in it—such as putting the battle of Jena after Tilsit—and so many mistakes as to time and place, that it would make a corporal in the old French army laugh. 'Notwithstanding this,' added he, 'it was written

[1] Napoleon had changed his bedroom some time before.
[2] Really written by the Marquis Lullin de Châteauvieux. It was disavowed by Napoleon in his will.

by a man of *esprit*, though in several passages he appears not to have had *sens commun*. In some places his assertion of the motives which actuated me is correct. What he says on the subject of my Nobility is correct. What he says about my intentions and wishes to do away with everything which had been established since Charlemagne is also right. That the Nobility I formed was that of the people is true, as I took the son of a peasant and made him a Duke or a Marshal when I found that he had talents. That I wanted to introduce a system of general equality is true, and that every person should be eligible to every situation, provided he had talents to fill it, whatever his birth might be. That I wanted to do away with all the ancient prejudices of birth is also correct. That I laboured to establish a Government of the People which, although *dur*, was still that of the people, is also true. That I ought to have deposed, for my own security, the House of Brandenburg, when I had it in my power, and all the ancient orders of sovereigns, and that they almost always combined against and attacked me, is also right. Probably I ought to have done so, and I should have succeeded. It is true that I wished to establish a Government of the People. It is a work which will much displease the oligarchy, because they do not wish that any person except one of themselves should be eligible for any important situation. With *their* will, birth, and not talents or capability, should regulate the choice. A worse, a more despotic or unforgiving government than an oligarchy never existed. Offend them once, you are never pardoned, and no treatment can be too cruel for you when in their power. The pamphlet is written with that lightness peculiar to Frenchmen, and consequently contains many mistakes. The *Edinburgh Review* will find out directly that I am not the author of it. They will take it to pieces as I have done. I see by the sketch[1] they have published of my life that they take pains to ascertain the truth. Most of it is true; and it is difficult for me to imagine from whence they had their information on some parts of my early life, which were very little known to any except my own family.

'That work,' continued he, 'was not written by Madame de Staël, or if it be, it was the work of a few hours, and was sent to the press without any correction. But there are in it *fautes trop grossières* for Madame de Staël. The sentiments expressed in it are such as Madame de Staël would *talk*, and though new in England, were for several years the subjects of discussion in France.

'The author,' continued he, 'has made a great mistake in saying that after Jena I never did anything worthy of my former actions. The greatest military manœuvres I ever made, and those for which I give myself most credit, were performed at Eckmühl, and were infinitely superior to Marengo, or to any other of my actions. It is the work of

---

[1] The sketch alluded to came from the classical pen of John Allen. Napoleon had read it with great attention in my presence, and made some pencil marks upon particular passages. — B. E. O'M.

some young *homme d'esprit* who has hurried it to the press without having submitted it to the revision of any of his friends. It is however composed with good intentions towards me.'

He added that such a work, by him, would make a great noise. 'It will be, or perhaps is written,' said he, 'but it will be for my son and for posterity.

'It rested only with me,' said he, 'to have deposed both the King of Prussia and the Emperor of Austria. When I was at Schoenbrunn' (I think he said), 'the Duke of Würtzburg frequently insinuated to me that the only means to secure the good faith of Austria would be to depose his brother Francis and place the crown on his head. These offers were repeated to me afterwards through a Minister, with an offer of his son as hostage, who should be placed as my aide-de-camp, with every other possible guarantee. I reflected upon it for some time; but the marriage with Marie Louise put a stop to any further consideration on the subject. I was wrong in not having accepted it. Nothing would have been easier to execute.'

I asked if he believed it to have been written by the Abbé de Pradt. 'No,' replied the Emperor; 'I do not think that he is the author. De Pradt,' continued he, 'may be said to be *une espèce de fille de joie qui prête son corps* to all the world for payment. Once, when he was giving vent to his customary *bavardage* and extravagant projects in my presence, I contented myself with humming a part of the air:

> Où courez vous donc, monsieur l'Abbé
> Vous allez vous casser le nez,

which disconcerted him so much that he had not another word to utter.'

Speaking about the badness of the house, and the offer said to have been made by Sir Hudson Lowe to build a new one, Napoleon observed that he had only refused the offer of making additions to the present wretched old house of Longwood and the design to build another on that miserable situation. 'With all the activity of Cockburn, the construction of a new house would take three years, and with this man, I daresay, six; and that a house might be healthy, it ought not to be inhabited for eighteen months after being built. I shall be dead long before that time. Plantation House is the only one in the island fit for me. The Governor, having a house himself in town, could easily retire to it for six months until improvements were made here, and having the command of everything himself, without being obliged to ask permission from anybody, he could soon render this habitable for some months in the year, which is all that it is adapted for. He could retire to town in the winter season.'

Napoleon then said that the English servants in the house had laughed at the French for eating lentils, and asserted that in England they fed horses with what the French eat here. He laughed very heartily while saying this, and at an anecdote which I related about Dr. Johnson, who, I informed him, had in the first edition of his *English Dictionary* defined oats to be 'food for horses in England and for men in Scotland.'

Count Montholon called Captain Blakeney[1] and myself this day to look at the state of his apartments. The rooms, especially the Countess's bedroom, the children's room, and bathroom, were certainly in a shocking state, from the extreme dampness of the place. The walls were covered with green fur and mould, notwithstanding the fires which were constantly kept in them. I never saw a human habitation in a more mouldy or humid state, in which opinion the orderly officer agreed.

September 8.—Saw Napoleon, who informed me that after I had left him yesterday, he had found himself very unwell with headache and general pains in his limbs; and had taken a warm bath, which had been very beneficial to him.

He was in very good spirits, spoke for a long time about the *Manuscrit de Ste Hélène*, and observed that it must have been written by a person who had heard him reason and was acquainted with his ideas. He added that he thought he knew the author, whom he supposed to be a man who had figured in the Revolution, and now lived retired.

He asked many questions about the number of bottles of wine we drank at our party the night before last. Blamed Mr. Boys's conduct for having preached in allusion to the Admiral.[2] Said that a

---

[1] Captain Blakeney had replaced Captain Poppleton as orderly officer on the departure of Captain Poppleton's regiment from St. Helena.

[2] Mr. Boys had thought it a duty to say something from the pulpit in censure of an important official, for having set an example of immorality in a small colony, by publicly living with a woman not his wife, and for absenting himself from church.—B. E. O'M.

man's conscience was not to be amenable to any tribunal ; that no person ought to be accountable to any earthly power for his religious opinions. ' Had you not persecuted the Catholics in Ireland,' added he, ' in all probability the greatest number of them would before now have become Protestants ; but persecution strengthens them in their belief. Even Pitt himself was aware of the necessity of giving the Catholics equal privileges with the Protestants.'

September 9.—Races at Deadwood. The Commissioners all present. None of the French from Longwood attended except the children and some of the domestics.

During the interval between the heats, Sir Hudson Lowe sent for me, and asked if 'some of General Bonaparte's horses were not on the raceground ?' I replied in the affirmative. His Excellency asked how they came there ? I replied that I had borrowed the horses from General Gourgaud, one of which I had lent to Miss Eliza Balcombe, and the other to the surgeon of the *Conqueror*. Sir Hudson immediately broke out into not the most moderate expressions, and his gestures attracted the attention of many of the spectators. He characterised my having dared to lend any of General Bonaparte's horses without his (the Governor's) permission as the greatest piece of presumption he had ever witnessed. I observed that I had come to St. Helena to learn that it was a crime to borrow a horse for the use of a young lady ; neither had I known that it was necessary to go to Plantation

House to ask permission from him to borrow a horse belonging to the Longwood establishment. Sir Hudson replied that 'I had no business to form any opinion about it.'

This was evidently only a pretext to have an opportunity of venting his spite, as not a week passed that horses were not sent down to town, and frequently to Sir Thomas Reade's, for Dr. Livingston and others to ride up to Longwood, without its having ever been signified that it was necessary first to apply to Sir Hudson Lowe for permission. Besides, General Gourgaud always directed that a horse should be in the stable at my command.

A little before the conclusion of the races the three Commissioners, Madame Sturmer, and Captain Gor came in as far as the inner gate of Longwood, where they remained for some time, during which the Governor approached and looked in at the outer gate. Shortly afterwards Count and Countess Bertrand, Count and Countess Montholon, and General Gourgaud went out to walk, and met the Commissioners outside the gate, with whom they had a long conversation. They afterwards proceeded together to Hut's Gate. It was nearly dark before they returned.

Napoleon in high spirits; looked out of a window at the races, with which he was much pleased. Told me that he had done everything in his power to establish races in France.

September 12.—Went to Plantation House, in consequence of orders communicated to me by Captain Blakeney. After some conversation relative to the late discussions respecting the quantity of fuel allowed to Longwood, Sir Hudson Lowe asked in an abrupt manner if I had not received some books from Dr. Warden? I replied that I had received seven or eight monthly publications containing reviews of his work. 'Did you not receive one, sir, with a view of Longwood?'[1] I replied, Yes. 'It is very extraordinary,' said Sir Hudson, 'that you did not inform me of it.' I replied that I was not bound to tell him of any or every book I received or purchased; that I was in the habit of having books and pamphlets of various descriptions from England which I was not obliged to give any account of. Sir Hudson said that I ought to have done so, and asked if I had lent any of them to the French, or if they had seen them. I replied that to my knowledge the French had not seen them; that they were at present in my inner apartment. He said that 'it was very extraordinary I should have had those pamphlets for two months without being able to tell whether the French had seen them; and that I might have books in my rooms, to be shown to them, of a very improper tendency, which they might read in my absence;' and after harping for a long time on those unlucky pamphlets, he said he supposed I had no objection to lend them to him. I replied, Certainly not; that they should be sent to him on my return. They consisted of

---

[1] A few days before I had lent this pamphlet to an officer of the staff.—B. E. O'M.

the *Monthly Review, Gentleman's Magazine, Eclectic Review, British Ladies' Magazine, European Magazine,* and *New Monthly.* His Excellency then said that Count Las Cases had given a pretty strong hint in the letter he had sent to Longwood from the Cape that he was in want of the money which he had lent them, which it did not appear to be *convenient* for them to understand. After which he made a long and abusive harangue upon the 'Character of Bonaparte,' extracted from the *Quarterly Review,* which publication His Excellency appeared to consider as a sort of political gospel.

September 14.—Napoleon in very good spirits. Asked many questions about the horses that had won at the races, and the manner in which we trained them; how much I had won or lost; and about the ladies, etc. 'You had a large party yesterday,' continued he. ' How many bottles of wine? *Drink, your eyes look like drink!*' he added in English. 'Who dined with you?' I mentioned Captain Wallis amongst others. 'What, is that the lieutenant who was with Wright?' I replied in the affirmative. 'What does he say about Wright's death?' I said, 'He states his belief that Wright was murdered by orders of Fouché, for the purpose of ingratiating himself with you. That six or seven weeks before Wright had told him that he expected to be murdered like Pichegru, and begged him never to believe that he would commit suicide; that he had received a letter from Wright about four or five weeks before his death, in which he stated that he was better treated, allowed to subscribe to a library, and to receive newspapers.'

Napoleon replied, ' I will never allow that Wright was put to death by Fouché's orders. If he was put to death privately, it must have been by my orders and not by those of Fouché. Fouché knew me too well. He was aware that I would have had him hanged directly if he attempted it. By this officer's own words, Wright was not *au secret*, as he says that he saw him some weeks before his death, and that he was allowed books and newspapers. Now if it had been in contemplation to make away with him, he would have been put *au secret* for months before, in order that people might not be accustomed to see him for some time, as I thought this . . . intended to do in November last. The Bourbons have every opportunity of proving it if it really took place. But your Ministers themselves do not believe it. The idea I have of what was my opinion at that time about Wright is faint; but as well as I can recollect it was, that he ought to have been brought before a military commission for having landed spies and assassins, and the sentence executed within forty-eight hours. What dissuaded me from doing so, I cannot clearly recollect. This affair of Wright,' added he, 'made so little impression upon me, that when Lord Ebrington spoke about him at Elba, I did not recollect the incident. My mind was so much occupied with great objects that I had little time to think of a poor English captain. Had the Bourbons, Moreau, or the Vendean chiefs been put to death, then indeed I might have been suspected. I might have tried and executed the Vendean chiefs for having carried arms against the country. They are all alive.

'My opinion is, if I had known Wright had been one of Sidney Smith's officers, and that he had fought against me at Acre, I should have sent for and questioned him about the siege and released him. I recollect perfectly well seeing an officer wounded and carried off at Acre, whose bravery I admired at the time. I think that I should have released him if I had found him to be that officer. It appears also that he killed himself when he was upon the point of being released, as I see that the Court of Spain had interceded for him. When you first spoke to me on the subject, I imagined that Wright had killed himself purposely to avoid giving evidence against your Ministers; and I attributed a degree of heroism to the act which I gave him great credit for; but since I see that it was a long time after, and when I was at Ulm, at the head of a hundred and fifty thousand men, and three hundred leagues from Paris. It takes but a trifle to make you English kill yourselves.'

Napoleon then rallied me upon my supposed attention to Miss ——, and said I ought to marry her. I replied that I was neither rich enough nor young enough to have pretensions to so fine a lady. He now recounted some of his own love adventures. 'The most beautiful woman I ever saw,' said he, 'was an Irish girl, Mademoiselle G——s; whether she had been born in Ireland or was only

of an Irish family I am not certain. It was during
Josephine's time, and long before I married Marie
Louise. One day, when I was hunting in St.
Germains, some of the Court intriguers contrived so
that she came with a petition in her hand to deliver
to me. When she presented herself, every one
made way for her, as I had given orders that persons bringing petitions should invariably be allowed
to approach me. She fell at my feet and presented it.
She was covered with a veil that did not conceal the
beauty of her countenance, which was really heavenly.
Certainly I was taken with her charms, and although I
suspected there was some intrigue, I was not displeased.

'Three or four times afterwards I saw and conversed with her, and used to pat her on the cheek.
At this time a letter from her mother to her was
brought to me from the Secret Post Office. This
mother was an old intriguer, and gave her daughter
directions which elucidated her character. I was
now convinced that it was not proper for me to
countenance this proceeding, and although I was
assuredly smitten with her, for she was as beautiful
as an angel, I gave such orders as prevented her
ever being again admitted to my presence. Since
that time I have been informed she really had a
regard for me, and would have been faithful. She
is now married to M——, a very rich man, but
still, I am led to believe, preserves an affection for me.[1]

---

[1] The conversation turned upon masked balls, of which the Emperor
was peculiarly fond, and frequently called for them. He was then
always sure of a certain rendezvous which never failed to take place.

'The evening before I left Paris for Waterloo,' continued Napoleon, 'a beautiful Englishwoman came to the palace and asked to see me. She saw

He was, he said, regularly accosted every year by the same mask, who reminded him of old intimacies, and ardently entreated to be received and admitted at Court. The mask was a most amiable, kind, and beautiful woman, to whom many persons were certainly much indebted. The Emperor, who continued to love her, always answered: 'I do not deny that you are charming, but reflect a little upon your situation; be your own judge and decide. You have two or three husbands, and children by several of your lovers. It would have been thought a happiness to have shared in the first fault; the second would have caused pain, but still it might be pardoned; but the sequel—and then, and then! . . . Be the Emperor and judge; what would you do in my place? I who am bound to revive and maintain a certain decorum. The beautiful suitor either did not reply or said: "At least do not deprive me of hope," and deferred her claims of happiness to the following year. And each of us,' said the Emperor, 'was punctual at the new rendezvous.'—*Las Cases*, vol. iii., part v., p. 145, English edition.

'Sire, it is understood, that when in the summit of your power, you suffered yourself to be bound in the chains of love. That fired by an unexpected resistance, you conceived an attachment for a lady in private life; that you wrote her above a dozen love-letters; and that her power over you prevailed so far as to compel you to disguise yourself, and to visit her secretly and alone, at her own residence, in the heart of Paris.'—'And how came this to be known?' said he, smiling, which of course amounted to an admission of the fact. 'And it was doubtless added,' continued he, 'that that was the most imprudent act of my whole life; for had my mistress proved treacherous, what might not have been my fate, alone and disguised, in the circumstances in which I was placed, amidst the snares with which I was surrounded? But what more is said of me?'—'Sire, it is affirmed that Your Majesty's posterity is not confined to the King of Rome. The Secret Chronicle states that he has two elder brothers: one the offspring of a fair foreigner, whom you loved in a distant country; the other the fruit of a connection nearer at hand, in the bosom of your own capital. It was asserted that both had been conveyed to Malmaison before our departure; the one brought by his mother, and the other introduced by his tutor; and they were

Marchand, who told her that it was impossible. She said she was an English lady, and a friend of Mademoiselle G———s, whom I well knew, and that she was persuaded I would see her; that I could not refuse to see a young lady who loved me and admired my character. Marchand told her that I was to leave Paris the next morning and could not be disturbed. At hearing this she appeared to be much afflicted, and with some reluctance she went away. Perhaps she was some beautiful intriguer, or one who had *la tête montée* for me.[1]

'When once a woman has *la tête montée*, all the world will not prevent her from attempting to succeed in her designs. Soon after I had taken Vienna, the Austrian Princess ——— got her head full of me, from hearing me so much talked of. She was one of those princesses of whom you know there are so many in Germany. Murat, who was a fine handsome fellow, tried to gain her affections, but she rejected him with disdain. I ordered her to be admitted, and represented myself as Maréchal Duroc. She could speak very little French or

described to be the living portraits of their father.'[1]—*Las Cases*, vol. i., part i., p. 330, English edition. [*See note at end.*]

[1] According to the Paris correspondent of the *Daily News*, Prince Napoleon made in 1887 another addition to the numerous relics of the First Emperor in purchasing a locket given by him to a Venetian beauty of high rank in 1809. It contains a portrait of himself made with his own hair. Such fanciful works of art were common enough early in the century. With the portrait is a hastily scrawled billet-doux establishing its authenticity.

[1] It is said that a codicil in the Emperor's will, which, however, is to remain secret, completely confirms the above conjectures.

Italian, and I could not converse in German. I told her not to speak so loud, as the Emperor would hear her, and pointed out Duroc as Emperor; but she was not to be deceived. She had seen me pass by a house where she was and cried, No, no ; *vous, vous Empereur.* She was extremely handsome, and very candid in her confessions.'

Napoleon then spoke about the assertion, said to have been made by Lord Castlereagh in the House of Commons, respecting him—viz. that he had made out a list of the richest heiresses in France whom he was in the habit of ordering to marry such of his generals as he pleased. That none of them could marry without his leave, and were obliged to espouse any persons to whom he thought proper to give them. These assertions he declared to be wholly false. 'So far from being true,' added Napoleon, 'it was not in my power to get even Caulaincourt married to a lady to whom I wished to see him united. She was the daughter of ——, who was President of the Chamber, a banker, and enormously rich. She was a beautiful girl, and he intended giving her a large portion. I asked the father myself as a favour to give her in marriage to Caulaincourt, but he gave me a positive refusal. At that time Caulaincourt was one of my greatest favourites. So much for Castlereagh's veracity.'

September 19.—Went to Plantation House, in obedience to directions received from Sir Hudson Lowe through Captain Blakeney, and instructed also to take with me a report of the state of Napoleon's

VIEW OF LONGWOOD, FROM THE FLOWER GARDEN

health. On my arrival, Sir Hudson Lowe asked for the report, which stated that, with the exception of a few slight catarrhal attacks, his health had been tolerably good. Sir Hudson Lowe asked if they had been of any consequence, to which I answered in the negative.

The Governor observed that others besides me had made reports relative to General Bonaparte's health. That Madame Bertrand had told the Commissioners that he was extremely unwell; that because they saw him standing in the verandah, they must not believe that he was in good health. I repeated that he had suffered some indisposition, but not of a serious nature. Sir Hudson Lowe then said that he had heard a great deal, though not all, of the conversation which had passed between the French and the Commissioners, and that all of the former except one had abused the opportunity. That every time Count Bertrand had had an opportunity of speaking to them he had abused it; that this last was the only time that Montholon had had an opportunity of speaking to them, which he (Sir Hudson) asserted he had fully availed himself of by cramming them with misrepresentations.

September 20.—Saw Napoleon in his bath. At first he was rather dull and out of spirits. Complained of pain in the right cheek, shooting from the diseased tooth. Great want of sleep at night. Explained to me several symptoms which convinced me that Corvisart had been right in prescribing to him exercise on horseback, which I strongly recommended myself in as forcible a manner as possible. Napoleon replied that under the present restrictions, liable to be insulted by a sentinel if he *budged* off the road, he could never stir out; neither did he think that I myself, or any other Englishman placed in his situation, would avail himself of the privilege to ride, fettered with such restrictions. I confined myself, therefore, to recommending antiscorbutic vegetables, etc.

He then made some observations about Mr. P——e's having sold his wife,[1] which he said would reflect but little credit on the Governor, and that, had such a circumstance occurred in France, the Procureur Général would have prosecuted the offending parties. That it appeared to be a most disgraceful circumstance, especially if, as was asserted, it had been sanctioned by the two organs of communication of the Governor, civil and military.

'My marriage with Marie Louise,' added Napoleon, 'produced no change in my habits. Never was woman more astonished than Marie Louise was after her marriage, when she observed the few precautions that I took to ensure my safety against any attempts upon my life. When she perceived that there were no sentinels except at the outer gates of the palace; that there were no *lords* sleeping before the doors of the apartments; that the doors were not even locked, and that there were no guns or pistols in the rooms where we slept, "Why," said she with astonishment, "you do not take half so

---

[1] A circumstance which actually happened at St. Helena.

many precautions as my father who has nothing to fear." I am,' continued Napoleon, 'too much of a fatalist to take any precautions against assassination. When I was in Paris I used to go out and mingle with the populace without my guards, receive their petitions, and was frequently surrounded by them so closely that I could not move.'

I asked the Emperor in what engagements he considered himself to have been in the greatest danger? He replied, 'In the commencement of my campaigns. At Toulon, and particularly at Arcola. At Arcola my horse was shot under me; rendered furious by the wound, the animal seized the bit between his teeth and galloped on towards the enemy. In the agonies of death he plunged into a morass and expired, leaving me nearly up to my neck in the swamp, and in a situation from which I could not extricate myself. I thought at one moment that the Austrians would have come and cut off my head, which was just above the surface of the morass, and which they could have done without my having been able to offer the least resistance. However, the difficulty of getting at me and the approach of my soldiers, who rescued me, prevented them.'

I asked if he had not been frequently slightly wounded. He replied, 'Several times, but scarcely more than once had I occasion for surgical assistance, or any fever in consequence of a wound.[1] At

---

[1] 'While he was dressing he put his hand on his left thigh, where there was a deep scar. He called my attention to it by

Marengo a cannon-shot took away a piece of the boot of my left leg, and a little of the skin,' said he,

laying in his finger in it, and finding that I did not understand what it was, he told me that it was the mark of a bayonet wound by which he had nearly lost his limb at the siege of Toulon. Marchand, who was dressing him, here took the liberty of remarking that the circumstance was well known on board the *Northumberland;* that one of the crew had told him on going on board that it was an Englishman who first wounded our Emperor.

',The Emperor, on this, observed that people had in general wondered and talked a great deal of the singular good fortune which had preserved him, as it were, invulnerable in so many battles. "They were mistaken," added he; "the only reason was that I always made a secret of all my dangers." He then related that he had had three horses killed under him at the siege of Toulon, several others killed and wounded in his campaigns in Italy, and three or four at the siege of Saint Jean d'Acre. He added that he had been wounded several times; that at the battle of Ratisbon a ball had struck his heel; and at the battle of Essling or Wagram, I cannot say which, another had torn his boot and stocking and grazed the skin of his left leg. In 1814 he lost a horse and his hat at Arcis-sur-Aube, or in its neighbourhood. After the battle of Brienne, as he was returning to headquarters in the evening in a melancholy and pensive mood, he was suddenly attacked by some Cossacks who had passed over into the rear of the army. He thrust one of them off with his hand, and was obliged to draw his sword in his own defence; several of the Cossacks were killed at his side. "But what renders this circumstance very extraordinary," said he, "is that it took place near a tree which at that moment caught my eye, and which I recognised as the very one under which, when I was but twelve years old, I used to sit during play-hours and read *Jerusalem Delivered*." ... Doubtless on that spot Napoleon had been first fired by the love of glory!

'The Emperor repeated that he had been very frequently exposed to danger in his different battles, but it was carefully kept secret. He had enjoined, once for all, the most absolute silence on all circumstances of that nature. He said it would be impossible to calculate the confusion and disorder which might have resulted from the slightest report or the smallest doubt relative to his existence. On his life depended the fate of a great empire, and the whole showing the mark to me, 'but I used no other application to it than a piece of linen dipped in salt and water.' I asked about a wound of which there was a deep mark in the inside of the left thigh, a little above the knee. He said that it was from a bayonet. I asked if he had not had horses frequently killed under him, to which he answered, eighteen or nineteen in the course of his life.

'The regiment de la Fère,'[1] said Napoleon, 'in which I commenced my career,[2] behaved so badly

policy and destinies of Europe.'—*Las Cases*, vol. i., part ii., p. 67, English edition. See also vol. i. p. 252 of this work.

'The night before the battle of Jena the Emperor said he had run the greatest risk. He might then have disappeared without his fate being clearly known. He had approached the bivouacs of the enemy in the dark to reconnoitre them; he had only a few officers with him. The opinion which was then entertained of the Prussian army kept every one on the alert; it was thought that the Prussians were particularly given to nocturnal attacks. As the Emperor returned, he was fired at by the first sentinel of his camp: this was a signal for the whole line; he had no resource but to throw himself flat on his face until the mistake was discovered. But his principal apprehension was that the Prussian line, which was very near him, would act in the same manner.'—*Las Cases*, vol. i., part ii., p. 143, English edition. See also footnote to English edition of 1885 of Bourrienne's *Memoirs*, vol. ii. p. 468.

'Napoleon during his military career fought sixty battles; Cæsar fought but fifty.'—*Las Cases*, vol. iv., part vii., p. 241, English edition.

[1] Artillery.

[2] 'On one occasion, on parade, a young officer stepped out of the ranks, in extreme agitation, to complain that he had been ill-used, slighted, and passed over, and that he had been five years a lieutenant, without being able to obtain promotion. "Calm yourself," said the Emperor, "I was *seven* years a lieutenant, and yet you see that a man may push himself forward for all that." Everybody laughed, and the young officer, suddenly cooled by those few

to the inhabitants of Turin that I was obliged to reduce them. I accordingly had them marched to Paris, and assembled on the parade, ordered the colours to be taken from them by some colonels, words, returned to his place.'—*Las Cases*, vol. ii., part iv., p. 103, English edition.

Some curious instances of the especial connection of the letter M with the two Napoleons, First and Third, may perhaps be noted. Marbœuf was one of the first to recognise the talent of Napoleon at the École Militaire. Montenotte was one of his earliest, Marengo one of his greatest, battles ; Mantua his principal siege, and Melas opened to him the way into Italy. He fought at Montmirail, Montereau, and Mont St. Jean, Paris was lost for him at the battle of Montmartre, and his troops were defeated at Maida. Other battles took place at Malo-jaroslowitz, Medina de la Rio Seco, Millessimo, the Mincio, Mohilow, Mohrungen, Mojaisk, Montebello, etc., and General Mack surrendered to Napoleon at Ulm, while both Malta and the Mauritius were lost to the French. Milan was the first, Madrid the middle, and Moscow the last capital of the enemy to be entered. Josephine was born at Martinique, and Marie Louise partook of his highest destinies ; Moreau and Murat betrayed him. Six of his Marshals (Macdonald, Marmont, Masséna, Moncey, Mortier, and Murat) and twenty-six of his generals of division had names beginning with the letter M—Maret, Mollien, Miot, Molé, Montalivet, and Melzi served him well in their diplomatic or civil capacities. Cardinal Maury represented the Church, and Mdlle. Mars the Stage. His first chamberlain was Montesquieu, his last sojourn Malmaison. He lost Egypt through the blunders of Menou, employed Miollis to arrest the Pope, and created Ney Prince of the Moskowa, and Regnier Duke of Massa. Malet conspired against him, and Metternich overcame him ultimately in the field of diplomacy. He gave himself up to Captain Maitland, was sent to St. Helena, where he had the company of Count Montholon and Sir Pulteney Malcolm, and the services of his valet Marchand. Two of his brothers took the titles of Montfort and Musignano, and his Mother had the official title of Madame Mére bestowed upon her by the Emperor. We leave it to the reader to trace out the coincidence further in regard to Napoleon III. The words Montijo, Morny, Magenta, MacMahon, Malakoff, Mexico, Maximilian, Montauban, Metz, Moltke, etc. will at once occur to him.

and lodged in the church of (the Invalides, I
think he said), 'covered with mourning. I divided
the officers who had not behaved so badly as
the principal offenders amongst other regiments.
Some months afterwards I formed the regiment
again under different officers, and the colours were
taken from the church with great pomp by a
number of colonels, each tearing a piece off, which
they burnt, and new ones were given in their
stead.

'When I was about seventeen years of age,' said
he, 'I narrowly escaped being drowned in the Saône.
While swimming, cramp seized me, and after several
ineffectual struggles I sank. I experienced at that
moment all the sensations of dying, and lost all
recollection. However, after I had sunk, the current
carried me upon a bank of sand, on the edge of
which it threw me, where I lay senseless for I know
not how long, and was restored to life by the aid of
some of my young companions, who by accident
saw me lying there. They at first gave me up for
lost, as they saw me sink, and the current had
carried me to a considerable distance.'[1]

While looking over a number of papers (chiefly
Portsmouth ones) he observed an article stating
that —— had made large purchases in the north of
Ireland. 'Ah,' said Napoleon, 'some of my money
has gone to pay for those estates! After the
abdication at Fontainebleau, upwards of forty
millions of francs, my private property, was seized

[1] See also footnote, vol. i. p. 273.

and taken from my treasurer, near Orleans.¹ Of this money about five and twenty millions of francs were divided amongst T——, M——, H——, and

¹ As narrator of Napoleon's conversations, I acquaint the public with the fact detailed by him of the seizure of his treasures; but it is evident that the *application* of them, as related by him, could have been only conjecture on his part.—B. E. O'M. .
See *Le Cabinet Noir*, English edition, pp. 280-295, for details regarding the disappearance of the Crown treasure in 1814.

'THE DEPOSIT AT THE HOUSE OF LAFITTE.

'On the Emperor's second abdication, somebody who loved him for his own sake, and who knew his improvident disposition, eagerly inquired whether any measures had been taken for his future support. Finding that no provision had been made, and that Napoleon remained absolutely destitute, a contribution was made, and four or five millions were raised for him, of which M. Lafitte became the depositary.

'At the moment of his departure from Malmaison, the solicitude of Napoleon's real friends was no less serviceable to him.

'An individual, aware of the disorder and confusion of our situation, wished to ascertain whether the little treasure had been forwarded to its destination. What was his astonishment on learning that the carriage in which it had been placed was left in a coach-house at Malmaison. A new difficulty arose: the key of the coach-house was not to be found; and the embarrassment occasioned by this unexpected circumstance delayed our departure for some moments. M. Lafitte wished immediately to give the Emperor a receipt for the sum; but Napoleon would not accept it, saying, "I know you, M. Lafitte. I know that you did not approve of my government, but I esteem you an honest man."

'M. Lafitte seems to have been doomed to be the depositary of the funds of unfortunate monarchs. Louis XVIII. on his departure from Ghent also placed a considerable sum of money in his hands. On Napoleon's arrival, on March 20, M. Lafitte was sent for by the Emperor, and questioned respecting the deposit, which he did not deny. On his expressing his apprehension lest a reproach should be intended to be conveyed in the questions which had been put to him: "None," said the Emperor; "that money belonged personally to the King, and private affairs are totally distinct from political matters."'—*Las Cases*, English edition, vol i., part i., p. 167.

C——[1] The money thus seized included the marriage portion of the Empress Marie Louise, which had been paid in gold sovereigns, an old German coin. The remainder was placed in the French Treasury. The whole of these sums had been guaranteed to me by the treaty of Fontainebleau. The share which C—— obtained was very large, and the exact amount of it is known to me.'[2]

The talents requisite in a good general then came under his observation. 'The mind of a general ought to resemble and be as clear as the field-glass of a telescope, *et jamais se faire des tableaux*. Of all the generals who preceded him, and perhaps all those who have followed, Turenne was the greatest. Maréchal Saxe, a mere general, *pas d'esprit;* Luxembourg *beaucoup; le grand Frédéric, beaucoup,* and a quick and ready perception of everything. Your Marlborough, besides being a great general, *avait aussi beaucoup d'esprit.* Judging from Wellington's actions, from his despatches, and above all from his conduct towards Ney, I should pronounce him to be *un homme de peu d'esprit, sans générosité, et sans grandeur d'âme.* Such I know to be the opinion of Benjamin Con-

[1] The same blanks and initials occur in the French edition. Napoleon probably intended by this imputation to attack Talleyrand, de Maubreuil, Hardenberg, and Castlereagh.

[2] 'Then there occurred at Orleans an incident as painful for the Empress as it was shameful for the Provisional Government. It was in want of money; what did it do? It contrived to seize this treasure under pretext that it was the property of the State —a thing absolutely false.'—*Le Cabinet Noir*, English edition, p. 294.

stant and of Madame de Staël, who said that, except as a general, he had not two ideas. As a general, however, to find his equal amongst your own nation, you must go back to the time of Marlborough; but as anything else, I think that history will pronounce him to be *un homme borné.*[1]

September 21.—At about six minutes before ten o'clock at night three distinct shocks of an earthquake were felt at Longwood. The whole of the house was shaken with a rumbling, clattering noise at first as if some heavy body like a loaded waggon was dragged along the upper apartments, succeeded by a tremulous motion of the ground, the glasses rattling on the table, and the pictures jumping from the walls. The duration of the whole might have been from sixteen to twenty seconds, as Captain

---

[1] Wellington on his part was outspoken in his appreciation of his great adversary. 'Lord Wellington was here [in Paris] for a few days,' writes the Hon. J. W. Ward to Miss Berry in May 1814; 'his dukedom met him on his arrival. He was received in a manner that could not but give great pleasure to every Englishman. He seems quite unspoilt by success. He has not even contracted that habit of silence and reserve which so often accompanies dignity and favour. But he is just as he was—gay, frank, and ready to converse. I counted myself lucky in meeting him one of the days he was here at Aberdeen's, with Schwartzenberg, Stadion, and Prince Maurice of Lichtenstein. Stadion observed that he believed he had never been engaged against Bonaparte in person. The Duke answered instantly: "No; and I am very glad I never was! I would at any time rather have heard that a reinforcement of forty thousand men had joined the French army than that he had arrived to take the command." I had heard the opinion ascribed to him before, but I was glad to find he had the liberality to repeat it after Bonaparte's fall.'—*Journals and Correspondence of Miss Berry*, edited by Lady Theresa Lewis, vol. iii. p. 16.

Blakeney and myself, who were sitting together at the time that it occurred, had sufficient time from its commencement until it was over to reason and reciprocally ask from what it could proceed, before we guessed at the right cause, which we discovered simultaneously before it ceased. No mischief was done.[1] Generals Montholon, Gourgaud, all the household attendants and English servants, came out. No alarm appeared to exist amongst them.

General Montholon informed me that his son Tristan, who was asleep, was awakened by the shock, and exclaimed that somebody was endeavouring to throw him out of the bed. General Gourgaud also felt three distinct shocks. Upon inquiry being made of some of the sentinels about the house, they replied that they had not experienced anything extraordinary. This may be accounted for by the fact of the wind having been so strong at the time that they were obliged to use considerable exertion in walking against it. The sensation was very strongly felt in our kitchen, about forty yards from the house, and at the guard-room, about five hundred yards distant, particularly by those men who were lying down on the ground.

Very little mischief was done in the island. It appeared that the direction of the shocks was perpendicular. Had it been lateral, Jamestown

[1] Although Napoleon was in bed, which he did not leave during the time of the shocks, some veracious person wrote to England that 'Bonaparte endeavoured to escape out of the house, but was stopped by the sentinels,' which falsehood was eagerly inserted in some of the ministerial papers.—B. E. O'M.

must have been overwhelmed with immense masses of rock.

September 22.—Saw Napoleon in his bedroom. When I entered it he was employed in making some calculations. He raised his eyes, looked at me, and said smiling, 'Well, Mr. Doctor, *tremblement de terre* last night.' I observed that I had experienced three distinct shocks. After he had remained a short time at his calculations he got up and said that he was in bed at the time it occurred. 'At the moment of the first shock,' continued he, 'I imagined, and said to myself, some accident has happened to the *Conqueror;* she has taken fire and is blown up,[1] or else some powder magazine on the island has exploded. At the second shock, however, I immediately perceived what it was, and said it was an earthquake.' I asked if he had heard the rumbling noise which accompanied it, and that I thought the duration of it had been from sixteen to eighteen seconds. Napoleon replied that he thought it had lasted altogether about twelve seconds. He mentioned that he had felt the shock of an earthquake once before at Ferrara at break of day.

Some further conversation about earthquakes then took place, during which I mentioned that a shock had been felt in St. Helena in the year 1756, and another in 1782. I said that it was likely the fanatics and the superstitious in the island would

---

[1] When this surmise was mentioned a short time afterwards to Admiral Plampin, the following remark was made: 'Ay, ay, the d——d rascal supposed so, because he wished it!'—B. E. O'M.

attribute the earthquake to his presence; for the Portuguese had said that the strong and destructive south-east wind which prevailed at Madeira in the autumn of 1815, when the *Northumberland* arrived off Funchal, and had done so much mischief, had been produced by his arrival. He laughed very heartily at this, and observed that to make a good tale of it the earthquake ought to have occurred upon his arrival.

Napoleon then said he had been informed that Lord Moira had demanded twenty thousand additional European troops in India. 'I do not believe it,' said he; 'but if there is any necessity to send troops to India, it is owing to the imbecility of your Ministers in having given up any possession beyond the Cape to the French. If true, it has been most probably caused by some intriguing French adventurers, of whom there are now many thousands without employment, who, joining necessity to their hatred of you, have stirred up the Mahrattas against you. Instead of having given up Pondicherry and the Isle de Bourbon to the French, you ought to have acted as the Romans did to the Carthaginians, and said, 'You shall not stir beyond such a latitude,' not for ever, because that would be an injustice, but for ten years or longer, until your fears for the safety of the Indies are over. My opinion is, that your having given up Pondicherry and Bourbon to the French will cost you ten thousand more Europeans in India, without benefiting France in the position she now is, under those incapables, the Bourbons.

'Even when *I* was in power, I would not have given a farthing for those possessions had it not been for the hopes that I always entertained of driving you out of India; to effect which, and to maintain a correspondence, the Isle of France or of Bourbon was so necessary. Every year I received Ambassadors from the Nabobs and other Indian princes, especially those of the Mahrattas, imploring help from me, and offering to drive you from India, provided I would assist them with fourteen or sixteen thousand infantry, artillery, and officers. They offered to find all the cavalry if I would send officers to instruct their troops. The hatred they expressed against you was astonishing. Possibly you may have some interested views in giving up Pondicherry, thinking that thereby you may smuggle some of your India goods by French tenders into France. But this cannot be of sufficient weight against the great injury arising from the proximity to your Indian possessions of a rival nation like the French. Your having given up that colony will also excite envy and a desire to recover all they formerly had, whereas, if they had none, they would forget that they ever had had any possessions in India.

'You ought not to have allowed the French or any other nation to have put their nose beyond the Cape. You ought to monopolise the whole China trade to yourselves. Instead of going to war with the Chinese, it were better to make war with the nations who desire to trade with them. You ought not to suffer the Americans to send a ship there. You gave up Batavia to the Dutch, whom, next to the French, it was your interest to shut out from India. The Dutch use a large quantity of tea, which should be supplied by you. The great object of every nation is to consider its own interests, especially when every other country gains something. After my fall, you might have had anything you liked to ask for; but whilst other nations were acquiring territory, you abandoned your interests, and even neglected to make a treaty favourable to your commerce, for which you are now suffering.'

September 25.—Napoleon sent for me in the evening about eight o'clock. Found him in his bedroom. He complained of slight headache and pain in the right side of the face, which he said he had felt immediately upon going into the garden, in consequence of the effect of the wind, and which had prevented him from staying out more than a quarter of an hour. He again asked me of what temperament I took him to be—what was necessary to be done to keep him in a state of good health? I replied that I conceived him to be of a temperament which required much activity; and that it was necessary for him to employ both his physical and mental faculties almost constantly. That he was a man who required to stir much about. 'You are right,' replied the Emperor; 'such has been necessary to me through my life, such is now, and such will be as long as the machine holds. Exercise of the mind I almost daily take in my writings and otherwise;

and exercise of the body I should take even in this island, were I not in the hands of a *boja*. But under the present system it can never take place. Never can I put myself in the way of being insulted by sentinels, or receiving a *fusillade* if I stirred off the high road.'

September 26.—Saw Napoleon at nine o'clock. He complained of a sensation of soreness in the lower extremities.

He ate his breakfast before me, which consisted of two or three radishes, a little toast and butter, followed by a little *café au lait*.

September 28.—Saw Napoleon at 11 A.M. Appeared to be in nearly the same state as yesterday. Ankles œdematous; appetite bad; ate nothing since breakfast yesterday. His body has been rendered so extremely sensible to external impressions that the slightest exposure to wind or cold produced a catarrhal or rheumatic affection. I proposed to call in Mr. Baxter, giving as a reason that when a person of so much consequence and in such peculiar circumstances was even slightly indisposed, it was proper to call in the first medical advice.

Napoleon replied, 'There is no necessity for it. If all the colleges of medicine in France and England were assembled, they would give the same advice that you have done, viz. to take exercise on horseback. I myself know as well as any physician what is necessary for me. It is exercise. Calling in Baxter to me would be like sending a physician to a man who was starving with hunger, instead of giving him a loaf of bread. I have no objection to your making known to him my state of health if you like, and I am well aware that he will say *exercise*. As long as the present system is in force I will never stir out.' He then repeated the conversation he held with Lord Amherst on this subject.

'The only one of us,' added he, 'who goes out, I may say, is Gourgaud, and he has been stopped upwards of fifty times. Had I been in his place, the same thing would have happened to me. Once during the Admiral's time I was stopped, but he instantly turned the island topsy-turvy on account of it; and I clearly saw that he was really displeased, and that he took every precaution to prevent the recurrence of a similar circumstance. Now this brute would, on the contrary, be pleased with it, or with anything else that would have a tendency to lower or to degrade my character.

'I am convinced,' added Napoleon, 'that the barbarous manner in which I am treated will be revenged by the blood of some innocent Englishmen. By the argument of your Ministers, that it is *useful* to keep me here, every act, however atrocious, may be justified. Would it not have been *useful* to me to have procured the assassination of Nelson or Wellington? Would it not now be *useful* to the French nation to get rid of all the Allied troops by poisoning the bread and the water? Would it not be *useful* to them to assassinate Wellington? It is not the *utility* of an act which is to be considered—it is its justice; for by the former principle every species of crime may be apparently justified as being useful, and *therefore* necessary. It is the doctrine of Talleyrand.'

Soon after this Sir Hudson Lowe came to Longwood, and having made some inquiries respecting Napoleon's health, asked if I had had any particular conversation with him upon the subject of his complaint? In reply, I communicated to him the foregoing conversation, avoiding the repetition of the epithet *bourreau*. His Excellency called Major Gorrequer to be a witness to some parts of it, viz. that about Lord Amherst, which he said he did not believe, and asked if I had made any reply? I said, No. He observed that a reply might easily have been made if I had been disposed to do so, but that it appeared I was of the same way of thinking as General Bonaparte asserted Lord Amherst had been; and asked if such were the case? I answered that as a medical man, I had strongly recommended Napoleon to take exercise on horseback.

After a tolerably long harangue, in which His Excellency accused Napoleon of having purposely delayed seeing the Ambassador until the day before his departure, in order that he (Sir Hudson) might not have an opportunity of refuting his calumnies, he concluded by saying, 'Do you not think, sir, that General Bonaparte has treated me most shamefully in that business?' I replied that

Napoleon had been so unwell as not to be in a situation to receive strangers; that until the last moment he had been undecided whether to receive his lordship or not; and that Lord Amherst had been at his (Sir Hudson's) house for several days, during which he must have had ample opportunities of making his lordship acquainted with every particular. That if I were rightly informed, Lord Amherst had seen and conversed with him for some hours after the interview his lordship had with Napoleon, with whom he had been only about two hours.

This reply excited His Excellency's wrath, who, looking at me with an expression of countenance that I shall never forget, said, 'If it were not that it would be made a subject of complaint, I should immediately and without waiting the orders of Government send you off the island, sir. I have received no official intelligence from Government concerning your appointment; you are not of my choosing; you are only permitted to visit General Bonaparte as a medical man.' I observed that I was acting according to his own instructions by confining myself to medical subjects. He repeated his threat of sending me off the island; to which I answered by telling him that a dismissal from St. Helena would not give me the smallest uneasiness. After this Sir Hudson went down to Count Bertrand's, where he remained about half an hour. On his return he sent for me, and after saying that General Bonaparte had been represented by Count Bertrand to be in a much worse state of health than I had mentioned, ordered me to send him a written report of his health.

About four o'clock Count Balmaine, with Baron and Madame Sturmer, came as far as the inner gate of Longwood, where they met General and Madame Bertrand, who with their little Arthur and a maidservant were walking out. Shortly afterwards General Montholon joined them. They remained together for nearly an hour, walking between the guard-room and the inner gate. It was amusing to observe the gestures of Sir Thomas Reade, who was all the time standing at or moving before Captain Blakeney's door, with a telescope in his hand; especially at a time when a thick fog came on which completely obscured them from the Knight's view, who was vainly endeavouring to penetrate it with his glass.

Sir Hudson Lowe's visit to Count Bertrand, I am informed, was to propose that a soldier's barrack should be put up at Longwood for Napoleon to walk under as a substitute for the continuous shade in which the spot was deficient. Some conversation also took place about the restrictions, in which observations of a nature similar to those of Napoleon to me in the morning were made to Sir Hudson Lowe by Count Bertrand, who also informed His Excellency of the opinion expressed by Lord Amherst.

Saw Napoleon in the evening. He was in much the same state as in the morning. Told me that he had seen Madame Sturmer through his glass, and commented on the bloom of her cheeks.

September 29. — Signal made for Captain Blakeney to proceed to Plantation House. Sent my report of Napoleon's health by him, and made application for some sea-water to be sent to Longwood for a bath for the use of Napoleon.

Saw Napoleon, who was in much better spirits.

Had a jocular conversation with him about patron saints. He asked who was my patron saint,—what was my Christian name? I replied that my first was a family name; that I was called after Barry, Lord Avonmore, an Irish peer. 'But,' said he laughing, 'you must have some patron saint to befriend you and plead your cause in the next world?' I mentioned my second Christian name. 'Ah!' said he, 'then *he* will plead for you. St. Napoleon ought to be very much obliged to me, and do everything in his power for me in the world to come. Poor fellow, nobody knew him before! He had not even a day in the Calendar. I got him one, and persuaded the Pope to give him the 15th of August, my birthday.

'I recollect,' continued he, 'when I was in Italy, a priest preaching about a poor sinner who had departed this life. His soul appeared before God, and he was required to give an account of all his actions. The evil and the good were afterwards thrown into opposite scales, in order to see which preponderated. That containing the good proved much the lightest, and instantly flew up to the beam. His wretched soul was condemned to the infernal regions, conducted by angels to the bottomless pit, delivered over to devils, and thrown into the flames. "Already," said the preacher, "had the devouring element covered his feet and legs and proceeded upwards even unto his bowels; in his vitals, oh! brethren, he felt them. He sank, and only his head appeared above the waves of fire, when he cried out to God, and afterwards to his patron saint. 'Oh! patron,' said he, 'look down upon me; oh! take compassion upon me, and throw into the scale of my good deeds all the lime and stone which I gave to repair the convent of ———.' His Saint instantly took the hint, gathered together all the lime and stone, threw them into the scale of good, which immediately preponderated; the scale of evil sprang up to the beam, and the sinner's soul into paradise at the same moment. Now you see by this, brethren, how useful it is to keep the convents in repair, for had it not been for the lime and stone bestowed by this sinner, his poor soul would even now, children, be consuming in hell fire; and yet you are so blind as to let the convent and the church, built by your forefathers, fall to ruin." At this time,' continued the Emperor laughing, 'these priests wanted to get a new convent built, and had recourse to this expedient to procure money which, after this, poured in upon them from all quarters.'

Napoleon then began to rally me about my profession. 'You medical people,' said he, 'will have more lives to answer for in the other world than even we generals. What will you say for yourself,' asked he laughing, 'when you are called to account for all the souls of poor sailors you have despatched to the other world? or what will your Saint say for you when the accusing angel proclaims, "Such a number you sent out of the world, by giving them heating medicines, when you ought to have given cooling ones, and *vice versâ?* so many more, because you mistook their complaints and bled them too much; others because you did not bleed them enough; numbers because they were poor people, and you did not pay them as much attention as you would have done to the captain or the admiral, and because you were over your bottle, or at the theatre, or with a fine girl, and did not like to be disturbed, or after *drink* (in English), when you went and distributed medicines haphazard. How many because you were not present at the time a change in the complaint took place, when a medicine given at the moment might have saved them? How many others because the provisions were bad, and you would not complain through fear of offending the *fournisseurs?*"'

I replied by observing that on the score of conscience I was perfectly easy in my mind; that human nature was liable to err; that very likely I had made mistakes but not intentional ones; nor had I ever paid less attention to the common people than to the officers; and endeavoured as much as possible, as I perceived that he was half in earnest, to uphold the honour of my profession. I also explained to him that in our service the surgeons could gain nothing by not complaining of the *fournisseurs*, etc. Napoleon answered that certainly a man ought always to be judged by his intentions; but that there were abuses in all departments which were principally kept up by people being either interested or afraid to complain; that he had endeavoured to eradicate them as much as possible, in which he had effected much, but had not been able perfectly to succeed. 'My opinion,' continued he, 'is that, when physicians despatch a number of souls to the other world either through ignorance, mistake, or not having properly studied their complaints, they are just as cool and as little concerned as a general with whom I am acquainted, who lost three thousand men in storming a hill. Having succeeded, after several desperate attempts, he observed with great *sang froid*, "Oh, it was not this hill I wanted to take; it was another; this is of no use," and returned to his former position.'

I remarked that it seemed as if he thought physicians as bad and as ignorant as they are described in Molière or *Gil Blas*. He laughed and said, 'I believe that there are a great many of Molière's physicians. Of surgery I have quite a different opinion; as there you do not work in the dark. There your senses guide and assist you. You recollect having heard of Sieyès?' I replied in the affirmative. 'Sieyès,' continued he, 'before the Revolution, was almoner to one of the princesses.

One day, when he was performing mass in the chapel before herself, her attendants, and a large congregation, something occurred which made the princess get up and retire. Her example was followed by her ladies-in-waiting, and by the whole of the nobility, officers, and others, who attended more out of complaisance to her than from any true sense of religion. Sieyès was very busy reading his breviary, and for some time did not perceive it. Raising his eyes, however, from his book, lo! he observed that the princess, nobles, and all the others *comme il faut* had disappeared. With an air of displeasure and contempt he shut the book, hastily descended from the pulpit, exclaiming, "*I* do not say mass for the *canaille!*" and went out of the chapel, leaving the service half finished. Now,' said he laughing very heartily, 'many of you physicians would leave a patient half-cured because he was one of the *canaille*.'

He then spoke of Larrey. 'Larrey,' said he, 'was the most honest man, and the best friend to the soldier, that I ever knew. Vigilant and indefatigable in his exertions for the wounded, Larrey was seen on the field of battle after an action, accompanied by a train of young surgeons, endeavouring to discover if any signs of life remained in the bodies. In the most inclement weather and at all times of the night and the day Larrey was to be found amongst the wounded; he scarcely allowed a moment's repose to his assistants, and kept them continually at their posts. He tormented the generals, and disturbed them in their beds at night whenever he wanted accommodation or assistance for the wounded or sick. They were all afraid of him, as they knew he would instantly come and make a complaint to me. He paid court to none of them, and was the implacable enemy of the *fournisseurs.*'

Speaking about service on board ships of war at sea during the winter, especially of a certain class, I remarked that the seamen were better off in point of being able to warm themselves at a fire than the officers. 'Why so?' said Napoleon. I replied 'Because they have the advantage of the galley fire,[1] where they can warm and dry themselves.'—'And why not the officers?' I said that it would not be exactly decorous for the officers to mix in that familiar way with the men. '*Ah! la morgue aristocratique, la rage aristocratique!*' exclaimed Napoleon. 'Why, in my campaigns, I used to go to the lines in the *bivouacs*, sit down with the meanest soldier, converse, laugh, and joke with him. I always prided myself on being the man of the people.'

I observed that a man in his exalted situation might do without impropriety that which if done by an inferior officer, especially on board a ship, might produce too much familiarity, perhaps contempt, and thereby relaxation of discipline. '*La morgue aristocratique*,' cried Napoleon again; 'you are the most aristocratic nation in the world. Had I been

[1] The galley is the kitchen on board a man of war.

one of those *principiotti* in Germany, your oligarchy would never have sent me here. But because *je suis l'homme du peuple;* because I may say that I raised myself from the mob to the greatest height of power without the aid of the aristocracy or hereditary rights; because a long line of nobles or of petty princes did not distinguish my name; because, in fact, I was not one of them, they determined to oppress and humiliate me when in their power. Lords Bathurst and Castlereagh, *la canaille de l'aristocratie*, are the persons who have ordered all these attempts. John Bull will comprehend that I am oppressed, *parceque je sors du peuple*, in order to prevent any of them from presuming to elevate themselves to a level with the aristocracy.'

He concluded by observing, 'That the Governor always took a witness with him to Bertrand's for the purpose, he supposed, of testifying to everything that he thought proper to assert. That in all probability he made a *procès verbal* as he liked, and got the other to sign it. That, therefore, to prevent his *making* conversations, he had ordered Bertrand to write an official letter to him, stating their grievances and what they wanted.'

September 30.—Napoleon much in the same state. Went to Plantation House to report. Found that Sir Hudson Lowe had gone out. Met him at Longwood on my return. Informed him of the state of Napoleon's health; and in reply to some of his observations, told him that there was nothing immediately dangerous, but that œdematous swellings of the extremities taking place with a man of Napoleon's time of life and of his temperament and present habits were always to be looked upon with a suspicious eye, as such were frequently the primary symptoms of dropsy.

His Excellency said that his principal object in coming to Longwood had been to obtain an answer from Count Bertrand to an offer which he had made on the 28th of the month to put up a soldiers' barrack seventy feet long, which might be formed into a temporary gallery to walk in until an answer arrived from England relative to building the new house. That he could get no reply from Bertrand but a shrug of the shoulders. That Count Bertrand had been very violent in his language, and had not merely asked for one or two things, but had insisted 'that everything should be put upon the same footing as during Sir George Cockburn's time. That the Emperor would not stir out unless permission were given to him (Bertrand) to admit persons by his pass into Longwood. That he should write and hold correspondence with whoever he liked, go where he liked, enter what houses he liked, in fact, do what he liked in the island without any restriction.' He then asked if I had heard anything from him of the conversation which they had held with the Commissioners? I replied that 'I had not heard him mention even their names.' His Excellency said that 'it was very extraordinary, as General Bonaparte had made some very strong remarks about them to Mr. Balcombe.'

Saw Napoleon again in the evening. He complained of pain in his teeth and cheeks, which he attributed to having taken a walk in the garden for ten minutes. Proposed to him that the barrack should be erected. He replied that he stood in need of exercise in the open air and not in a covered gallery. That he had once caused a gallery of a league in length to be built for him in France, but that it had not answered the purpose. Moreover, that in summer the billiard-room became so hot at five o'clock in the afternoon from the rays of the sun penetrating it as to render it impossible to remain there; that a wooden barrack would be worse; that it would therefore be useless to erect it, as the shade of the trees was what was desired.

October 1.—Saw Napoleon in his bedroom at 8 A.M. He complained of a dull pain immediately under the ribs, which he said he experienced yesterday morning for the first time. Sensation in the right shoulder, which he described to be more of numbness than of pain. Pulse 68. Slight inclination to cough. Want of rest at night. He said that he felt as if he wanted to lean or press his side against something. Told him that if it increased and were accompanied by other symptoms, there could not be a doubt of its being hepatitis; in which case it would be necessary to have recourse to proper remedies, which I specified, together with abstinence from wine and a suitable diet. He shook his head at the proposal of physic. I told him that if it were hepatitis, it must not be neglected, as if not taken in time, it would terminate fatally.[1] He replied, '*Ce qui est écrit, est écrit*, from above,' looking up. '*Nos journées sont comptées.*' I answered that according to that doctrine all medical aid was useless. He made no reply.

With respect to diet and abstinence from wine he observed that he was a man who had never committed any excesses either in eating or drinking. That he drank very little wine ; however, that he found the little he took was absolutely necessary, always finding himself better after it, and was convinced that if he left it off, he should sink rapidly. He then went into a salt-water bath, and had a long conversation with me upon medical subjects.

October 2.—Napoleon felt relieved by the salt-water bath yesterday. Continued much in want of

[1] From November 20, 1815, to the 20th of the same month 1816 there were admitted into the regimental hospital four hundred and thirty-eight patients, one hundred and seventy-nine of whom were afflicted with bowel complaints. The regiment was between five and six hundred strong.

The loss of life among the crews of the following small ships, whilst they were on the St. Helena station, was also very great, viz. twenty-four in the *Mosquito*, complement one hundred men ; sixteen in the *Racoon*, one hundred men ; eleven in the *Leveret*, seventy-five men ; fifteen in the *Griffon*, eighty-five men ; besides numbers invalided and sent to England on account of the same complaints. It is well known to naval officers that, unless in *very sickly stations*, small vessels are generally very healthy, frequently not losing a man in a year. I was myself surgeon of a sloop of war in the West Indies, in which ship not a single death occurred during twelve months, though exposed for a considerable portion of that time to the influence of the noxious climate of Surinam.—B. E. O'M.

rest. Recommended exercise on horseback, etc. Saw him again at ten in bed. His legs were a little more swollen than in the morning. He would have taken another bath, but there was no water. Had eaten scarcely anything. Slight headache.

October 3.—Examined the right side, and perceived that it felt firmer to the touch than the left. There was also a tumefaction evident to the sight, which when pressed hard gave a little pain. Napoleon said that this was observed about two months since. That he had thought nothing of it, and attributed it to obesity, but that now, from its being attended with pain, he imagined it might be connected with enlargement of the liver.[1]

Napoleon said that the Governor had written to Count Bertrand yesterday stating that he (Napoleon) might go off the road and down into the valley, but that the same privilege, unless when with him, was not to be extended to his officers. 'Mere *tracasserie*,' said he, when I recommended him to profit by it; 'it would only expose me to more insults; for the sentinels do not know me, and every old soldier who wished to fulfil his duty, so as to clear himself of all responsibility, would say, "*Halte là*, is General Bonaparte amongst you? Are you him? Oh, then, if you are him, you may pass." Thus should I be exposed to daily insults and be

---

[1] As it is not the intention of the author to tire the reader with the detail of a medical journal, the enumeration of the symptoms will for the future be discontinued unless where absolutely necessary.—B. E. O'M.

obliged to give an account of myself to every sentinel who thought it right to perform his duty properly. Besides, he has no right to impose more restrictions upon *questi signori* than upon me. By the paper which they have signed, they only agree to subject themselves to such restrictions as are or may be imposed upon me. I never would go out without sending Gourgaud to ascertain that there was no danger of being stopped and insulted by sentinels.'

I asked permission to call in Mr. Baxter to see him. He said that if the symptoms increased, he probably would, as I wished it, provided that the Governor did not interfere with it; if he did interfere, never.

October 4.—Went to Plantation House, according to order, and gave Sir Hudson Lowe a written report of the state of Napoleon's health. After having read it, he said that there were too many details in it, and that I must make out one which could be made public. Said that he had received a long letter from Count Bertrand, containing arguments similar to those which I was in the habit of using, and in which there was an allusion to Lord Liverpool, which, when coupled with circumstances that had taken place some time ago, looked as if there were some correspondence in that quarter. I said that Napoleon had always declared that he believed Lords Liverpool and Sidmouth to be better disposed towards him than any other of the English Ministers. That, indeed, I had never heard him speak ill of any of the English Ministers excepting Lords Bathurst and Castlereagh.

October 6.—Napoleon nearly the same. Again recommended him exercise most strongly, and told him that if he deferred it much longer, the swellings in his legs might increase so much as to render him incapable of taking it. That if he mounted on horseback and rode, I was convinced all the swellings in the lower extremities would soon disappear. He assented to this, but declared that until things were put on the footing they had been in Sir George Cockburn's time he would not go out, and repeated his apprehensions of annoyance from the Governor.

I took the liberty of observing that he was like a man tumbling down a precipice who would not lay hold of a rope within his grasp, by which he might save himself from inevitable death. He laughed at this comparison and said, '*Que le sort se fasse, nos journées sont complées.*'

October 7.—Napoleon nearly the same. Observed that the Governor had insinuated that he (Napoleon) wanted to kill himself. 'Had I intended this,' continued he, 'I would have fallen upon my sword long ago and died like a soldier; but I am not fool enough to attempt to purposely kill myself by the slow agonies of a lingering disease. I never loved tedious warfare. But there is no death, however slow and painful, that I would not prefer to dishonouring my character. A man who was once capable of imposing the restrictions of the 9th of

October and the 14th of March, is capable of laying them on again, or even worse, according to his caprice or his fears, real or imaginary. If I were to go out and be once insulted by a sentinel, it would have a more injurious effect on my health than six months' confinement. But this man is insensible to any moral feeling.'

Communicated the substance of what Napoleon had said to Sir Hudson Lowe, to whom I repeated that whenever Sir George Cockburn made any regulations relative to the French, he was accustomed to discuss the matter with Counts Bertrand or Montholon, by means of which they were enabled to make arrangements in a manner likely to give the least offence. Sir Hudson said that *his own measures* had been approved of by the British Government, and that most of the letters which he had received commenced by stating that the Prince Regent had commanded that such and such measures should be adopted.

October 8.—Napoleon walked for a short time in the garden. Being so unaccustomed to exercise, this fatigued him so much that he was obliged to sit down on the steps before the verandah. He was, however, in better spirits than yesterday, and felt benefited by the salt-water baths and such of the other remedies as he would consent to use.

October 9.—The Emperor not so well. Got cold yesterday, and complains of pains in the lower extremities, and had been very unwell in the night. 'I was going to send for you early in the morning,' said he, 'but then I considered this poor devil of a doctor has been up all night at a ball and has need of sleep. If I disturb him, he will have his eyes so heavy and his intellects so confused that he will not be able to form any correct opinion. Soon after this I fell into a perspiration and felt much relieved.'

Immediately after I had left him, he went to bed again, where he remained for some hours.

October 10.—Napoleon in rather bad spirits.

Had some conversation with the Emperor afterwards. 'When I returned from Italy,' said he, ' I went to live at a small house—in the Rue Chantereine [I think]. A few days afterwards the municipality of Paris ordered that it should be called *Rue de la Victoire*. Every one sought to manifest the national gratitude to me. It was proposed to give me a fine hôtel in Paris and a magnificent estate. Although I had maintained and paid the army for two years, and even paid the arrears for some time before, and sent more than thirty millions to the treasury of France, I was scarcely worth three hundred thousand francs. The Directory, however, influenced probably by jealousy, would not consent, and said that my services were such as could not be rewarded by money. Every description of person tried to see me. The enthusiasm was *au comble*. I rarely however associated with others than Kléber, Desaix, Caffarelli, and some *savans*. The Directory gave me a splendid fête. Talleyrand, who was Minister of Foreign Affairs, gave another. I remained but a short time at either. I was afterwards nominated to the command of the Army of England, which was so named to deceive your Ministers as to its real destination, which was Egypt.

'Talleyrand had been Bishop of Autun during the Revolution, and was one of the three bishops who swore to the civil constitution of the clergy. He was afterwards sent to England, but becoming suspected during the fury of the Revolution, he fled to America, where he remained until after the 13th Vendémiaire, when his name was erased from the list of emigrants. He insinuated himself into the confidence of the Directory, and was made Minister of Foreign Affairs, and as such had constant communication with me. It was then customary to celebrate the anniversary of the execution of Louis the Sixteenth, at which Talleyrand wished that I should attend. I replied that I had no public functions; that I did not like the ceremony; that fêtes were celebrated for victories, but that the victims left on the field of battle were lamented with tears; that celebrating the death of a man was not the policy of a Government but that of a faction. Talleyrand maintained that it was just because it was politic; that all countries had rejoiced at the death of tyrants, and that my presence was expected. After a long argument it was arranged that the Institute should attend, which I was to accompany as a member of the Mechanical

Section to which I belonged. Although I avoided public notice, the multitude, which paid no attention to the Directory, but had waited to see me go out, filled the air with cries of "*Vive le général de l'armée d'Italie.*" Never yet,' added he, 'was a general more beloved by his troops!'[1]

'To show you the confidence that I had in the disposition of the army,' said he, 'I need only recount to you an event which will be perpetuated in history. Five or six days after my landing at Cannes in 1815, the advanced guard of my little army met the advance of a division marching from Grenoble against me. Cambronne, who commanded my troops, wanted to address them, but they would not listen to him. They also refused to receive Raoul, whom I sent afterwards.

'When I was informed of this, I went to them myself, with a few of my Guard, with their arms reversed, and called out, "The first soldier who pleases may come forward and kill his Emperor." It operated like an electric shock, and "*Vive l'Empereur!*" resounded through the ranks; the division and my Guards fraternised, all joined me,

---

[1] 'One day at dinner, while describing one of his engagements in Egypt, he named numerically the eight or ten semi-brigades which had been engaged. On hearing this, Madame Bertrand could not refrain from asking how, after so long a lapse of time, he could possibly recollect all these numbers. "Madam, this is a lover's recollection of his former mistresses," was Napoleon's reply.'—*Las Cases*, vol. ii., part iv., p. 277, English edition.

'"A regiment, sir, is never destroyed by the enemy; it is immortalised," said the Emperor on one occasion.'—*Las Cases*, vol. iii., part v., p. 72, English edition.

and advanced together to Grenoble. Close to Grenoble the brave Labédoyère, a young man, animated by the noblest sentiments, and disgusted by the conduct of the *misérables*, against whom France had fought and bled for so many years, joined me with his regiment. At Grenoble I found the regiment, in which, twenty-five years before, I had been captain, and some others, drawn up on the ramparts to oppose me. No sooner did they see me than enthusiastic cries of *Vive l'Empereur!* were heard, not only from them, but from the whole of the National Guard and the populace: the gates were torn down, and I entered in triumph. What is singular and strikingly shows the sentiments of the troops is, that in a moment the six thousand men by whom I was thus joined mounted old tricoloured cockades, which they had kept as treasures when the army had been obliged to adopt the Bourbon anti-national flag. I advanced to Lyons, where I was joined by the troops charged to defend it against me, and the Comte d'Artois was happy to escape, escorted by a single dragoon,[1] from the city he had commanded a few hours before. To all his entreaties, offers, and prayers, *Vive l'Empereur!* was the reply.'

Sir Hudson Lowe and Major Gorrequer were for some time at Count Bertrand's this day.

---

[1] The National Guards who deserted the Comte d'Artois applied afterwards to the Emperor to be enrolled, and were refused. The one soldier who had remained faithful to his former commander was promoted and decorated by the Emperor.

Sir Thomas Reade told me that Sir Hudson Lowe had received a sealed parcel from Bertrand, addressed to Lord Liverpool, which he would forward, although he knew that it contained complaints against himself. That he did not care what complaints they made. That if it were not for the d——d Commissioners, things would be better. He then asked me if I had much conversation with them? I said very little; that I had observed a marked alteration in their conduct towards me latterly; instead of asking me numerous questions as before, they rarely spoke except upon commonplace subjects. He observed that 'it was very likely they (the Commissioners) would tell the French the tenor of my reports on Bonaparte's health, as the French had represented him to be worse than I had described him.'

Major Gorrequer came to Longwood by signal, and had a long conference with Count Bertrand.

October 12.—Saw Napoleon with his legs in a tub of hot water. Told me that he felt uneasy and in a bad humour.

Sir Hudson Lowe had a long interview with Count Bertrand; the latter endeavoured to explain to him the point in dispute, viz. that being obliged to send all letters through him open to such persons resident on the island, as he (the Governor) might allow to visit them, was considered a useless humiliation. If he wished to forward a letter privately to England, or to carry on an illicit correspondence with an individual or individuals in the island, he (Bertrand) having the power of inviting a certain number of persons to visit Longwood, and to retain them there some hours (as the Governor said he would allow), would surely embrace *that* as the proper moment to give them such letters, rather than hazard compromising himself and them by sending a sealed letter containing improper communications through the orderly officer when, should suspicions arise, it might be opened and ruin the person to whom it was addressed. Sir Hudson Lowe, however, would not understand this. Count Bertrand also mentioned to him that the Emperor considered a free intercourse with the inhabitants as the only guarantee he had for his life.

When Major Gorrequer was at Count Bertrand's on the 10th, the latter informed him that the Governor's proceedings had been so illegal and involved in such mystery and obscurity that some of the officers of the 53d Regiment, conceiving that there might be criminal intentions in view, had signified to them not to be afraid, for that in the 53d Regiment there were neither assassins nor executioners to be found. Also that Sir George Cockburn had said soon after the arrival of Napoleon, 'If I put sentinels in such a manner, and insist upon such and such measures, this man will shut himself up and never stir out. He will not live six months. I will not be the means of assassinating anybody. I will arrange matters so that he shall have liberty and at the same time not afford the least chance of escaping from the island, which is all that I can effect, or indeed care about.'

October 14.—This morning, on presenting myself according to custom to call upon Napoleon, I was informed that he was asleep, and had left word for me to go down to Count Bertrand. Had a conversation with the latter, the purport of which was that the Emperor had been given to understand that I was in the habit of writing bulletins of his health daily, or at more distant periods, and that it was his desire that every bulletin should be shown to him (the Emperor) before being sent. That any person acting as his physician must necessarily have a portion of his confidence; and that he would not consent to be styled General Bonaparte in reports made by him, as such would appear in Europe to be an acquiescence on his part to the use of such a title, which he would rather die than consent to; that the words *l'Empereur* must be used, and that I had better make the Governor acquainted with it. I observed that with respect to the title of *l'Empereur*, I knew that it would be inadmissible.

Saw Napoleon afterwards, who told me that he had always thought I might be required to make out reports of the state of his health, especially when labouring under indisposition; that, however, as it was only a surmise, he did not take any notice of it; but that some days ago Generals Montholon and Gourgaud were asked how were certain symptoms (palpitations), which they were totally ignorant he had ever been afflicted with, as he (Napoleon) had only made me acquainted with them, and had professed their surprise ; that a reply was made, stating that such symptoms were described in the bulletins of health sent to the Governor.

I informed Napoleon that I had often made reports of the state of his health. He asked to see one. I immediately brought him one of the 10th. Looking over it, he observed the word 'General,' and said that he would never consent to be so styled by me or by any other person acting as his physician ; that as such I must possess a certain share of his confidence, without which I could not be acquainted with the symptoms ; that a physician was to the body what a confessor was to the soul, and was bound to keep such confession equally sacred unless permitted to divulge it. For the future, therefore, he insisted I should submit to him all reports which I should make of his health previous to sending them to the Governor. That he did not wish to influence me in their compilation; on the contrary, if I conceived any observations made by him to be incorrect, I was not to insert them, but that I should not render an account of such symptoms as delicacy or other motives might induce him to wish should be kept secret. After this warning, if I were to send any more bulletins without their having been previously shown to him, it would be acting the part of a spy and not that of a physician, which, he added, was what the gaoler of St. Helena wanted, and had done everything in his power to make me. My reports were transmitted to the Commissioners, and by them to their courts. He could not therefore consent to allow a person in my situation to style him 'General' in reports which might be sent to France, where he had been once sovereign; or to the Courts of Vienna and Petersburg; as coming from me, it would appear to be an acquiescence on his part in such title, which he would rather die than consent to. Therefore I must give my word of honour not to make any reports in future without complying with what he thus required, and leaving the original in Bertrand's possession; if I did not consent to this arrangement, that I must not write any more; if I did, he would never see me again as a physician.

I replied that I never should be permitted by the Governor to style him *l'Empereur*, and suggested that I might use Napoleon or Napoleon Bonaparte. That as to showing the reports to him, I must first communicate with the Governor, to which he consented, but not to the appellation. In my verbal reports, he said he cared not if I called him *generale*, *boja*, or *tiranno Bonaparte*.

Communicated the purport of the above to Sir Hudson Lowe at Plantation House. As I had foreseen, he decidedly refused to consent to the use of the title required; that he was willing he should be styled Napoleon Bonaparte. As to showing the reports to Napoleon previous to their being sent to him, he said that he saw no objection for the present; however, it was a matter he could not decide upon on the spot as it required some consideration, etc.

He added that it was some deep-laid scheme of the Commissioners.

Informed Napoleon in the evening of the answer made by the Governor. He observed that he could not think of allowing himself to be insulted by his physician. That after the proposal he had made to the English Government to assume the *incognito*, to which no answer had been given, it was the height of insult to insist upon naming him as they liked. The more they endeavoured to humiliate him, the more tenacious would he be of the title. 'I lost my throne for a point of honour, and would lose my life a hundred times rather than allow myself to be debased by consenting to be designated as my oppressors please.'

After some time I proposed dropping all titles and using the word *personage*, which I said I thought might remove all difficulties. He approved of my suggestion, but said that *patient* would answer better and satisfy him, provided the bulletins were first shown to him, and his consent obtained to send them.

It was signified to Count Bertrand this day by Sir Hudson Lowe that Sir George Cockburn used to cause the notes and papers which were sent by the French to town to be shown to him before they were allowed to be transmitted to the persons to whom they were directed.

October 15.—Communicated the proposal of yesterday to Sir Hudson Lowe, who refused his consent, saying that he must be styled Napoleon

Bonaparte or General Bonaparte in any bulletins or reports made of the state of his health.

October 17.—Napoleon was lying on his sofa, looking low and melancholy, with a cup of chicken-broth before him. Marchand told me that he had been very unwell in the morning, and that he was obliged to chafe his temples and forehead with *eau de Cologne*. Napoleon would not answer the inquiries which I made relative to his complaints.

The *Griffon* sloop arrived this day, bringing the intelligence of the loss of the *Julie* sloop of war on the island of Tristan d'Acunha on the 2d, with all the officers, except Captain Jones and two midshipmen.

October 18.—Napoleon in his bath. Still persisted in refusing to consult me on his complaints. Told me that I had been remarked to go regularly every Tuesday and Saturday to Plantation House; and that, were it not for the confidence he had in me, he would, the moment it had been noticed, have dispensed with my services, as it was evident from the regularity of the periods that I went by order of the Governor. 'The fact is,' continued he, 'that all this is only an artifice to deprive me of medical assistance *e d'arrivare più presto alla fine;* for it was well known that as soon as I found it out, I would not submit to it, and that no man of feeling or honour would do so.'

Communicated the sentiments expressed by Napoleon to Sir Hudson Lowe at Plantation House, who after some hesitation authorised me to say that for the future no more bulletins would be demanded without first having made him (Napoleon) acquainted that such were asked for.

October 19.—Reported this reply of the Governor to Napoleon; after which, and after having assured him that I would not send any bulletins without having shown them to him, he entered into particulars with me touching his malady. There was some degree of anxiety evident, and a tinge of melancholy probably caused by his complaint, and perhaps increased by the information in the last paper sent him by Sir Hudson Lowe, containing the decision of the Allied Powers that his son should not succeed to the Duchies of Parma, etc.

October 28.—Went to Plantation House, where Sir Hudson Lowe, after some inquiries touching Napoleon's health, demanded if I had had any remarkable conversations with General Bonaparte, what length of time they lasted, and on what subjects? This led to a discussion, in which His Excellency was more than ordinarily violent and abusive. Amongst other elegant expressions, he said that he conceived me to be a jackal, running about in search of news for General Bonaparte.

In reply to this expression I said that I would neither be a jackal, nor a spy, nor informer for him or for any one else. 'What do you mean, sir,' said he, 'by a spy, nor an informer?' I said that if I complied with his directions to inform him of the conversations which passed between Napoleon and myself I should conceive myself to be both. In a paroxysm of rage he said that I was to consider myself prohibited from holding any communication whatsoever with Napoleon Bonaparte except upon medical subjects. That I was to have no sort of communication with him upon other points.

I asked him to give me this order in writing, which he refused, and after some further abuse told me to wait outside the room for some time. In about a quarter of an hour I was called in again and informed by Sir Hudson Lowe that I was to conduct myself as before, observing, however, that he (Sir Hudson) only authorised me to hold medical communication with General Bonaparte; that as to other subjects, I was myself responsible; that I was not to refuse to answer General Bonaparte upon any subject on which he might question me; but that I *was not to ask him any questions other than medical ones*, etc.

Afterwards he asked what I thought myself bound to divulge? I replied as I had formerly done when similar questions had been put to me. He then told me that he would in future dispense with my attendance twice a week, but that he expected me to confer with Mr. Baxter every week on the state of Napoleon Bonaparte's health; to which I consented, as Napoleon had no objection to verbal communications being made, and I need not say that I was heartily glad that my presence at Plantation House was dispensed with.

November 2.—Napoleon reclining on the sofa with some newspapers lying before him and his snuff-box in his hand.[1] He looked very melancholy and low. After the customary inquiries about his health, my advice was given as usual, in as forcible a manner as I could, especially as to exercise on horseback. He replied that he felt no confidence in the Governor, who he was convinced would find out some pretext to insult him, or make some insinuations before he went out four times. 'The letter,' continued he, 'which you saw at Bertrand's the other day, came from him, and contained a paper with the account that my son had been disinherited from the succession to the Duchies of Parma, etc. Now this coming from another person would be nothing; but as he invariably culls out all the news that might prove agreeable, which he retains at Plantation House, and sends whatever may wound my feelings, it is easy to see the motives by which he is actuated.

'You see,' added he, with emphasis, 'that he lost no time in sending that news to me. I was always prepared to expect something of the kind from the wretches who compose the Congress. They are afraid of a prince who is the choice of the people. However, you may yet see a great change—that is, provided they continue to give him a good education,

[1] It has been asserted that Napoleon took snuff in such immoderate quantities that he was in the habit of cramming his waistcoat pocket full of that article, as no snuff-box could contain sufficient for his consumption. The reader may form his own opinion upon the correctness of this assertion when he is informed that twelve pounds of the only kind of snuff he used were brought by Marchand from Paris in July 1815, of which rather more than one half remained when I left St. Helena in July 1818.—B. E. O'M.

or that they do not assassinate him. If they brutify him by a bad education, there is little hope. As for me, I may be considered as dead, as already in the sepulchre. I am certain that before long this body will be no more. I feel that the machine struggles, but cannot last.

'I,' added he, 'could listen to the intelligence of the death of my wife, of my son, or of all my family without change of feature. Not the slightest sign of emotion or alteration of countenance would be visible. Everything would appear indifferent and calm. But when alone in my chamber, then I suffer. Then the feelings of the man burst forth.

'I suppose,' added he, 'that that Montchenu is very glad to hear of my illness. By what channel does he send his letters to France?' I replied that he sent them through the Governor and Lord Bathurst. 'Then they are all opened and read in London by your Ministers.' I replied that I was ignorant of their having recourse to such practices. 'Because,' said Napoleon, 'you never have been in a situation to know anything about it. I tell you that the despatches of all the Ambassadors and other diplomatists that pass through the Post-Office are opened. Otto told me that when in London he ascertained this to be a fact beyond a doubt.' I said that I had heard that in all the States on the Continent official letters were opened. 'Certainly they are,' answered Napoleon, 'but they have not the impudence to deny it like your Ministers, although it is carried to as great an extent among you as anywhere else.

'In France,' continued the Emperor, 'an arrangement was made, so that all the letters sent by the Ambassadors or other diplomatic characters, all their household, and all persons connected with Foreign Affairs, were sent to a secret department of the Post-Office in Paris, no matter in what part of France they were put in. All letters or despatches, in like manner, for Foreign Courts or Ministers were sent to this office, where they were opened and deciphered. The writers sometimes made use of several different ciphers, not continuing the same for more than ten lines, in order to prevent their being understood. This, however, did not answer, as in order to decipher the most ingenious and difficult, it was only necessary to have fifty pages of the same cipher, which, from the extent of the correspondence, was soon to be had. So clever were the agents employed, and so easily did they read the ciphers, that latterly only fifty louis were paid for the discovery of the means of deciphering any new one. By opening all the letters addressed to diplomatic persons, the Post-Office police got acquainted with their correspondents, all subsequent letters to whom were treated in a similar manner. The Ambassadors suspected that some liberties were taken with their correspondence, and to preserve secrecy used generally to change their cipher every three months. But this only gave a little additional trouble. They sent their letters sometimes to a post-office town a few miles distant from where they actually resided, thinking that they were very cunning, and would thus escape observation, not knowing of the arrangement I have mentioned to you. The Ambassadors of the Lesser Powers, such as Denmark, Sweden, and even Prussia, used, through avarice, to save the expense of couriers, to send their despatches through the Post-Office in cipher, which were opened and deciphered, and the most important part of their contents copied and communicated to me (never to the Ministers) by [? Savary].

'By these means I knew the contents of the despatches that Bernstorf, ———, and others sent to their Courts before they arrived at their destination; for they were always sealed up, and sent on after we had done with them. Several of them, especially those of Bernstorf, were full of injurious reflections upon me, censures on my conduct, and fabricated conversations with me. How often have I laughed within myself to see them licking the dust from under my feet at my *levée*, after having read in the morning the *bêtises* they had written of me to their Sovereigns! We used also frequently to discover important matters which they had communicated to them in confidence from the Ambassadors of Russia and Austria, and of your country (when you had one in Paris), who always sent their despatches by couriers of their own, which prevented me from being acquainted with their nature. Through the correspondence of the Lesser

Powers I thus became acquainted with the opinions of the Greater.

'The cleverness of those who conducted this machinery was astonishing. There was no species of writing which they could not imitate perfectly; and in the Post-Office were kept seals similar to those used by the Ambassadors of all the Powers of Europe, independently of an immense number of others belonging to families of different countries. If they met with a seal for which they had not a facsimile, they could get one made in twenty-four hours. This arrangement,' continued he, 'was not an invention of mine. It was first begun by Louis the Fourteenth, and some of the grandchildren of the agents originally employed by him filled in my time situations which had been transmitted to them from their fathers. But,' added he, 'Castlereagh does the same in London. All letters to and from diplomatic persons, which pass through the Post-Office, are opened, and the contents forwarded to him or some other Minister, and they must be aware that a similar practice is followed in France.'[1]

I asked if it was a general rule to open at the French Post-Office letters addressed to persons not diplomatic. 'Rarely,' said he, 'and never unless a man was strongly suspected. Then the first thing that was done was to open every letter directed to him, by means of which his correspondents were discovered, and all letters addressed to them in-

[1] See debates in the House of Commons in June and July 1844, nithe Mazzini case.

spected; but this was an odious measure and very seldom resorted to with Frenchmen. As to foreigners, enemies of France, it was proper to adopt every means of becoming acquainted with their secret machinations.'

Napoleon then told me that he had resolved for the future only to have one regular meal daily at about two or three o'clock. For some time past he has eaten very sparingly.

November 3.—Napoleon much the same. According to his general custom, when newspapers were before him, he asked me now and then the meaning of any word which he did not comprehend.

Some conversation took place about Lord Cochrane, and the attempt which his Lordship had made to capture or destroy the ships in the Charente. I said that it was the opinion of a very distinguished naval officer whom I named, and who was well known to him, that if Cochrane had been properly supported, he would have destroyed the whole of the French ships. 'He could not only have destroyed them,' replied Napoleon, 'but he might and would have taken them out, had your Admiral supported him as he ought to have done. For, in consequence of the signal made by L'Allemand' (I think he said) 'to the ships to do the best in their power to save themselves, *sauve qui peut* in fact, they became panic-struck and cut their cables. The terror of the *brûlots* (fire-ships) was so great that they actually threw their powder overboard, so that they could have offered very little resistance. The

French Admiral was an *imbécile*, but yours was just as bad.¹ I assure you that if Cochrane had been supported, he would have taken every one of the ships. They ought not to have been alarmed by your *brûlots*, but fear deprived them of their senses, and they no longer knew how to act in their own defence.'

When asking the Emperor some medical questions, he recounted the following anecdote : ' About seven years ago the Persian Ambassador in Paris fell ill and ordered a physician to be sent for. The messenger, not properly comprehending what he meant, thought that he wished to see a Minister of the Treasury, to whom he went and informed him that the Persian Ambassador desired to speak to him. The Minister, surprised, said, " This is a curious mode of acting, but those barbarians know nothing of etiquette, and perhaps he has something important to communicate." On his arrival the Ambassador held out his wrist that he should feel his pulse, and described his ailments. You may judge how the Minister was confounded at such a reception !'

November 5.—Napoleon remained in bed very late, not having had any sleep during the night. Found him not risen at eleven.

Saw him later in the day, and had some conversation about his brother Lucien.² He deprecated

---

[1] His name deserves to go down to history—Lord Gambier.

[2] ' Some one present informed the Emperor that Lucien had ready for the press another poem similar to his Charlemagne, to be entitled "Charles Martel in Corsica." It was added that he had likewise written a dozen tragedies. " Why, the devil's in him !" ex-

the cruelty and injustice of persecuting a literary character who did not meddle in politics, and who had even quarrelled with him. To persecute a man from whom no danger was to be apprehended two years after he (Napoleon) had been sent to St. Helena was the height of injustice. Such fear of an individual shows that they are conscious of acting contrary to the will of the people. '*Les tyrans tremblent pour leurs seuils.*' Here he made a quotation about Pluto trembling lest the earth should open and expose to view all the horrors of the infernal regions. 'What a degradation,' added he, 'to see the Ambassador of one of the greatest Powers in Europe persecuting an individual who has never been nor ever desired to be a sovereign.'

He also told me that one Ignatio Lorri (I think was the name), a Corsican and a foster-brother of his, had early in life entered the English sea-service. He was ignorant, though *un bravissimo uomo*, and an excellent seaman. He commanded an English storeship, and landed in ——,[1] where he went disguised as a peasant to see the French Consul. 'When he came into his presence,' continued Napoleon, 'he threw off his *cappotto*, showed the English uniform, and told him who he was. He claimed the Emperor. He was then informed that his brother Louis was the author of a novel. " His work may possess spirit and grace," said he; " but it will not be without a mixture of sentimental metaphysics and philosophic absurdity." '—*Las Cases*, vol. iii., part vi., p. 177, English edition.

[1] The name of the place is illegible in the manuscript of my journal.—B. E. O'M.

made many inquiries concerning me, without, however, offering to enter my service. The Consul did not believe him, and wrote a long history to Paris of an impostor who had presented himself to him, and claimed to be the Emperor's foster-brother. He was much astonished to find that I admitted it to be perfectly true. It is surprising that during all the height of my power this man never asked a favour of me, although in his childhood he loved me, and knew that, since my elevation, I had loaded his mother with favours and money.'

November 6.—Napoleon in rather better spirits, otherwise much the same. Spoke to me about an article which he had seen in the papers, stating that Talma had paid a reckoning for him at a tavern once, when through the want of money he had offered his sword in pledge. This he declared to be untrue, and he did not believe Talma had ever said so. 'I did not know Talma personally,' continued he, 'until I was First Consul. I then favoured and distinguished him very much as a man of talent and the first in the profession. I sometimes sent for him in the morning to discourse with me while I was at breakfast. The libellers said that Talma taught me how to act the Monarch! When I returned from Elba, I said one morning at my breakfast to Talma, who was present with some men of science, "*Eh bien, Talma*, so they say that you taught me how to sit upon my throne. *C'est un signe que je m'y tiens bien.*"'

Count Balmaine and Baron Sturmer had a long

interview with General Montholon yesterday. They rode up to the inner gate, where they remained for some time looking in. Signals are made to Plantation House whenever they come near Longwood, and a spy is generally sent to dog them from the town; but no direct attempts are made to prevent their intercourse with the inhabitants of Longwood.

November 8.—Napoleon observed that I walked lame, and asked if I had the gout. I replied in the negative, and said that it had been caused yesterday by a tight boot; that I never had the gout, and never had been confined to my bed a day in my life by illness. He then asked if my father had ever had that disease, and said that he would prescribe for my present complaint, by ordering me to eat nothing, drink barley-water, and keep my leg up on a sofa during the day. He then made some observations about his son, and said that his having been disinherited from the succession to Parma gave him little uneasiness. ' If he lives,' added he, ' he will be something. As to those contemptible little States, I would rather see him a *private gentleman*, with enough to eat, than Sovereign of any of them. Perhaps it may, however, grieve the Empress to think that he will not inherit after her; but it does not give me the smallest trouble.

'The Emperor Francis,' added he, 'whose head is crammed with ideas of high birth, was very anxious to prove that I was descended from some of the old tyrants of Treviso; and after my marriage with Marie Louise, employed divers persons to search into the old musty records of genealogy, in which they thought they could find something to prove what they desired.[1] He imagined that he had succeeded at last, and wrote to me, asking my consent that he should publish the account with all official formalities. I refused. He was so intent upon this favourite object that he again applied, and said, "*Laissez-moi faire*," that I need not appear to take any part in it. I replied that this was impossible, as, if published, I should be obliged to take notice of it; that I preferred being the son of an honest man to being descended from any little tyrant of Italy. That I was the Rodolph of my family.

'There was formerly,' added he, 'one Buonaventura Bonaparte, who lived and died a monk. The poor man lay quietly in his grave; nothing was thought about him until I was on the throne of France. It was then discovered that he had been possessed of many virtues which never had been attributed to him before, and the Pope proposed to me to canonise him. "*Saint Père*," said I, "*pour l'amour de Dieu épargnez-moi le ridicule de cela;*" you being in my power, all the world will say that I forced you to make a saint out of my family.'[2]

[1] See Chapter VII. of *Le Cabinet Noir* (d'Hérisson).
[2] 'When on his way to Florence, after the expedition to Leghorn, Napoleon slept at the house of an old Abbé Buonaparte, at San Miniato, who treated the whole of his staff with great magnificence. Having exhausted all the family recollections, the Abbé told the young General that he was going to bring forth the most precious document of all. Napoleon thought he was about to show him a fine

November 25.—Signal made for me to go to Plantation House, where I found Sir Hudson Lowe, who interrogated me upon various matters that had taken place at Longwood, and the conversations I had had with Napoleon. I replied that I had formed a determination not to meddle with what did not concern me, and only troubled myself about my professional pursuits. He said that I must have had some conversations not medical with him, and demanded to be informed of the subject of the con-

genealogical tree, well calculated to gratify his vanity (said he, laughing), but it was a memorial regularly drawn up in favour of Father Buonaventura Buonaparte, a capuchin friar of Bologna, long since beatified, but who had not yet been canonised, owing to the enormous expense it required. "The Pope will not refuse you," said the good Abbé, "if you ask him; and should it be necessary to pay the sum now, it will be a mere trifle for you." Napoleon laughed heartily at this simplicity, so little in harmony with the manners of the day; the old man never dreamt that the saints were no longer in fashion.

'On reaching Florence, Napoleon conceived it would be very satisfactory to his namesake to send him the ribbon of the Order of St. Stephen, of which he was merely a knight; but the pious Abbé was much less anxious about the favours of this world than the religious justice which he so pertinaciously claimed; and, as it afterwards appeared, not without reason. The Pope, when he came to Paris to crown the Emperor, also recurred to the claims of Father Buonaventura. "It was doubtless he," said the Pope, "who, from his seat amongst the blessed, had led his relative, as it were, by the hand through the glorious earthly career he had traversed, and who had preserved Napoleon in the midst of so many dangers and battles." The Emperor, however, always turned a deaf ear to these remarks; leaving it to the holy father's own discretion to provide for the glory of Buonaventura. As to the old Abbé of San Miniato, he left his fortune to Napoleon, who presented it to one of the public establishments in Tuscany.'—*Las Cases*, vol. i., part i., p. 101, English edition.

versations I had with General Bonaparte. I replied that in the first place nothing important had taken place; that in the next, I did not think myself bound to repeat the subject of such conversations as I had with Napoleon unless permitted, or unless matters came to my knowledge connected with my allegiance, or of great importance to my own Government.

Sir Hudson replied, 'You are no judge, sir, of the importance of the conversations you may have with General Bonaparte. I might consider several subjects of great importance which you consider as trifling or of no consequence.' I observed that if I was not at liberty to use my own discretion or judgment, I must necessarily repeat to him everything I heard, which would place me in the situation of a man acting a most dishonourable and disgraceful part. The Governor replied, 'That it was my *duty* to inform him of what circumstances came to my knowledge, and of the subject of my conversation with General Bonaparte; for if I did not, it was easily in his power to prohibit me from holding any communication with him except on medical subjects, and then only *when sent to* for that purpose. That it was a duty I owed to the English Government.' I answered that it would be acting the part of a spy, an informer, and a *mouton*. That I never understood the Government had placed me about him for other than medical purposes; that my duty did not require me to commit dishonourable actions; and that I would not do so for any person.

Sir Hudson remained silent for a few moments, eying me furiously, and asked what was the meaning of the word *mouton?* I replied, '*Mouton* means a person who insinuates himself into the confidence of another for the purpose of betraying it.' Sir Hudson then broke out into a paroxysm of rage; said that I had given him the greatest possible insult in his official capacity that could be offered, and concluded with ordering me to leave the room, saying that he would not permit a person who had made use of such language to sit in his presence. I told him that I did not voluntarily come into nor ever would have entered his house unless compelled to do so. He walked about in a frantic manner, repeating in a boisterous tone, 'Leave the room, sir,' which he continued bawling out for some moments after I had actually quitted it.

December 4.—Miss V——, a pretty girl, and *femme de chambre* to Lady Lowe, came to Longwood this day from Plantation House mounted on one of the Governor's horses, and furnished with a letter from Major Gorrequer, stating that Sir Hudson Lowe had forgotten to leave a pass for her before he went to town, and directing Captain Blakeney to admit her. She went to Longwood House, where she remained for near two hours, during which time she passed through almost every room in the building; the French domestics were so much enchanted with the apparition of a young and pretty girl, that their gallantry could scarcely refuse her anything. She was very desirous of obtaining admission to Napoleon, and at one time had partly opened the door of the room where he was, for the purpose of going in to him, but was prevented by St. Denis. She persuaded them, however, to allow her to peep at him for some time through the keyhole.[1]

December 7.—Informed Mr. Baxter that Napoleon had at last agreed to take some medicine, which I administered myself, and by which he had been temporarily benefited. Mr. Baxter agreed as to the propriety of affording him some other winter abode than the dreary and exposed situation of Longwood, where, in consequence of the bleak and eternal south-east wind, he generally caught cold whenever he went out. Mr. Baxter himself mentioned Rosemary Hall or Colonel Smith's as being the most suitable.

December 9.— Signal made for me to proceed to Plantation House. Soon after my arrival Sir Hudson Lowe said, with a serious air, that he had sent for me on business not medical, that he had grave occasion to censure my conduct, and then proceeded to ask if I had not kept up a correspondence, or was not the medium of communication for the French at Longwood, with persons on the island? I felt surprised at the question, and replied that I was ignorant of his meaning. He repeated his interrogations more than once, adding that he

[1] A few months afterwards the young woman left the island *enceinte*, if report be true, by one of the inmates of Plantation House, and was accompanied on board ship by Sir Thomas Reade, and great attention paid to her by the Governor.

did not mean communications to favour General Bonaparte's escape from the island, but of another nature. I replied that if going into shops and buying articles for Countesses Bertrand and Montholon, or others at Longwood, could be construed into carrying on communications or correspondence for them, I must certainly plead guilty. He then asked if I had not written to town to a person to send up some articles for Madame Bertrand? I replied, Certainly, that I had written to Mr. Darling to send up some articles of household use. The Governor said that it was a breach of orders, as he had prohibited me from being the bearer of any message or communication not medical. 'What business had I to do so? If Madame Bertrand wants anything of the kind, let her apply to the orderly officer; and why had she not done so?'

I replied that, in the first place, cleanliness was necessary to prevent sickness, and consequently everything relating to it was medical; that, in the next place, the orderly officer was absent from Longwood when the request was made to me; that, even if he had been present, delicacy would prevent a lady from making demands to him for articles which she could with propriety mention to her surgeon; and that I did not conceive it to be a crime to desire a tradesman to purchase similar articles either for Madame Bertrand or myself. His Excellency, as usual, flew into a violent passion, and said that he would not allow me to insult him in his capacity of Governor, and was otherwise very violent; asked me, 'How dare I order articles to be sent out of the King's stores without consulting him? or to have them charged to those stores?' I replied that I had said nothing about charging them to the King's stores. A reference was then made to my letter to Mr. Darling, which the Governor had in his possession, and which confirmed my statement.

I asked for written instructions in order to prevent the possibility of a mistake, which he refused to give. I then asked if the ladies required me to purchase articles for them in the shops, what reply was I to make? After some hesitation he said that 'if they wished me to purchase anything for them myself, I need not refuse, but that if they asked me to apply to another to purchase anything for them, I was not to comply with it!!'

Masséna, the Emperor observed on one occasion, when I was at Longwood, lost himself in the campaign of Portugal, owing to the bad state of his health, which did not permit him to sit on horseback, or inspect himself what was going on. 'A general who sees with the eyes of others,' added he, 'will never be able to command an army as it should be. Masséna was then so ill that he was obliged to trust to the reports of others, and consequently failed in some of his undertakings. At Busaco, for example, he attempted to carry a position almost impregnable in the manner he attacked it; whereas, if he had commenced by turning it, he would have succeeded. This was owing to his not being able to reconnoitre personally.' He added, 'That if Masséna had been what he was formerly, he would have followed Wellington so closely as to be able to attack him,[1] while entering the lines before Lisbon, before he could have taken up his position properly.

December 14.—Sir Hudson Lowe came to Longwood. Asked me several questions about Napoleon's health. Observed that it was very extraordinary he did not take exercise; that if he expected, by confining himself, to obtain any further relaxation in the system adopted, he was mistaken. He then inquired if the want of sleep was caused by mental or by bodily disease. I said that I thought it was chiefly caused by the want of exercise; that no active man, leading such a life as Napoleon did, could possibly remain long in a state of health. The Governor said with a sneer that *he* believed *laziness* was the cause of his not taking exercise. I replied that when he first came to the island he had taken a great deal. He then said that he wanted to have information of his state of health more frequently, and desired me to mention anything extraordinary to Captain Blakeney. I said that it would be very easy to arrange matters, by sending him bulletins describing Napoleon as 'the patient,' giving copies to Count Bertrand at the same time. This he refused to allow, saying that as long as verbal reports could be got, he did

[1] Speaking of the Duke of Wellington on a former occasion, he observed that all generals were liable to err, and that whoever committed the least number of faults should be esteemed to be the greatest, and that Wellington had committed them as seldom as most others.—B. E. O'M.

not think written ones of consequence. He also made some insinuations about his not having seen Mr. Baxter.

In the course of conversation this day Napoleon expressed his disapprobation of our custom of shutting up shops and prohibiting people from working on Sundays. In reply to what I said he remarked, 'For those who are at their ease, it may be very right and proper to discontinue working on the seventh day, but to oblige a poor man who has a large family, without a meal to give them, to leave off labouring to procure them food, is the height of barbarity. If such a law be enforced, provision ought to be made by your Government to feed those who, on that day, have not wherewithal to purchase food, and who could obtain it if permitted to labour. Or let your greedy priests give a portion of their dinners on that day to the starving poor whom they will not allow to work. They would have an apoplexy or an indigestion the less. Besides, it does not serve the cause of morality. Idleness is the mother of mischief, and I will wager that there is more drunkenness to be seen, that there is more vice, and that more crimes are committed in England on a Sunday than on any other day of the week.'

Speaking of the possibility of amalgamating the negroes with the whites, Napoleon observed that it had occurred to him that the only mode of effectually reconciling the two colours would be to allow polygamy in the colonies, and that every black or white man should be permitted to have a wife of each colour. By such means he thought that, in the next generation, nearly all would be alike, and consequently all jealousy and hatred dispelled.[1] He added that it would have been easy to have obtained a dispensation from the Pope to that effect.

Saw Napoleon again in the evening; he made some observations about the Governor, who, he observed, had passed by his windows. 'I never see that Governor,' said he, 'without thinking I behold the man heating the poker for your Edward the Second in Berkeley Castle. *La nature m'a prévenu contre*, and gave me a friendly warning the first day I saw him. *Comme Caïn, la nature l'a bien cacheté.* If I were in London, and Sir H. Lowe were presented to me *en bourgeois*, and I were asked, Whom do you conceive that man to be? I should reply, *C'est le bourreau de la municipalité.* You cannot say,' added he, 'that it arises from prejudice against your nation, as I have never been so with Cockburn. Never did I for a moment, as you well know, suspect or distrust him in the slightest manner. From him I would readily have received a surgeon or anything else. I had every confidence in him, even after we had differed. This Governor wanted to encircle the house with *grilles de fer*, in order to make the second *cage de fer de Bajazet*, for which purpose he put his Government to the useless expense of sending out a shipload of iron rails.'

[1] See Froude's recently published work, *The English in the West Indies.*

I recommended him to see Mr. Baxter, adding that it would be a satisfaction to me to have the assistance of the advice and opinion of another medical man. He replied, 'He has been recommended by the Governor, and that, is sufficient to prevent me from ever seeing him.

'If I, *malheureusement*,' added he, 'had such a physiognomy, the world would then believe the libellers. Look, they would say, oh, look at the countenance of the *scélérat!* See the murders of Wright, of Pichegru, and of a thousand others stamped on the visage of the monster!'[1]

[1] The acrimony entertained towards the Emperor Napoleon even when deceased is exemplified by a reply which it is said escaped from the lips of an Under-Secretary of State, who, when informed that, a short time before his dissolution, Napoleon ordered that his body should be opened, his heart taken out, preserved in spirits of wine, and sent to the Empress Marie Louise, replied, '*It ought to have been thrown into quick-lime.*' When Napoleon was sent to St. Helena, it was expressly stated, in the regulations for his safe custody, that should he die in that island, his body should be interred wherever he thought proper to order it in his will. This promise, however, was not kept for many years. In the codicil to his will, which was made known to the Ministers, the following words are to be found:—

'LONGWOOD, *Avril le* 16, 1821.,

'*Ceci est un codicille de mon testament.* 1°. *Je désire que mes cendres reposent sur les bords de la Seine, au milieu de ce peuple Français que j'ai tant aimé.*

(*Signé*) 'NAPOLÉON.'

His remains were refused, a year after his demise, to the prayers of his aged mother, and nearly twenty years elapsed before the French Government permitted them to be transferred to the banks of the Seine.

CHAPTER IV

1818

JANUARY 1.—Napoleon nearly in the same state as yesterday.

Some conversation took place upon Mr. Hobhouse's book, which, as has been already stated, had been sent by the author and detained by Sir Hudson Lowe.[1] I said that it had been seen by accident in Sir Hudson's library by the person who had acquainted him (Napoleon) with the circumstance. 'It was a *bêtise* in the Governor,' said he, 'after he had illegally detained it, to leave it where any person might see it.

'In Cardinal Richelieu's time, a nobleman who waited upon him to ask some favour was ushered into his private cabinet. While they were conversing a greater personage entered the room. After some conversation with Richelieu, the great man took his leave, and the Cardinal, in compliment to him, attended him to his carriage, forgetting that he had left the other alone in his cabinet. On his return he rang a bell, and one of his confidential

[1] See *ante*, vol. i. p. 88

secretaries entered, to whom he whispered something. He then conversed with the other very freely, appeared to take an interest in his affairs, accompanied him to the door, shook hands, and took leave in the most friendly way, telling him that he might make his mind easy, as he had determined to provide for him. The poor man departed highly satisfied and full of gratitude. As he was going out of the door he was arrested, not allowed to speak to any person, and conveyed in a coach to the Bastille, where he was kept *au secret* for ten years; at the expiration of which time the Cardinal sent for him, and expressed his great regret at having been obliged to adopt the step he had taken; that he had no cause of complaint against him; on the contrary, that he believed him to be a good subject to His Majesty; but the fact was, he had left a paper on the table when he quitted the room containing State secrets of vast importance, which he was afraid he might have perused in his absence; that the safety of the kingdom obliged him to adopt measures to prevent the possibility of its contents being known. That as soon as the safety of the country permitted, he had released him; he begged his pardon for the uneasiness he had caused him, and would be happy to make him some amends.'

Sentiments relative to the French Revolution were also expressed by Napoleon, and arguments adduced in favour of the validity of the Imperial title. 'The Republic sent to and received from all the Powers of Europe ambassadors. It was sanctioned by the will of the people, by victory, by religion, and by all the nations of Europe. Louis, driven from one state to another, was at last obliged to seek for refuge in England, but was received there as a private person, and on the express stipulation that he should only assume the title of the Comte de Lille. None of the Powers ever acknowledged Louis the Seventeenth, or Louis the Eighteenth. Every legitimate Government cancels the rights and the legitimacy of the Governments which precede it. The French Revolution was a general movement of the mass of the nation against the privileged classes. The nobles retained the administration of justice and other feudal rights; enjoyed the privilege of being exempt from the burthens of the community, and exclusively possessed all honourable employments. The chief object of the Revolution was to destroy those privileges and abuses, to abolish the manorial courts, suppress the remains of the ancient servitude of the people, and render all citizens equally liable to bear the expenses of the State. It established equality of rights. Any citizen might succeed to any office according to his talents. Before, France was composed of provinces unequal in extent and in population. They had a great variety of legal customs and peculiar laws for the administration of civil as well as criminal justice. France was an assemblage of several states without amalgamation. The Revolution destroyed those little nations and formed a new one. There was one France, with an homogeneous division of territory, the same civil and criminal laws, and the same regulations for taxes throughout the land.

'Subsequently the French nation established the Imperial throne, and placed me upon it. No person ever ascended a throne with more legitimate rights. The throne of France was granted before to Hugues Capet by a few bishops and nobles. The Imperial throne was given to me by the desire of the people, whose wishes were three times verified in a solemn manner. The Pope crossed the Alps to crown and anoint me.[1] Kings hastened to acknowledge me. England acknowledged the Republic and sent Ambassadors to the First Consul. Before she violated the Peace of Amiens, the English Ministers offered, through Malhouet, to acknowledge me as King of France if I would agree to the cession of Malta; and in 1806 Lord Lauderdale came to Paris to treat for a peace between the King of Great Britain and *the Emperor Napoleon*, exchanged his powers, and negotiated with the Plenipotentiary of *the Emperor*. If Fox had lived, peace would have been made.[2] Moreover, the Imperial title was acknowledged by Lord Castlereagh when he signed the *ultimatum* at Chaumont.'

[1] Upon this occasion the Lord's prayer was printed in two hundred different languages at the Imperial Press, and a copy magnificently bound for the occasion, with studs and bosses of solid gold upon fine morocco emblazoned with the arms of the Pope.

[2] A draft of the proposed terms in the autograph of Fox is at Upton.

January 2.—Went to Plantation House by order of the Governor, whom I saw in the library. He asked a great many questions concerning my appointment as surgeon to Napoleon, and concluded by asserting that I was not his surgeon, but only *tolerated to visit him*. I observed that the bills which I drew for my pay on the Navy Board, the form of which had been ordered by Sir George Cockburn, were worded, 'as surgeon to Napoleon Bonaparte and suite.' I also took the liberty of asking him for what object I was at St. Helena?

He asked me 'if I conceived myself to be independent of him as Governor, and of the Government under whose orders I acted?' I replied that no British officer could be independent of the Government of his country. He then asked, 'Whether I conceived myself independent of *him*, and if it were not in his power as Governor, and having charge of Napoleon Bonaparte, if he thought that my conduct was not correct, to send me away if he pleased?' I told him that he could reply to that himself, as he best knew what the extent of his authority was. This answer did not please him, and after walking about the room for a little time exclaiming against my conduct, he stopped, crossed his arms, and after looking at me with an expression of countenance which I shall never forget, said, 'This is my office, sir, and there is the door leading to it. When I send for you on duty, you will come in at that door; but do not put your foot in any other part of my house, or come in at any other entrance.'

I replied that it was not for my own pleasure, or by my own desire, that I ever set foot in any part of his house; and after suffering this paltry abuse of authority, departed.

Saw Napoleon, who was nearly in the same state as yesterday. Had some conversation relative to the capture of Rome by the French. 'After the treaty which I had concluded at Tolentino with that incapable yet intriguing Court of old women at Rome,' said Napoleon, 'they endeavoured by all means to assist the Austrians, and even placed an Austrian general at the head of their troops. Everywhere the populace were excited by all the means generally put in practice by superstition and bigotry to massacre the French. General Duphot, who was residing at Rome as a private person, was murdered at the door of my brother Joseph, who was Ambassador there. However, under all the circumstances, and concluding that a rupture with Rome would infallibly lead to one with Naples, I was of opinion that we ought only to punish but not destroy her; that we ought to demand that an example should be made of the guilty; that Provera, the Austrian General, should be obliged to depart, and an Ambassador sent to Paris to beg pardon. The Directory, however, decided that we should march against the Pope, and said that the time was come to overturn that idol. Berthier was sent with an army to revolutionise Rome and establish a Republic, which was done. The people at first were transported with joy at the thought of the re-establishment of the Roman Republic, and fêtes were given, and a *Te Deum* celebrated with great pomp; at which last a number of the Cardinals attended, although the act of re-establishment was the annihilation of the Pope's temporal power. Their joy, however, was of short duration, as the troops, who were little restrained by their generals, and excited by agents of yours and of the Austrians, plundered the Vatican and the palaces of the nobles of their pictures and pieces of art of all kinds, and finished by mutinying against the *imbéciles*, who saw their error too late, and endeavoured in vain to put a stop to these abuses.

'When the Venetians,' continued Napoleon, 'deceived by false reports that Joubert's army had been defeated and cut to pieces, and duped by the traitorous and Machiavellian policy of the court of Vienna, armed a number of Sclavonians and peasants, the priests preached destruction to the French, and another Sicilian Vespers. All the French in Verona were massacred, and their bodies thrown into the Adige. Four hundred of the sick and wounded in the hospitals were barbarously murdered. In other towns in the Venetian territories similar cruelties were practised. As soon as they discovered that the army of Joubert was intact, that Augereau was marching against them, and that the Austrians, defeated everywhere, had sent to me to supplicate for peace, their fright knew no bounds. A deputation waited upon me, making the most submissive proposals; pledging themselves to agree to everything I should require, and offering me millions if I would grant their prayers. Finding this useless, orders were despatched to their Minister at Paris to corrupt the Directory, in which they succeeded, as orders were sent of a nature favourable to their wishes.[1] The despatches of their Ambassador, however, were seized and brought to me, and the whole intrigue was discovered, together with the amount of the bribes they had given. I ordered the French Minister to quit their territories within twenty-four hours, and declared war against Venice. Baraguay d'Hilliers entered it with his division, upset the oligarchy, and the whole of the States were soon republicanised.'

January 9.—Another series of interrogations at Plantation House, partly about Lord Amherst, during which the Governor said that 'General Bonaparte would not have dared to make use of the insulting expressions he did before any other.persons than Lord Amherst and myself; that General Bonaparte had so expressed himself, because he knew that his Lordship had received the Governor's permission to listen to any complaints which he might make; that a listener was as bad as a repeater; and that Count Bertrand had told him (Sir Hudson) in October last that General Bonaparte was influenced by the persons about him, amongst whom I formed one.' I could scarcely help smiling

[1] See also p. 190 of this volume.

at the supposition that *I* could have influenced such a person as Napoleon, and contented myself with replying that, as far as I knew him, he was not a man to let himself be guided by the opinion of others. Sir Hudson, however, insisted that Count Bertrand had confessed it, and said that *I* should be responsible for a great deal of what might happen, etc.

January 13.—More interrogations at Plantation House. Sir Hudson Lowe took out of his pocket a *Morning Chronicle* of September 17, 1817 (I think), containing a detail of a conversation stated to have taken place between Napoleon and some English gentlemen, and was desirous, he said, 'to know from me whether such a conversation had ever taken place between General Bonaparte and myself, or if I had ever communicated it to other persons. That he inferred from the commencement of the article, viz.—

'*After the usual salutations,*' . . . that the conversation had taken place between General Bonaparte and some person who was in the habit of seeing him frequently; that Admiral Malcolm and myself were the only persons who had *tête-à-tête* conversations with him; therefore that it must have been communicated by one of us.' I replied that I had neither written nor communicated it, and reminded him that others besides the Admiral and myself had communications with Napoleon. His Excellency appeared to be very anxious that I should assist him to saddle it upon the Admiral; in which, however, he did not succeed. Indeed, on the first glance I had of it, I saw that it must have come from Mr. Ellis; it, however, contained some misrepresentations.

January 15.—Saw the Governor at Plantation House, to whom I reported that Napoleon's indisposition had rather increased, and that I had been that morning under the necessity of giving him physic. Communicated the same to Mr. Baxter.

January 16.—Saw Napoleon, who felt somewhat relieved by the effect of the physic administered yesterday.

January 20.—Went to Plantation House, according to orders. While speaking to Mr. Baxter in the library, the Governor came in, looking very angry, and asked in a rough and abrupt manner what communications I had to make respecting General Bonaparte's health? I replied that no permanent change for the better had taken place. 'Has he been out of the house?'—'He has not.'—'Has he been in the billiard-room?'—'He spends a considerable portion of his time there every day.'—'How does he employ his time there?'—'I cannot tell, sir.'—'Yes, you can, sir,' replied the Governor, regarding me in his customary manner; 'you well know what he does there; you do not do your duty to Government.'

His Excellency then walked about the room, stopping occasionally with his arms crossed over his breast and regarding me in a manner which it is difficult to describe, and uttering furious exclamations.

I contented myself with taking out my watch to ascertain how long he contemplated me in this manner. I thought more than once that he meditated some act of violence. This composure and silence appeared not to be what he wished, and he began another series of interrogations relative to the name of the person who had given me information about twelve months ago, that Lord Liverpool had interfered to prevent my removal from St. Helena. I answered that I had, at the time I had first mentioned it to him in July last, offered to show to a third person that part of the letter which stated that application had been made to Lord Liverpool to prevent my being removed. The Governor renewed in a violent tone his demand that I should forthwith give him the name of the person who had informed me, and said that the offer I had then made of showing it to a third person was an insult to him. I answered as before, which drew forth another demand for the name with an increase of violence. I said then that as my replies only brought upon me bad language and bad treatment, I must decline giving him any more answers on the subject. 'Put down, Major Gorrequer, that Mr. O'Meara refuses to answer,' was the Governor's reply. After a long and abusive harangue about my improper conduct since he had catechised me about a newspaper (*id est*, since I had refused to be an instrument to calumniate Admiral Malcolm), I was permitted to depart.

January 28.—Saw Napoleon, who was rather

better than on the preceding day. Had some conversation about Châteaubriand. 'Châteaubriand,' said he, 'is an old *émigré*, who was appointed secretary to Cardinal Fesch, when the latter was Ambassador to the Vatican, where he contrived to render himself disliked by the Pope and the Cardinals, notwithstanding the *galimatias* which he had published upon Christianity. While he was there, he endeavoured to persuade the old King of Sardinia, who had abdicated and turned *religieux*, to renew his claims to the throne of Sardinia. The King, suspecting him to be a *mouton, le mit à la porte*, and made a complaint to me of his conduct, which caused his disgrace. While I was in power, he was one of the most abject of my flatterers. *C'est un fanfaron sans caractère, qui a l'âme rampante, et qui a la fureur de faire des livres.'*

I asked him some questions about Bernadotte's conduct. 'Bernadotte,' said he, 'was ungrateful to me, as I was the author of his greatness; but I cannot say that he betrayed me; he in a manner became a Swede, and never promised that which he did not intend to perform. Neither Murat nor he would have declared against me had they thought that it would have lost me my throne. Their wish was to diminish my power, but not to destroy me altogether.

'Labédoyère,' said he, 'was animated by the noblest sentiments and a sovereign contempt for a race which had surrounded itself with all that was most foreign to the manners and rights of the French; and with a set of *misérables* who, to avoid starvation, had vegetated for twenty-five years in inferior and disgraceful situations. His attachment to me was enthusiastic, and he declared himself at the moment of the greatest danger.'

Drouot he described as one of the most virtuous and unassuming characters in France, though possessed of talent rarely to be met with. Drouot was a man who would live as contentedly, as far as regarded himself personally, upon forty sous a day as if he had the revenues of a sovereign. He was charitable and religious; and a man whose morals, probity, and simplicity would have been honoured in an age of stern republicanism.[1]

[1] 'To-day the Emperor again reviewed the character of his generals. He passed an eulogium on several of them who are now no more. He also bestowed the highest praise on the talents of General Drouot. He observed that Drouot possessed every quality necessary to make a great general. He had reasons for supposing him superior to many of his marshals, and had no hesitation in believing him capable of commanding one hundred thousand men. "And, perhaps," added he, "he was far from thinking so himself, which, after all, can only be regarded as an additional good quality." He again alluded to the prodigious valour of Murat and Ney, whose courage, he said, so often exceeded their judgment, that they might have been capable of the greatest absurdities if it could have been supposed possible in a case in which they had well considered the danger. Such is the mystery, said he, of certain actions in certain individuals: the inequality between temper and understanding explains all. The conversation turned on the battle of Hohenlinden. The Emperor remarked that it was one of those great triumphs that are brought about by chance and obtained without plan: Moreau, he repeated, was destitute of invention; he was not sufficiently decided; and, therefore, he was most fit to be employed on the defensive. Hohenlinden was a confused sort of affair; the enemy had been unexpectedly attacked amidst his own operations, and was conquered by troops whom he had himself penetrated and nearly destroyed. The merit rested chiefly

January 30.—Went to Plantation House. After some questions relative to Napoleon's state of health, Sir Hudson Lowe said that he had heard, in an indirect manner, that General Bonaparte was in a much worse state of health than I had reported; that he desired, therefore, whenever I went to town, that I would mention to Mr. Baxter or Sir Thomas Reade the state of his health, which might prevent the necessity of my then coming to Plantation House to report. That I might now mention to Major Gorrequer what I had to say about his health. Accordingly, I gave the Major full medical details. I also applied for a small still, in order to make some orange-flower water, as there was none to be had on the island; which to Napoleon would have been very grateful, and indeed necessary.[1]

February 3.—The *Cambridge* storeship arrived bringing the melancholy news of the death of the Princess Charlotte.

Napoleon expressed his affliction at the unfortunate event: as, independent of the feelings which naturally arose at the fate of a princess, cut off in the prime of youth and beauty, and with such prospects before her, he said that he had not been without hope that she would have caused a more liberal policy to be adopted towards himself. He

with the troops and generals of the partisan corps who had been most exposed to danger, and who had fought like heroes.'—*Las Cases*, vol. ii., part iv., p. 290, English edition.

[1] This request was never complied with, although frequently repeated.—B. E. O'M.

inveighed against the accoucheurs, and expressed his surprise that the populace had not stoned them to death. He observed that the business had a strange appearance, and that precautions appeared to have been taken to deprive the princess of everything necessary to support and to console her on a first accouchement. It was unpardonable in the old Queen not to have been on the spot. 'What signified, Leopold,' said he ; 'he is a *garçon*, and knew not what to do. Had it not been for me,' added he, 'Marie Louise would have died in a similar manner. Dubois came to me with great alarm painted on his countenance, and said "that the Empress was in a state of great danger—that there was a wrong presentation." I asked him if he had ever seen anything of the kind before. Dubois replied "that he had but very rarely, perhaps not one in a thousand, and that it was very afflicting to him that so extraordinary a case should happen with the Empress."—"Forget," said I, "that she is Empress, and treat her as you would the wife of a petty shopkeeper in the Rue St. Denis. This is the only favour I ask of you." Dubois then asked, " If it were necessary that one should be sacrificed, which should he save, the mother or the child ?"—" The mother certainly," I replied ; "it is her right." I then accompanied Dubois to the bedside, and encouraged and tranquillised the Empress as much as possible. The child was apparently dead when born, but by frictions and other means he was restored to life. His birth produced a delirium of joy in the nation.

On the discharge of the first gun that announced the interesting event all the population of Paris, in the greatest suspense, ran into the streets, the public walks, and the parks, counting the number of guns. Twenty-one guns were to have been fired for the birth of a princess, and one hundred and one for a prince. At the discharge of the twenty-second gun the Parisians rent the skies with acclamations and expressions of universal delight. Almost all the powers of Europe sent Ambassadors extraordinary to compliment me on the happy event. The Emperor of Austria was represented by his brother, the Duke of Würtzburg, and the Emperor Alexander sent his Minister for the Home Department to Paris to express his satisfaction on the occasion.[1]

[1] Shortly after the birth of young Napoleon, his father contemplated building a superb palace nearly opposite to the *Pont d'Jena*, which was to have been called *Le Palais du Roi de Rome*. The Government consequently endeavoured to purchase all the houses situated upon the ground where it was intended to be built. One of these belonged to a poor cooper named Bonvivant, which, at the highest estimation, was not worth more than a thousand francs. The owner demanded ten thousand francs. The Emperor ordered that it should be purchased at that price. When the proper persons waited upon the cooper to conclude the agreement, he said that, upon reflection, he should not sell it for less than thirty thousand francs. It was referred to Napoleon, who directed that it should be given to him. The cooper next increased his demand to forty thousand. The architect was greatly embarrassed, and did not know how he could again approach the Emperor on the subject; at the same time he knew that it was impossible to conceal anything from him. He therefore addressed him again on the subject. '*Ce drôle là abuse*,' said he, '*pourtant il n'y a pas d'autre moyen; allons il faut payer.*' The architect returned to the cooper, who increased his price to fifty

'No sooner was it known,' continued Napoleon, 'that the interests of France had induced me to dissolve the ties of my marriage than the greatest sovereigns of Europe schemed for an alliance with me. As soon as the Emperor of Austria heard that a new marriage was on the tapis, he sent for Narbonne, and expressed his surprise that his family had not been thought of. At this time an union with a Princess of Russia or of Saxony was contemplated. The Cabinet of Vienna sent instructions on the subject to Prince Schwartzenberg, who was Ambassador at Paris.[1] Despatches were also received from the Ambassador in Russia, stating the willingness of the Emperor Alexander to offer his sister, the Grand Duchess Anne. A Privy Council

thousand francs. Napoleon, indignant, when informed of it said. ' *Cet homme là est un misérable, et bien je n'achetterai point la maison, et elle restera comme un monument de mon respect pour les loix.*' The Bourbons returned, razed the foundation of the intended palace, and threw down what had been erected ; the cooper's hovel fell to ruins, and its master, M. Bonvivant, retired to Passy, Rue Basse, No. 31, where he earned a miserable subsistence by his trade.—B. E. O'M.

[1] 'The Emperor, at one of his levees, having been obliged to wait some time for the Comte de S——, attacked him on his arrival, openly, in the presence of all. It happened to be precisely at the time when five or six kings (and among others, those of Bavaria, Saxony, and Würtemberg) were at Paris. "Sire," replied the guilty courtier, "I have no doubt a million of excuses to make to Your Majesty, but at this time one is not at perfect liberty to go through the streets as one pleases. I just now had the misfortune to get into a *crowd of kings*, from which I found it impossible to extract myself sooner. This, Sire, was the cause of my delay." Every one smiled, and the Emperor contented himself with saying, in a very softened tone of voice, "Whatever, sir, may be the cause, take proper precautions for the future, and above all, never make me wait again."'[1]—*Las Cases*, vol. iii., part v., p. 138, English edition.

was held upon the subject, and the votes of the majority were for an Austrian princess. I consequently authorised Prince Eugene to make the overture to Prince Schwartzenberg, and articles of marriage, similar to those between Louis the Sixteenth and Marie Antoinette, were signed. The Emperor Alexander was not pleased that his overtures were slighted, and thought that he had been deceived, and that two negotiations had been carried on at the same time, in which he was mistaken.'

February 10.—No improvement has taken place in Napoleon's health. Had some conversation with him relative to the marriage of the Princess Elizabeth with the Prince of Hesse Homburg. 'The English royal family,' said he, '*va incanagliarsi*[1] with little petty princes, to whom I would not have given a brevet of *sous-lieutenant*. When I marched upon Ulm in 1805, I passed through Stuttgardt with my army, where I saw your Princess Royal, the Queen of Würtemberg,[2] with whom I had several

---

[1] A word probably invented by Napoleon, and intended to convey degradation in a very strong manner.—B. E. O'M.

[2] I have been informed, from a source entitled to the highest credit, that the Queen of Würtemberg wrote an account of this interview to her mother, Queen Charlotte, in which she expressed very favourable opinions of Napoleon, and, in describing his person, concluded in the following manner : '*and he has so bewitching a smile.*' [See also the *Memoirs of Napoleon*, by the Duchesse d'Abrantés, in which she says, 'It is difficult, if not impossible, to describe the charm of his countenance when he smiled; his soul was upon his lips and in his eyes. The magic power of that expression is well known. The Emperor of Russia had experienced it when he said to me, "I never loved any one more than that man !"'—1836 edition, vol. ii. p. 297.]

conversations, and was much pleased with her. She soon lost whatever prejudices she might have originally entertained against me. I had the pleasure of interfering to her advantage when her husband, who was a brute, though a man of talent, had ill-treated her, for which she was very grateful to me. She afterwards contributed materially towards effecting the marriage between my brother Jerome and the Princess Catherine, daughter of the King by a former marriage.'

February 16.—While in Jamestown, I was asked by Mr. Barber of the Cambridge, who had opened a shop in the town, 'How did Bonaparte like the portraits?' Being ignorant of his meaning, I asked for explanations. He said that I surely must know what he alluded to, and after some further conversation informed me that he had brought out two engravings of young Napoleon for sale, thinking that it would please the French, and induce them to give him some custom. That on his arrival he had mentioned the circumstance, and that both the portraits had been taken by the Governor and Sir Thomas Reade, Sir Hudson Lowe declaring that he was glad to have an opportunity of sending such articles to Bonaparte. Mr. Barber appeared much surprised and disappointed when he learned from me that they had not reached Longwood.[1]

February 17.—Went to Plantation House. The

---

[1] On my departure from St. Helena in August 1818, neither of the engravings had been sent to the father. B. E. O'M.

Governor, after having made some inquiries about the state of Napoleon's health and that of General Gourgaud, asked whether I had complied with the desire he had expressed on the 21st, that I should show to Captain Blakeney the letter in which Lord Liverpool's name was mentioned? I replied that as he had left it to my option, whether to show it or not, I had preferred the latter, seeing that the business had occurred a long time ago; that at the *time* I had offered to show it, which he had refused, and also because he had said he considered the offer to show it as an insult. That it was necessary for me to be very cautious, and as I did not know why I was now required to show the letter, I had declined doing so. His Excellency was not pleased with this reply, and began to abuse me in his customary manner, saying that 'I constantly insulted him as Governor.' I replied that it never had been my intention to insult him either in word or deed; that I was very sorry if constructions, so foreign to my intentions, should have been put upon them.

Sir Hudson Lowe then got up, and, looking at me in a menacing manner, said, 'Upon your word of honour, sir, I ask you if you have had any conversations with Napoleon Bonaparte upon other than medical subjects for a month past?' I replied, 'Perhaps there may have been on other subjects not interesting!'—'I do not allow *you*, sir, to be a judge of whether they were interesting or otherwise. You have no authority for holding any communications with Napoleon Bonaparte unless upon medical subjects, and then only when sent to for that purpose. Have you had any communication with any other person of his household?'—'Certainly, sir, I have had.' Without waiting to know whether those communications were medical or otherwise, he burst out with, 'You have no authority, sir, to hold any communication whatsoever with any of his household who are subject to the same restrictions as himself unless upon medical subjects, and then only when sent for; and when finished, you are to leave them. You have no business to go amongst them unless for medical purposes. Have you, sir, had any communication with any of them upon other subjects?' I replied by referring His Excellency to his own orders, that I should not hold any other communication than medical with them. 'This reply, sir, as usual, is not a direct one. You make it a practice to go to town when ships arrive, which I do not approve of. You go to collect news for General Bonaparte.' I answered, 'That I was an English officer, and as such would not give up my rights; moreover, that I, as well as others, was desirous of purchasing the necessaries of life as soon as they were landed, and before any monopoly took place to increase the price. That, if he intended to prohibit me from going to town, I had to request orders to that effect in writing.'

This Sir Hudson refused, saying with a sneer, 'The request is worthy of the place you came from and the people with whom you associate. I do not think a person under a pledge to Napoleon Bonaparte ought to be received in society, and I do not approve of your going to town when ships arrive. You are suspected by me, sir.' I replied, 'That I was under no other pledge to Napoleon than one which was tacitly understood in every society of gentlemen.' The Governor said, 'That it was presumption and insolence for me to dare to judge of the line of conduct His Majesty's Government had thought proper to pursue with respect to Napoleon Bonaparte.' I replied that I did not attempt to judge of that—that I merely mentioned what was the custom of society. 'You are a suspected man, sir; you are suspected by *me.*'—' I cannot help that, sir. It is a consolation to me, however, under such circumstances to have the *mens conscia recti.*' This the Governor said was a fresh insult. 'You took an opportunity, sir, of staying in town the other day when a ship arrived instead of coming here to report, as you ought to have done,' said His Excellency, after he had a little recovered his breath. 'It was in compliance with your own instructions, sir, of the 30th of January. You then told me, in the presence of Major Gorrequer, that when I saw Mr. Baxter or Sir Thomas Reade in town, it might supersede the necessity of my coming to Plantation House on that day. Having, therefore, seen and explained to Mr. Baxter on that day what I had to say, I did not think it necessary to come up here.' He endeavoured to shuffle this off. I appealed to Major Gorrequer, if I had not repeated His Excellency's own words? The Governor said, in not the most moderate manner, that this appeal was an insult to him, and burst forth into a fresh paroxysm of invective, which lasted for a considerable time.

February 18.—Napoleon more lively than he has been for a few days.

He spoke of the plans which he had upon England.

'Had I succeeded in effecting a landing,' said he, 'I have very little doubt that I should have accomplished my views. Three thousand boats, each to carry twenty men and one horse, with a proportion of artillery, were ready. Your fleet having been decoyed away, as I before explained to you, would have left me master of the Channel. Without this I would not have made the attempt. Four days would have brought me to London. In a country like England, abounding in plains, defence is very difficult. I have no doubt that your troops would have done their duty, but one battle lost, the capital would have been in my power. You could not have collected a force sufficiently strong to beat me in a pitched battle. Your ideas of burning and destroying the towns and the capital itself are very plausible in argument, but impracticable in their accomplishment. You would have fought a battle and lost it. "Well, then," you would say, "we have been beaten, but we have not lost our honour. We shall now endeavour *de tirer le meilleur parti* from our misfortune. We must make terms." I would have offered you a Constitution of your own choice and have said, "Assemble in London deputies from the people to fix upon a Constitution." I would have called upon Burdett and other popular leaders to organise one according to the wishes of the people. I would have declared the King fallen from the throne, abolished the nobility, proclaimed liberty, freedom, and equality. Think you, that in order to keep the house of Guelph on the throne, your rich citizens, merchants, and others of London would have consented to sacrifice their riches, their houses, their families, and all their dearest interests, especially when I had made them comprehend that I only came to give them liberty? No, it is contrary to history and to human nature. You are too rich. Your principal people have too much to lose by resistance, and your *canaille* too much to gain by a change. If they supposed that I wanted to render England a province of France, then indeed *l'esprit national* would do wonders. But I would have formed a Republic according to your own wishes, required a moderate contribution, barely sufficient to have paid the troops, and perhaps not even that. You talk of your freedom! Can anything be more horrible than your pressing of seamen? You send your boats on shore to seize upon all the males that can be found who, if they have the misfortune to belong to the *canaille*, if they cannot prove themselves *gentlemen*, are hurried on board your ships, to serve as seamen in all quarters of the globe. And yet you have the impudence to talk of the conscription in France; it wounded your pride because it fell *upon all ranks*. Oh, how shocking that a *gentleman's* son (in English) should be obliged to defend his country, just as if he were one of the *canaille!* And that he should be compelled to expose his body, or put himself on a level with a *plebeian!*

'That conscription,' continued Napoleon, 'which offended your *morgue aristocratique* so much, was conducted scrupulously according to the principle of equal rights. Every native of a country is bound to defend it. The conscription did not *écraser* a particular class like your press-gang, nor the *canaille*, because they were poor. It was the most just, because the most equal mode of raising troops. It rendered the French army the best composed in the world.[1] The conscription would have become a national institution instead of being regarded as a punishment or a servitude. It would have been

---

[1] I was informed by the Duke of Rovigo, and by many other officers who had served with the Emperor, that the humanity he displayed to his soldiers was on all occasions exemplary. That he was frequently in the habit of riding over the field of battle after an action, accompanied by members of his staff, and by persons carrying restoratives of different kinds for the purpose of resuscitating any of the wounded, in whom signs of life appeared, and that Napoleon had often spent hours in this pious employment. Amongst other instances, the Duke of Rovigo mentioned that after the battle of Wagram, Napoleon, accompanied by him and several others, rode over the field, and pointed out many of the wounded for assistance. While employed in this manner, the body of a colonel named Pepin, who had fallen under his displeasure for some misconduct several years before, and had not been actively employed until a short time before the battle of Wagram, attracted his attention, though he had not seen him for a number of years. He was on his back, a ball had perforated his head, and life

a point of honour to have served the country, and the time would have come that a girl would not have married a youth that had not paid the debt he owed to it. The love of glory is the inheritance of a Frenchman.'

February 20.—Underwent a few more interrogations from Sir Hudson Lowe, in which I had the good fortune to leave his house without having been assailed with any outrageous language.

February 23.—Cipriani complained this day of inflammation of the bowels, which, from the moment he made it known to me, presented most formidable appearances. Recourse was had to all the vigorous remedies usually administered in such cases. Only temporary relief, however, was obtained; and the unfavourable symptoms returned with increased aggravation. It was soon evident that his life was in imminent danger; and other professional men were called in. All, however, was useless, and the complaint was rapidly hurrying him on to dissolution. Cipriani himself, although conscious of his danger, preserved the greatest composure. Napoleon, who had an affection for him as his countryman and a man wholly devoted to his service, was extremely anxious for his recovery and frequent in his inquiries. On the 25th Napoleon, with whom I had been repeatedly during the day to report the state of the patient, sent for me at twelve o'clock at night.

was not extinct, though he was insensible. 'Ah, Pepin! poor fellow,' said Napoleon, 'I am sorry to see him here, and still more so that, before he met his fate, I had not an opportunity of letting him know that I had forgiven him.'—B. E. O'M.

I mentioned that Cipriani was lying in a kind of stupor. 'I think,' said he, 'that my appearance before poor Cipriani would act as a stimulus to slumbering nature, and rouse her to make new efforts which may finally overcome the disease and save the patient.' He endeavoured to illustrate this by describing the electric effects which had been produced in many instances by his appearance on the field of battle at most critical moments and times. I replied that Cipriani was still sensible; and that I knew the love and veneration he had for his master to be so great that on his appearance before him he would make an effort to rise in his bed, which exertion, in the weak state in which he was, would probably produce syncope, during which his soul would most probably take its departure.[1] After this and other explanations on the subject, Napoleon acquiesced in my opinion that he should not try the experiment; observing that in such cases *les hommes de l'art* were the best judges.

About four o'clock next day poor Cipriani was numbered with the dead.

Cipriani was a man possessed of great but uncultivated talents. Though artful, he had the appearance of openness and candour. He had, however, many good qualities. He was generous and charitable. Like most of his countrymen, he was an ardent friend and a bitter enemy, and had

[1] It is well known to professional men that, in cases of great debility, the mere raising of a patient's head from the pillow has sometimes produced dissolution.—B. E. O'M.

strong national spirit. He was a republican in principle, and manifested more attachment to Napoleon in his misfortunes than he had ever shown for him in his grandeur. He was regarded by his master in a very confidential light. His corpse was followed to the grave by Counts Bertrand and Montholon, by myself, and by all the household who could attend. So much was he esteemed at St. Helena, that several of the most respectable of the inhabitants and some of the officers of the 66th Regiment voluntarily joined the funeral procession. Had he been buried *within* the limits, Napoleon himself would have attended.

Immediately after his death I reported the circumstance to Napoleon, who remarked, 'Where is his soul? Gone to Rome, perhaps, to see his wife and child, before it undertakes the long final journey.'

Some days before his demise, Cipriani told me that not long after the Governor had put into execution his rigorous measures towards the inmates of Longwood, Santini, who was of a merry disposition, had been observed to be much altered and apparently thoughtful and melancholy. One day he came into Cipriani's room and avowed his intention of shooting the Governor the first time that the latter came to Longwood. Cipriani asked him if he was mad, and endeavoured to dissuade him from the attempt by using all the arguments in his power. Although Cipriani had much influence over him, Santini was unmoved. He had his double-barrelled gun loaded with ball, with which he intended to despatch the Governor, and then to shoot himself. Cipriani, finding his arguments fruitless, went to Napoleon, to whom he communicated the affair. The Emperor immediately sent for and questioned Santini, who avowed his intentions. Napoleon then commanded him, as his Emperor, to drop all thoughts of injuring Sir Hudson Lowe, and succeeded, though not without some reluctance on the part of Santini, in making him abandon his project. Santini was a most determined character and brave as a lion. Besides being master of the small sword, he had a sure and deadly aim with fire-arms; and there is little doubt that, had it not been for this prohibition, he would have effected his intentions.[1]

March 6.—The progress of disease in the Emperor slowly continues its advance. Found him reading a volume of Corneille, upon whom he pronounced some warm eulogiums, observing that to the sentiments which he inspired France was indebted for some of her glorious deeds, and adding that if Corneille had lived in his time, he would have made him a prince.

He then conversed about himself, saying that he believed Nature had destined him for great reverses—that he had a soul of marble. After which he made some comparisons of his own conduct with that adopted by his enemies towards him similar to those already recorded.

[1] During dinner the Emperor, turning with a stern look to one of the servants in waiting, exclaimed, to our utter consternation,

'Maitland,' said Napoleon, 'was not an accomplice in the snare that was laid for me by your Ministers when they gave him orders to receive me on board his ship. He is *un brave homme*, and incapable of participating in the infamous transaction that took place. He was deceived as well as myself, and probably thought, in bringing me to England, that I should have been allowed to live there, subject to such restrictions as had been imposed upon my brother Lucien. Previous to going on board the *Bellerophon*,' added he, 'debates were held upon the propriety of the measure. Some naval officers, to whom it was mentioned, strongly urged that I should not venture on such a step.'

He then gave some explanation of the causes which had produced his fall: 'Had it not been for that fatal suspension of arms in 1813, to which I was induced to consent by Austria, I should have succeeded. The victories of Lutzen and Wurtzen had restored confidence in the French forces. The King of Saxony was triumphantly brought back to his capital; one of the corps of the French army was at the gates of Berlin, and the enemy had been driven from Hamburg. The Russian and Prussian armies were preparing to pass the Vistula when

'So then, assassin, you resolved to kill the Governor! Wretch!— If such a thought ever again enters your head, you will have to do with me; you will see how I shall behave to you.' And then addressing himself to us, he said, 'Gentlemen, it is Santini there who determined to kill the Governor. The rascal was about to involve us in a sad embarrassment. I found it necessary to exert all my authority, all my indignation to restrain him.'—*Las Cases*, vol. iii., part v., p. 83, English edition.

the Cabinet of Austria, acting with its characteristic perfidy, advised the suspension of hostilities at a time when it had already entered into engagements with Russia and Prussia; the armistice was only a delusion to gain the time necessary to make preparations, it being intended to declare against France in May. The unexpected successes obliged Austria to act with more circumspection. It was necessary to gain more time, and negotiations went on at the Congress of Prague. Metternich insisted that Austria should have the half of Italy, and made other exorbitant conditions which were only demanded in order to be refused.

'As soon as she had got her army ready, Austria declared against France. After the victory of Dresden I was superior, and had formed a project of deceiving the enemy by marching towards Magdeburg, of then crossing the Elbe at Wittenberg and marching upon Berlin. Several divisions of the army were occupied in these manœuvres when a letter was brought to me from the King of Würtemberg, announcing that the Bavarian army had joined the Austrians, and, to the number of eighty thousand men, were marching towards the Rhine, under the command of Wrede; that he, being controlled by the presence of that army, was obliged to join his contingent to it, and that Mayence would soon be invested by a hundred thousand men.

'This unexpected defection entirely changed the plan of the campaign, and all the preparations made to fix the war between the Elbe and the Oder became useless. At Leipsic, afterwards, I was victorious on the 16th, and should have succeeded on the 18th had not the whole Saxon army, which occupied one of the most important positions in the line, deserted to the enemy, with a train of sixty pieces of cannon, which were immediately turned against the French. Notwithstanding this, the field of battle remained in our possession, and the Allies made a retrograde movement on the same day. During the night I ordered the army to retire upon our supplies behind the Elster. The defection of some other German corps afterwards and the premature blowing up of the bridge at Leipsic caused the most disastrous effects.

'When the army had passed the Saale, it should have rested to recover from its fatigues and receive ammunition and other supplies from Erfurth. Intelligence, however, arrived that the Austro-Bavarian army under Wrede had arrived on the Main by forced marches, and it was necessary to march against it. Wrede was driven from his position at Hanau, completely beaten and himself wounded. Conferences afterwards took place at Frankfort, and proposals for peace were offered on condition that I should renounce the Protectorate of the Confederation of the Rhine, Poland, and the departments of the Elbe, but that France should be preserved in her limits of the Alps and the Rhine. Those conditions were accepted as bases. This Congress, however, like the others, turned out to be a delusion, as at the moment that those pacific proposals were made the Allies violated the neutrality of Switzerland, which they entered in large force. At Châtillon, afterwards, they presented their *ultimatum*, in which they demanded that France should be reduced to the limits she had previous to 1792, which I rejected. Had it not been for the subsequent treachery of Talleyrand, Marmont, and Augereau, the Allies would not have succeeded in forcing upon the throne a detested family, against whom, for twenty-five years, the nation has combated; and France would not·have been degraded by the spectacle of a King upon the throne who had the baseness publicly to declare that he owed it to the Prince Regent of England.'

March 28.—Twenty-seven volumes of books were sent to Longwood by Sir Hudson Lowe on the 12th, and seven on this day, with some numbers of the *Lettres Normandes et Champenoises*. These formed the whole supply of books and pamphlets sent by His Majesty's Ministers[1] (or through

---

[1] Mr. Goulbourn promised Count Las Cases, on the return of the latter to Europe, that every interesting book and new publication should be sent to Longwood, with a copious and regular supply of newspapers, French and English, of different descriptions. Whether the worthy secretary performed his promise or not, I am unable to say. None except some odd numbers of the *Times* and *Courier*, *Observer*, etc., with a few French papers of very old date, reached Longwood during my residence there. In one instance—in March 1817, I think—the Governor permitted me to take the *Morning Chronicle* for some weeks, as a great favour, which was not again repeated.—B. E. O'M.

them) since the arrival of the *Phaeton* in 1816. Napoleon observed, '*C'est une bassesse dont je ne croyais pas même que Lord Bathurst fût capable.*'

It has been a rule for some time that all captains of merchant ships which arrive are obliged to submit a list of their books, newspapers, etc. to Sir Hudson Lowe, and those of a political nature are specifically required to be sent to him, under a pretext of desiring to forward them to Longwood, where, however, none of the books have arrived, and but very few newspapers. The *Edinburgh Review* is specially sought after by His Excellency and staff.

April 4. — Some days ago a circumstance occurred which threw some light upon the motives which had induced the Governor to oblige me to visit Plantation House twice a week. One of the foreign persons residing in the island informed Count Montholon that the Commissioners had seen an account of the state of Napoleon's health in the bulletin of that day. Count Montholon, knowing that no bulletins were issued by me, asked for explanations, which were given; and by which it appeared that surreptitious bulletins were made by a person who never saw Napoleon, and who consequently could not judge of his complaint. Those fictitious reports were sent from Plantation House to the Commissioners, and transmitted by them to their respective courts. I apprehend that every conscientious reader will be of opinion that those bulletins ought to have been shown to me, I being the only medical man who saw the patient, and consequently the only person capable of judging of their correctness.[1]

April 10.—Sir Hudson Lowe, having failed in the application that he made in London to procure my removal from St. Helena, had recourse to an expedient which ensured him success. He caused a letter to be written to me this day by Sir Thomas Reade, in which he informed me that I was not to pass out of Longwood, without assigning any reasons for a measure by which it appeared that the Governor had imposed upon me restrictions even more arbitrary and vexatious than those which he had inflicted upon the French; for by confining me to Longwood, within the precincts of which he allowed no persons to enter without a pass, he deprived me of English society; while at the same time he prohibited me from holding any other intercourse even with the French than that relating to my profession. It is almost unnecessary for me to explain to the reader that I was neither able nor inclined to obey this arbitrary mandate. As soon as I received this letter I went to the Briars, with the intention of laying the affair before Admiral Plampin, who sent word by his secretary that he would not see me. I then wrote a letter to Sir Hudson Lowe, tendering my resignation, and another to Count Bertrand, in which I explained

[1] Sir Hudson Lowe, when he could no longer refrain from giving some account of this transaction, stated to Count Bertrand that the fictitious bulletins were merely repetitions of my conversations with Mr. Baxter. If this were true, why conceal them from me?—B. E. O'M.

the step that I had been compelled to take, and the motives which induced me to adopt it.

April 14.—Napoleon sent for me to give me an audience prior to my departure, during which he declined receiving any more medical advice from me in the situation in which I was placed by Sir Hudson Lowe, and addressed me in the following words : '*Eh bien, Docteur, vous allez nous quitter. Le monde concevra-t-il qu'on a eu la lâcheté d'attenter à mon médecin ? Puisque vous êtes un simple lieutenant, soumis à tout l'arbitraire et à la discipline militaire, vous n'avez plus l'indépendance nécessaire pour que vos secours puissent m'être utiles ; je vous remercie de vos soins. Quittez le plutôt possible ce séjour de ténèbres et de crimes ; je mourrai sur ce grabat, rongé de maladie et sans secours ; mais votre nation en sera déshonorée à jamais.*' He then bade me adieu.

May 9.—Sir Hudson Lowe—finding that he could not succeed in his plan of establishing another surgeon with Napoleon (and that the latter was determined not to receive him); and having been made to comprehend by the Commissioners [1] that if Napoleon died while he kept me in confine-

[1] I have been informed that some very animated discussions took place at Plantation House on this subject, in one of which the Governor, while debating with Baron Sturmer, burst forth into one of the paroxysms of anger he so frequently manifested towards me. The Baron very coolly made His Excellency stop opposite to a large looking-glass, in which he begged him to contemplate his own features, adding that he should not desire to afford his court a better representation of what was occurring at St. Helena than the figure in the mirror before him.—B. E. O'M.

ment (without bringing me to a trial, or even preferring any charge against me) or under the hands of any surgeon forced upon him, strange surmises would arise in England and in Europe respecting his death, of which they themselves would be unable to render a satisfactory explanation,—decided upon removing the restrictions he had imposed upon me.

Accordingly he released me, after having kept me in confinement twenty-seven days; during which time I was successively assailed, in correspondence, by all his staff; and in order to ensnare me frequently required to return, by a dragoon who waited, answers to letters composed after several days' reflection by the united wisdom of Sir Hudson Lowe and his staff. As this correspondence has been already before the public, I shall not now trouble the reader with it. In the letter containing the order for my release, His Excellency felt himself obliged to acknowledge me as Napoleon's private surgeon, a point which he had contested before.

A despatch was sent by Sir Hudson Lowe to Longwood, containing some extracts from a correspondence of Lord Bathurst, stating, amongst other matters, that permission would be given that a list of persons not exceeding fifty in number, resident on the island, should be drawn up by Count Bertrand and submitted to the Governor for approval, and that such persons should be admitted to Longwood, at suitable hours, with no other pass than the invitation of General Bonaparte; it being understood that they were on such occasions to deliver in their invitations, with their names, as vouchers at the barrier, and that the Governor was to reserve a discretionary power to erase from the list any individuals to whom he might consider it inexpedient to continue such facility of access.

May 10.—Previous to allowing me to resume my medical functions at Longwood, Napoleon, in order to put a stop to the fabrication of bulletins, required that I should make a report of the state of his health once a week or oftener if necessary, a copy of which should be given to the Governor if he required it. This I immediately communicated to Sir Hudson Lowe, who not only did not require it, but absolutely prohibited me from making him (Sir Hudson) any written report.

Napoleon's state of health had become worse since last month; the pain was more constant and severe.

May 16.—A proclamation issued by Sir Hudson Lowe, and placarded in the most conspicuous places, interdicting all officers, inhabitants, and other persons whatsoever from holding any correspondence or communication with the foreign persons under detention on the island.

Considerable indignation was excited in the island at the conduct which had been pursued towards Napoleon.

May 18.—Captain Blakeney ordered by Sir Hudson Lowe to assemble all the English servants at Longwood, and read to them the proclamation of the 16th. This was done without notice being given to their masters. Napoleon, when informed of this, ordered that the English servants employed at Longwood House, in place of Santini and the others sent away by Sir Hudson Lowe, should be discharged.

May 20.—Had some conversation with the Emperor about the work published by Mr. Ellis upon the Embassy to China, and the conversation at Longwood which that gentleman had published. Napoleon observed, that having learned that Mr. Ellis had been secretary to a mission to Persia a short time after General Gardanne had quitted Ispahan, he had questioned him as to the progress that Russia had made on the Persian side. 'I told him,' added Napoleon, 'that if Russia succeeded in attaching the brave Polish nation to her, she would no longer have a rival, because she would restrain England by menacing the latter's possessions in India ; and Austria, by the great moral superiority of her troops, and by the followers of the Greek Church, who are so numerous in Hungary and Galicia ; and that appearances rendered it probable that a Greek patriarch would one day officiate in St. Sophia.

'During all the conversations I had with Mr. Ellis,' continued he, 'which lasted about half an hour, not one word was said about St. Helena. Count Montholon had no conversation on the subject with Mr. Ellis or any members of the legation. Mr. Ellis made no inquiries on the spot, never visited the interior of the establishment, knew nothing, saw nothing, and heard nothing about it, at least from the French. And yet in his work he has the impudence to play the part of a judge who had heard the complaining parties on the spot. But that passage has not been written by his hand. It is the invention of some *commis* to Lord Bathurst who has imposed the insertion of it upon him. Such a prostitution of his name reflects but little credit upon the diplomatic character.'[1]

He made some observations upon the contrast between the Governor's proclamation and conduct and the despatches sent by Lord Bathurst; and said that the despatch was merely got up to have the appearance of doing something to benefit him, while in reality nothing was done.

In the course of the conversation, Napoleon observed that but little reliance was to be placed on the writings of a man, in forming a judgment of his private character or conduct, which he illustrated by informing me that Bernardin St. Pierre, whose writings were so sentimentally beautiful, and breathed principles of humanity and morality in every page, was one of the worst private characters in France.

June 7.—The *Mangles* storeship arrived.

June 11.—With the exception of the painful inflammatory affection of the cheeks, the recurrence

---

[1] Mr. Ellis has since been appointed to a lucrative situation at the Cape of Good Hope, which, I believe, is the gift of Lord Bathurst.—B. E. O'M.

of which has been prevented by the extraction of two more teeth, Napoleon's state of health has become much worse. He has been confined almost entirely to his apartments for nearly six weeks.

June 20.—The officers of the 53d Regiment had done me the honour to elect me an honorary member of their mess ; and on the departure of that regiment from the island, the officers of the 66th had conferred a similar honour upon me. Sir Hudson Lowe employed Sir Thomas Reade to fill the mind of Lieutenant-Colonel Lascelles (the commanding officer) with the most insidious calumnies against me, in consequence of which Lieutenant-Colonel Lascelles called upon Lieutenant Reardon of the regiment (a friend of mine), to whom he said it had been insinuated to him by Sir Thomas Reade that I had become displeasing to the sight of the Governor, that the officers of the regiment ought to expel me from their mess as a person who had submitted to insults from the Governor, who had turned me out of his house, and consequently that I was unfit for their society ; insinuating also that my expulsion would be very agreeable to Sir Hudson Lowe, who, he observed, had said that he should consider any person who was seen to associate with me as his personal enemy. Lieutenant-Colonel Lascelles concluded by begging Lieutenant Reardon to persuade me to withdraw privately from the mess, as my presence there was obnoxious to the Governor ; protesting, however, that personally he had a great esteem for me, and that he would be one of the first to invite me to dine there as a guest.

Reflecting that, if I slunk away secretly, opportunity would be furnished to my enemies to paint me in the blackest colours, and to represent that my conduct had been such as to compel the officers of the 66th to turn me out of the mess, and being conscious of upright intentions, I immediately wrote to Lieutenant-Colonel Lascelles, claiming a full and open investigation, and referring the matter to the decision of the officers of the 66th. In the evening I met him coming to see me. He made many professions of friendship and esteem for me, but said that, as the Governor was displeased with me, he begged I would withdraw privately from the mess, that Sir Hudson Lowe desired it, and that he was afraid of his resentment being exercised upon himself and upon the officers of the regiment if I did not comply with his wishes. He concluded by stating that Sir Thomas Reade had shown him part of my correspondence with the Governor, and some secret documents which had never been communicated to me, and professing his esteem, in which sentiment he said he knew he was joined by every officer in the regiment.

I replied that clandestine misrepresentations, from their being unknown to me, might remain unrefuted; that no person was secure from the breath of calumny; that, however, I was ready to submit the whole of the correspondence between the Governor and myself to the judgment of the officers of the regiment, or to submit to any other scrutiny that he or they might desire, and to abide by their decision; but that I never would renounce the honour which the officers of the 66th had conferred upon me in granting me a seat at their table, unless (according to the custom of the army) by a vote of the mess, or by an order from the Governor.

This reply was communicated to Sir Hudson Lowe, who, probably having his own reasons for not allowing the correspondence to be submitted to the judgment of a corps of officers, sent an order by Brigadier-General Sir George Bingham (as I have been informed) to Lieutenant-Colonel Lascelles, to exclude me from the mess, which was communicated to me by letter without assigning any reason for the act.

Being desirous of obtaining every authentic information to establish the fact that this new outrage had been effected by the order of Sir Hudson Lowe, I waited upon Sir George Bingham, by whom I was very politely received, and informed that he had been commanded to carry the order into execution.

June 25.—Sent a letter to the Deadwood camp, thanking the officers for the courtesy and kindness I received from them whilst an honorary member of their mess.

June 26.—The officers of the 66th Regiment replied that they always conceived my conduct while with them to be perfectly consistent in every respect with that of a gentleman, and felt much indebted for the expressions of esteem contained in my letter.

June 27.—Napoleon much affected by a severe catarrhal affection, caused by the humidity of his rooms. Discontinued some of the remedies he was taking, and reported the state of his health to the Governor.

July 15.—Several cases of wine sent by the Princess Borghèse through Lady Holland arrived last month. A few were sent to Longwood, and the remainder deposited in the Government stores by order of Sir Hudson Lowe. Napoleon expressed on this as well as on many other occasions sentiments of great affection towards his sisters, Eliza and Pauline, and declared his conviction that no sacrifice would be too great for the latter to make for his benefit; adding that he had no doubt she would endeavour to obtain permission to come out to St. Helena.[1] He also spoke of the Princess Hortense in very high terms, and praised her great talent. He expressed a very strong sense of the attention and kindness manifested for him in his misfortunes by Lady Holland, at a time when he was abandoned by many from whose gratitude he had reason to expect some little notice. He observed that the members of the family of the great Fox abounded in liberal and generous sentiments.

July 20.—Went to town and tried to procure a

[1] The Princess subsequently demanded permission to proceed to the place of her brother's exile.

copy of the observations on Lord Bathurst's speech, some of which I was informed had arrived on the island. Captain Bunn, of the *Mangles*, to whom I applied for one, professed his surprise that such an application should be made from a person belonging to Longwood, for immediately after his arrival Sir Hudson Lowe and Sir Thomas Reade had taken five copies of the pamphlet from him, saying that they wanted to send two or three to Longwood. He added that those two persons had been very particular in requiring him to render an account of the books that he had brought out, and had possessed themselves of all the modern publications on political subjects, and all the copies of the *Edinburgh Review* he brought with him.

July 25.—After having paid a professional visit to Napoleon, who was no better, and while entering my room at about half-past four o'clock, Captain Blakeney delivered to me the following letter:[1]

PLANTATION HOUSE, *July 25, 1818.*

SIR—I am directed by Lieutenant-General Sir Hudson Lowe to inform you that by an instruction received from Earl Bathurst, dated the 16th of May 1818; he has been directed to withdraw you from your attendance upon General Bonaparte, and to *interdict you all further interviews with the inhabitants at Longwood.*

Rear-Admiral Plampin has received instructions from the Lords Commissioners of the Admiralty as to your destination when you quit this island.

---

[1] A letter of a similar import was sent to Count Montholon by Sir Hudson Lowe, containing instructions from Lord Bathurst that Mr. Baxter should be directed to attend in my place.

You are in consequence to leave Longwood immediately after receiving this letter without holding any further communication whatsoever with the persons residing there.—I have the honour, etc.

       EDWARD WYNYARD, *Lieut.-Col.*,
                Military Secretary.

Barry O'Meara, Esq.,
 Longwood.

Humanity and the duties of my profession alike forbade a compliance with this unfeeling command, especially as my situation was of a civil nature, similar to other naval officers in the employ of the excise or customs. I determined to disobey it whatever might be the consequences; Napoleon's health required that I should prescribe a regimen for him, and prepare the medicines which it would be necessary for him to take in the absence of a surgeon, an absence likely to be of long duration, as I was perfectly sure he would accept of no one recommended by Sir Hudson Lowe. I accordingly went instantly to Napoleon's apartment. Having obtained admission, I communicated to him the order which I had received. '*Le crime se consommera plus vite,*' said Napoleon, 'I have lived too long for them. *Votre ministère est bien hardi,*' added he; 'when the Pope was in France, I would have cut off my right arm rather than have signed an order for the removal of his surgeon.'

After some more conversation had taken place, and I had given him such medical instructions as I could upon the moment, Napoleon said, 'When you arrive in Europe, you will either go yourself, or send to my brother Joseph. You will inform him that I desire he shall give to you the parcel containing the private and confidential[1] letters of the Emperors Alexander and Francis, the King of Prussia, and the other sovereigns of Europe, with me, which I delivered to his care at Rochefort. You will publish them, to *couvrir de honte* those sovereigns, and manifest to the world the abject homage which those vassals paid to me when asking favours or supplicating for their thrones. When I was strong and in power, *ils briguèrent ma protection et l'honneur de mon alliance*, and licked the dust from under my feet. Now, in my old age, they basely oppress and take my wife and child from me. I require you to do this, and if you see any calumnies published of me during the time that you have been

[1] On my return to Europe, I used every exertion to obtain the important letters in question. Unfortunately, however, for posterity, my efforts have not been attended with success. Before the Comte de Survilliers (Joseph Bonaparte) had left Rochefort for America, apprehensive that he might be seized by the Allied Powers, he judged it prudent to deposit his precious charge in the hands of a person upon whose integrity he thought he could rely; but who it has appeared since basely betrayed the Count, as some months ago a person brought the original letters to London for sale, for which he demanded £30,000. This was immediately communicated to some of His Majesty's Ministers, and to the Foreign Ambassadors, and I have been credibly informed that the Russian Ambassador paid £10,000 to redeem those belonging to his master. Amongst other curious passages, which have been repeated to me by those who have been favoured with their perusal, the following occurs in reference to Hanover: His Majesty of Prussia stated that '*he always entertained a paternal regard for that country;*' and it appeared that the sovereigns in general *made earnest supplications for territory.*—B. E. O'M.

with me, of which you can say, "I have seen with my own eyes that this is not true," contradict them.'

He soon after dictated to Count Bertrand a letter which he signed, adding a postscript in his own handwriting, and assuring me that those few words would say more to the Empress for me than if he had written pages in quarto; he then presented me with a superb snuff-box and a statuette of himself; desired me, on my arrival in Europe, to make inquiries about his family, and communicate to its members that he did not wish that any of them should come to St. Helena to witness the miseries and humiliations under which he laboured.

'You will express the sentiments which I preserve for them,' added he. 'You will bear my affections to my good Louise, to my excellent mother, and to Pauline. If you see my Son, embrace him for me; may he never forget that he was born a French prince! Testify to Lady Holland the sense I entertain of her kindness, and the esteem which I bear to her. Finally, endeavour to send me authentic intelligence of the manner in which my Son is educated.' The Emperor then shook me by the hand and embraced me, saying,

'Adieu, O'Meara, nous ne nous reverrons plus. Soyez heureux.'

July 25, 1818.

CHAPTER V[1]

THE CLOSING YEARS OF NAPOLEON'S LIFE

ONE by one the faithful adherents who had followed Napoleon as readily to his rocky prison as to the steps of the Imperial throne, and the new sympathisers he had found in the island, were being driven from St. Helena. In December 1816 Count Las Cases was banished from the island; death removed Cipriani, the *maître d'hôtel*, in February 1818;[2] General Gourgaud's health having broken down during his residence at Longwood, he, in the following month, obtained permission to return to Europe, charged by Napoleon to represent his position to the Emperors of Austria and Russia;[3]

[1] This chapter appears for the first time in the present (1888) edition.

[2] 'The whirligig of Time brings round its revenges.' Count Montholon, in his *History of the Captivity of Napoleon* (English edition 1847, vol. iii. pp. 12-17), attributes Sir Hudson Lowe's loss of Capri in 1807 to the successful machinations of Cipriani, who was then employed as a spy by Salicetti, the Neapolitan Prime Minister. If the story was true, it is curious that Cipriani should have died when practically Lowe's prisoner at St. Helena.

[3] Gourgaud's departure has also been attributed to 'jealousy of the favour shown to others.'—See Bourrienne's *Napoleon*, edition 1885, vol. iii. p. 489.

the vessel in which Gourgaud embarked also conveyed Mr. Balcombe and his family, Mrs. Balcombe's illness being the ostensible reason for their departure, though the suspicious hostility of the Governor towards persons in whose society Napoleon took so much pleasure, and the perpetual panic about 'conspiracies' and 'secret correspondence' also had much to do with it; and in July of the same year O'Meara was dismissed from his appointment, having shown himself—sometimes, perhaps with imprudence—too zealous on his patient's behalf to please the nervous and splenetic Governor.

These changes, and the persistent animosity shown towards all who evinced sympathy for the exiles, naturally increased their resentment and alarm.[1] Napoleon, incensed at the removal of O'Meara, whose society appears to have amused, and whose enthusiasm must have pleased him, though he paid small heed to his medical authority, refused to see any doctor recommended by the Governor. 'During more than two months,' says Montholon (*History of the Captivity of Napoleon*, vol. iii. p. 37), 'the contest with Sir Hudson Lowe, concerning the admission of an English physician into the service of the Emperor, was incessant. To all his offers the Grand Marshal or I answered, "Let us choose for ourselves, and place the person chosen

---

[1] In June 1818 Baron Stürmer, the Austrian Commissioner, was removed, 'in consequence,' says Mr. Forsyth (*Captivity of Napoleon*, vol. iii. p. 31), 'of his persisting in unauthorised communications with the French at Longwood.'

in the same position as was at first enjoyed by Dr. O'Meara."'

While this matter was pending, an interval of rather more amicable relations between Longwood and Plantation House occurred. The Governor 'enlarged the circle of our free walks,' says Montholon, 'and left us for a time at rest;' Napoleon resumed his walks in the garden, and his morning dictations; and the foundations of the long-talked-of new house were traced without opposition in the garden of Longwood.

In December, however, Napoleon grew rapidly worse; altercations recommenced as to the conditions on which the resident doctors should be allowed to attend at Longwood ; and more difficulties than ever were thrown in the way of Captain Nicholls, the orderly officer whose duty it was to see Napoleon daily.[1]

There can be no doubt that Napoleon and those

[1] Captain Nicholls's letters and journals at this time and during the following year contain amusing instances of the straits to which Napoleon's dislike of this inspection reduced him : 'I was nearly twelve hours on my legs this day,' he writes, 'endeavouring to see Napoleon Bonaparte before I succeeded, and I have experienced many such days since I have been stationed at Longwood.' . . . . '*I believe* that I saw Napoleon Bonaparte to-day in the act of strapping his razor in his dressing-room.' . . . 'I have not seen General Bonaparte to-day. At this moment there is a person sitting in the General's billiard-room with a cocked hat on. I however can only see the hat moving about. *If the French are accustomed to sit at dinner with their hats on*, probably this is Napoleon Bonaparte at his dinner !' And Montholon is said to have told Captain Nicholls 'that if he could not see Napoleon through the window, he might do so through the keyhole.'—(See *Forsyth*, vol. iii.)

about him exaggerated trifles, were hypersensitive to small annoyances, and were disposed to retaliate in any manner possible, no matter how devoid of dignity or good sense. How could it be otherwise in so artificial, monotonous, and isolated a life, whilst clinging pertinaciously to every rag of their former importance — even such importance as could be obtained by making themselves disagreeable? If Sir Hudson Lowe had been a man of more tact, able to give way in small matters with generosity, he would have met with far less opposition in great ones. 'The want of due forms,' said Montholon, 'affects the Emperor more than the thing itself—it is everything with him. Observe due form, and you may do with him whatever you please. Madame Bertrand wishes to have a cap, a handkerchief; she cannot get it as quickly as she would—that puts her into a rage—she excites her husband, who does the same by the Emperor, and he gets *jusqu'au* 36° *de furie*.'[1]

At the beginning of July 1819 the Countess Montholon, who had long been in ill-health, left St. Helena with her children; and just after she sailed her husband sent the Governor a note for her in which he said: 'L'Empereur témoigne un grand regret pour ton départ; ses larmes ont coulé pour toi, peut-être pour la première fois de sa vie!'[2]

In August Dr. Arnott, the principal medical officer at St. Helena, went to Longwood to offer his services to the ex-Emperor, and was received by

[1] Forsyth, vol. iii. p. 83.   [2] *Ibid.* vol. iii. p. 168.

Count Bertrand, who produced a paper containing a series of conditions to which he required the doctor's assent.[1] Arnott replied that he would agree to no conditions whatever; that Napoleon should have the full benefit of his professional skill, but that he would enter into no other engagement; and the interview ended.[2]

It must have been a great relief to all parties when a successor to O'Meara, nominated by Cardinal Fesch at the request of the British Government, arrived at St. Helena. This was Professor Antommarchi, a Corsican by birth, and Prosecuteur d'Anatomie at the Hospital of Sainte Marie Neuve at Florence. He was accompanied by the Abbés Buonavita and Vignale,[3] by a *maître d'hôtel* from

[1] These 'conditions' were probably of the same nature as the oath required from Antommarchi before he was allowed to see Napoleon, that he 'would not communicate with the English, and that he would more especially avoid giving them the least information respecting the progress of Napoleon's disorder.'—See Bourrienne's *Napoleon*, edition 1885, vol. iii. p. 507.

[2] *Forsyth*, vol. iii. p. 178.

[3] Antommarchi makes bitter complaint of the delays occasioned by the infirmities of Buonavita, who, he says, 'after a residence of twenty-six years in Mexico, had returned to Europe and had been successively almoner to Madame Mère at Elba, and chaplain to Princess Pauline at Rome. He was full of zeal, but feeble, gouty, and infirm, he could not possibly fulfil the object of his mission. A recent attack of apoplexy had also affected his tongue and almost entirely deprived him of speech. Nevertheless he did not hesitate to accept the appointment. His wish to serve the Emperor made him forget his weakness.'—*Last Days of Napoleon*, Colburn, 1825, vol. i. p. 9.

The Abbé Vignale's chief recommendation would appear to have been some knowledge of surgery, which, however, according to Antommarchi, he was soon forbidden by Napoleon to exercise.

the establishment of Madame Mère, and a cook supplied by that of the Princess Pauline.[1] On Antommarchi's arrival at St. Helena in September Sir Hudson Lowe received him with an amiability which he seems to have found quite alarming. But at Longwood he was regarded with some distrust, and not until Bertrand and Montholon had seen him more than once, and he had, by direction of the former, written a full account of his life and professional experience, for the inspection of his illustrious patient, would Napoleon consent to receive him. Antommarchi was then conducted to a 'small and very dark' bedroom, and ordered to go very close to the bed, in order to be seen and heard. 'For,' said Napoleon, 'on this miserable rock I am become quite deaf.' Napoleon then asked repeated questions about his family, of whom Antommarchi was able to give him many particulars, as Madame Mère had entertained him and the two Abbés at 'a magnificent dinner' before their departure from Rome, and he had been cordially received and

[1] Antommarchi and the other passengers suffered much on the voyage from the wretched vessel in which they sailed and the brutality and greed of the captain. It gave him, therefore, no small satisfaction, when he again went on board for his luggage, to find the captain a prisoner on his own ship. It seemed that at Deptford some one had put on board several sealed packets addressed to inhabitants of St. Helena, alleging that they were religious publications, which, when opened, proved to be copies of O'Meara's 'Exposition' full, says Mr. Forsyth (*Captivity of Napoleon*, vol. iii. p. 185), of 'the grossest calumnies against the Governor.' He adds that every recipient sent his copy 'back to the publisher with the leaves uncut.' A most remarkable instance of want of curiosity —or fear.

charged with many affectionate messages by Princess Pauline, Louis, and Lucien, and had seen the Comtesse de Survilliers (wife of Joseph) and her handsome daughters at Frankfürt, where he had met Las Cases, about whom also Napoleon made many inquiries. They talked at great length of Corsica, Napoleon seeming pleased to find that Antommarchi knew the places familiar to his own childhood, and expressing regret that he had not gone there, where he might have been content to remain, instead of to Elba, while yet he had some liberty of choice. Finally he discussed his symptoms with his new doctor, expressing his usual scepticism as to medical science, but promising to try the effect of obeying his directions. 'You have given up everything to come and attend me,' he said; 'it is but fair that I should also do something.'

At that time Napoleon had not lost his liking for a little practical joke. A few hours after leaving the deaf and suffering invalid in the darkened bedroom, Antommarchi was again sent for, and was startled to find him fully dressed in the drawing-room. 'He came towards me, took me by the ears, and said, laughing, "You thought I had lost all my strength in this horrible climate!" I was struck with astonishment and remained motionless.'

Antommarchi, like O'Meara, expressed disgust at the discomfort of Longwood, and he minutely catalogues the meagre and insufficient furniture: 'The door leading into the bath-room was concealed by an old screen, next to which was an equally old sofa covered with calico. Upon this sofa Napoleon usually reclined, and sought shelter from dampness and the gnats; his legs thrust into a sack of flannel, and a shabby table by his side, on which were his books or his breakfast. . . .. The dampness of the two rooms was excessive. It attacked and destroyed everything; the paltry nankeen which served as tapestry was hanging in rags against the walls.'

It must be admitted that Napoleon's habits did not add to the orderliness of his apartments. 'The carpet of his room was strewed with books; there were some round the bed, some in the middle of the apartment, some close to the walls. I could not understand why they were thus scattered about, and asked the cause of this confusion. "The Emperor has read all night. When he wishes to read he covers his bed with books, takes them up, turns them over, and throws them away when he has done with them."—" But why not pick them up?" —" Because he was still reading. As long as the Emperor holds a book in his hand he will not suffer anybody to interrupt him. Good works are allowed to slide down on the floor, indifferent ones are disdainfully pushed aside, and bad ones thrown against the wall,—but it is only when the Emperor is out of the room that we are allowed to touch them."'

It took some time for the new doctor to understand and become accustomed to the etiquette observed by Napoleon's attendants. He tells us that on October 9 'the Emperor was walking round Longwood. I observed him looking about, peeping into the interior of the apartments to see what was going forward there, and visiting, one after the other, every room occupied by his suite. I was going up to him, when I was stopped by one of the servants. "You must not go near the Emperor; His Majesty is incognito. Do you not see that he has not his usual dress on, nor the cocked hat, which he never leaves off, except during the short time he is at table? Well, whenever the Emperor puts on that long green greatcoat, and buttons it up to the neck, and takes that large round hat, he does not wish to be approached by anybody, and even the Grand Marshal himself does not disturb him."'[1]

When Antommarchi's boxes arrived, Napoleon seized with enthusiasm the books which had been sent him—'an unsatisfactory collection,' says the doctor, 'containing duplicates of some that he already had, and omitting others for which he was most anxious. Some bundles of newspapers which the doctor brought he eagerly seized, exclaiming, "Ah! these will bring up the arrears of my information about the state of affairs. It is curious enough to see the wise measures which were to cancel the recollection of my tyranny! Poor Europe — what convulsions are preparing for it!"'

Antommarchi relates an amusing scene which took place when, the last box from Europe having

[1] *Last Days*, vol. i. p. 126.

been broken open, it proved to contain 'the vases and church ornaments. "Stop," said Napoleon, "this is the property of Saint Peter; have a care who touches it; send for the Abbés."' He then proposed to make Buonavita, in spite of his agitated protests, 'Bishop of the Jumna,' and ordered Count Montholon to procure the necessary dress; as, however, St. Helena could not furnish the scarlet and violet vestments, nothing more was heard of the imaginary bishopric.[1]

In a more serious mood Napoleon desired to have the dining-room made available for divine worship, which he ordered to be celebrated on Sundays 'and the holidays appointed by the Concordat,' but not daily.

Napoleon's religious opinions have been variously represented. We have seen that he was displeased with his little friend, Miss Balcombe, for accusing him of atheism;[2] and in his conversations with Las Cases he said, 'I never doubted the existence of God; for, if my reason was inadequate to comprehend it, my mind was not the less disposed to adopt it;'[3] whilst on another occasion, according to the same authority, 'The Emperor ended the conversation by desiring my son to bring him the New Testament and . . . read as far as the Sermon on the Mount. He expressed himself struck with the highest admiration of the purity,

[1] See *Antommarchi*, vol. i. p. 101, and *Bourrienne*, edition 1885, vol. iii. p. 508.
[2] See *ante*, vol. ii. p. 9.
[3] *Las Cases*, English edition 1836, vol. iii. p. 126.

the sublimity, the beauty of the morality which it contained.'

But perhaps the fullest record of Napoleon's religious sentiments is that referred to by Lacordaire, who concludes the magnificent peroration to the first of his 'Conferences' on Jesus Christ in the following words :—[1]

'Our age commenced by a Man who outstripped all his contemporaries, and whom we who have followed have not equalled. A conqueror, a soldier, a founder of empire, his name and his ideas are still everywhere present. After having unconsciously accomplished the work of God he disappeared, that work being done, and waned like a setting sun in the deep waters of the ocean. There upon a barren rock he loved to recall the events of his own life; and from himself going back to others who had lived before him, and to whom he had a right to compare himself, he could not fail to perceive a form greater than his own upon that illustrious stage whereon he took his place. He often contemplated it; misfortune opens the soul to illuminations which in

[1] Taken from a note in the *Catéchisme de Persévérance*, by the Abbé Gaume. It is quoted also in *Les Etudes*, by M. Nicholas. General Montholon—who with General Bertrand was present at the conversations which are recorded by the Chevalier de Beauterne— writes from Ham, on May 30, 1841, to that author: 'I have read with lively interest your *brochure* entitled "The Sentiments of Napoleon on the Divinity of Jesus Christ," and I do not think it would be possible to express more accurately the religious belief of the Emperor.'

Dr. Newman also refers, in his *Grammar of Assent*, to the same memorable utterance.

prosperity are unseen. That form constantly rose before him—he was compelled to judge it. One evening in the course of that long exile which expiated past faults and lighted up the road to the future, the fallen Conqueror asked one of the few companions of his captivity if he could tell him what Jesus Christ really was. The soldier begged to be excused ; he had been too busy during his sojourn in the world to think about the question.' Thereupon, added Lacordaire, speaking from the pulpit of Notre Dame, ' he (Napoleon) opening the Gospel, not with his hands, but from a heart filled by it, compared Jesus Christ with himself and all the great characters of history ; developed the different characteristics which distinguished Jesus Christ from all mankind, and after uttering a torrent of eloquence which no Father of the Church would have disclaimed, ended with these words, " In fine, I know men, and I say that Jesus Christ was not a man!"'

Lacordaire clearly proved that he was justified in uttering this panegyric. ' These words of Napoleon,' he added, ' sum up all I would say to you on the inner life of Christ, and express the conclusion which sooner or later every man arrives at who reads the Gospel with just attention. And the day will come when the youngest among you will say from the experiences of life, when life is drawing to its close, " I, too, know men, and I say that Jesus Christ was not a man." And the day also will come when, upon the tomb of her great Captain, France will grave these words, and they will shine with more immortal lustre than the sun of the Pyramids and Austerlitz.'

[THE EXACT WORDS OF NAPOLEON ARE HERE REPRODUCED.

One of Napoleon's generals was one day discussing in his presence the divinity of our Lord. Napoleon remarked: 'I know men, General, and I can tell you that Jesus Christ is not a man. Superficial minds see a resemblance between Christ and the founders of empires, the conquerors and the gods of other religions. The resemblance does not exist; the distance between Christianity and any other religion whatever is infinite.

'Any one who has a true knowledge of things and experience of men will cut short the question as I do. Who amongst us, General, looking at the worship of different nations, is not able to say to the different authors of those religions—"No, you are neither gods, nor the agents of the Deity; no, you have no mission from Heaven. You are formed of the same slime as other mortals; your own lives are so entirely one with all the passions and all the vices which are inseparable from humanity, that it has been necessary to deify them with you; your temples and your priests themselves proclaim your origin." Abominations, fables, and rotten wood; are these religions and gods which can be compared with Christianity?

'I say No.

'In Lycurgus, Numa, Confucius, and Mahomet I see lawgivers, but nothing which reveals the Deity. They did not themselves raise their pretensions so high. They surpassed others in their times, as I have done in mine. There is nothing about them which announces Divine beings; on the contrary, I see much likeness between them and myself. I can testify to common resemblances, weaknesses, and errors, which bring them near to me, and to human nature.

'It is not so with Christ. Everything in Him amazes me; His mind is beyond me, and His will confounds me. There is no possible term of comparison between Him and anything of this world. He is a Being apart. His birth, His life, His death, the profundity of His doctrine, which reaches the height of difficulty, and which is yet its most admirable solution, the singularity of this mysterious Being, His empire, His course across ages and kingdoms—all is a prodigy, a mystery too deep, too sacred, and which plunges me into reveries from which I can find no escape; a mystery which is here, under my eyes, which I cannot deny, and neither can I explain.

'Here I see nothing of man.

'You speak of Cæsar and of Alexander, of their conquests, and of the enthusiasm which they were able to awaken in the hearts of their soldiers, and thus draw them with them on adventurous expeditions; but this only shows us the price of the soldier's affection, the ascendency of the genius of victory, the natural effect of military discipline, and the result of able commandership. But how many years did the empire of Cæsar endure? How long was the enthusiasm of the soldiers of Alexander maintained? Their prestige lasted a day, an hour, the time of their command, and followed the chances of war. If victory had deserted them, do you doubt whether the enthusiasm would not immediately have ceased? I ask you, yes or no? Did the military influence of Cæsar and Alexander end with their life? Was it prolonged beyond the tomb?

'Imagine a man making conquests with a faithful army, devoted to his memory—after his death! Imagine a phantom, who has soldiers without pay, without hopes for this world, and who inspires them to submit to all kinds of privations. Turenne was still warm when his army broke up before Montecuculi; and as to myself—my armies forgot me whilst I still lived, as the Carthaginian army forgot Hannibal. Such is the power of us great men! A battle lost casts us down and carries away our friends. How many a Judas have I seen around me!

'In short, and this is my last argument, there is not a God in Heaven, if any man could conceive and execute with full success the gigantic design of seizing upon the supreme worship by usurping the name of God. Jesus is the only one who has dared to do this. He is the only one who has said clearly, affirmed imperturbably, Himself of Himself, *I* AM GOD; which is quite different from the affirmation, *I am a god.* History mentions no other individual who qualified himself with the title of God, in the absolute sense. How, then, should a Jew to whose existence there is more testimony than to that of any of His contemporaries, He alone, the son of a carpenter, gave Himself out as God Himself, for the Self-existent Being, for the Creator of all beings? He claims every kind of adoration, He builds His worship with His own hands, not with stones, but with men. And how was it that by a prodigy surpassing all prodigies, He willed the love of men—that which it is most difficult in the world to obtain—and immediately succeeded? From this I conclude His Divinity. Alexander, Cæsar, Hannibal, all failed. They conquered the world, but they were not able to obtain a friend. I am perhaps the only person of the present time who has any love for Hannibal, Cæsar, or Alexander. It is true we love our children; but how many children are ungrateful! Do your children love you, General? You love them, but you are not sure of a return.

'Christ speaks, and from that time generations are His by ties more strict, more intimate, than those of blood; by a union more sacred, more imperative, than any other could be. All those who sincerely believe in Him feel that superior love, of which time, the great destroyer, can neither exhaust the strength nor limit the duration. I, Napoleon, admire this the more that I have so often thought of it; and it proves to me absolutely the Divinity of Christ.

'I have inspired multitudes to die for me. God forbid that I should form any comparison between the enthusiasm of my soldiers and Christian charity; they are as different as their causes. And then my presence was required; the electricity of my look, my voice, a word from me, then the sacred fire was kindled in all hearts. I certainly possess the secret of that magic power which carries away other people's minds; yet I could never communicate it to others. Not one of my generals ever received it from me, or guessed at it; neither have I the power to eternalise my name and my love in the heart.

'Now that I am at St. Helena—now that I am alone, nailed to this rock, who fights and conquers empires for me? What courtiers have I in my misfortune? Does any one think of me? Does any one in Europe move for me? Who has remained faithful? Where are my friends? Yes, you, two or three whose fidelity immortalises you, share my exile.' Here the voice of the Emperor assumed a peculiar tone of melancholy irony and deep sadness. 'Yes, our existence has shone with all the brilliancy of the diadem and of sovereignty, and yours, General, reflected this splendour, as the dome of Les Invalides reflects the rays of the sun. But reverses have come. By degrees the golden hues are effaced, the floods of misfortune and the outrages to which I am every day subjected carry away the last tints. Only the copper remains, General, and soon I shall be dust.

'Such is the destiny of great men; of Cæsar, and of Alexander; we are forgotten, and the name of a conqueror like that of an emperor is only the subject of a college theme. Our exploits come under the ferule of a pedant, who either praises or insults us. A few moments and this will be my fate; what will happen to myself? Assassinated by the English oligarchy, I die prematurely, and my body will be returned to the earth to become pasture for worms. This is the destiny, now very near, of the great Napoleon. What a gulf between my misery and the eternal reign of Christ, preached, praised, loved, adored, living in the whole universe! Is this to die? Is it not rather to live? Such is the death of Christ—such the death of God.']

But perhaps the department of the Abbé's duties in which Napoleon took the strongest interest, was the education of Count Bertrand's children, for whom he always showed great affection. They visited him whenever he felt well enough to talk and play with them, and at a rather later period Antommarchi describes how he was summoned to the garden to pierce the ears of Hortense Bertrand, in order that she might wear a pair of earrings Napoleon had got for her, whilst Count Montholon supported the little girl, the ex-Emperor exhorted her to be brave, and her brother Arthur 'stamped and stormed,' declaring in broken English that he would not allow his sister to be hurt.

Another of Dr. Antommarchi's pictures shows us Napoleon at work : ' The Emperor was at his desk, around him were rulers and compasses, and he twisted in his fingers a pencil which he habitually wrote with, very seldom using pen and ink. I perceived plans, sketches, and algebraic formulæ; but he whistled, and that announced a storm. We always guessed the sensations which agitated him by his manner of applying to work. If he was serious, we could judge that he was suffering and the subject difficult. If we heard him hum a few lines of some lively Italian air, we knew that his sufferings and recollections were suspended, and that he was restored to his usual amenity. But if the air resounded through his lips, he was cross, displeased, out of temper, and only waited an opportunity or a word to break out. Woe to whoever was then in the way—he had to weather a squall!'[1]

With Antommarchi's entreaties that Napoleon would leave the house and take more air and exercise, Napoleon compromised by beginning to turn

[1] *Last Days*, vol. i. p. 149.

vigorously to gardening; the doctor's narrative and the orderly officer's notes in November and several subsequent months being largely filled with descriptions of his digging, planting, and watering, the Abbés, the gentlemen of his suite, and his attendants being all pressed into the service, and a party of Chinese labourers engaged to help.¹ These operations were frequently followed by *al fresco* meals, and the change in Napoleon's habits made the orderly's duties so easy of accomplishment that he records it with pious thankfulness: 'God send he may always continue in this humour during my residence at Longwood!'

In January 1820 an enlargement of the limits to 'about thirteen miles' (according to Captain Nicholls) gave Napoleon some satisfaction, and he took some long rides, on several occasions breakfasting at the house of Sir William Doveton, on the other side of the island.

A favourite occupation of Napoleon, says Mr. Forsyth, was to write or dictate papers 'on the

¹ 'It was a picture worthy of being represented by a celebrated artist, to see the conqueror of so many kingdoms, who had dictated laws to so many sovereigns, at dawn of day, spade in hand, a broad straw hat on his head, and his feet clad in red morocco slippers, directing our labours, and those, assuredly more useful, of the Chinese gardeners. . . . The turf walls being finished, the Emperor had twenty-four large trees purchased, and caused them to be planted with two yards square of earth round their roots. The artillery company transported them to Longwood, with the help of several hundred Chinese. . . . The library garden was shut in to the height of the steps of the billiard cabinet by semicircular grass steps, each range of steps being planted with rose trees. . . . A space six feet wide, being made with a double row in the centre, made a cabinet with grassy seats.'—*History of the Captivity of Napoleon*, Colburn, 1847, vol. iii. p. 114.

subject of defensive operations by field-works, and the depth of formation of troops. The French formed their line three deep, but as the rear rank could not fire over the two others in its front, he preferred the English method of forming two deep only, so long as effect could not be given to the fire of the third rank. Count Bertrand mentioned, shortly after Napoleon's death, that he would get up as often as seven times in the middle of the night to write notes on this question. . . . He used to trace out his plans and field-works in his little garden, with his officers and attendants around him. He described the mode in which he would give effect to the fire of a line drawn up in ranks even ten deep, by placing the rows of men on inclined positions, or drawing them up with the men of lowest stature in the front rank, and the tallest in the rear. With these ranks, eight or ten deep, he thought himself perfectly unassailable, and would hear of no objection to his plan. He proposed that in those places where the ground did not slope, the men should be made to dig away some of the earth where they were to stand, so as to form steps which would give sufficient elevation to the rear ranks to enable them to fire over those in front, and this he said he would have done in a minute. When Bertrand asked for another minute, he replied, "No! in war half a minute is too much to lose. You would have the cavalry upon you and be cut in pieces." To prove the practicability of such depths of formation he sometimes called out, "Come here, Noverraz, you are the tallest; place yourself there, and you others

THE EMPEROR IN HIS GARDEN.—From a Picture by Horace Vernet.

come here." Having arranged them according to size on a declivity, he stood behind, saying, " I who am the smallest will be in the last rank." He then, said Bertrand, levelled a stick and took aim over our heads, exclaiming in triumph, " Eh bien! Don't you see that I fired over the head of Noverraz?"'[1]

About this time Napoleon appears to have had *one* welcome visitor from Plantation House. 'Miss Susanna Johnson, the young and pretty daughter of Lady Lowe, ventured to come alone to Longwood,' says Montholon, 'and begged me to show her the gardens newly created, as if by magic, by the manual labour of the Emperor. . . . Believing I might be certain of not meeting the Emperor, I yielded to her wishes and conducted her to the private gardens. We had scarcely gone a hundred paces, however, before, on making a turn in the covered walk, we found ourselves face to face with the Emperor who, seated on a bench, appeared to be watching us. My surprise was great, but less so, I think, than the impression made on Miss Johnson. Her pretty face was lighted up with animation, and expressed at once her timid embarrassment and her joy at seeing the Emperor. His manner was amiable and kind; he had a plate of sweetmeats brought to her, appeared to take pleasure in showing her his gardening labours, and, as she was taking her departure, plucked a rose and offered it to her as a souvenir of what he termed *her pilgrimage.*'[2]

[1] *Captivity of Napoleon,* vol. iii. pp. 207, 208.
[2] *Ibid.,* vol. iii. pp. 122, 123.

Napoleon's long and frequent conversations with Antommarchi, as with O'Meara, turned frequently on the sins of the English Government, the tyranny of Sir Hudson Lowe, and the uselessness of medicine. 'We are,' he said on one occasion, 'machines made to live. Do not counteract the living principle. . . . The art of healing consists only in lulling and calming the imagination. That is the reason why the ancients adopted an imposing costume. That costume you have unadvisedly abandoned, and in so doing you have exposed the imposture of Galen. Who knows whether, if you were suddenly to appear before me with an enormous wig, a cap, and a long train, I should not take you for the god of health? Whereas you are only the god of medicines.'

In July 1820 Antommarchi writes: 'The progress of the Emperor's complaint was slow but unceasing and visible; and it was on the mind that its effect was particularly marked. He now only spoke of the objects that had arrested his attention during his infancy, and of his friends and relations.' To his mother his thoughts turned continually. 'You are very much attached to me, Doctor,' he said to Antommarchi; 'you care not for contradiction, pain, or fatigue when you can relieve my sufferings; yet all this is not maternal solicitude. Ah, Mamma Letizia!' Of his old Corsican nurse he also spoke with great affection, and told many anecdotes of his childhood.

On November 1, says Montholon, 'the Emperor, seeing that there were no workmen employed about the new house, yielded to a feeling of curiosity to see it. The fine dimensions of the apartments destined for him struck him, and he could not refrain from saying that he would be much more comfortable there than at the old Longwood, and that it would be like the children who quarrel with their bread and butter to refuse to inhabit it when it was finished.' Unfortunately Sir Hudson Lowe heard of this inspection and, with his usual want of tact, called next day on Montholon to know 'how General Bonaparte had liked his new habitation.' That, of course, was quite enough to make him, *dis*like it at once: 'The Emperor's displeasure was extreme. He dictated to me a letter full of bitterness, in which he declared that he would never, unless forced to do so, enter the iron cage which was being constructed by the English Government. This referred to the iron railing destined to enclose the garden, terrace, and pasture surrounding the house. This time we were again victorious. The works relating to the iron railing were suspended.'[1]

Montholon proceeds to relate several proposals for aiding Napoleon to leave the island, which reached him in spite of all the Governor's vigilance. 'To all these offers of escape the Emperor always replied, when speaking to me, "I should not be six months in America without being assassinated by the Comte d'Artois's creatures . . . and besides, we should always obey our destiny . . . it is my martyrdom which will restore the crown of France

[1] *Captivity*, vol. iii. pp. 140, 141.

to my dynasty. I see in America nothing but assassination or oblivion. I prefer St. Helena."'[1]

In December Napoleon received intelligence of the death of his sister Eliza, formerly Grand-Duchess of Tuscany. Antommarchi says that the shock almost overpowered him, and that his comment was: 'Well, Doctor, you see Eliza has just shown me the way! Death, which had forgotten my family, has begun to strike it; my turn cannot be far off.'[2]

To Montholon he said, 'She had noble qualities and a remarkable mind, but no intimacy ever existed between us. Our characters were opposed to this.'

In curious contrast with the many friendly expressions which Antommarchi attributes to Napoleon respecting himself, is a correspondence which took place in January, when the doctor wrote to Montholon of his desire to return to Europe, as he regretted his 'inability to gain the confidence of the Emperor,' and the reply dictated by Napoleon to Montholon, in which he tells Antommarchi, 'During the fifteen months which you have spent in this country, you have given His Majesty no confidence in your moral character; you can be of no use to him in his illness,' and suggests that he should accompany the Abbé Buonavita when he sailed for Europe, Napoleon having dismissed him (with a small pension) on account of his continuous ill-health. Bertrand and Montholon, however, interceded for Antommarchi, and at length obtained

[1] *Captivity*, vol. iii. p. 142. [2] *Last Days*, vol. i. p. 371.

his pardon. 'He was really a good young man, and much devoted to the Emperor; it was a pity that he was not ten years older.'[1]

On March 17 Napoleon went out for the last time. Soon afterwards he consented to see Dr. Arnott, but the time had past when the most able of physicians could have relieved his sufferings or prolonged his life. Still, amidst weakness and cruel pain, Napoleon retained his gratitude for personal devotion, and his kindly memory for past services. Antommarchi relates how, when the end was drawing very near, 'the Emperor ordered the door of his apartment to be closed to everybody except General Montholon and Marchand, who both remained with him until six o'clock. When I entered the room I found the carpet strewn with papers torn up, and observed that everything was ticketed and bore an address. Napoleon had made an inventory of all his effects, and assigned to each object a special destination. "My preparations are made, Doctor," he said; "I am going; it is all over with me." I was representing to him that there were still many chances in his favour, and that his case was not desperate, but he stopped me: "No more illusion. I know the truth, and am resigned."'

The zeal and solicitude of his servants, who insisted on sharing the sad night-watches of Bertrand, Montholon, and the doctor, greatly touched Napoleon, who, says Antommarchi, 'recommended them to his officers, enjoining that they might be assisted and

[1] *Captivity*, vol. iii. pp. 155, 156.

taken care of. "And my poor Chinese," said he; "do not let them be forgotten. Let them have a few scores of Napoleons. I must take leave of them also."[1]

Many interesting details of Napoleon's last illness, too long and numerous to be given here, will be found in each of the works already so freely quoted. A less familiar account, so condensed as to bring it within the space now available, is given in the following letter, written by Count Bertrand to Joseph Bonaparte, which we extract from *Du Casse* (Letters of Joseph Bonaparte) :—[2]

LONDON, *September 16, 1821.*

PRINCE—I write to you for the first time since the awful misfortune which has been added to the sorrows of your family. Your Highness is acquainted with the events of the first years of this cruel exile; many persons who have visited St. Helena have informed you of what was still more interesting to you—the manner of living and the unkind treatment which aggravated the influences of a deadly climate. In the last year of his life the Emperor, who for four years had taken no exercise, altered extremely in appearance; he became pale and feeble. From that time his health deteriorated rapidly and visibly. He had always been in the habit of taking baths; he now took them more frequently and stayed longer in them: they appeared to relieve him for the time. Latterly Dr. Antommarchi forbade him their use, as he thought that they only increased his weakness.

In the month of August he took walking exercise, but with

---

[1] *Last Days*, vol. i. p. 145.
[2] *Du Casse* (English edition; Murray, 1852), vol. ii. pp. 272-275.

difficulty; he was forced to stop every minute. In the first years he used to walk while dictating; he walked about his room, and thus did without the exercise which he feared to take out of doors lest he should expose himself to insult; but latterly his strength would not admit even of this. He remained sitting nearly all day and discontinued almost all occupation. His health declined sensibly every month.

Once in September, and again in the beginning of October, he rode out, as his physicians desired him to take exercise; but he was so weak that he was obliged to return in his carriage. He ceased to digest; his debility increased. Shivering fits came on, which extended even to the extremities; hot towels applied to the feet gave him some relief. He suffered from these cold fits to the last hour of his life. As he could no longer either walk or ride, he took several drives in an open carriage at a foot-pace, but without gaining strength. He never took off his dressing-gown. His stomach rejected food, and at the end of the year he was forced to give up meat; he lived upon jellies and soups. For some time he ate scarcely anything, and drank only a little pure wine, hoping thus to support nature without fatiguing the digestion; but the vomiting continued, and he returned to soups and jellies. The remedies and tonics which were tried produced little effect. His body grew weaker every day, but his mind retained its strength.'

He liked reading and conversation; he did not dictate much, although he did so from time to time up to the last days of his life. He felt that his end was approaching, and he frequently recited the passage from *Zaïre* which finishes with this line—

. · . À revoir Paris je ne dois plus prétendre.

Nevertheless the hope of leaving this dreadful country often presented itself to his imagination; some newspaper articles and false reports excited our expectations. We sometimes fancied that we were on the eve of starting for America; we read travels, we made plans, we arrived at your house, we wandered over that immense country, where alone we might hope to enjoy liberty. Vain hopes! vain projects! which only made us doubly feel our misfortunes.

They could not have been borne with more serenity and courage, I might almost add gaiety. He often said to us in the evening, 'Where shall we go? to the Théâtre Français, or to the Opera?' And then he would read a tragedy by Corneille, Voltaire, or Racine; an opera of Quinault's, or one of Molière's comedies. His strong mind and powerful character were perhaps even more remarkable than on that larger theatre where he eclipsed all that is brightest in ancient and modern history. He often seemed to forget what he had been. I was never tired of admiring his philosophy and courage, the good sense and the fortitude which raised him above misfortune.

At times, however, sad regrets and recollections of what he had done, contrasted with what he might have done, presented themselves. He talked of the past with perfect frankness; persuaded that on the whole he had done what he was required to do, and not sharing the strange and contradictory opinions which we hear expressed every day on events which are not understood by the speakers. If the conversation took a melancholy turn, he soon changed it; he liked to talk of Corsica, of his old uncle Lucien, of his youth, of you, and of all the rest of the family.

Towards the middle of March fever came on. From that time he scarcely left his bed except for about half an hour in the day; he seldom had the strength to shave. He now, for the first time, became extremely thin. The fits of vomiting became more frequent. He then questioned the physicians on the conformation of the stomach, and about a fortnight before his death he had pretty nearly guessed that he was dying of cancer. He was read to almost every day, and dictated a few days before his decease. He often talked naturally as to the probable mode of his death; but when he became aware that it was approaching, he left off speaking on the subject. He thought much about you and your children. To his last moments he was kind and affectionate to us all; he did not appear to suffer so much as might have been expected from the cause of his death. When we questioned him, he said that he suffered a little, but that he could bear it. His memory declined during the last five or six days; his deep sighs and exclamations from time to time made us think that he was in great pain. He looked at us with the penetrating glance which you know so well; we tried to dissimulate, but he was so used to read our faces that no doubt he frequently discovered our anxiety. He felt too clearly the gradual decline of his faculties not to be aware of his state.

For the last two hours he neither spoke nor moved; the only sound was the difficult breathing, gradually but regularly decreasing; his pulse ceased; and so died, surrounded only by a few servants, the man who had dictated laws to the world, and whose life should have been preserved for the sake of the happiness and glory of our sorrowing country. Forgive, Prince, a hurried letter, which tells you so little, when you wish to know so much, but I should never end if I attempted to tell all.

You are so far off that I know not when I shall have the honour of seeing you again. I must not omit to say that the Emperor was most anxious that his correspondence with the different sovereigns of Europe should be printed; he repeated this to us several times. In his will the Emperor expressed a wish that his remains should be buried in France; however, in the last days of his life, he ordered me, if there was any difficulty about it, to lay him by the side of the fountain whose waters he had so long drunk.

*   *   *   *   *   *   *

And both the wishes expressed by Napoleon as to his place of interment were fulfilled: first laid to rest, with the honours of a military funeral, and the tears of a sorrowing household, 'under the beautiful willows which overhung the spring,' by whose side he had often sat,—nineteen years later his country reclaimed his body, a request responded to on behalf of the British Government with Lord Palmerston's characteristic generosity, and a great pageant accompanied its transference from St. Helena to the Invalides in Paris. Louis Philippe received the body of the great Emperor with a respect which did honour to himself; and when in 1855 the Queen of England stood with Napoleon III. beside the First Napoleon's tomb, her silent homage to the memory of a great enemy typified the national feeling, which could well afford to let old hatreds die, and dwell chiefly on the great achievements of the soldier and monarch, and the kindly impulses of the man.

'. . . . . since he had
The genius to be loved, why let him have
The justice to be honoured in his grave.
I think this nation's tears thus poured together,
Better than shouts. I think this funeral
Grander than crownings, though a Pope bless all.
I think this grave stronger than thrones.'

[*NOTE*]

THE BATTLE OF WATERLOO

(*Vol. i. p.* 334, *and Vol. ii. p.* 26)

THE following letter from the Rev. G. de Grouchy appeared in one of the London journals as the last sheets of this work were passing through the press, and appears to be of sufficient interest and importance to be subjoined to O'Meara's record :—

To the Editor of the '*Standard.*'

SIR—In your article of the 30th you say that 'Grouchy has been accused of want of energy in not vigorously marching to strike the Prussians, whom he discovered to be moving on Napoleon's right flank.' It was not want of energy, but want of time, that absolutely prevented his doing that which Napoleon most imprudently ordered him to do. I received the following information from Marshal de Grouchy's own mouth :—

Napoleon summoned him at one o'clock A.M. on the 18th, and requested him to advance against the Prussians under Blucher, whom he believed to be in the neighbourhood of Wavre, some twelve or fifteen miles distant. Grouchy prayed the Emperor not to send him, at such a time, on so uncertain an errand, with thirty-one thousand men whom he commanded. The only reply he got was, 'Grouchy, am I commander or not?' The distance was too great, in the swampy state of the country, for him to meet the Prussians till late in the day. He sent several messages during that day to Napoleon, one at nine o'clock, another at eleven. Of these Napoleon took no notice.

At one o'clock P.M. he sent word that there seemed to be a general cannonade; but the instructions he then received were too late, and could not be carried into effect.

I write this from memory; but further and more precise details can be obtained from the *Historical Fragments*, relative to the Battle of Waterloo, by Grouchy himself, which are in my possession.—I am, Sir, your obedient servant,

G. DE GROUCHY.

Stoke St. Milburgh, Ludlow,
August 31, 1888.

Napoleon

An abstract of personal details concerning him, or of opinions upon persons or events expressed by him.

₊ *For particulars of persons mentioned in these volumes (unless especially referred to by the Emperor) see the General Index.*

His patron saint, ii. 245, 282, (283)
His parentage and childhood, i. 343, 344; ii. 282, 347
His foster-brother, ii. 279, 280
Boyhood, i. 232, 274; ii. 187, 188, 228, 231
The opening of his career, i. 202, 233; ii. 229
The campaigns and career of Napoleon—
Toulon (1793), i. 187-190; ii. 227
13th Vendémiaire, year IV. (1795), ii. 6, 7
Italy (1796), i. 199, 233, 244; ii. 35, 60, 61, 101, 102, 227, 230, 231, 259, 298, 299, 300
Egypt and Syria (1798-99), i. 64, 199, 281, 296-300; ii. 4, 5, 6, 31, 32, 96-99, 160, 171
[Walcheren (1799), i. 238]
Marengo (1800), ii. 211
Hohenlinden (1800). *See* Moreau in General Index
[St. Domingo (1802-1803), ii. 207]

Campaigns, etc., continued—
Ulm and Austerlitz (1805), i. 211
Jena and Auerstädt (1806), i. 192
Eylau and Friedland (1807), ii. 187
Spain. *See* Ferdinand, in General Index
Eckmühl, Essling, and Wagram (1809), i. 33, 199, 252, 354; ii. 211
Moscow (1812), i. 32, 176-181; ii. 51, 75, 107
Lützen, Bautzen, Dresden, and Leipzig (1813), i. 34, 251, 252; ii. 180, 322, 323, 324
France (1814), ii. 181
The return from Elba (1815), ii. 261, 262
Ligny and Waterloo (1815), i. 161, 334-338, 359; ii. 24, 25, 26, 35, 143, 185, 186, 371, 372
His escapes and wounds, i. 198, 199, 253, 273, 274, 362, 363;

ii. 61, 227, 228, 229, 231. *See* also Conspiracies

Conspiracies against Napoleon, i. 303-311, 355; ii. 13-17, 79, 80, 86, 167, 168, 195, 218-220

⁎ *See also Pichegru, Georges, Moreau, etc., in General Index.*

His national works, ii. 108, 109

His personal appearance,—Prefatory Note referring to Cameo. *See* also Illustrations,—i. 7, 8, 114; ii. 24, 53, 58, 75, 310, 348, 349, 357

Knowledge of languages, ii. 8, 74

Characteristics, i. 216, 283, 304, 307, 345, 365; ii. 145, 344, 349

Habits, manners, customs, etc., i. 14, 15, 24, 27, 31-35, 39, 44, 68, 74, 85, 86, 87, 91, 126, 148, 204, 209, 215, 267, 280, 282, 283, 293, 327, 353; ii. 24, 31, 57, 67, 74, 89, 95, 102, 141, 146, 178, 179, 194, 208, 250, 254, 272, 277, 302, 317, 343, 357, 358, 359

Napoleon's flirtations, ii. 66, 221-224

The Empress Josephine, i. 165; ii. 23, 27, 139

For other than special references see General Index.

The Empress Marie Louisa, ii. 27, 183, 184, 226, 281, 307, 340

For other than special references see General Index.

His son (the King of Rome), ii. 281, 308, 340; his bust detained by Lowe, ii. 128, 136, 137, 139, 140, 144, 150, 151, 161; his portrait, ii. 311

For other than special references see General Index.

Anecdotes of Napoleon, i. 50, 107, 108, 119, 183, 188, 189, 208, 232, 351; ii. 45, 68, 88, 102, 129, 137, 149, 158, 221, 222, 224, 228, 229, 232, 261, 282, 283, 308, 309, 318, 322, 344, 347, 350, 357, 365, 366

Agreeable traits of his character, i. 25, 108, 166, 217, 218, 274, 275, 284, 287, 360; ii. 59, 89, 153, 172, 174, 262, 308, 317, 318, 321,'336, 340

Religious sentiments, i. 167, 168, 169, 171; ii. 3, 4, 9, 36, 198, 320, 350-355

Robbery of his funds in 1814, ii. 232

Napoleon at Elba, ii. 20, 21, 22, 34, 50, 56, 84

His surrender in 1815, i. 4, 260; ii. 322

Duke of Wellington and St. Helena, ii. 195

Voyage to St. Helena, i. 1, 2, 3, 4, 6, 7, 8, 9, 39; ii. 237

'The Briars,' i. 11, 13, 14, 16, 24, 166

'Longwood,' i. 11, 12, 17, 18, 19 (plan), 20, 21, 22, 47, 49, 50, 51, 76, 79 (fire there, 83), 166, 243, 321, 339, 340, 349; ii. 18, 46 (rats, etc., 47), 169, 208, 213, 214 (earthquake, 234, 235, 236), 347, 348

New House at Longwood, ii. 363

Disagreeable relations with Sir Hudson Lowe, i. 36, 37, 47, 48, 49, 53, 54, 55, 57, 58, 82, 95, 96, 97, 99, 100, 101, 102, 103, 109, 118, 119, 128, 129, 130, 132, 134, 135, 136, 137, 138, 139, 141, 143, 145, 146, 147, 150, 151, 152, 156, 157, 173, 174, 196, 197, 204, 205, 206, 207, 213, 219, 226, 227, 228, 229, 230, 240, 244, 246, 247, 248, 249, 255, 257, 258, 259, 262, 263, 264, 265, 276, 277, 285, 286, 287, 289, 290, 291, 316, 317, 318, 319, 320, 321, 322, 323, 324, 326, 327, 333, 361, 366; ii. 1, 30, 76,

PERSONAL DETAILS 375

77, 83, 84, 103, 111, 113, 119, 125, 126, 147, 153, 161, 162, 163, 164, 165, 170, 197, 203, 217, 218, 241, 242, 243, 244, 252, 256, 257, 263, 264, 265, 266, 267, 268, 270, 271, 284, 285, 289, 291, 300, 301, 312, 313, 314, 327, 329, 343
_{*} *The above are the more important instances only.*
The removal of Count Las Cases by Governor Lowe, i. 205, 268; ii. 193
The removal of Dr. O'Meara by Governor Lowe, ii. 340
Napoleon's suite dismissed, i. 158
The Imperial plate, at Longwood, broken up, to obtain money, i. 113, 121, 123, 143, 167, 175, 204, 270
Health of Napoleon (*see* also 'Wounds'—reported attempt at suicide in 1814, i. 131), i. 33, 56, 61, 67, 87, 117, 129, 131, 144, 155, 156, 160, 164, 165, 166, 167, 173, 197, 220, 253, 254, 259, 266, 271, 275, 287, 317, 341, 342, 344, 349; ii. 19, 20, 96, 115, 151, 199, 208, 214, 225, 226, 239, 240, 245, 252, 253, 255, 257, 258, 259, 263, 269, 270, 272, 278, 286, 289, 293, 302, 306, 310, 318, 326, 330, 336, 338, 342, 346, 347, 362, 365, 366, 367, 368, 369
His last moments, ii. 362, 365, 366, 367, 368, 369, 395
The last return to France, ii. 370, 396

Conversations or comments of Napoleon (*see* under 'Campaigns,' etc.) Opinions upon Marriage, i. 67 — English cookery, i. 69 — English seamen, i. 163, 164, 277, 278; ii. 55, 72, 99, 172, 173, 250

—Jewish and other religions, i. 167, 169, 171, 181, 182, 183 [ii. 42]—Freemasons, i. 170—Jesuits, i. 170—Poles, i. 175, 176—Predestinarianism, i. 184—English soldiers, i. 97, 185; ii. 100 — Italian, Russian, Austrian, and Prussian troops, i. 186, 187—Spain, i. 195—The Expedition to Copenhagen, i. 234; ii. 77—Dunkirk pilots, i. 235—Breaches of parole, i. 237—Walcheren expedition, i. 238—Prisoners in pontoons, i. 294, 295—Attempted invasion of England, i. 312, 313, 314, 315; ii. 315, 316—The French Revolution, i. 242; ii. 295—Egypt and England, i. 325, 326—The assassination of the Emperor Paul, i. 328, 329, 330—Intended invasion of India, i. 330, 331; ii. 204, 205, 206, 237, 238—Russian aggression, i. 331, 332; ii. 104, 105, 106, 115, 116, 331 — South America, i. 317, 358—English Embassy to China, ii. 28, 29—English manufactures, ii. 31—The 'Army of Italy,' ii. 35—Exercise of patronage, ii. 38, 39—Well-deserved reproof to a bigot, i. 169; ii. 42—The Bourbons, ii. 41, 42, 43—Dey of Algiers, ii. 53, 54, 55—On doctors, ii. 62, 63, 247, 248—Curious accidents, ii. 64, 65—Eunuchs, ii. 65, 66—The Peace of Amiens, ii. 52, 78, 296—The exchange of prisoners, ii. 80, 81, 82—Prince Leopold's appearance, ii. 85—Anecdote of French women, ii. 101, 102—'Folly' of England, ii. 116, 117, 118—'A nation of shopkeepers,' ii. 121, 122 — On prisons, ii. 124, 125 (*see* 'Pontoons' above) — English

ABSTRACT OF PERSONAL DETAILS

habits at dinner, ii. 201—Wellington's sieges, ii. 202, 289—New French nobility, i. 155; ii. 210—Imperial matchmaking, ii. 224—Amusing stratagem of monks, ii. 245, 246—Postal espionage, ii. 273, 274, 275, 276—Lord Cochrane in the Charente, ii. 277—Anecdote of Persian Ambassador, ii. 278—On the observance of Sunday, ii. 290—Anecdote of Cardinal Richelieu, ii. 293, 294—On the death of the Princess Charlotte, ii. 306, 307—On conscription, ii. 317—His gratitude to his family, ii. 336—And also to the Holland family, i. 73; ii. 336—Injunctions to Dr. O'Meara, ii. 339—His sister's death (Eliza), ii. 364—Opinion of Antommarchi, ii. 364—His last wishes, ii. 365

∗ *For individuals see fuller references in the General Index.*

Special mention of—The Pope, ii. 139—Madame Mère, ii. 138, 340—Czar Alexander, i. 231—King of Prussia, i. 104, 231; ii. 100, 101, 212—Queen of Prussia, ii. 175, 176—Emperor of Austria, ii. 68, 96, 212, 309 Marie Antoinette, ii. 193—Comte d'Artois, i. 106—Ferdinand of Spain, ii. 154, 186, 187—Prince Leopold, ii. 85—Prince of Orange, ii. 174—The Arch-Duke Charles, i. 187—Metternich, ii. 52—Schwarzenberg, i. 187—Stein, ii. 50, 51—Wurmser, ii. 157, 158, 159—Blucher, i. 184—Wellington, ii. 289 (*see* Campaigns)—Washington, i. 153 —Pitt, i. 163—Cornwallis, ii. 48, 49—Fox, ii. 155, 156—Sir John Moore, i. 62, 160—Sir Sidney Smith, i. 193, 194; ii. 195—Robespierre, Marat, etc., ii. 189—Barras, i. 172; ii. 190—Fouché, i. 154; ii. 191, 219—Moreau, i. 220, 221, 250; ii. 87, 88, 92, 93, 305—Pichegru, i. 225, 301; ii. 89-92, 94—Georges, i. 75—Bernadotte, ii. 95, 304—Hoche, ii. 37, 38—Desaix, i. 222, 223, 280; ii. 91, 92—Menou, i. 63; ii. 6—Kléber, i. 63, 222—Carnot, i. 171, 172—Sieyès, ii. 191, 249—His suite at St. Helena, i. 153—Various generals, i. 221; ii. 45, 60, 233—Berthier, i. 341—Clarke, i. 343, 344—Davoût, ii. 44—Drouot, i. 72; ii. 305—Grouchy, i. 334, 335; ii. 371—Jourdan, ii. 202—Lannes, i. 222, 223—Masséna, i. 221, 222, 224, 354; ii. 288—Murat, i. 30, 191; ii. 68, 69, 70, 71, 133, 134, 135, 141, 142, 223—Ney, i. 336; ii. 11—Oudinot, i. 203—Savary, i. 153—Soult, i. 107, 335; ii. 202—Talleyrand, i. 197, 198, 302, 350, 358; ii. 2, 11, 188, 192, 260—Barré, i. 64—Brueys, ii. 97—Villeneuve, i. 63—Denon, ii. 2, 139—Talma, ii. 280—Lafitte, ii. 232—Chateaubriand, ii. 304—Madame de Staël, ii. 113, 114, 211—Abbé de Pradt, ii. 212—Larrey, ii. 249—Narbonne, ii. 184

∗ *For other allusions to the above see General Index.*

INDEX

OF PERSONS MENTIONED IN THE PRELIMINARY MATTER TO THE FIRST VOLUME

SEE ALSO LIST OF PRINCIPAL PERSONS AT ST. HELENA, PREFIXED TO VOLUME I.

ABELL, Mrs., lxxiv, lxxv
Abercromby, Sir Ralph, xvi
Alexander, Emperor of all the Russias, xviii, xxiv, lxix
Alison, Sir Archibald, xx
Anglès, Count, xxiv

BAIRD, Sir David, xl
Balcombe, Mr., xxiv, lxxiv
Balcombe, Miss Betsy, xliv, lxxiv
Balmaine, Count, xxxiv, xlvii, xlviii, lxv, lxvi, lxvii, lxviii, lxxiii
Barrow, Mr., Secretary, xiii, xiv
Bathurst, Benjamin, l
Bathurst, Earl, xix, xx, xxi, xxxiv, xxxvii, xxxviii, xlviii, xlix, l, lxi, lxiii, lxvi, lxvii, lxxv, lxxvi, lxxvii
Baxter, Dr., lx
Beauharnais, Eugène, xxiv
Beauharnais, Hortense, lxxv
Bernadotte, Prince of Ponte-Corvo, xviii
Bertrand, Count, xxi, li, lii. *See* also biographical note prefixed to vol. i.
Bertrand, Countess, lxxv
Blackwood, xxvi
Blucher, Prince, xviii
Bonaparte, Joseph, xxiv

Bonaparte, Pauline, xvi, xli
Broglie, de, Duc, xlvii
Brunswick, House of, lxxvi
Byron, Lord, xxvi

C——, Sir George, xxv
Carlyle, Thomas, xxvii
Campbell, Lord, xx
Carnot, lxxix
Caroline, Queen, xxvi
Charles, Archduke, xxxii, xxxiii
Cipriani, xvii
Clough, A., xxxix
Cockburn, Sir George, xix, xxv, xxxvii
Croker, John Wilson, xxv, xxix, xxx, xxxi, xxxii, xxxiii, xxxv, xxxvi, xli, xlvii, lviii, lxiv

DE BUTTS, Lieutenant, xvi
Dickens, Charles, xlviii
Dudley, Lord, xxiv
Dumouriez, General, xlix
[Duroc, xlviii]

EAST INDIA CO., xix
Eliott, Sir G. A., xv
Elysée Père, xxxvii

Eugène, Prince, xxiv
Exmouth, Lord, xviii

FINLAISON, Mr., lviii, lix
Ford, Mr., xvi
Forsyth, Mr. William, Q.C., xvii, xxi, xxxiv, xxxvii, xlvii, xlviii, lii, liii, liv, lv, lviii, lix, lxi, lxii, lxiii, lxiv, lxx
Francis, the Emperor, xxiv, lxvii, lxviii
Frederick the Great, xlvii

GEORGE III., xx, lv. (*See* George IV. under Prince Regent)
Gneisenau, Count, xviii
Goulburn, Mr., xliii
Gourgaud, General Baron, xliii. *See* also biographical note prefixed to vol. i.

HAMAN, liii
Heathfield, Lord, xv
Hérisson, Count, xxiii, xxiv
Holmes, Mr., xii
Hope, Sir A., xviii

JACKSON, Colonel, xx
Jomini, lxxix
Josephine, the Empress, xxxix

KEITH, Lord, xxiii

LA MARQUE, General, xvii
Lamb, Charles, lxxvi
Las Cases, Count, xxvi, xliv, xlv, xlvi, xlvii, lvii, lxxiv. *See* also biographical note prefixed to vol. i.
Lascelles, Colonel, liv, lv
Llandaff, Bishop of, xxv
Louis XVIII., xlix, lxix
Lowe, Sir Hudson, xv, xvi, xvii, xviii, xix, xx, xxi ; Introduction and elsewhere
Lowe family, xv, xix
Lyndhurst, Lord, xx
Lyster, Colonel, li, lii

MADAME MÈRE, vii, xvi
Malcolm, Admiral Sir Pulteney, xxv, lxxvii
Maria Louisa, lxviii
Melville, Lord, xxv, lix
Metternich, Prince, xxi, xxxi, lxii, lxviii, lxix, lxxi, lxxiii
Montchenu,· Marquis de, xxxiv, xlvii, lxv, lxvi, lxvii, lxviii, lxix
Montholon, Count, xx, xlvii, xlviii, lii, liii, liv. *See* also biographical note prefixed to vol. i.
Moore, Sir John, xvi, xvii
Moore, Thomas, xxvi
Mordecai, liii
Moreau, General, xxxv, xxxvi
[Muiron, Colonel, xlviii]

NAPIER, Colonel, xvii
'North, Christopher, xxvi

O'CONNELL, Daniel, xxv
O'Hara, General, xv
O'Meara, Dr., Preface ; xxiii, xxiv, xxv, xxvi, xxvii
O'Meara, Miss Kathleen, xxvi
Orchardson, xliv

PEEL, Sir Robert, xxi, xxxvii
Pellew. *See* Lord Exmouth
Pichegru, General, xxxv
Plampin, Admiral Robert, xiv
Poppleton, Major, lv
Prince Regent, the, xviii, lviii

RÉMUSAT, Madame de, xxxi, xxxix
Revelli, M., vii
Roederer, Count, xxx, xxxi
Rome, King of, liv, lxviii

SAINTE BEUVE, xlvii, lxxvi
Schwarzenburg, Prince, xxxii, xxxiii
Scott, Sir Walter, xx
Smith, Sir Sidney, xvii
Soult, Duke of Dalmatia, lxxvi
Southey, Robert, lxxvi,
Stodart, J. G., vii
Stokoe, Dr., xxxvi, lv, lx, lxxvii

Sturmer, Baron, xxxiv, xxxviii, xliv,
    xlv, xlvi, liii, lix, lxiii, lxiv, lxv,
    lxvi, lxvii, lxviii, lxix, lxx, lxxi,
    lxxii, lxxiii, lxxiv
Sturmer, Baroness, xliv
Suzzarelli, xvii

TALBOT, Sir John, xxiii
Teynham, Lord, xxi
Tindal, Mr., xx

VERLING, Dr., lx
Victoria, Queen, xxi
Voltaire, xlvii

WARDEN, Mr. (Dr.), xiii, xiv
Wellington, Duke of, xviii, xxi, xxxii, xxxiii, lvi, lvii
Wilson ('Christopher North'), xxvi
Woolnoth, T., vii

INDEX

TO NAMES OF PERSONS MENTIONED IN THE BODY OF THIS WORK

Names of Persons printed in the Kalendar and Roll of Honour in violet ink at the end of the Second Volume are not included

* See also Index to Preliminary Matter, and Special Abstract, for 'Napoleon'

ABELL, Mrs., i. 14, 15, 45, 166, 327, 353; ii. 3, 10
Abercrombie, General, i. 115
Aberdeen, Earl of, ii. 234
Abrantés, Duchess of, i. 131, 169; ii. 310
Abrantés, Duke of. *See* Junot
Alexander, Emperor of Russia, i. 124, 125, 159, 171, 177, 180, 181, 193, 212, 231, 251, 260, 264, 328, 331; ii. 22, 105, 106, 107, 115, 168, 175, 184, 308, 310, 339, 341
Alexander the Great, ii. 354, 355, 356
Algiers, Dey of, i. 275
Ali (*see* St. Denis), i. 258
Ali Pasha, i. 102
Alison, Sir Archibald, i. 127
Allen, John, ii. 211
Alvinzi, General, ii. 158
Amherst, Earl, ii. 24, 28, 29, 30, 76, 79, 118, 147, 148, 151, 152, 162, 164, 169, 241, 242, 243, 244, 300
Anglesea, Marquis of, ii. 185
Anne, Grand Duchess of Russia, ii. 309

Antommarchi, Dr., ii. 345, 346, 347, 349, 350, 357, 362, 364, 365, 366
Arbuthnot, Mr., i. 57
Archambaud, the Brothers, i. 2, 156, 157, 158, 204, 258
Archduke Charles. *See* 'Charles'
Aréna, i. 303
Arnott, Dr., ii. 344, 345, 365
Artois, Comte d', i. 105; ii. 17, 262, 363
Augereau, Marshal, i. 221; ii. 299, 325
Austria, Emperor of, i. 191, 231, 260, 310, 341; ii. 22, 51, 68, 95, 96, 116, 135, 141, 157, 168, 181, 183, 184, 212, 281, 308, 309, 339, 341
Avonmore, Lord, ii. 245

BAJAZET, ii. 291
Balcombe, Mr., i. 11, 13, 14, 15, 24, 28, 111, 121, 123, 124, 126, 143, 144, 204, 361; ii. 126, 140, 253, 342
Balcombe, Miss (*see* also Mrs. Abell), ii. 350

Balcombe family, the, i. 14, 28, 260, 327, 334, 342, 353; ii. 9, 199, 215, 342
Balcombe, Cole, and Co., i. 175, 360; ii. 132
Ballantyne, Mr., ii. 132
Balmaine, Count, i. 70, 118, 158, 159; ii. 32, 57, 60, 66, 67, 73, 215, 216, 244, 280 (326, 328)
Balston, Captain, ii. 128, 129, 131
Banks, Sir Joseph, ii. 129
Baraguay d'Hilliers, General, ii. 300
Barber, Mr., ii. 311
Baring Brothers, ii. 194
Barker, Mr., i. 206
Barras, i. 172, 233; ii. 190
Barré, Commodore, i. 64, 65; ii. 98
Barrére, ii. 190
Barry, Lord Avonmore, ii. 245
Bathurst, Lord, i. 40, 90, 94, 123, 129, 130, 133, 140, 145, 151, 214, 247, 255, 303, 340; ii. 119, 120, 125, 127, 147, 151, 160, 163, 165, 168, 204, 251, 257, 273, 326, 329, 332, 337
Bathurst, Mr. Benjamin, i. 145
Baxter, Mr. (Surgeon), i. 35, 75, 102, 201, 256, 261, 271; ii. 240, 256, 271, 286, 290, 291, 302, 306, 314, 327, 337
Bauer, Herr, i. 232
Bavaria, King of, i. 197, 212, 358; ii. 309
Bavaria, Princess of, i. 341
Beauharnais, Eugène, Viceroy of Italy, i. 165, 358; ii. 21, 310
Beauharnais, Hortense, i. 203; ii. 336
Beauharnais, Josephine. *See* Josephine, Empress
Beauharnais family, the, ii. 12
Bedford, Duke of, i. 302
Bernadotte, Prince of Ponte-Corvo, i. 221; ii. 89, 95, 304
Bernard, a servant, i. 2, 77, 94, 156

Bernardin de St. Pierre, ii. 332
Bernstorf, Count, ii. 275
Berri, Duc de, i. 66, 355
Berri, Duchesse de, i. 203
Berry, Miss, ii. 85, 93, 334
Berthier, Prince of Neufchâtel, i. 274, 308, 341; ii. 89, 298
Bertrand, General Count (Henri Gratien), i. 2, 5, 7, 8, 10, 11, 15, 20, 23, 24, 25, 26, 38, 46, 47, 48, 53, 56, 57, 60, 66, 74, 76, 77, 79, 80, 81, 82, 83, 84, 90, 94, 107, 119, 123, 129, 130, 132, 134, 135, 138, 141, 142, 143, 144, 146, 147, 148, 150, 151, 152, 153, 156, 158, 160, 173, 203, 204, 208, 214, 229, 230, 246, 247, 248, 249, 253, 254, 255, 256, 257, 259, 262, 263, 264, 266, 267, 268, 275, 276, 286, 293, 317, 318, 320, 322, 323, 324, 333, 347, 351, 353, 357, 360, 361; ii. 1, 18, 24, 57, 58, 60, 71, 83, 84, 103, 119, 120, 129, 136, 140, 141, 143, 144, 145, 147, 150, 151, 152, 153, 161, 168, 185, 196, 197, 198, 209, 216, 225, 243, 244, 251, 252, 255, 256, 258, 262, 263, 264, 265, 267, 268, 272, 289, 300, 301, 320, 327, 329, 340 (342), 345, 346 (349), 351, 359, 361, 364, 365, 366
Bertrand, Countess, i. 2, 10, 15, 16, 20, 23, 40, 45, 46, 57, 80, 85, 99, 101, 107, 124, 147, 158, 202, 209, 240, 241, 260, 266, 275, 285, 287, 288, 302, 320, 321, 351, 357, 360, 361; ii. 9, 24, 33, 59, 60, 83, 84, 103, 136, 147, 162, 193, 196, 197, 203, 216, 225, 244, 261, 287, 344
Bertrand children (Arthur, Hortense, and Napoleonne), i. 2, 23, 241, 285, 302, 341; ii. 59, 136, 172, 244, 356, 357

Bertrand, Mons., i. 360
Besborough, Lady, ii. 93
Bessières, Duke of Istria, i. 305
Bessières, Madame, ii. 17
Billaud de Varennes, i. 242; ii. 189, 190
Bingham, Sir George, i. 26, 43, 122, 135, 185, 215, 219, 228, 229, 230, 257, 258; ii. 84, 335
Bingham, Lady, i. 43; ii. 1
Blacas, Duc de, i. 208, 347; ii. 41, 43
Blakeney, Captain, i. 205; ii. 196, 200, 214, 216, 224, 235, 244, 245, 285, 289, 312, 331, 337
Blood, Lieutenant, i. 22, 70
Blucher, Prince, i. 57, 96, 184, 363; ii. 371
Bonaparte, Abbé, ii. 282
Bonaparte, Bonaventura, ii. 282, 283
Bonaparte, Caroline, Queen of Naples, i. 191; ii. 85, 194
Bonaparte de Cianfardo, i. 343
Bonaparte, Eliza, Princess of Piombino, ii. 336, 364
Bonaparte, François de, i. 343
Bonaparte, Jerôme, King of Westphalia, ii. 311
Bonaparte, Joseph, King of Spain, i. 216, 224, 225, 237, 317; ii. 113, 121, 202, 298, 339, 347, 366
——— his wife and daughters, ii. 347
Bonaparte, Josephine. *See* Josephine, Empress
Bonaparte, Letitia (Ramolino), MADAME MÈRE, i. 191, 279, 351; ii. 22, 138, 154, 230, 292, 340, 345, 346, 362
Bonaparte, Louis, King of Holland, ii. 12, 53, 279, 347
Bonaparte, Lucien (senior), ii. 368
Bonaparte, Lucien, Prince of Canino, i. 18; ii. 278, 322, 347
Bonaparte, Maria Louisa. *See* Maria Louisa, Empress

Bonaparte, Napoleon I. *See* separately
Bonaparte, Napoleon II. (King of Rome), i. 18, 50, 71 (145), 149, 288, 289, 300, 353; ii. 21, 30, 128, 136, 137, 139, 140, 154, 179, 222, 270, 272, 273, 281, 339, 340
——— 'his brother,' i. 315
Bonaparte, Napoleon Louis, ii. 53
Bonaparte, Napoleon III., ii. 230
Bonaparte, Napoleon Jerôme, Prince Napoleon, ii. 223
Bonaparte, Pauline, Princess Borghese, i. 208; ii. 336, 340, 345, 346, 347
Bonvivant, M., ii. 308, 309
Bourmont, General, and Traitor, i. 334
Bourrienne, Fauvelet de, i. 9, 67, 88, 154, 198, 203, 209, 210, 216, 250, 304, 311, 356, 364; ii. 3, 5, 22, 66, 67, 74, 174, 229, 341, 345, 350
Bouvet de Lozier, ii. 15
Boys, Major, ii. 145, 147
Boys, Rev., ii. 214
Brandenburg, House of, ii. 210
Breame, Mr., ii. 87
Broglie, Duc de, ii. 114
Brooke, Mr., i. 45, 94; ii. 196, 197
Brougham and Vaux, Lord, i. 66
Brueys, Admiral, i. 64; ii. 97, 98, 99
Brune, Marshal, i. 221
Brutus, ii. 191
Bulow, General Count, ii. 25
Bunbury, Sir Henry, i. 1, 37, 71
Bunn, Captain, ii. 337
Buonavita, Abbé, ii. 345, 346, 350, 358, 364
Burdett, Sir Francis, i. 66; ii. 124, 316
Burnet, Bishop, i. 182

CÆSAR, Julius, ii. 229, 354, 355, 356

Cæsar (a servant), i. 307
Caffarelli-Dufalga, i. 273 ; ii. 259
Cambacérès, Duke of Parma, i. 279; ii. 68, 69
Cambronne, General, ii. 261
Campan, Madame, i. 242, 348 ; ii. 138, 193
Campbell, Captain, ii. 60
Campbell, Colonel Sir Neil, ii. 21
Canning, Mr., i. 358
Canova, i. 304
Capet, Hugh, ii. 296
Caracciolo, Prince, i. 278
Carbon, i. 308
Carlos, Don, ii. 186
Carnot, Count, i. 171, 172, 238, 343; ii. 191
Carnot, President, i. 171
Caroline, Queen of Naples (Bourbon), i. 278 ; ii. 71, 167
Castellentini, ii. 96
Castlereagh, Lord, i. 90, 103 ; ii. 21, 22, 43, 49, 50, 109, 122, 123, 127, 182, 183, 224, 233, 251, 257, 276, 296
Cathcart, Lord, i. 251
Caulaincourt, Duke of Vicenza, i. 362 ; ii. 44, 50, 182, 183, 224
Ceracchi, i. 303
Chameroi, Mdlle, i. 169; ii. 143
Championnet, General, i. 190
Charles (servant), i. 243
Charles, the Arch-Duke, i. 187 ; ii. 93
Charles I. (of England), i. 240, 242
Charles II. (of England), i. 182, 249
Charles IV. (of Spain), i. 152 ; ii. 77, 187
Charles Martel, ii. 278
Charlotte, Queen (of England), ii. 307, 310
Charlotte, the Princess, ii. 85, 174, 306
Charras, Colonel, i. 335
Chartres, Duc de (son of Louis Philippe), ii. 167

Châteaubriand, i. 281 ; ii. 19, 75, 304
Chatham, Earl of, i. 238 ; ii. 79, 116, 155
Chaumette, ii, 189
Chesborough, Miss, i. 202
Chesney, Colonel, i. 335
Chesterfield, Earl of, i. 39
China, Emperor of, ii. 28, 29
Christ, the Divinity of, ii. 351, 352, 353, 354, 355, 356
Churchill, Mr. and Misses, ii. 33
Cicero, ii. 155
Cipriani, i. 2, 22, 25, 87, 121, 175, 204, 245, 270, 279, 285, 291, 324, 327 ; ii. 73, 115, 126, 128, 184, 199, 200, 318, 319, 320, 321, 341
Clarke, Duke of Feltre, i. 283, 343, 344
Clausel, General, i. 222 ; ii. 45
Clavering, Lady, i. 78
Clayden, P. W., i. 7
Cochrane, Lord, ii. 72, 277, 278
Cockburn, Admiral Sir George, i. 1, 7, 20, 11, 13, 15, 16, 17, 21, 22, 23, 25, 26, 28, 36, 37, 38, 39, 40, 42, 54, 66, 89, 127, 128, 130, 136, 149, 196, 201, 215, 217, 227, 229, 247, 262, 263, 270, 319, 322, 351, 365 ; ii. 24, 83, 84, 111, 113, 163, 195, 209, 213, 241, 252, 257, 258, 264, 268, 291, 297
Cockburn, Sir George's brother, i. 127
Coffin, Captain, ii. 69
Cole, Mr., ii. 110, 132, 198
Collot d'Herbois, i. 241 ; ii. 189
Condorcet, ii. 177
Confucius, ii. 353
Constant, Benjamin, ii. 204, 233
Cook, Captain (of the *Tortoise*), i. 349 ; ii. 33, 34
Cooper, Mr., i. 22
Corneille, i. 20, 34 ; ii. 321, 368
Cornwallis, Earl of, i. 258 ; ii. 48, 49, 57

Corvisart, Baron, i. 42, 67, 131, 310; ii. 31, 225
Coster, ii. 13, 16
Courland, Duchess of, ii. 11
Couthon, i. 172
Crescentini, ii. 65, 66
Croker, John Wilson, i. 157
Cromwell, Oliver (His Highness the Lord Protector), ii. 5, 86

DANTON, ii. 190
Darling, Mr., ii. 287, 288
Daru, Count, i. 283; ii. 88, 89
Davie, Captain, ii. 148
Davoût, Prince of Echmühl, i. 238, 365; ii. 44, 133
Del Guasto, ii. 117
Denon, Baron, i. 126; ii. 2, 139
Desaix, General, i. 220, 221, 222, 223, 280; ii. 20, 91, 92, 259
Desgenettes, Baron, i. 299
Dey of Algiers, i. 275
Dillon, Madame, i. 351
Dorset, Duchess of, ii. 156
Douglas, Major, i. 194
Doveton, Mr. and Miss, i. 28
Doveton, Sir William, ii. 358
Drake, Mr., i. 91, 258; ii. 13, 17
Drouet, Comte d'Erlon, i. 72
Drouot, General, i. 72, 85; ii. 133, 185, 305
Dubois, Dr., ii. 307
Du Casse, i. 98, 125, 224; ii. 202, 366
Dugommier, General, i. 234
Dumesnil, General, i. 199; ii. 181
Dumourier, General, i. 237
Dundonald, Earl of, ii. 72, 277, 278
Duphot, General, ii. 298
Duroc, Duke of Friuli, i. 5, 85, 148, 202, 203, 216; ii. 103, 104, 223, 224

EBRINGTON, Lord, i. 302; ii. 219
Edward II. (of England), ii. 291
Elizabeth, Princess, ii. 310
Elliot, Mr., i. 344; ii. 148

Ellis, Mr., ii. 152, 302, 331, 332
Elphinstone. *See* Mountstuart Elphinstone
Elphinstone, Captain, ii. 153
Emmett, Major, i. 35
Enghien, Duc d', i. 233, 302, 350, 355; ii. 14, 17
Entraigues, Comte d', ii. 89, 90, 91
Esterhazy, Prince, ii. 151
Exmouth, Lord, ii. 54, 55, 142

FABRE d'Eglantine, ii. 190
Fagan, Colonel, ii. 145, 146
Fehrzen, Major, ii. 58, 59, 103
Ferdinand, King of Naples, i. 190; ii. 69
Ferdinand, King of Spain, i. 198; ii. 23, 154, 186, 187
Fersen, Count, ii. 193
Fesch, Cardinal, i. 352; ii. 304, 345
Festing, Captain, ii. 24
Finlaison, i. 113, 132
Fitzgerald, Lieutenant, i. 107
[Fleurus, Duke of, i. 225; ii. 202]
Fleury, Duc de, ii. 20
Flinders, Captain, ii. 129
Forsyth, William, Q.C., i. 9, 16, 37, 55, 71, 95, 109, 114, 121, 124, 126, 127, 129, 132, 174, 206, 214, 255; ii. 151, 342, 343, 344, 345, 346, 358
Fouché, Duke of Otranto, i. 153, 154, 307; ii. 114, 189, 190, 191, 192, 218, 219
Fouquier Tinville, i. 242
Fourreau de Beauregard, i. 3
Fowler, Mr., i. 89
Fox, Charles James, i. 192 (mispaged); ii. 94, 154, 156, 159, 296, 336
Fox, Mrs., ii. 155
Foy, General, i. 222
Francis the First, i. 50; ii. 117, 118
Francis, Sir Philip, ii. 3
Frederick the Great, i. 50; ii. 59, 74, 175, 233

Froude, J. A., ii. 291
Fuller, Captain, ii. 45

G——s, Mdlle, ii. 220, 221, 223
Galen, ii. 362
Gambier, Lord, ii. 278
Gardanne, General, ii. 331
Gardner, Dorsey, i. 334; ii. 25
Gasparin, i. 234
Gaume, Abbé, ii. 351
Gell, Sir William, ii. 85
Gengis-Khan, i. 50
Gentilini (servant), i. 2, 156, 204
George I. (of England), ii. 149
George III. (of England), i. 240; ii. 38, 80, 149, 296, 316
George IV. (of England). *See* under Prince Regent
Georges (Père), i. 275
Georges (Fils), i. 221, 235, 250, 251, 275; ii. 13, 14, 15, 16, 94
Gerard, General, i. 222; ii. 45
Germany, Emperor of. *See* Austria
Glauber, i. 167
Goldsmith, ii. 27
Gor, Captain, i. 71, 158; ii. 57, 60, 66, 216
Gorrequer, Major, i. 35, 45, 89, 94, 110, 111, 112, 113, 121, 122, 123, 128, 132, 205, 259, 269, 271, 285, 333; ii. 32, 67, 87, 126, 132, 166, 208, 242, 262, 263, 264, 285, 303, 306, 314
Goulburn, Mr., ii. 325
Gourgaud, General, Baron (Gaspard), i. 2, 5, 11, 15, 20, 24, 95, 117, 120, 122, 135, 173, 180, 268, 276, 278, 285, 286, 316, 325, 351, 357; ii. 35, 57, 58, 62, 66, 67, 73, 121, 145, 185, 186, 187, 215, 216, 235, 241, 256, 265, 312, 341, 342
Gourgaud, mother of General, i. 351; ii. 121
Gourgaud, sister of General, i. 351

Graham, Sir Thomas, ii. 202
Grandt, Madame, ii. 2, 3, 11
Grassini, Madame, ii. 66
Grenier, General, ii. 70
Grey, Captain, i. 109
Griffiths, Rev. Mr., ii. 152
Grouchy, Marshal the Marquis de (and Count), i. 161, 334, 335; ii. 26, 37, 371, 372
Grouchy, Rev. G. de (or de Gruchy), ii. 371, 372
Guelph, House, ii. 316
Guizot, M., i. 171; ii. 86
Guyot, General Count, ii. 26

HALL, William (servant), ii. 119
Hamilton, Captain, i. 42, 133
Hamilton, Duke of, ii. 138
Hamilton, Lady, i. 278
Hamley, General, i. 335
Hampden, John, ii. 155
Hannibal, ii. 354, 355
Hardenberg, Prince, ii. 127, 233
Harrison, Major, i. 285, 286
Hartington, Lord, ii. 93
Haugwitz, Count, i. 211
Heaviside, Captain, ii. 153
Hébert, i. 242; ii. 189
d'Hérisson, Count, i. 23, 32, 343; ii. 96, 232, 233, 282
Hesse Homburg, Prince of, ii. 310
Hobhouse, Mr., i. 88, 90; ii. 293
Hoche, General, i. 220; ii. 37, 38
Hodson, Major and Mrs., i. 24, 366
Hoffman the Novelist, i. 34
Holland, Lord, i. 73, 255, 345; ii. 119, 120
Holland, Lady, i. 77; ii. 136, 140, 336, 340
Hugh Capet, ii. 296

IMPETT, Captain, ii. 45
Innes, Captain, ii. 60
Iung, Colonel, i. 234
Ivan (Surgeon), i. 67

JACKSON, Lieutenant, i. 36, 83

Jackson, Sir George, ii. 175, 176, 180, 184, 192
Jackson, Lady, ii. 176, 180, 184
James, William (the Historian), i. 278; ii. 72, 77
Johnson, Dr. Samuel, ii. 213
Johnson, Miss Susanna, ii. 361
Jones, Captain, ii. 145, 147, 269
Jones, Rev. Mr., i. 65
Josephine, the Empress, i. 50, 165, 166, 209, 305, 306, 307; ii. 11, 23, 27, 53, 87, 139, 175, 221, 230
Josephine (a servant), i. 2, 22
Joubert, General, ii. 299
Jourdan, Marshal Count, i. 225; ii. 202
Julien, Captain, ii. 96, 97
Junot, Duc d'Abrantés, i. 188; ii. 20
Junot, Madame, i. 131, 169; ii. 310

KEATING, Colonel, i. 87
Keith, Lord, i. 2, 5, 6, 39, 193; ii. 153
Kléber, General, i. 63, 193, 220, 221, 222, 223, 225; ii. 6, 20, 259
Klinglin, or Klingspor, ii. 91
Köller, Baron, ii. 182
Kolli, Baron, ii. 154

LABAUME, i. 181
Labédoyère, ii. 59, 185, 262, 304·
Labouillerie, ii. 22
Lacordaire, Père, ii. 351, 352
Lafayette, General, ii. 143
Lafitte, Baron, ii. 232
La Haye, ii. 13
L'Allemand, Admiral, ii. 277
L'Allemand, General, ii. 59
Lamarque, General, i. 48, 223
Lamb, Captain, ii. 144, 145, 149, 150, 151, 161
Lanfrey, i. 250; ii. 207
Lannes, Duke of Montebello, i 203, 222, 223, 305

Lanusse, General, i. 223
Larrey, Baron, i. 298, 299; ii. 249
La Sahla, i. 311
Las Cases, Count and Marquis de (Emmanuel, Augustin, Dieudonné, Martin, Joseph), i. 2, 7, 10, 11, 13, 18, 20, 21, 22, 24, 49, 51, 78, 82, 94, 125, 131, 135, 136, 144, 146, 153, 164, 200, 201, 205, 206, 207, 208, 209, 212, 214, 215, 218, 226, 227, 230, 240, 245, 246, 247, 248, 249, 254, 255, 256, 257, 258, 259, 261, 264, 265, 266, 267, 268, 269, 286, 291, 296, 324, 354, 361; ii. 18, 130, 193, 198, 218, 325, 341, 347
Las Cases's narrative quoted, i. 2, 4, 31, 33, 37, 40, 48, 50, 85, 91, 103, 108, 109, 118, 120, 131, 154, 160, 173, 188, 192 (mispaged), 220, 221, 222, 232, 268, 273, 274, 283, 352; ii. 45, 69, 88, 89, 108, 109, 137, 158, 175, 222, 223, 228, 229, 232, 261, 279, 283, 305, 306, 309, 322, 350
Las Cases, the younger, i. 2, 11, 13, 18, 20, 22, 24, 94, 117, 118, 200, 201, 206, 209, 214, 244, 245, 246, 256, 261, 269, 341; ii. 193, 350
Las Cases, Madame, i. 18, 20, 206
Lascelles, Colonel, ii. 333, 334
Lauderdale, Earl of, i. 192 (mispaged); ii. 296
Lauriston, General, ii. 102
Lavalette, Count, i. 59, 281; ii. 12
Lavalette, Madame, i. 59; ii. 12
Leclerc, General, ii. 206
Lefebvre-Desnouettes, General, i. 237, 295
Le Musa, ii. 54
Le Normand, Mdlle, ii. 10
Leopold, Prince, ii. 85, 86, 306

INDEX OF NAMES IN THE

Le Page (a servant), i. 2, 204
Le Sage (*Gil Blas*), ii. 248
Le Sage. *See* also Las Cases
Leslie, Mr., i. 92
Lewis, Lady Teresa, ii. 85, 234
Lichtenstein, Prince Maurice of, ii. 234
Lille, Comte de (*see* Louis XVIII.), ii. 295
Limoelan, i. 306
Littré, i. 217
Liverpool, Earl of, i. 103; ii. 163, 256, 263, 303, 312
Livingston, Dr., ii. 216
Llama, the Grand, ii. 127, 128, 130, 131
Lorri, Ignatio, ii. 279
Louis Napoleon. *See* under Bonaparte
Louis XIV., ii. 276
Louis XV., ii. 184, 260
Louis XVI., i. 242; ii. 96, 113, 177, 193, 310
Louis XVII., ii. 295
Louis XVIII., i. 107, 225, 226, 236, 249, 264, 335, 336, 337, 347, 356; ii. 21, 22, 36, 37, 41, 43, 78, 86, 110, 167, 182, 232, 295, 325
Louis Philippe (ii. 167), ii. 370
Louis (Prince of Prussia), i. 211
Lowe, Sir Hudson, *passim*.
Lowe, Lady, i. 35, 240, 321, 333, 354; ii. 11, 57, 58, 203, 285, 361
Löwenstern, Count Otto, ii. 183
Lullin de Châteauvieux, Marquis, ii. 209
Luxembourg, Duke of, ii. 233
Lycurgus, ii. 353
Lyster, Colonel, i. 35

M, Curious List of Names commencing with 'M,' ii. 230
Macdonald, Duke of Tarentum, i. 221; ii. 230
Macdonald, General, ii. 194
Macirone, Colonel, ii. 133, 141

Mack, General, ii. 230
Mackay, Lieutenant, i. 107
Mackenzie, Mr., ii. 33, 34
M'Lean, Dr., i. 216
MacMahon, Marshal, ii. 230
Madox, Mr., i. 116
Magenta, Duke of, ii. 230
Mahomet, ii. 353
Maingaud, M. (Surgeon), i. 3, 4, 52
Maitland, Captain, R.N., i. 1, 5, 6; ii. 230, 322
Malakoff, Duke of, ii. 230
Malcolm, Admiral Sir Pulteney, i. 72, 74, 76, 93, 94, 95, 97, 123, 124, 205, 207, 209, 215, 219, 230, 257, 263, 264, 265, 266, 271, 280, 281, 285, 286, 287, 288, 290, 291, 315, 316, 317, 319, 324, 352; ii. 30, 72, 76, 77, 78, 79, 112, 115, 119, 127, 145, 147, 148, 149, 160, 166, 230, 301, 302, 303
Malcolm, Lady, i. 76, 266, 288, 319; ii. 24, 127, 145, 146, 147, 148, 149
Malet, General, ii. 230
Malouet, ii. 78, 296
Manning, Mr., ii. 128, 129, 130, 131, 136, 140
Marat, ii. 189
Marbœuf, ii. 230
Marceau, General, i. 220, 221
Marchand (servant), i. 2, 14, 22, 32, 49, 56, 86, 87, 204, 218, 266; ii. 56, 137, 145, 149, 223, 228, 230, 269, 272, 365
Maret, Duke of Bassano, i. 131, 357; ii. 230
Maria Louisa, Empress, i. 18, 50, 51 (145), 289, 350, 352; ii. 21, 27, 28, 55, 68, 69, 85, 96, 150, 153, 183, 184, 212, 221, 226, 230, 233, 273, 281, 292, 307, 339, 340
Marie Antoinette, i. 242, 243, 348; ii. 138, 189, 193, 310
Marius, ii. 169

Marlborough, Duke of, i. 195; ii. 233, 234
Marmont, Marshal, the Duke of Ragusa, ii. 181, 182, 230, 325
Mars, Mdlle, ii. 230
Mary Queen of Scots, i. 328
Mason, Miss, i. 142, 276, 285, 286, 316, 366; ii. 30
Massa, Duc de (Regnier), ii. 230
Masséna, Marshal, Prince of Essling, i. 220, 221, 222, 224, 337, 354; ii. 44, 45, 230, 288
Masseri[a], i. 239, 279
Maubreuil, Marquis de, ii. 233
Maunsell, Colonel, i. 84, 99, 121, 122, 158
Maury, Cardinal, ii. 230
Maximilian, the Emperor, ii. 230
Maxwell, Captain Murray, ii. 152
Mazzini, ii. 276
Meade, General, i. 114, 115, 116, 117, 118, 119, 120
Meade, Mrs., i. 115, 116
Mehée de la Touche, ii. 13, 17
Melzi, Duke of Lodi, ii. 230
Meneval, Baron, i. 67, 282, 283
Menou, General, i. 63, 223; ii. 4, 6, 7, 230
Merry, Mr., ii. 156
Metternich, Prince, i. 71; ii. 50, 51, 52, 68, 127, 135, 184, 230, 323
Meynel, Captain, i. 72, 280, 319; ii. 79, 80
Mina, i. 195
Miollis, General, ii. 230
Miot, i. 290, 291, 296; ii. 230
Miot, brother of, i. 296
Moira, Lord, ii. 60, 237
Moira, Lady, i. 56, 57
Molé, Count, i. 342; ii. 230
Molière, i. 20; ii. 63, 249, 368
Molleville, Bertrand de, i. 242
Mollien, Count, ii. 230
Moltke, General, ii. 230
Moncey, Duke of Conegliano, i. 221; ii. 230
Montalivet, ii. 230

Montauban, General (Duke of Palekao), ii. 230
Montchenu, Marquis de, i. 71, 80, 104, 201, 202, 203, 249, 271, 272, 364, 365; ii. 57, 58, 83, 103, 104, 120, 197, 215, 216, 273 (326), (328)
Montecuculi, ii. 354
Montesquieu, ii. 230
Montesquieu, Abbé, i. 356
Montfort, Count (Jerôme, brother of Napoleon), ii. 230
Montholon, General Count (Charles Tristan), i. 2, 10, 11, 15, 18, 20, 21, 24, 37, 38, 39, 41, 79, 82, 92, 93, 94, 102, 110, 111, 112, 113, 116, 117, 120, 121, 123, 125, 128, 135, 149, 152, 153, 156, 204, 209, 218, 219, 255, 266, 274, 275, 276, 293, 332; ii. 24, 58, 61, 75, 79, 84, 125, 126, 127, 129, 132, 144, 168, 199, 203, 207, 208, 214, 216, 225, 230, 235, 244, 258, 265, 281, 320, 326, 331, 337, 341, 342, 343, 344, 346, 350, 351, 357, 361, 362, 363, 364, 365
Montholon, Countess, i. 2, 10, 15, 16, 18, 20, 21, 57, 119, 240, 260, 266, 275, 333, 334, 364; ii. 18, 19, 24, 48, 62, 127, 198, 208, 214, 216, 287, 344
Montholon, Tristan de, i. 2; ii. 59, 62, 172, 235
Montholon (children), ii. 344
Montijo, Comtesse de, ii. 230
Montvérant, ii. 147
Moore, Sir John, i. 62, 63
Moore, Tom, i. 70
Moreau, General, i. 220, 221, 222, 224, 225, 250, 251; his boot, 252; 301, ii. 15, 16, 87, 88, 91, 92, 93, 219, 230, 305
Moreau, Madame, ii. 88
Morny, Comte de, ii. 230
Mortier, Marshal, Duke of Treviso, ii. 230

Mounier, Baron, ii. 96
Mountstuart Elphinstone, Right Hon., ii. 153
Mouton Duvernet, General, i. 336, 337
Muiron, Colonel, i. 126, 148, 199
Murat, Joachim, King of Naples, i. 30, 190, 191, 221, 315; ii. 16, 68, 69, 70, 71, 133, 134, 135, 141, 142, 194, 223, 230, 304, 305
Musignano, Prince of (Lucien, brother of Napoleon), ii. 230
Mussey, ii. 13

NANTES, Bishop of, i. 181
Naples. *See* under Bonaparte, Caroline (Bourbon), Murat, etc.
Napoleon. *See* separate Index
Napoleon, St., ii. 245 (283)
Narbonne, Count, ii. 184, 309
Necker, M., ii. 113
Nelson, Viscount and Duke of Brontë, i. 64, 278; ii. 4, 38, 77, 97, 98, 99, 155, 241
Newman, Cardinal, ii. 351
Ney, Marshal, the Prince of the Moskowa, i. 30, 221, 336, 337; ii. 11, 12, 134, 230, 233, 305
Nicholas, M., ii. 351
Nicholls, Captain, ii. 343, 358
Noverraz (servant), i. 2, 37, 86, 147, 339; ii. 199, 359, 361
Numa, ii. 353

O'CONNOR, Mr. C., ii. 38
O'Hara, General, i. 187, 188, 189
Oldenburg, Duke of, ii. 184
O'Meara, Barry E. *See* Prefatory Memoir, and *passim*
Orange, Prince of, ii. 173, 174, 175
Orange, mother of the Prince of, ii. 173, 174, 175
Ordener, Colonel, ii. 17
Orleans, Duchess of, ii. 174
Orleans. *See* under Louis Philippe
Otto (Comte de Mosloy), ii. 273

Oudinot, Marshal, Duke of Reggio, i. 203, 204, 221, 252, 253, 336
Oudinot, Madame, i. 203

P——E, Mr., ii. 226
Palm, a bookseller, i. 365
Palmerston, Viscount, ii. 107, 370
Paoli, i. 234, 338
Pardoe, Miss, ii. 118
Paul, Emperor of Russia, i. 125, 327, 329, 330; ii. 104
Pellew, Sir Edward (Lord Exmouth), ii. 54, 55, 142
Pelletier (or Peltier), i. 333, 334, 366
Pepin, Colonel, ii. 317, 318
Peraldi, i. 279
Peyran (a servant), i. 2 (*see* also 'Piéron')
Phillipeaux, Engineer, i. 194
Phipps, Colonel, ii. 22; and also note to Roll of Titles at end
Pichegru, General, i. 220, 225, 250, 251, 301; ii. 13, 15, 16, 88, 89, 90, 91, 92, 93, 94, 166, 218, 292
Pichegru's brother, ii. 15
Pichon, ii. 19, 27, 75
Piéron, i. 284 (*see* also 'Peyran')
Pillet, i. 291, 292, 293, 294; ii. 81, 200
Piontkowski (*alias* Piontowski), Captain, i. 65, 69, 92, 117, 119, 120, 138, 146, 156, 157, 158
Pirie, Mrs., i. 72
Pitt, William, i. 163, 301, 314; ii. 20, 189, 215
Plampin, Admiral, ii. 24, 30, 145, 148, 204 (? 214), 236, 327, 337
Planat, Colonel, i. 4
Plon, M. Eugène, ii. 22
Plutarch, i. 234
Polignac, Prince Jules, ii. 16
Poniatowsky, Marshal Prince, i. 176
Pope, the (Pius VI. and Pius VII.), i. 169, 181; ii. 29, 65, 139,

159, 245, 282, 283, 291, 296, 298, 299, 304, 338
Poppleton, Captain, i. 61, 76, 77, 82, 84, 94, 95, 99, 107, 108, 109, 116, 121, 123, 125, 138, 147, 157, 174, 200, 205, 249, 253, 267, 269, 279, 364, 366; ii. 8, 45, 66, 67, 111, 132, 147, 151, 214
Porteous, Mr., i. 10, 11, 15, 47
Portugal, Queen of, i. 66
Poussielgue, brothers, ii. 171
Pozzo di Borgo, Count, i. 264, 279
Pradt, Abbé de, i. 70; ii. 212
Prichard, aide-de-camp, i. 128, 132, 205
Prince Regent, the, i. 89, 91, 201, 207, 246; ii. 77, 163, 170, 177, 258, 325
Provera, General, ii. 298
Prussia, King of (Frederick William III.), i. 104, 192 (mispaged), 210, 211, 212, 231, 312, 328, 330, 346; ii. 50, 51, 100, 101, 168, 175, 212, 339
Prussia, Queen of (Louisa), i. 104, 211; ii. 175, 176

QUEREL, ii. 14
Quinault, ii. 368

RACINE, i. 20; ii. 368
Raffles, Mr. (Sir S.), i. 59
Rainsford, Inspector, i. 201, 205; ii. 58
Raoul, General, ii. 261
Rapp, Count, i. 307, 309; ii. 27
Raucourt, Mdlle, ii. 42
Raynal, Abbé, ii. 187
Reade, Colonel Sir Thomas, i. 35, 41, 45, 46, 74, 77, 84, 88, 94, 107, 117, 119, 120, 123, 124, 128, 129, 130, 132, 133, 134, 135, 136, 137, 138, 142, 143, 175, 202, 205, 214, 249, 267, 269, 270, 281, 291, 326, 339, 342; ii. 33, 57, 60, 73, 110, 126, 128, 133, 137, 144, 145, 147,

150, 151, 166, 216, 244, 263, 286, 306, 311, 314, 327, 333, 334, 337
Réal (not Grand Juge), ii. 14, 166
Reardon, Lieutenant, ii. 333
Regnier (Duke of Massa), ii. 230
Rémusat, Madame de, i. 7, 8, 67, 87; ii. 52, 53, 75
Reynier, General, ii. 100
Richelieu, Cardinal, ii. 293, 294
Ripsley, Captain, ii. 60
Rivière, ii. 13, 16
Robespierre, i. 172, 241, 242, 243; ii. 188, 189
Robinson, Mr., i. 65
Robinson, Sir George, ii. 3
Rogers, Samuel, i. 7
Romanzoff, Count, ii. 184
Rome, King of. *See* under Bonaparte
Rose, Captain, ii. 17
Ross, Captain, i. 65, 68
Rostopchin, Count, i. 179
Rousseau (a servant), i. 2, 156, 157, 158, 259
Rumboldt, Sir George, i. 127, 128
Russia, Emperor of. *See* 'Alexander' and 'Paul'

SAINT DENIS (*see* also 'Ali'), i. 2, 22, 86, 148, 215, 216, 258; ii. 286
Saint Helens, Lord, ii. 103
Saint Hilaire, ii. 13
Saint Just, i. 172
Saint Napoleon, ii. 245 (283)
Saint Pierre, Bernardin, ii. 332
Saint Priest, General, i. 252
Saint Régant (or Rejant), i. 306, 308
Saint Roche, Curé of, i. 169; ii. 42, 43
Saint Victor, ii. 13
Saint Vincent, Earl, i. 39, 55
Salicetti, ii. 341
Salms, Princess of, ii. 176
Santini (a pamphleteer), ii. 131
Santini (a servant), i. 2, 147, 156

157, 158, 258; ii. 320, 321, 322, 331
Sardinia, King of, i. 360; ii. 304.
Sarrazin, General, i. 98, 237
Savary, Duke of Rovigo, i. 5, 153, 154, 198, 355; ii. 15, 166, 167, 194, 275, 317
Saxe, Marshal, ii. 233
Saxony, King of, i. 212, 251, 311; ii. 309, 322
Schwartzenberg, General Prince, i. 187
Schwartzenberg, Prince (ambassador), i. 268; ii. 234, 309, 310
Scott (a servant), i. 206 (214), 324
Scott, Sir Walter, ii. 131, 132
Sebastiani, General, i. 57
Shaftesbury, Earl of, i. 182
Shah Nadir, i. 50
Shah of Persia, i. 330; ii. 206
Shakespeare, ii. 18
Siborne, Captain, i. 335, 359
Sidmouth, Lord, ii. 256
Sidney, Algernon, ii. 155
Sieyès, Abbé, ii. 191, 192, 248, 249
Skelton, Colonel and Mrs., i. 15, 22, 28, 219; ii. 18
Smith, Admiral Sir Sidney, i. 190, 193, 194, 199, 299; ii. 6, 32, 33, 59, 194, 195, 220
Smith, Colonel, i. 80; ii. 286
Solomon, Mr., ii. 115, 147, 162
Soult, Duke of Dalmatia, i. 107, 221, 224, 274, 335; ii. 45, 60, 185, 202
Souvaroff, Marshal, i. 224
Spain, King of. *See* Charles
Spain, Queen of, ii. 186
Stadion, Count, ii. 234
Staël (Holstein), Madame de, ii. 113, 114, 204, 211, 234
Stanfell, Captain, i. 35, 98; ii. 24
Staps, i. 310
Stein, Baron, ii. 50, 51
Strange, Sir Thomas, i. 245, 246, 247, 248, 257
Stuart, General, ii. 100

Sturmer, Baron, i. 70, 71, 81, 158, 159, 204, 206, 209, 271, 272, 340; ii. 32, 57, 75, 215, 216, 244, 280 (326), 328, 342
Sturmer, Baroness, i. 70, 71, 81, 104; ii. 32, 57, 199, 216, 244, 245
Suchet, Duke of Albufera, i. 222; ii. 44, 45
Sultan, the, ii. 55
Survilliers, Count of (Joseph, brother of Napoleon), ii. 339
Survilliers, Countess of, and daughters, ii. 347
Sussex, Duke of, i. 73
Sweden, King of. *See* Bernadotte
Sweeny, Lieutenant, i. 119
Sylla, ii. 169

TALBOT, Captain, ii. 64
Talleyrand de Perigord, Prince, i. 182, 197, 198, 302, 350, 358; ii. 1, 2, 3, 11, 21, 127, 188, 190, 192, 233, 242, 259, 260, 325
Talleyrand, Madame, ii. 2, 3
Talma, ii. 280
Tamerlane, i. 50
Thiers, Adolphe, i. 127, 250, 251
Thorvaldsen, ii. 22
Toby, i. 25
Toussaint l'Ouverture, ii. 206
Turenne, ii. 233

URMSTON, Mr., i. 59; ii. 128
Ussher, Captain, ii. 33, 34, 56, 57

V——, Miss, ii. 285
Vandamme, General, i. 98, 124, 125
Vendean chiefs, the, ii. 219, 220
Verestchagin, ii. 127
Vernon, Rev. Mr., i. 341
Victor, Marshal, Duke of Belluno, ii. 60, 88
Victoria, Queen (𝔚𝔥𝔬𝔪 𝔊𝔬𝔡 𝔓𝔯𝔢𝔰𝔢𝔯𝔳𝔢), ii. 370

Vignale, Abbé, ii. 345, 346, 350, 358
Villeneuve, Admiral, i. 63, 64
Virion, i. 294
Vitzthum, Count, ii. 34
Voltaire, i. 290 ; ii. 368

WALES, Princess of, ii. 84
Walker, Mr., i. 179
Wallis, Captain, ii. 218
Ward, Lord Dudley and, ii. 182, 234
Ward, Dr., i. 84
Warden, Dr., i. 7, 65, 68, 70, 288, 349, 350, 352, 353, 354, 357, 364 ; ii. 3, 11, 13, 14, 18, 217
Washington, General, i. 153 ; ii. 155
Wauchope, Captain, i. 280
Webb, Mr., ii. 60
Wellington, Duke* of, i. 70, 161, 162, 224, 298 ; ii. 24, 25, 35, 102, 174, 195, 202, 233, 234, 241, 242, 289, 396, 397
Whitaker, Joseph, F.S.A., i. 210
Whitworth, Lord, i. 163 ; ii. 52, 53, 78, 155, 156
Wilberforce, Bishop, ii. 196
Wilks, Colonel (H.E.I. Co.'s governor), i. 11, 15, 26, 42, 215, 228, 397

Wilks, Mrs., i. 15
Wilks, Miss, i. 42
William III. (of England), ii. 148
Williams, Miss, i. 31
Wilson, Sir Robert, i. 59, 281
Wilton, Mr., ii. 72
Wortham, Lieutenant, i. 36
Wrede, General, ii. 323, 324
Wright, Captain, i. 269
Wright, Captain John, i. 59, 301, 355 ; ii. 13, 14, 15, 79, 80, 166, 194, 195, 218, 219, 220, 292
Wurmser, Marshal, ii. 157, 158, 159
Würtemberg, King of, i. 197, 212, 358 ; ii. 309, 323
Würtemberg, Queen of, ii. 310
Würtemberg, Princess Catherine of, ii. 311
Würtzburg, Duke of (brother of Emperor Francis), ii. 212, 308
Wynyard, Colonel, i. 83, 128, 132, 138, 142, 269 ; ii. 338

YORK, Duke of, i. 140 ; ii. 100
Younghusband, Colonel and Mrs., i. 28 ; ii. 57

ZAYONCHEK, General, i. 175

Postscript

THE FIRST FUNERAL OF NAPOLEON

A CORRESPONDENT, says the *St. James's Gazette* in November 1888, has favoured us with the following extract from a letter, dated St. Helena, 12th May 1821, and written by an officer serving on board one of the East India Company's ships:—

'On Tuesday we came in sight of St. Helena, and anchored next day about eight in the morning. Imagine an immense rock, without the slightest marks of vegetation save a few bushes in one valley where the town stands, and forming a barrier to the sea, which may wash upon it for ages, for millions of years, and make no impression on it. On the Saturday after our arrival Bonaparte died, and on Monday morning I rode to Longwood, where I saw the poor remains of that once great man. He was lying dressed in full uniform. I could have known him among fifty thousand. His face at first sight appeared familiar, so striking are the likenesses I had seen of him. He was dressed with a short green coat, which only came down as far as the end of the breast-bone, with a very long waistcoat, such as was worn in the days of King Charles, a pair of white leather breeches, long boots, covering the knees, with long spurs; he had a cocked hat upon his head. A fine cross was placed upon his body, with the figure of Christ nailed to it; a sword lay by his side. He lay like a poor ordinary mortal, and it was difficult to conceive that that poor smelling carcass was the being who once spread fear and terror over a quarter of the globe; that this was the identical man whose ambition caused the death of so many thousands of his fellow-creatures; that that dull eye which death has now closed was the same whose glance awed the world. He had not yet entered his new house, which is now quite finished, and ready. It is a most elegant house, and is placed in a beautiful part of the island. His principal amusement for a long time past had been gardening, a which he wrought with his own hands. The divisions and walks in the garden were very beautiful, and were principally made by himself. His burial was on the 9th of May (Wednesday), but which I had not the pleasure of attending. According to the account I hear, very little pomp or parade was made on the occasion. At two o'clock the man-of-war ship stationed here fired minute-guns, the echo of which amongst the rocks of St. Helena resembled.the loudest peals of thunder and had a fine effect. His death will make a wonderful alteration in the island; it is supposed the greater part of the military will be sent home immediately to England. I cannot but think I have been very fortunate in arriving at St. Helena at such a time—it is not every day that such a man as Bonaparte makes his exit from this world.'

A FAMOUS CRAFT FALLEN ON EVIL DAYS.

'The famous French nautical monument, *La Belle Poule*, is in a sad condition. It was *La Belle Poule* that carried home the remains of the First Napoleon from St. Helena in 1840. · It was *La Belle Poule* that came up the Seine to Rouen with Napoleon's remains, and passed under the old suspension bridge which was converted for the occasion into a triumphal arch. The ship has ever since been moored in Toulon Harbour, where it was used as a floating barracks for old sailors, and there is now some talk of breaking up the venerable craft, as it costs the State too much for constant caulking and general patching up.'—*Pall Mall Gazette*, 3d *November* 1888.

THE DUKE OF WELLINGTON'S OPINION ABOUT SIR HUDSON LOWE AND THE ARRANGEMENTS AT ST. HELENA.

As the Duke of Wellington's attitude towards Sir Hudson Lowe has already been referred to (Introductory matter to Vol. I.), it may be serviceable to append here some remarks which fell from his lips in 1848 and are recorded in Earl Stanhope's *Notes of Conversations with the Duke of Wellington*, just published.

Referring to the impending publication of Sir H. Lowe's papers—

"The Duke said he was confident that the principal charges against Sir Hudson Lowe would prove to be false. I agreed to this, and observed that I supposed the Duke had scarcely known Sir Hudson personally. "Yes I did; I knew him very well. He was a stupid man."[1]—"I conceive," said I, "that he had a bad, irritable temper, and in that point was ill qualified for his post."—"He was not an ill-natured man, but he knew nothing at all of the world, and like all men who know nothing of the world he was suspicious and jealous." "What I wanted them," continued the Duke, "to do at St. Helena—and I knew the Island—was this: I would have let Bonaparte go about it wherever he pleased and speak to whoever he pleased, provided only that he showed himself to an English officer every night and every morning—twice in the twenty-four hours. I would also have stationed in each of the six or seven creeks from which alone he could have embarked, a guardhouse with a serjeant and twelve men. If any boats were seen approaching without authority the guard would have fired, and in the same way they would have prevented any boats putting off. By such a plan I was confident from my knowledge of the Island—I was there I think a fortnight—that Napoleon might have been left at liberty to ramble over the Island, and could not have escaped from it. We used to hear every now and then of plans formed in America and elsewhere for effecting his escape." The Duke said also that he thought that the Government had been mistaken in removing the old East India Company's Governor, Colonel Wilks. He was a very intelligent, well-read man, and knew everything that had been passing in Europe, and Napoleon had become really attached to him. After he was gone, Napoleon (as the Duke mentions) said more than once, *Pourquoi n'ont-ils pas laissé ce vieux gouverneur? Avec lui je me serais arrangé, nous n'aurions pas eu de querelles'* (*p.* 327). *See also pp.* 67, 104, *and* 260 *of Lord Stanhope's Work.*

[1] 'He was a man wanting education and judgment,' said the Duke on another occasion.—*Earl Stanhope*, p. 67.

THE END

Printed by R. & R. CLARK, *Edinburgh.*

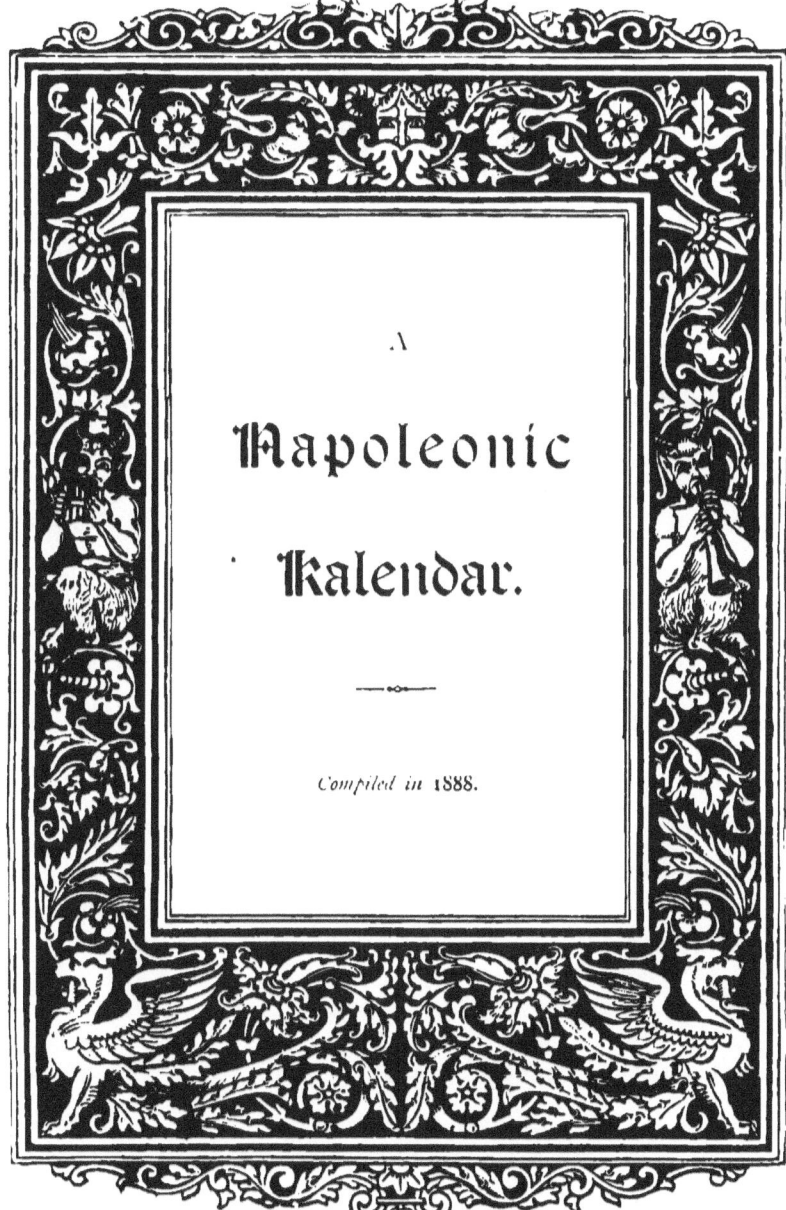

A Napoleonic Kalendar.

Compiled in 1888.

"*MA MÉMOIRE SE COMPOSE DES FAITS, ET DES SIMPLES PAROLES NE SAURAIENT LES DÉTRUIRE.*"—
Napoleon at St. Helena.

DECLARATION OF NAPOLEON AT ST. HELENA.

"The historian of France cannot pass over the Empire, and, if he have any honesty, he will not fail to render me my share of justice. His task will be easy; for the facts speak for themselves—they shine like the sun. I closed the gulf of anarchy and cleared away chaos. I purified the Revolution, dignified nations, and established kings. I excited every kind of emulation, rewarded every kind of merit, and extended the limits of glory. This is at least something. On what point can I be assailed on which an historian could not defend me? Can it be for my intentions? But even here I can find absolution. Can it be for my despotism? It can be demonstrated that the Dictatorship was absolutely necessary. Will it be said that I restrained liberty? It can be proved that licentiousness, anarchy, and the greatest irregularities still haunted the threshold of freedom. Shall I be accused of being too fond of war? It can be shown that I always received the first attack. Will it be said that I aimed at universal monarchy? It can be proved that this was merely the result of fortuitous circumstances, and that our enemies themselves led me step by step to this determination. Lastly, shall I be blamed for my ambition? This passion I must doubtless be allowed to have possessed, and that in no small degree; but, at the same time, my ambition was of the highest and noblest kind that ever, perhaps, existed—that of establishing and of consecrating the empire of reason, and the full exercise and complete enjoyment of all the human faculties! And here the historian will probably feel compelled to regret that such ambition should not have been fulfilled and gratified." Then, after a few moments of reflection, "This," said the Emperor, "is my whole history in a few words."

JANUARY.

1 Napoleon entered the College of Autun at the age of nine, 1779.
2 Surrender of Dantzic, 1814. [Napoleon entered Warsaw, 1807.
3 Combat at Capua, 1799. The Duke of Albuféra died, 1826.
4 Louis Bonaparte married to Hortense Beauharnais, 1802. The Battle of Albufera, 1812.
5 Count Miot de Melito died, 1841
6 Combat at La Bastide, 1814.
7 Joseph Bonaparte born, 1768. Suchet, Duke of Albufera, died, 1826.
8 Eliza Bonaparte born, 1777. General Cambronne died (in his bed),
9 Valentia captured by Suchet, 1812. [1842.
10 Ney, Prince of the Moskowa, born at Sarrelouis, 1769. Sir Hudson Lowe died, 1844.
11 Murat deserts Napoleon and declares war against France, 1814. Baron Gérard, painter, died, 1837.
12 Count Daru born, 1767.
13 Second Concordat between the Pope and Napoleon signed, 1813.
14 Battle of Rivoli, 1797. Marriage of Eugène Viceroy of Italy with a daughter of the King of Bavaria, 1806. [1806.
15 François Joseph Talma, tragedian, born 1763. Venice occupied,
16 Battle of La Favorita, 1797. Battle of Corunna, 1809.
17 Napoleon restricts the Paris newspapers to thirteen, 1800.
18 La Vendée pacified, 1800. Goree captured, 1804.
19 Bernardin de Saint Pierre, author of "Paul and Virginia," born, 1737.
20 Murat married Caroline Bonaparte, 1800.
21 [Louis XVI. guillotined, 1793.] Kehl annexed, 1807.
22 Pius VII. released from his imprisonment at Fontainebleau.
23 [William Pitt died, 1806.]
24 Count Molé born, 1781.
25 Battle of Mohrungen, 1807. Drouet, Count d'Erlon, died, 1844.
26 Bernadotte, afterwards King of Sweden, born at Pau, 1764. General Bonaparte made President of the New Italian Republic, 1802.
27 [The Battle of St. Dizier, 1814.
28 Langlès, the Orientalist, died, 1824.
29 The Battle of Brienne, 1814.
30 Combat of Cagliano, 1797.
31 Seville taken by Victor, 1810.

FEBRUARY.

1 Battle of La Rothière, 1814.
2 The Surrender of Mantua, 1797. Letitia Bonaparte, mother of Napoleon, died, 1836.
3 General Count Pajol born, 1772. General Foy born, 1775.
4 Abortive negotiations for peace commenced at Chatillon-sur-Seine,
5 Mademoiselle Mars born, 1779. [1814.
6 Combat of Hoff, 1807.
7 Battle of Bar-sur-Aube, 1814. Fauvelet de Bourrienne, ex-Secretary to Napoleon, died, 1834.
8 Battle of Preussisch-Eylau, 1807. Catalonia and Northern Provinces of Spain decreed part of the French Empire, 1810. Prince Eugène's
9 Treaty of Luneville, 1801. [victory at Valeggio, 1814.
10 General Berthier entered Rome, 1798. Dalberg, Grand Duke and Archbishop, died, 1817.
11 Admiral Verhuell born, 1764. Battle of Montmirail, 1814.
12 Combat of Château-Thierry, 1814.
13 Mortier, Duke of Treviso, born at Cambrai, 1768. Battle of Kalitsch,
14 Battle of Vauchamps, 1814. [1813.
15 Baron Corvisart born, 1755. Joseph Bonaparte made King of Naples, 1806. Berthier made Prince of Neufchâtel, 1806.
16 Battle of Ostrolenka, 1807. P. P. Prud'hon, historical painter, died 1823.
17 The Annexation of Rome and the Papal States to the Empire, 1810.
18 Battle of El Arisch, 1799. Battle of Montereau, 1814.
19 Jourdain, the Orientalist, died, 1818. Caulaincourt, Duke of Vicenza, died, 1827.
20 Andreas Hofer, the Defender of the Tyrol, shot, 1810.
21 Trial of Peltier for libel on the First Consul, 1803. Saragossa surrendered, 1809.
22 [French landing in Pembrokeshire, 1797.] Prince Eugène, Viceroy
23 Battle of Orthes, 1814. [of Italy, died, 1824.
24 Charles Bonaparte, father of Napoleon, died, 1785.
25 Louis S. C. Xavier Girardin died, 1827.
26 Napoleon quitted Elba, 1815.
27 General Reynier died, 1814.
28 Marmont, Duke of Ragusa, died, 1852.

MARCH.

1 The New French Nobility created, 1808. Napoleon landed in France, 1815.
2 Suchet, Duke of Albuféra, born at Lyons, 1772. Napoleon appointed Commander-in-Chief of the Army of Italy, 1796.
3 Victor, Duke of Belluno, died, 1841.
4 Stephanie Beauharnais (P. of Baden) adopted by Napoleon, 1806.
5 The Civil Code (code Napoléon) decreed, 1803. Battle of Barrosa,
6 Baron Jomini born, 1779. Volta, the electrician, died 1826. [1811.
7 Battle of Craon, 1814. Entry of Napoleon into Grenoble, 1815.
8 [Pozzo di Borgo born, 1764.] The assault on Bergen-op-Zoom, 1814. Cambacérès died, 1824.
9 Marriage of Napoleon to Vicomtesse de Beauharnais, 1796.
10 Jaffa taken by assault, 1799. Battle of Laon, 1814.
11 Combat of Redinha, 1811.
12 Marshal Gouvion St. Cyr died, 1830.
13 Napoleon's conversation with Lord Whitworth, 1803.
14 [General Dumouriez died, 1823.]
15 General Murat made Grand Duke of Berg, 1806.
16 Battle of the Tagliamento, 1797. Madame Campan died, 1822.
17 Marquis de Fontanes died, 1821. [1805.
18 Napoleon lays siege to St. Jean d'Acre, 1799. Admiral Bruix died,
19 Le Brun, Duke of Placentia, born at St. Sauveur Landelin, 1739. Louis XVIII. leaves Paris, 1815.
20 The King of Rome born, 1811. Battle of Arcis-sur-Aube, 1814. Napoleon re-enters Paris, 1815.
21 Lucien Bonaparte, Prince of Canino, born, 1775. Greuze, the painter, died, 1805. The Duc d'Enghien shot at Vincennes, 1804.
22 Arrighi, Duke of Padua, died, 1853.
23 Laplace, the astronomer, born, 1749. War declared by France against United States of America, 1810.
24 Trieste taken by Bernadotte, 1797. General Drouot died, 1847.
25 Murat born at Bastide, 1767. Battle of La Fere Champenoise, 1814.
26 Caroline Bonaparte born, 1782.
27 Mirbel, the botanist, born, 1776. The Treaty of Amiens signed, 1802.
28 General Count Bertrand born, 1773. Battle of Medellin, 1809.
29 Soult, Duke of Dalmatia, born at St. Aurans, 1769. Oporto captured by Marshal Soult, 1809. The Slave Trade abolished by Napoleon,
30 The Capitulation of Paris, 1814. [1815.
31 The disaster at the Princess Schwartzenburg's ball, 1811. The entry of the Allies into Paris, 1814.

APRIL.

1. Count Portalis born, 1745.
2. Oudinot, Duke of Reggio, born at Bar-sur-Ornain, 1767. First portion of the Papal States annexed to the French Empire, 1808. Marriage of Napoleon and Marie Louise, 1810. Napoleon dethroned by the Senate, 1814.
3. Combat of Sabugal, 1811. [1817.
4. Napoleon I. abdicated, 1814. Massena, Prince of Essling, died,
5. Battle of Mockern, 1813.
6. Regnier, Duke of Massa, born, 1736. General Pichegru committed suicide (?) in prison, 1804.
7. François M. C. Fourier, born, 1772. Princess Stephanie Beauharnais married to the Prince of Baden, 1806.
8. Joseph Fievée, journalist and novelist, born, 1767.
9. The Duc d'Angoulême released by Napoleon, 1815.
10. Count Lagrange, the geometer, died, 1813. Battle of Toulouse, 1814. Prince Borghèse died, 1832. Hortense Beauharnais, Queen of Holland, born, 1783.
11. Lannes, Duke of Montebello, born at Lectoure, 1769.
12. Battle of Montenotte, 1796.
13. Gouvion St. Cyr born, 1764. Battle of Millesimo, 1796.
14. Battle of Dego, 1796. The Bank of France established, 1803.
15. [Prince Schwartzenburg born, 1771.] Napoleon makes his will at St.
16. Battle of Mount Thabor, 1799. [Helena, 1821.
17. General (afterwards Marshal) Gérard died, 1852.
18. The Treaty of Leoben signed, 1797. Isabey died, 1855.
19. Hamburg holds out under Marshal Davoust, 1815 (?).
20. Napoleon III. born, 1808. The Battle of Abensberg, 1809. Napoleon takes leave of the Old Guard, 1814. Moncey, Duke of Conégliano, died, 1842.
21. Battle of Mondovi, 1796. Battle of Landshut, 1809.
22. Admiral Villeneuve committed suicide, 1806. Battle of Eckmühl, 1809. [1809.
23. The Abbé de Pradt born, 1759. Napoleon wounded at Ratisbon,
24. Sérurier (afterwards Marshal) made Governor of the Invalides, 1804.
25. Napoleon entered the School of Brienne, aged nine, 1797. The "Additional Act" to the Constitution published, 1815.
26. Savary, Duke of Rovigo, born at Mare, 1774. Amnesty granted to
27. Denon, the scientist, died, 1825. [the Emigrés, 1802.
28. General Bernard, engineer, born, 1779.
29. Jourdan, Marshal, born at Limoges, 1762.
30. General Count Souham born, 1760. Louisiana sold by France to the United States, 1803.

MAY.

1 [Duke of Wellington born, 1769.] [Sir Sydney Smith escaped from Paris, 1798.] Marshal Bessières killed, 1813.
2 Battle of Lutzen, 1813.
3 Sieyès born, 1748. Battle of Ebersberg, 1809. Louis XVIII. entered Paris in 1814. Paer, Master of the Imperial Chapel,
4 Napoleon landed at Elba, 1814. [died, 1839.
5 The abdication of Charles IV. of Spain, 1808. Battle of Fuentes d'Onoro, 1811. Death of Napoleon at St. Helena, 1821.
6 The abdication of Ferdinand VII. of Spain, 1808.
7 Passage of the Po, 1796.
8 The burial of Napoleon at St. Helena, 1821. [1808.
9 Battle of Lodi, 1796. The Grand Duke of Berg made King of Naples,
10 Count Monge born, 1746. Davoust, Prince of Eckmühl, born at Annaux, 1770. [General Kutusoff died, 1813.]
11 Cardinal Maury died, 1817. Madame Récamier died, 1849.
12 Louis Dupetit Thouars, botanist, died, 1831.
13 Carnot born, 1753. Baron Cuvier, the naturalist, died, 1832. Cardinal Fesch, and Maret, Duke of Bassano, died, 1839.
14 Napoleon's passage of the Great St. Bernard commenced, 1800.
15 [Prince Metternich born, 1773.] Entry of General Bonaparte into Milan, 1796. Count Las Cases died, 1842.
16 Massena, Prince of Essling, born at Nice, 1758. Venice occupied, 1797. Battle of Albuera, 1811.
17 The (remaining) portion of the Papal States annexed to the French Empire, 1809. Talleyrand, Prince of Benevento, died, 1838.
18 War declared between England and France, 1803. Napoleon I. declared Emperor of the French, 1804. Caroline Murat died, 1839.
19 Napoleon sailed from Toulon for Egypt, 1798. The Legion of Honour established, 1802.
20 Battle of Bautzen, 1813. Prince Talleyrand de Périgord died, 1838.
21 Battle of Wurtzchen, 1813.
22 The Siege of Acre raised by Napoleon, 1799. The defeat of Aspern-Essling, 1809.
23 Duroc, Duke of Friuli, died of his wounds, 1813.
24 Louis Bonaparte made King of Holland, 1806.
25 Genoa annexed, 1805. [Prince Barclay de Tolly died, 1818.]
26 Napoleon crowned King of Italy at Milan, 1805. Laffitte, the
27 Jacques Halévy, composer, born, 1752. [banker, died, 1844.
28 Capture of Fiume, 1809.
29 Fouché born at Nantes, 1763. The Empress Josephine died, 1814. Marshal the Marquis de Grouchy died, 1847.
30 The First Treaty of Paris, 1814.
31 Lannes, Duke of Montebello, died of his wounds, 1809.

JUNE.

1. The gathering in the Champ de Mai, 1815. Berthier, Prince of Wagram, tumbled out of a window at Bamberg. Davoust, Prince of Eckmühl, died, 1823. Count Lamarque died, 1832.
2. Napoleon entered Milan, 1800. Savary, Duke of Rovigo, died, 1833.
3. Barry E. O'Meara died, 1836.
4. Chaptal, the minister, born, 1756. Massena's defence of Genoa terminated, 1800. Genoa annexed to France, 1805.
5. Cabanis, the philosopher, born, 1757. Louis Bonaparte made King of Holland, 1806. Hanover occupied by the French, 1803.
6. Joseph Bonaparte made King of Spain and the Indies, 1808. General Lasalle killed, 1809.
7. Madame Junot, Duchesse d'Abrantès, died in indigence, 1838. [Frederick William III. of Prussia died, 1840.]
8. Combat of Wolfsdorff, 1807.
9. Battle of Montebello, 1800.
10. Napoleon excommunicated by Pius VII. in 1809.
11. The King of Rome born, 1811. General Lauriston died, 1828.
12. Napoleon captured Malta, 1798. The yielding of Burgos, 1813. Napoleon left Paris for Belgium, 1815. Augereau, Duke of Castiglione, died, 1816.
13. Napoleon entered Cairo, 1799.
14. Battle of Marengo. Desaix killed. Kléber assassinated, 1800. Battle of Friedland, 1807.
15. Regnier, the mechanician, born, 1751.
16. The Battles of Ligny and Quatre Bras, 1815. Le Brun, Duke of Placentia, died, 1824.
17. [Thorvaldsen completes his "Triumph of Alexander" for Napoleon in June, 1812.]
18. Battle of Mont St. Jean, Marshal Grouchy's victory at Wavres, and intended advance on Brussels, 1815.
19. H. J. F. de Lammenais born, 1752.
20. First attack upon the Tuileries (Napoleon an eye-witness), 1792.
21. The Battle of Vittoria, 1813. [The Abbé Sieyès died, 1836.]
22. Napoleon I. abdicated in favour of Napoleon II., 1815.
23. Napoleon crossed the Niemen, 1812.
24. Josephine born at Martinique, 1763. Regnier, Duke of Massa, died, 1814. Jerôme Bonaparte, King of Westphalia, died, 1860.
25. Georges Cadoudal executed, 1804. Sismondi, the historian, died, 1842.
26. Baron Gros, painter, died, 1835.
27. Latour d'Auvergne killed in battle, 1800. Napoleon II. proclaimed, 1815.
28. Tarragona taken by General Suchet, 1811. King Joseph quitted Spain, 1813.
29. Lucien Bonaparte, Prince of Canino, died, 1840.
30. Barras born, 1755.

JULY.

1 General Bonaparte landed in Egypt, 1798.
2 General Bonaparte took Alexandria, 1798.
3 Louis Napoleon abdicated the throne of Holland, 1810.
4 Battle of Maida, 1806. Chateaubriand died, 1848.
5 Battle of Enzersdorf, 1809.
6 Battle of Wagram, 1809. The Pope removed from Rome, 1809.
7 J. M. Jacquard, mechanician, born, 1752. The Treaty of Tilsit
8 Napoleon embarks at Rochefort, 1815. [signed, 1807.
9 Holland annexed to the French Empire, 1810.
10 Surrender of Ciudad Rodrigo to Ney, 1810.
11 Lalande, the astronomer, born, 1732. Combat of Znaim, 1809.
12 The formation of the Confederation of the Rhine, 1806. Napoleon made Protector.
13 Battle of Chébréïsse, 1798. Soult made prisoner at Genoa, 1800.
14 Battle of Medina de Rio Seco, 1808. Madame de Staël-Holstein died, 1817.
15 The Concordat with the Pope, 1801. Napoleon surrendered to the Prince Regent, 1815.
16 Pierre Jean de Béranger died, 1857.
17
18 The capture of Gaeta by Massena, 1806.
19 [Louisa Augusta, Queen of Prussia, died, 1810.]
20 Marmont, Duke of Ragusa, born at Chatillon, 1774. General Sebastiani died, 1851.
21 Baptism of Napoleon at Ajaccio, 1771. Battle of the Pyramids, 1798.
22 Maret, Duke of Cadore, born at Dijon, 1763. General Dupont's surrender at Baylen, 1808. Battle of Salamanca, 1812. Death of the Duke of Reichstadt (the King of Rome), 1832.
23 Battle of Mohilow, 1812.
24 Admiral Villaret de Joyeuse died, 1812.
25 Battle of Aboukir, 1799. Mr. O'Meara left St. Helena, 1818. Baron Larrey died, 1841. General Gourgaud died, 1852
26 Arrival of Napoleon at Plymouth, 1815.
27 The battles of Ostrowno (25th, 26th, and 27th), 1812.
28 Battle of Talavera, 1809. Battle of the Pyrenees, 1813. Mortier, Duke of Treviso, killed by Fieschi's bomb, 1835.
29 The Imperial Guard decreed, 1804. Junot, Duke of Abrantès, died insane, 1813.
30 Chaptal, the chemist, died, 1832. Baron Norvins, the historian, died, 1854.
31 Moncey, Duke of Conegliano, born at Besançon, 1754.

AUGUST.

1 Battle of the Nile. Admiral Brueys blown up, 1798
2 Marshal Brune murdered, 1815. Carnot died, 1823
3 Battle of Lonato, 1796
4 Napoleon created First Consul *for life*, 1802.
5 The Battle of Castiglione, 1796.
6 Bessières born at Preissac, 1768. Napoleon arrested (and not released until August 20), 1794.
7 Eliza Bacchiochi, Princess of Piombino, died, 1820. Jacquard, inventor, died, 1834.
8 Napoleon sailed for St. Helena in the *Northumberland*, 1815.
9 Jacques Antoine Dulaure, archæologist, died, 1835.
10 First battle of Krasnoi, 1812.
11 [Moreau born at Morlaix, 1763.]
12
13 General Menou died, 1810.
14 Pius VII. born, 1742. The New Louvre (commenced by Napoleon I.), completed by Napoleon III., 1857.
15 Birth of Napoleon Bonaparte at Ajaccio, 1769. General Joubert killed at the Battle of Novi, 1799.
16 Lord Nelson's attack upon the Invasion Flotilla at Boulogne, 1801.
17 Battle of Koliça, 1808. Battle of Smolensko, 1812.
18 Jerôme made King of Westphalia, 1807.
19 General Labédoyère shot by the Bourbons, 1815.
20 Pius VII. died, 1823.
21 Battle of Vimiera, 1808. Count Montholon died, 1853.
22 Prince Jerôme Bonaparte married to eldest daughter of the King of Wurtemburg.
23 Baron Cuvier born, 1769. [General Wurmser died, 1797.] Battle of Gross Beeren, 1813.
24 Napoleon left Egypt, 1799
25 Portalis, legislator, died, 1807.
26 Palm, the bookseller, shot, 1806. Battle of the Katzbach, 1813.
27 Battle of Dresden. General Moreau killed, 1813.
28 Battle of Kulm, 1813.
29 [Pius VI. died at Valence, 1799.]
30 Convention of Cintra, 1808.
31 David, the painter, born, 1748.

SEPTEMBER.

1 Napoleon entered the Army at the age of sixteen, 1785.
2 Louis Bonaparte born, 1778.
3 Prince Eugène, Viceroy of Italy, born, 1780. Charles James Fox's interview at the Tuileries, 1802.
4 Évariste Dumoulin, journalist, died, 1833.
5 Battle of Dennewitz, 1813. Count Daru died, 1829.
6 Engagement at Juterbock, 1813.
7 Battle of Borodino. Marshal Davoust wounded, 1813.
8 Combat of Bassano, 1796.
9 Combat of Mojaisk, 1812.
10 Ugo Foscolo died, 1827. General Andreossi died, 1828.
11 Piedmont united to France, 1802. [1820.
12 [Marshal Blucher died, 1819.] Kellermann, Duke of Valmy, died,
13 Oudinot, Duke of Reggio, died, 1847.
14 Napoleon entered Moscow, 1812. Lefebvre, Duke of Dantzic, died, 1820. [The Duke of Wellington died, 1852.]
15 [General Hoche died, 1797.]
16 [Louis XVIII. died, 1824.]
17 The burning of Moscow—September 15th to 20th, 1812. Breguet, mechanician, died, 1823.
18 Sitting of the great Sanhedrim at Paris, 1806. Doctor Antommarchi arrived at St. Helena, 1819.
19
20 Pauline Bonaparte born, 1780.
21 The Republic proclaimed, 1792.
22
23
24 Junot, Duke of Abrantès, born at Bussy les Forges, 1771. Macdonald, Duke of Tarentum, died, 1840.
25
26 [Massena's victory at Zurich, 1799.]
27 The Conference at Erfurt commenced, 1808. Battle of Busaco, 1810. "Carle" Vernet, painter, died, 1836.
28 Edmé François Jomard, engineer and geographer, died, 1862.
29
30 Napoleon anchored at Ajaccio, 1799.

OCTOBER.

1 Louisiana acquired by France, 1800.
2
3 The Ionian Islands transferred, 1809.
4 The Day of the Sections. Intervention of General Bonaparte, 1795.
5 Hortense, Queen of Holland, died, 1837.
6 Landing of General Bonaparte in France from Egypt, 1799. Battle of Donauworth, 1805. Meeting between Napoleon and Goethe and Weiland at Weimar, 1808. Lacépède, the naturalist, died, 1825. Lesueur, the composer, died, 1837.
7
8 Alfieri died, 1803.
9 Napoleon entered upon power, 1799. The Provisional Consulate. Wellington retreated to the lines of Torres Vedras, 1810.
10 Plot of Cerrachi, Aréna, etc., to assassinate Napoleon frustrated.
11 Ouvrard, the financier and contractor, born, 1770.   [1800.
12 Canova, the sculptor, died, 1822.
13 Murat shot, 1815.
14 Battle of Elchingen, 1805. Battles of Jena and Auerstadt, 1806. Treaty of Schœnbrunn, 1809. Attempted assassination of Napoleon by Staps, 1809. Illyrian Provinces organized, 1809.
15 Napoleon arrived at St. Helena, 1815.
16 Battle of Leipsic (the "Battle of Nations") commences, 1813.
17 Clarke, Duke of Feltre, born at Landrecies, 1765. The Treaty of Campo Formio, 1797. Battle of Halle, 1806.
18 Cambacérès, Prince of Parma, born at Montpelier, 1755. Surrender of Sir Hudson Lowe at Capri to Murat, 1808.
19 The retreat from Russia commenced, 1812. The retreat after Leipsic commenced. Prince Poniatowski drowned, 1813. Talma died, 1826.
20 The surrender of General Mack at Ulm, 1805.
21 The revolt at Cairo, 1798. The Battle of Trafalgar and death of Lord Nelson, 1805.
22 The conspiracy of General Malet at Paris, 1812.
23 Napoleon entered the Military School at Paris, aged fifteen, 1784.
24 Battle of Malo-Jaroslowitz, 1812.
25 Lefebvre, Duke of Dantzic, born at Rufac, 1755. General Duroc
26   [born, 1772.
27 Napoleon entered Berlin in state, 1806.
28 The Marquis of Grouchy born at Paris, 1766. Clarke, Duke
29 Stettin surrendered, 1806.   [of Feltre, died, 1818.
30 Merlin de Douai born, 1754. General Junot married Mdlle. Laura Permon, 1800. Battle of Hanau, 1813.
31

NOVEMBER.

1 [The French Directory elected, 1795.]
2
3 [The Congress of Vienna opened, 1814.]
4 Lacuée, Count Cessac, born, 1752.
5 General Vandamme born, 1770. The Convention of Berlin, 1808.
6 Pauline Leclerc married to Prince Borghèse, 1803. Count Berthollet, the scientist, died, 1822.
7
8 Capture of Magdeburg, 1806. Count Rapp died, 1821.
9 Count Berthollet, chemist, etc., born, 1748.
10 The Council of the Five Hundred deposed by Bonaparte, 1799.
11 Augereau, Duke of Castiglione, born at Paris, 1757. Battle of Caldiero, 1796. Flushing ceded to France, 1807.
12 The Valais united to France, 1810.
13 General Excelmans born, 1775. Napoleon entered Vienna, 1805.
14 Battle of Witepsk, 1812.
15 The body of Napoleon disinterred at St. Helena, 1840.
16 Battle of Arcola (three days, 15th, 16th, and 17th), 1796. Tallien died, 1820.
17 Macdonald, Duke of Tarentum, born at Sancerre, 1765. General Dugommier died, 1794.
18 Second Battle of Krasnoi (16th to 18th), 1812.
19 Battle of Ocana, 1809.
20 Berthier, Prince of Wagram, born at Versailles, 1753. The Second Treaty of Paris, 1815.
21 Battle of Castelnuovo, 1796. The Berlin Decrees against England issued, 1806. General Mouton (Count Lobau), afterwards Marshal, died, 1838.
22 Talleyrand appointed Foreign Minister under Napoleon, 1799.
23 Latour d'Auvergne born, 1743. General Mathieu Dumas born, 1753. Battle of Tudela, 1808. Marshal Jourdan died, 1833.
24 Bertrand Andrieu, the great medallist, born, 1761. Victor Du Cange, dramatist and novelist, born, 1783.
25 Count Las Cases' last interview with Napoleon, 1816.
26 Gaudin, Duke of Gaëta, died, 1844. Soult, Duke of Dalmatia, died, 1851.
27 Napoleon himself passed the Beresina, 1813.
28 Béranger born, 1749. [Battle of Hohenlinden, 1799.] General Foy died, 1825. Vernet, the painter, died, 1836.
29 The Battles of the Beresina (25th to 29th), 1812.
30 The House of Braganza "ceased to reign." French entry into Lisbon, 1807.

DECEMBER.

1 Jerôme appointed King of Westphalia, 1807. [Alexander I. of Russia died, 1825.]
2 General Leclerc died, 1802. Napoleon crowned by the Pope, 1804. Battle of Austerlitz, 1805.
3 The Distribution of Eagles to the Army in the Champ de Mars, 1804. The Twenty-Ninth Bulletin of the Grand Army issued, 1812.
4 Napoleon entered Madrid and suppressed the Inquisition, 1808.
5 Napoleon left the Grand Army for Paris, 1812.
6 Victor Perrin, Duke of Belluno, born, 1764.
7 Marshal Ney, Prince of the Moskowa, shot by the Bourbons, 1815.
8 Marshal Count Sérurier born, 1742.
9 Girodet, the painter, died, 1824.
10 Count Segur, the historian, born, 1753. Napoleon removed from James Town to Longwood, 1815. Benjamin Constant died, 1830.
11 Ferdinand VII. of Spain liberated, 1813.
12 General Clausel born, 1772. Maria Louisa born, 1791. Gerona captured, 1809.
13 The Hanse Towns annexed to the French Empire, 1810. The French and Allied troops recross the Niemen, 1812.
14
15 Napoleon sailed from Corsica on his first visit to France, 1778. Jerôme Bonaparte born, 1784. The body of the Emperor Napoleon deposited under the Dome of the Invalides, 1840.
16 [Prince Blucher born, 1742.] The Empress Josephine divorced, 1809.
17 Reynier, the historian, died, 1824. Count Rœderer died, 1835.
18 The Empress Maria Louisa died, 1847.
19 Toulon recaptured, Bonaparte assisting, 1793. The Emperor Napoleon arrived in Paris from Moscow, 1812.
20 Count Lavalette escaped, 1815.
21 General Eblé, engineer, born, 1758.
22 General Bonaparte at Suez superintending the Survey for the Canal,
23 General Count Mathieu Dumas born, 1753. [1798.
24 Attempt to assassinate General Bonaparte in Rue St. Nicaise, 1800. Jerôme Bonaparte married Elizabeth Paterson at Baltimore, 1803.
25 Napoleon made First Consul, 1799. Fouché, Duke of Otranto, died, 1820.
26 The Treaty of Presburg, 1805. Battle of Pultusk, 1806.
27 Battle of the Mincio, 1800. The Duke Decrès died, 1820.
28 Napoleon made a member of the Institute, 1797.
29
30 Convention between General Yorck and the Russians, 1812.
31 Madame de Genlis died, 1830. Jean Durand, architect, died, 1834.

THE
CAPITALS OF EUROPE
AND THE EAST

ENTERED BY OR UNDER THE INFLUENCE OF

THE EMPEROR NAPOLEON.

PARIS.	MADRID.
BRUSSELS.	GENEVA.
MILAN.	VENICE.
BERLIN.	VIENNA.
DRESDEN.	MUNICH.
FRANKFÜRT.	HANOVER.
WARSAW.	MOSCOW.
DAMASCUS.	CAIRO.
ROME.	NAPLES.
AMSTERDAM	HAMBURG.
COPENHAGEN.	LISBON.

Napoleon when in the vicinity of Jerusalem purposely avoided entering it.

THE

NAPOLEONIC ROLL

OF HONOUR.

The Men & Women of the First Empire.

NOTE.

THE indulgence of the reader is asked for the following list. The reason for its presence is that no perfect list is accessible to the general public, either in any English or, apparently, French work, of the honours conferred by Napoleon I.

Some of the more conspicuous titles are recorded in "Court and Camp of Buonaparte" (Murray, 1829) and in Bourrienne's "Memoirs," English edition of 1836 (Bentley). A more extended list is also given in the last English edition of Madame Junot's "Memoirs" (Bentley, 1883). Owing to the defective arrangement of the French Annuaires (which take the place of our Peerages), while all the titles are given in them, they have to be collected from a great number of volumes. The last important work published in France upon Napoleon, by Roger Peyre (Firmin-Didot), in the list of titles gives only a small portion of those quoted here. With some exceptions in the cases of Counts and Barons, the following list is believed to be complete, and will at all events prove serviceable until the more extended record by Colonel Phipps is published.

The dates of the creation are appended in as many cases as possible. The Christian names are not quoted, owing to the number usually borne by each person.

β

TITLES
CONFERRED BY NAPOLEON I.

EMPEROR	PROTECTOR	KING
OF THE	OF THE	OF
FRENCH.	CONFED^{N.} OF THE RHINE.	ITALY.

Abrantes, Duke of, 1808. General Junot.
Albert, Baron, 1809.
Albufera da Valencia, Duke of, 1812. Marshal Suchet.
Alix, Baron.
Almeras, Baron.
Ameys, Baron.
Archbishops of the Catholic Church.
Aubrey, Baron.
Auerstadt, Duke of, 1808. Marshal Davout.
Augereau, Baron.
Aulard, Baron.
d'Aure, Count.
Avy, Baron.

Bachelu, Baron.
Baden, Elector of, 1803 (from Margrave).
—— Grand Duke of, 1806 (from Elector).
Bailly de Monthion, Baron, 1808 ; Count, 1809.
Baraguay d'Hilliers, Count.
Barbé-Marbois, Count, 1806.
Barrois, Count.

Bassano, Duke of, 1811. Maret.
Baste, Count.
Bauduin, Baron.
BAVARIA, KING OF, 1806 (from Elector).
Bechaud, Baron.
Belliard, Count.
Belluno, Duke of, 1808. Marshal Victor.
Benevento, Prince of. Charles Maurice de Talleyrand-Périgord, 1806-14.
Berg and Cleves, Grand Duchess of. Caroline Bonaparte, 1806-8.
——————— Grand Duke of. Joachim Murat, 1806-8.
——————— Grand Duke of. Charles Napoleon Louis Bonaparte, 1809-14.
Berkheim, Baron.
Bernard, Baron.
Berthollet, Count.
Bertrand, Count.
Beugnot, Count.
Bigarré, Baron, 1810.
Bignon, Baron.
Bigot de la Préameneu, Count.
Bishops of the Catholic Church.
Blamont, Baron.
Bologna, Princess of, 1807. Josephine Beauharnais (daughter of the Viceroy of Italy).
Bonami, Baron.
Bondy, Count.
Bordesoulle, Baron, 1813.
Boudet, Count, 1807.
Bougainville, Count, 1808.
Boulay de la Meurthe, Count, 1808.
Breissard, Baron.
Broussier, Count.
Brune, Count (and Marshal).
Bruyères, Count.

Cacault, Baron.
Cadore, Duke of, 1810. Champagny.

Cambronne, Baron, 1810 ; Count, 1815.
Campredon, Baron, 1815.
Carnot, Count, 1815.
Castex, Baron, 1808.
Castiglione, Duke of, 1808. Marshal Augereau.
Caulaincourt, Baron, 18 ; Count, 1810.
Cessac, Count. General Lacuée, 1808.
Chamorin, Baron, 1809.
Champmol, Count, 1808. Emmanuel Crétet.
{Chanteloup, Count. (*See the following entry.*)}
{Chaptal, Count, 1808. }
Charpentier, Count.
Chastel, Baron.
Chouard, Baron.
Claparede, Count.
Clausel, Count, 1813.
Cleves. (*See* Berg.)
Cochorn, Baron.
Colbert, Baron.
Compans, Count.
Compere, Baron.
Conegliano, Duke of, 1807. Marshal Moncey.
Corbineau, Baron, 1808 ; Count, 1813.
Corvisart, Baron.
Costaz, Baron.
Couloumy, Baron.
Coutard, Baron, 1811.
¡Craon, Prince of. Murat.] *Only one authority for this title.*
Curial, Count.

Dalberg, Duke of, 1810. Emmerich von Dalberg.
Dalmatia, Duke of, 1808. Marshal Soult.
Dalton, Baron.
Danthouard, Count.
Dantzig, Duke of, 1807. Marshal Lefebvre.
Daru, Count, 1811.
Daumesnil, Baron, 1812.
Décres, Duke, 1813. Admiral Denis Decres.
Defrane, Count.

Dejean, Count.
Delaborde, Count, 1808.
Delantre, Baron.
Delfanti, Count.
Delonne, Baron. (*See* Franceschi.)
Delort (de Gléon), Baron.
Delzons, Baron.
Denon, Baron.
Deseve, Count.
Desgenettes, Baron, 1812.
Desgraviers-Berthollet, Count.
Des Michels, Baron.
Dessaix, Count.
Desvaux, Baron.
Dode, Baron.
Dommarget, Baron.
Domon, Baron.
Donop, Baron.
Donzelot, Count, 1807.
Doumerc, Baron.
Duhesme, Count, 1814.
Dumas, Count Mathieu, 18
Dunesme, Baron.
Duperré, Baron, 1810.
Duprés, Baron.
Duruttė, Count.

Eblé, Baron, 1804, afterwards Count,
Echmühl, Prince of, 1809.   Marshal Davout.
Elchingen, Duke of, 1808.   Marshal Ney.
d'Erlon, Count.   General Drouet.
Esclavin, Baron.
d'Espagne, Count.
Essling, Prince of, 1810.   Marshal Massena.
ETRURIA, KING OF, 1801-3.   Louis, Prince of Parma.
—— KING OF, 1803-7.   Charles Louis, son of above.
—— QUEEN OF, 1801-7.   Marie Louise Josephine de Bourbon.
Exelmans (or Excelmans), Baron, 1812.

Fain, Baron.
Feltre, Duke of, 1809.   Henry James William Clarke.
"First Grenadier of France," * 1800.   General Latour
    d'Auvergne.
Fischey, Baron.
Florence. (See Tuscany.)
Fontane, Baron.
Fontanes, Count, 1809.
Fouché, Baron.
Fournier (-Sarvolese), Count, 1809.
Foy, Count, 1811.
Franceschi, Count Delonne.
Frankfort, Prince of, 1810.   Eugène Beauharnais.
———— Grand Duke of, 1806.   Dalberg.
Friant, Count.
Friuli, Duke of, 1808.   General Duroc.

Gaëta, Duke of, 1809.   Michel Charles Gaudin.
Gassendi, Count, 1813.
Gauthier, Baron.
Gazan, Count, 1808.
Gérard, Baron, 18   ; Count, 1813.
Gifflenga, Baron.
Girard, Baron, 18   ; Count, 18
Grabowkski, Baron.
Graindorge, Baron.
Grandeau, Baron.
Grandjean, Baron.
Gregoire, Count.
Grenier, Count.
Grillot, Baron.
Grouchy, Count, 1809 (Marquis de).
Guastalla, Duchess of, 1806-14.   Pauline Bonaparte.
———— Duke of, 1806-14.   Prince Camille Borghese.

---

* This title conferred before the Empire. " Il reçut en 1800 du Premier Consul un sabre d'honneur et le titre de Premier Grenadier de France. Un arrêté du Premier Consul ordonna que son cœur serait porté par le fourrier de la compagnie dans laquelle il servait, que son nom serait maintenu sur les contrôles, qu'il serait nommé dans tous les appels et que le caporal de son escouade devrait répondre " Mort au champ d'Honneur."

Gudin, Count.
Guilleminot, Baron and Count.
Guyon, Baron.
Guyot, Baron and Count.
Guyot de Lacour, Baron.

Habert, Baron.
Harispe, Count, 1813.
d'Hautpoul, Count.
Haxo, Baron.
Hédouville, Count, 1805.
l'Heritier, Baron.
Hesse-Cassel, Elector of, 1803 (from Landgrave).
Hesse Darmstadt, Grand Duke, 1806.
Heyligers, Baron. ?
HOLLAND, KING OF, 1806-10. Louis Bonaparte.
———— QUEEN OF, 1806-10. Hortense Eugénie de Beauharnais.
Houard, Baron.
Huber, Baron, 1813; Count.
Hunebourg, Count, 1808. Henry James William Clarke. (*See* Feltre.)

Istria, Duke of, 1809. Marshal Bessières.
ITALY, VICE-REINE OF, 1805-14. Princess Augusta Amelia of Bavaria.
—— *VICEROY OF*, 1805-14. Eugène Beauharnais.

Jacquard, ? Baron.
Janin, Baron.
Jaquinot, Baron.
Jeannin, Baron.
Jourdan, Count, 1814. (Marshal.)

Keramelin, Baron.
Klein, Count, 1808.

Labédoyère.
Lacépède, Count, 1808. ?

Lacoste, Count.　André Bruno Fréval.
Lacroix, Baron.
Lafitte, Baron.
Lagrange, Count, 1808.
Lahoussaye, Baron.
Lamotte, Baron Paultre de, 1808.
Lamarque, Count.
Lanabère, Baron.
Lanchartin, Baron.
Lapagerie, Count Tascher.
Laplace, Count, 1808.
Lariboissière, Count.
Larrey, Baron.
Lasalle, Count, 1808.
Las Cases, Count.
Latour d'Auvergne.　(*See* " First Grenadier of France.")
Latour de Pré, Baron.　J. L. Savettier de Candras.
Latour Maubourg, Count.
Laurency, Baron.
Lauriston, Count, 1808.
Lavalette, Count.
Le Camus, Baron.
Ledru, Baron.
Lefebvre-Desnouettes, Count.
Lefol, Baron.
Legrand, Count.
Lemarois, Count.
Lemoine, Count.
Lepic, Count, 1815.
Letort, Baron, 1808.
Levie, Baron.
Leyen, Prince de, 1806.　(From Count.)
Lobau, Count, 1810.　Georges Mouton.　(*See* Count Mouton.)
Lodi, Duke of, 1807.　Francesco Melzi d'Eril.
Loison, Count.
Louis, Baron.
Lucca.　(*See* Piombino.)
　Lyons, Archbishop of, 1802-39.　Cardinal Joseph Fesch.]

MADAME MERE. Letitia Bonaparte (*née* Ramolino).
Maison, Count, 1813.
Mallet, Baron.
Marcognet, Baron, 1808.
Marion, Baron.

MARSHALS OF THE EMPIRE (26).

FAMILY NAME.	HIGHEST TITLE.	BORN IN	MAR-SHAL IN	AGE AT NOMIN-ATION.	DIED IN	CAUSES.
Augereau	Castiglione	1757	1804	47	1816	natural.
Bernadotte	[Sweden]	1763	1804	41	1844	natural.
Berthier	Neufchâtel	1753	1804	51	1815	accident.
Bessières	Istria	1768	1804	36	1813	wounds.
Brune	Count	1763	1804	41	1815	murder.
Davout	Eckmühl	1770	1804	34	1823	natural.
Grouchy*	Marquis	1766	1815	49	1847	natural.
Jourdan*	Count	1762	1804	42	1833	natural.
Kellermann†	Valmy	1735	1804	69	1820	natural.
Lannes	Montebello	1769	1804	35	1809	wounds.
Lefebvre	Dantzig	1755	1804	49	1820	natural.
Macdonald	Tarentum	1765	1809	44	1840	natural.
Marmont	Ragusa	1774	1809	35	1852	natural.
Massena	Essling	1756	1804	48	1817	natural.
Moncey	Conegliano	1754	1804	50	1842	natural.
Mortier	Treviso	1768	1804	36	1835	bomb.
Murat	Naples	1767	1804	37	1815	shot.
Ney	Moskowa	1769	1804	35	1815	shot.
Oudinot	Reggio	1767	1809	42	1847	natural.
Perignon†	Count	1754	1804	50	1818	natural.
Perrin (See Victor) Poniatowski	Prince	1762	1813	51	1813	drowned.
Saint Cyr	Count	1764	1812	48	1830	natural.
Sérurier†	Count	1742	1804	62	1819	natural.
Soult	Dalmatia	1769	1804	35	1851	natural.
Suchet	Albuféra	1770	1811	41	1826	natural.
Victor Perrin	Belluno	1764	1807	43	1841	natural.

* *Rank annulled, afterwards reinstated.*   † *Honorary Marshals.*

Massa, Duke of, 1809 (Massa-Carrara). Claude Antoine Regnier.
Maureillan, Baron (General Poitevin).
Mejean, Count.
Mejean, Count Maurice.
Meneval, Baron.
Merle, Baron.
Mermet, Baron, 1809.
Michel, Count. (? Baron des Michels.)

Milhaud, Count.
Miot de Melito, Count.
Missiessy, Count Burgues, 1811.
Molé, Count.
Molitor, Count, 1808.
Mollien, Count, 1806.
Montalivet, Count, 1809. Jean Pierre Bachasson.
Montbrun, Count.
Montebello, Duke of, 1808. Marshal Lannes.
Montholon, Count.
Morand, Count, 1805.
Moskowa, Prince of the, 1813. Marshal Ney.
Mouton, Count, 1809. (See Count Lobau.)
Mouton-Duvernet, Baron.
Muraire, Count, 1808.

Nagle, Baron.
Nansouty, Count.
NAPLES, KING OF. Joseph Bonaparte, 1806-8.
——— KING OF. Joachim Murat, 1808-15.
——— QUEEN OF. Marie Julie Clary, 1806-8.
——— QUEEN OF. Caroline Bonaparte, 1808-15.

Napoleon II., 1814.

Nassau, Duke of, 1806. (From previous title.)
Neufchâtel, Duke and Prince of, 1806. Marshal Berthier.
Norvins, Baron.

Ornano, Count.
Otranto, Duke of, 1809. Joseph Fouché.
Oudinot, Count, 1808. (Duke of Reggio, 1810.)
Ouvrard, Baron.

Padua, Duke of, 1808. Jean Toussaint Arrighi.
Pajol, Baron, 1808; Count, 1814.
Pampelone, Baron.
Parma, Duke of, 1806. Jean Jacques Régis de Cambacérès.
Partouneaux, Count.
Pecheux, Baron.

Pelusium, Count of. Gaspard Monge.
Penne, Baron.
Percy, Baron.
Perignon, Count, 1811. (Marshal.)
Pernetti, Baron.
Petit, Baron, 1813.
Piacenza. (*See* Plaisance.)
Pino, Count.
Piombino and Lucca, Prince of, 1805-14. Felix Pascal Bacchiocchi.
——————————— Princess of, 1805-9. Marie Anne Elisa Bonaparte.
Piré, Baron.
Plaisance, Duke of, 1806. Charles François le Brun.
Plauzonne, Baron.
Poltre, Baron.
Ponte Corvo, Prince of, 1805. Jean Baptiste Bernadotte, afterwards King of Sweden.
Portalis, Count.
Princes of the French Empire. (*See severally*.)

Ragusa, Duke of, 1808. Marshal Marmont.
Rampon, Count.
Rapp, Count, 1809.
Reggio, Duke of, 1810. Marshal Oudinot.
Regnaud de Saint-Jean-d'Angely, Count.
Regnier, Count, 1809.
Reille, Count, 1808.
Reiset, Baron.
Ricard, Baron.
Richmont, Baron.
Rioult Davenay, Baron.
Rivoli, Duke of, 1808. Marshal Massena.
Roederer, Count.
Roguet, Count.
ROME, KING OF, 1811-14. Napoleon Francis Charles Joseph Bonaparte.
Romeuf, Baron.
Roussel, Baron.

Rovigo, Duke of, 1808. General Savary.

Saint-Charles, Baron.
Saint-Croy, Count.
Saint-Cyr, Count Gouvion, 1808. (Marshal.)
Saint-Geniez, Baron.
Saint-Germain, Baron de.
Saint-Hilaire, Count.
Salzburg, Elector of, 1803.
Sanson, Count, 1808.
SAXONY, KING OF, 1806. (From Elector.)
Sébastiani, Count, 1811.
Ségur, Count.
Senarmont, Baron.
Sérurier, Count, 1808. (Marshal.)
Sicard, Baron.
Sieyes, Count.
Simmer, Baron.
Songis, Count, 1808.
Sorbier, Count, 1808.
Sortin, Count.
Souham, Count.
Soules, Count, 1808.
Soult, Baron (brother of the Marshal).
SPAIN, KING OF, 1808-13. Joseph Bonaparte.
———— QUEEN OF, 1808-13. Marie Julie Clary.
Subervie, Baron.
Suchet, Count, 1808. (See Duke of Albuféra.)
Sussy, Count, 1808. Jean Baptiste Collin.

Taranto,
Tarentum, } Duke of, 1809. Marshal Macdonald.
Teste, Baron.
Tharreau, Baron.
Thiry, Baron.
Thomieres, Baron.
Treviso, Duke of, 1807. Marshal Mortier.
Triaire, Baron.
Truguet, Count, 1814.

Tuscany, Grand Duchess of, 1809-14. Marie Anne Eliza
    Bonaparte.
————— Grand Duke of, 1809-14. Felix Bacchiocchi.

Unebourg, Count, 1812. General Vandamme.

Valée, Baron, 1811 ; Count, 1814.
Valence, Count. Cyrus M. A. de Timbrune.
Valengin, Duke of, 1806. Marshal Berthier.
Valentin, Baron, 1809.
Valmy, Count of.
————— Duke of, 1808. François Christopher Kellermann.
Vandamme. (*See* Unebourg.)
Van Marizy, Baron.
Venice, Prince of, 1807. Eugène Beauharnais.
Verdier, Count, 1808.
Vial, Baron, 1811.
Vicenza, Duke of, 1808. General Caulaincourt.
Vichery, Baron.
Villata, Baron.

Wagram, Prince of, 1809. Marshal Berthier.
Warsaw, Grand Duke of, 1807-13. Frederick Augustus IV.,
    King and Elector of Saxony.
Wathier, Baron.
WESTPHALIA, KING OF, 1807-13. Jerôme Bonaparte.
————— QUEEN OF, 1807-13. Frederica Catherine (of
    Würtemburg).
Würtemburg, Elector of, 1803. (From Margrave.)
————— KING OF, 1806. (From Elector.)
Wurzburg, Grand Duke of, 1805.

VIVE L'EMPEREUR

The Dignitaries of State.

THE CONSTABLE OF FRANCE.—Louis Bonaparte, 1804-14.
THE VICE-CONSTABLE OF THE EMPIRE. Berthier, 1807-14.
THE GRAND ELECTOR.—Joseph Bonaparte, 1804-14.
THE VICE GRAND ELECTOR.—Talleyrand de Périgord, 1807-14.
THE HIGH ADMIRAL OF FRANCE.—Joachim Murat, 1805-14.
THE ARCH-CHANCELLOR OF THE EMPIRE.—Cambacérès, 1804-14.
THE ARCH-CHANCELLOR OF STATE. Eugène Beauharnais, 1805-14.
THE ARCH-TREASURER OF THE EMPIRE.—Le Brun, 1804-14.
THE GRAND JUDGE.—Regnier, 1802-13. Molé, 1813-14.

THE VICEROY OF ITALY.—Eugène Beauharnais, 1805-14.
THE CHANCELLOR OF THE KINGDOM OF ITALY.—Melzi d'Eril, 1805-14.

THE MASTER OF HORSE.—Caulaincourt, 1804-14.
THE GRAND ALMONER.—Cardinal Fesch, 1804-14.
THE GRAND CHAMBERLAIN. Talleyrand de Périgord, 1804-9, and Anatole de Montesquiou, 1809-14.
THE MARSHAL OF THE PALACE.—Duroc, 1804-13, and Bertrand, 1813-21.
THE MASTER OF CEREMONIES.—Ségur, 1804-15.
THE CHIEF RANGER.—Berthier, 1804-14.
THE GOVERNESS OF THE KING OF ROME.

THE MINISTERS AND COUNCILLORS OF STATE.

THE CAMPAIGNS OF NAPOLEON.

First Epoch.

1796-7.—C. of Italy.
1798-9.—C. of Egypt.
1800.—C. of Marengo.

Second Epoch.

1805.—C. of Austerlitz.
1806.—C. of Jena.
1807.—C. of Friedland.
1808.—C. of Spain.
1809.—C. of Wagram.

Third Epoch.

1812.—C. of Moscow.
1813.—C. of Leipsic.
1814—C. of France.
1815.—C. of Waterloo.

(O'Meara's "Napoleon at St. Helena,
at end of volume ii.)

[*ADVERTISEMENT.*]

AT ALL BOOKSELLERS.

THE HISTORY OF THE GREAT FRENCH REVOLUTION, FROM 1789-1801.

BY

ADOLPHE THIERS.

TRANSLATED BY FREDERICK SHOBERL.

With Forty-one Fine Engravings and Portraits of the most eminent Personages engaged in the Revolution, engraved by W. GREATBACH. In 5 vols. Demy 8vo. 36s.

LIST OF PLATES IN EACH VOLUME.

VOL. I.

The Attack on the Bastile.
Portrait of the Duc d'Orleans.
Portrait of Mirabeau.
Portrait of Lafayette.
Orgies of the Gardes du Corps.
Portrait of Marie Antoinette.
Return of the Royal Family from Varennes.
Portrait of Marat.
The Mob at the Tuileries.
Attack on the Tuileries.

VOL. II.

Murder of the Princess de Lamballe.
Portrait of the Princess de Lamballe.
Portrait of Madame Roland.
Louis XVI. at the Convention.
Last Interview of Louis XVI. with his Family.
Portrait of Louis XVI.
Portrait of Dumourier.
Triumph of Marat.
Portrait of Larochejaquelin.

VOL. III.

Assassination of Marat.
Portrait of Charlotte Corday.
Portrait of Camille Desmoulins.
Condemnation of Marie Antoinette.
Portrait of Bailly (Mayor of Paris).
Trial of Danton, Camille Desmoulins, etc.
Portrait of Danton.
Portrait of Madame Elizabeth.
Carrier at Nantes.
Portrait of Robespierre.

VOL. IV.

Last Victims of the Reign of Terror.
Portrait of Charette.
Death of the Deputy Feraud.
Death of Romme, Goujon, Duquesnoi, etc.
Portrait of Louis XVII.
The 13th Vendémiaire (Oct. 5, 1795).

VOL. V.

Summoning to Execution.
Portrait of Pichegru.
Portrait of Moreau.
Portrait of Hoche.
Portrait of Napoleon Bonaparte.
The 18th Brumaire (Nov. 10, 1799).

'The palm of excellence after whole libraries have been written on the French Revolution has been assigned to the dissimilar histories of Thiers and Mignet.' WILLIAM H. PRESCOTT.
' I am reading Thiers' History of the French Revolution, which I find difficult to lay down.' —Rev. SYDNEY SMITH.

LONDON:

RICHARD BENTLEY & SON, NEW BURLINGTON STREET,

Publishers in Ordinary to Her Majesty the Queen.

[*ADVERTISEMENT.*]
AT ALL BOOKSELLERS.

THE PRIVATE LIFE OF MARIE ANTOINETTE, QUEEN OF FRANCE AND NAVARRE.

By JEANNE LOUISE HENRIETTE CAMPAN,
First Lady-in-Waiting to the Queen.

With a short Memoir of Madame Campan, by MM. BARRERE and MAIGNE. An entirely New and Revised Edition, with additional Notes, in Crown 8vo. With Portrait on Steel. 6s.

'Despite the stupendous mass of literature which exists in reference to the French Revolution and its antecedents, Madame Campan's "Memoirs of Marie Antoinette" still supply the most vivid, and, as some writers say, "matterful" collection of statements about the Queen. Perhaps there is no single book of anecdotic history which may be read with such advantage by the average student.'—PALL MALL GAZETTE.

'The work is a clever collection of sketches and anecdotes of the Courts of Louis XIV., Louis XV., and Louis XVI. Madame Campan's position was undoubtedly unsurpassed for this process of collection, holding from an early period the position of first lady-in-waiting to the beautiful and much-maligned Marie Antoinette. Moving all her life in Court circles, she has plenty to say, and says it in a manner at once light and pointed.'—DAILY TELEGRAPH.

MEMOIRS OF NAPOLEON BONAPARTE.

By LOUIS ANTOINE FAUVELET DE BOURRIENNE,
His Private Secretary.

Edited, with Preface, Supplementary Chapters, and Notes, by Colonel R. W. PHIPPS, late Royal Artillery. In 3 vols. Demy 8vo, with the following Thirty-eight Illustrations (except two) on Steel. 42s.

VOL. I.	VOL. II.	VOL. III.
Napoleon I. (*a*).	Josephine (*b*).	Marie Louise (*b*).
Letitia Ramolino.	Napoleon I. (*b*).	Massena.
Josephine (*a*).	Duc d'Enghien.	Macdonald.
Prince Eugène.	Pichegru.	The Abdication.
Kléber.	Ney (*a*).	Napoleon I. (*c*).
Lannes.	Caulaincourt.	Suchet.
Talleyrand.	Davoust.	Wellington.
Duroc.	The Cuirassiers at Eylau.	Plans of Waterloo.
Murat.	Junot.	Blucher.
Desaix.	Soult.	Gouvion St. Cyr.
Moreau.	Marie Louise (*a*).	Ney (*b*).
Hortense.	Lasalle.	The King of Rome.
	Napoleon's Empire.	Bessieres.

METTERNICH, who must have been a good judge, as no man was better acquainted with what he himself calls the 'Age of Napoleon,' says of these Memoirs:—'If you want something to read both interesting and amusing, get the "Memoires de Bourrienne." These are the only authentic Memoirs of Napoleon which have yet appeared.'

'Bourrienne is admirable. He is the French Pepys, and has done more than any one else to show Bonaparte to the world as he really was.'—TABLE TALK OF SAMUEL TAYLOR COLERIDGE.

LONDON:
RICHARD BENTLEY & SON, NEW BURLINGTON STREET,
𝔓𝔲𝔟𝔩𝔦𝔰𝔥𝔢𝔯𝔰 𝔦𝔫 𝔒𝔯𝔡𝔦𝔫𝔞𝔯𝔶 𝔱𝔬 𝔥𝔢𝔯 𝔐𝔞𝔧𝔢𝔰𝔱𝔶 𝔱𝔥𝔢 𝔔𝔲𝔢𝔢𝔫.

www.ingramcontent.com/pod-product-compliance
Lightning Source LLC
Chambersburg PA
CBHW032138010526
44111CB00035B/606